# Transnational Organised

The perceived threat of 'transnational organised crime' to Western societies has been of huge interest to politicians, policy-makers and social scientists over the last decade. This book considers the origins of this crime, how it has been defined and measured, and the appropriateness of governments' policy responses. The contributors argue that while serious harm is often caused by transnational criminal activity - for example, trafficking in human beings - the construction of that criminal activity as an external threat obscures the origins of these crimes in the markets for illicit goods and services within the 'threatened' societies. As such, the authors question the extent to which global crime can be controlled through law enforcement initiatives and alternative policy initiatives are considered. The authors also question whether transnational organised crime will retain its place on the policy agendas of the United Nations and European Union in the wake of the 'war on terror'.

Peter Gill is Professor of Politics and Security at Liverpool John Moores University.

Adam Edwards is Lecturer in Criminology and Criminal Justice in the School of Social Sciences, Cardiff University.

**Transnational Crime**
Series Editor: Vincenzo Ruggiero
*University of Middlesex*




**Transnational Organised Crime**
Perspectives on global security
*Edited by Adam Edwards and Peter Gill*

# Transnational Organised Crime

## Perspectives on global security

Edited by Adam Edwards and Peter Gill

London and New York

First published 2003
by Routledge
2 Park Square, Milton Park, Abindon, Oxon, OX14 4RN

Simultaneously published in the USA and Canada
by Routledge
270 Madison Ave, New York NY 10016

New in paperback, 2006

*Routledge is an imprint of the Taylor & Francis Group*

© 2003, 2006 Selection and editorial matter, Adam Edwards and Peter Gill,
the chapters, the contributors

Transferred to Digital Printing 2007

*British Library Cataloguing in Publication Data*
A catalogue record for this book is available from the British Library

*Library of Congress Cataloging in Publication Data*

ISBN 0-415-40339-1 (pbk)
ISBN 0-415-30095-9 (hbk)

Adam Edwards:
For my parents, Patricia and Michael, thank you.

Peter Gill:
In loving memory of my parents, Gladys and Ken.

# Contents

# Figures

# Tables

# Contributors

**Estella Baker**, Senior Lecturer in Law, Faculty of Law, University of Leicester.

**Barbara Bogusz**, Lecturer in Law, Nottingham Law School, Nottingham Trent University.

**Bill Burnham**, Senior Research Fellow, John Grieve Centre for Police Studies, Buckingham College of the University of the Chilterns.

**Nicholas Dorn**, Honorary Research Fellow, School of Social Sciences, Cardiff University.

**Adam Edwards**, Senior Lecturer, Department of Social Sciences, Nottingham Trent University.

**Paul Ekblom**, Principal Research Officer, Home Office Research and Statistics Directorate.

**Martin Elvins**, Senior Research Associate, Department of Sociology and Social Policy, Durham University.

**Peter Gill**, Reader in Politics and Security, School of Social Science, Liverpool John Moores University.

**Jo Goodey**, Centre for International Crime Prevention, United Nations, Vienna.

**Frank Gregory**, Jean Monnet Chair in European Integration, Department of Politics, University of Southampton.

**Mike King**, Assistant Director, Scarman Centre, University of Leicester.

**Peter Klerks**, Senior Researcher, National Police Academy, the Netherlands.

**Michael Levi**, Professor of Criminology, School of Social Sciences, Cardiff University.

**Valsamis Mitsilegas**, Research Associate, Centre for European Politics and Institutions, University of Leicester.

**Paddy Rawlinson**, Lecturer in Criminology, Scarman Centre, University of Leicester.

**James Sheptycki**, Lecturer in the Sociology of Law, Durham University.

**Peter Stelfox**, Detective Chief Superintendent, Head of Crime Investigations, Greater Manchester Police.

**Michael Woodiwiss**, Senior Lecturer, School of History, University of the West of England.

# Acknowledgements

The editors would like to thank the UK Economic and Social Research Council (ESRC) for their support in funding the research seminar series, entitled, 'Policy Responses to Transnational Organised Crime' (Grant No. R45126479698), upon which this book is based. They would also like to thank all the participants in the seminar series and the contributors to this book for their commitment to the project. Finally, special thanks go to Mari Shullaw and James McNally of Routledge, an imprint of the Taylor & Francis Group, for their patience and support in helping us to realise this book.

# Introduction

*Adam Edwards and Peter Gill*

The chapters in this book were initially written as papers for a series of seminars organised under the heading of 'Policy Responses to Transnational Organised Crime' and funded by the UK Economic and Social Research Council (ESRC). A programme of six seminars was held over a two-year period, from February 1999 to February 2001, but the genesis of this programme came earlier. As convenors of two specialist groups of the UK Political Studies Association – respectively, the *Politics of Law and Order Group* and the *Security and Intelligence Studies Group* – we agreed in 1996 that the growing salience of the issue of transnational organised crime (hereafter, TOC), in particular the apocalyptic tone of much of the official and media discussion, called for careful examination. At a one-day conference held in October 1996, two main themes were addressed: how could TOC be defined and measured and, second, what were the implications of the way the issue was being discussed for the policy responses being generated? Papers were presented at the conference by a mixture of academics and practitioners and were subsequently published as a special edition of the *International Journal of Risk, Security and Crime Prevention* (3(2) April 1998).

These discussions indicated clearly that our initial suspicions had not been misplaced; that is, careful examination is required of a political issue that emerges so suddenly, from relative obscurity to being within a few years the subject of special UN Conferences along with weighty pronouncements as to the magnitude of the threat posed. A prime example of this was provided by a conference held at the Center for Strategic and International Studies (CSIS) in Washington DC in 1994 that included presentations from the heads of the FBI, CIA and FinCEN and the proceedings of which, when published, were entitled: *Global Organized Crime: the New Empire of Evil* (Raine and Cilluffo, 1994). These preliminary conferences demonstrated the absence of any consensus around the official policy agenda. Advocates of the immediacy and extent of the problem asserted the reality of the threat posed by criminal organisations whose global reach and capacity to threaten legitimate political economies was enabled by rapid developments in communication, information and

transport technologies, the abolition of internal border controls within
continental trading blocs, such as the Association of South East Asian
Nations (ASEAN), European Union (EU) and North American Free
Trade Association (NAFTA), and the deregulation of international
markets. Sceptics challenged the over-homogenised imagery of TOC, contrasting this with the findings of case study research into the nature of
organised criminality within predominantly local markets for the
exchange and consumption of illicit goods and services. The lacunae
between prevailing policy assumptions about the threat of TOC and criminological research on the actual practice of organised crime provided the
objectives for the ESRC seminar series.

1    To examine the evolution of policy responses to transnational organ-
     ised crime including processes of definition, symbolic reassurance,
     failure, adaptation and innovation.
2    To question these processes of policy change and learning in terms of
     the available empirical evidence for the incidence, prevalence and
     concentration of transnational organised crime.
3    To explore conceptual and methodological innovations in the identi-
     fication, measurement and explanation of transnational organised
     crime.
4    To explore alternative methods of governing transnational organised
     crime with particular reference to the 'new governance'.
5    To examine the ethics and accountability of policy responses to trans-
     national organised crime.
6    To cultivate a dialogue amongst academics and policy-makers inter-
     ested in transnational organised crime and disseminate findings from
     the seminar series to a broader audience of interested parties.

This volume addresses the sixth objective and complements articles by the
editors that provided an interim review of findings from the ESRC
seminar series and their relation to wider debates concerning organised
crime (Edwards and Gill, 2002a, b). Throughout, the goal was to cultivate
dialogue between academic research and public policy-making in order to
produce knowledge relevant to governing security threats, notwithstanding substantial disagreements over the conceptualisation of these threats,
the different technologies of control they imply and their consequences.
A general organising principle of the seminar series was, therefore, to generate policy-relevant knowledge that could establish the foundations for
subsequent policy change and learning; to cultivate, in the parlance of
contemporary policy analysis, a more 'reflexive' approach to government
that is always critical of what we study, how we study it and to what ends
(Rhodes, 1997; Rose, 1993).
    Those presenting papers to the seminar series addressed some or all of
the first five objectives of the series with regard to the specific research on

which their papers were based. As a consequence, there was a productive cross-fertilisation of ideas reflected in the contributions to this text. It is possible to identify four themes that distinguish the basic orientation of the individual contributions and these have informed the organisation of the book into discrete parts. Readers are directed to the prefaces for each of these parts: these summarise the key arguments presented by contributors, contain critical observations generated by minutes of the series' meetings and references to the broader literature on organised crime. In turn, these four parts of the book explore the relationship between organised crime and broader debates over global security. These have provided the context for the emergence of TOC as a priority for international relations and the extension of responsibilities for intervention beyond home affairs to foreign and defence policy.

## Organisation of the book

Part I examines the origins of TOC as a concept that has acquired such high political salience amongst key institutions of global governance, such as the United Nations, Council of Europe, European Union, Organisation for Economic Co-operation and Development, the Organisation of American States, Group of Seven (Canada, France, Germany, Italy, Japan, United Kingdom and United States of America) major industrialised countries and the Political Eight (G7 plus Russia) Senior Experts Group on TOC. A recurrent theme is the historical and continuing significance of the United States. As well as being, in some senses, the 'home' of the concept and phenomenon of organised crime, the US has also, since the Second World War, been the pre-eminent source of the idea that criminal law enforcement must dominate approaches to organised crime control. Thus, the 'internationalisation' of US perspectives on security is considered an important motor of policy change and learning.

In the 1990s, as TOC rose rapidly up the policy-making agenda, including being the subject of a special UN Conference in Naples in 1994, it appeared that this might be explained most simply by the demise of the USSR and thus the Cold War and the consequent search by assorted security agencies for some new threat by which to justify their existence. This may well have been a factor, but contributions to this book suggest a more subtle analysis of the articulation of transnational crime within a more general array of security threats. Thus, the identification of organised crime with the Italian–American Mafia in the US in the early 1950s needs to be understood within the broader context of McCarthyism and the perceived Communist threat. Similarly, in Europe, during the twenty years *before* the end of the Cold War, a range of issues, such as drugs trafficking, political violence and asylum-seeking, were increasingly conflated in official discourse as matters of organised criminal threats to nations and populations. This 'security continuum' (Bigo, 1994) alerts us to the place of TOC within the broader political discourse on global security. Initially it seemed that the impact of the attacks on New York and Washington DC on 11 September 2001 and the subsequent 'war on terrorism' might return TOC to the relative obscurity it had enjoyed prior to 1991. However this was not to be: at the time of writing, the US Office of National Drug Control Policy is running advertisements telling people that by buying drugs they may be funding terrorists (the *Guardian*, August 8, p. 15) and the security continuum remains intact.

As contributions to Part I argue, the most frequent presentation of TOC is as a foreign threat to otherwise law-abiding and peaceful countries. The most obvious manifestation of this is the frequent identification of major organised crime groups in terms of specific ethnic or national origins – Chinese, Jamaican, Russian, Turkish and so on. This characterisation embodies the perception of TOC as an external security threat that must be challenged through criminal law enforcement and, if necessary, military means. Conversely, others argue that crime is, everywhere, ultimately a local phenomenon and that policy responses must be predicated on the reality that organised crime groups and networks, even if they sometimes cross borders, operate within particular local social, political and economic contexts.

Part II examines the interrelationship between the definitions of organised crime and the development of research instruments for its measurement and interpretation. Because crime statistics are constructed in terms of specific offences, proscribed in different national criminal legal codes, whether the crime was 'organised' or not, there are no direct figures. The tendency in official reports and pronouncements is to provide telephone number estimates of the purported 'costs' of organised crime. These 'guesstimates' usually originate within law enforcement and security agencies where, for example, seizures of specific drugs by police or customs will be subject to multiplication by ten in order to provide the 'real' value of the trade. In Part II it is debated whether such figures can provide a real estimate of the extent of TOC and whether alternative research methods are needed to recognise the social harms caused by these criminalised activities.

The focus of debates over the measurement and interpretation of TOC is on the possibility of quantifying the activities of organised crime groups (OCGs) and their principal actors or 'core nominals'. Proponents of the focus on OCGs explore the potential of surveys and statistical inference as tools of measurement whilst critics argue for a methodological shift in focus toward networks of relations between criminal actors operating in markets for the production, exchange and consumption of illicit goods and services.

Part III explores the utilisation of different methodological approaches through case studies of organised criminal activity in Europe. These case studies suggest the importance of placing the operation of illicit markets in a broader social and political context. In doing so, they question the depiction of organised criminality as divorced from the operation of licit markets and their regulation to suggest that governmental interventions, for example those of the European Union's strategy of creating an area of 'freedom, security and justice' within its external borders, can have the unintended consequence of generating organised criminal activity within and without national boundaries. The implication of this research is that illicit markets must be understood as embedded within certain social and political arrangements and not as a simple external threat to these arrangements.

In Part IV, current and prospective policy responses to TOC are re-examined in the light of the preceding conceptual, methodological and case study discussions of organised crime. A key focus of current debates is the adequacy of predicating policy change and learning on principles of criminal justice. This question is not just restricted to TOC but can be found more generally in the literature on crime control and *prevention*. While it is understandable that national governments and supranational bodies feel it necessary to try to reassure publics that they are tackling problems of crime, there are major questions that must be borne in mind. Specifically, on what grounds should approaches based on attempts to suppress criminal activity through criminal law, policing, prosecution and disruption be evaluated as successful? What are the implications of strategies premised on the reduction and prevention of crime as distinct from the enforcement of criminal law? What value is there in broadening debates over security to encompass activities that may not be proscribed by various criminal legal codes but can, nonetheless, be considered harmful according to criteria of social, as opposed to criminal, justice?

Finally, in the concluding chapter we present our own observations on the debates generated by the seminar series and contributions to this text. It is argued that security is an inherently political and moral, not just technical, issue and that eliciting the political assumptions, contexts and consequences of security strategies and their attendant technologies of control is a necessary prerequisite of enlightened policy change and learning. Prospects for policy reform are examined in relation to three generic narratives about organised crime that are distinguished in terms of their focus on the *external threat* of ethnically-defined groups, the apprehension of *increased opportunities* for crime by rational actors and the *internal challenge* of organised crime to specific social and political arrangements that generate differential associations for criminal activity. Each of these narratives embodies political value judgements about the principal causes of threats to security and each presupposes certain strategies for controlling these threats. It is not, in our view, possible to escape such value judgements, hence the centrality of political and normative debate to the contribution that criminological research can make to policy change and learning. However, it is possible to arbitrate between the competing claims of these, and subsequent, narratives by questioning the intelligibility of their objects. Whether TOC is successfully defended as an appropriate object of global security, or whether it is replaced by narratives that identify other governable places and objects, will depend on political debates over the possibility of security: whose security, accomplished how and at what social costs?

## References

Bigo, D. (1994) 'The European internal security field: stakes and rivalries in a newly developing area of police intervention', in M. Anderson and M. den Boer (eds) *Policing Across National Boundaries*. London: Pinter.

Edwards, A. and Gill, P. (2002a) 'Crime as enterprise? The case of "transnational organised crime"', *Crime, Law and Social Change* 37, 3: 203–33.

—— (2002b) 'The politics of "transnational organized crime": discourse, reflexivity and the narration of "threat"', *British Journal of Politics and International Relations* 4, 2: 245–70.

Raine, L.P. and Cilluffo, F.J. (1994) *Global Organized Crime: The New Empire of Evil*. Washington, DC: Center for Strategic and International Studies.

Rhodes, R.A.W. (1997) *Understanding Governance: Policy Networks, Governance, Reflexivity and Accountability*. Buckingham: Open University Press.

Rose, R. (1993) *Lesson-Drawing in Public Policy: A Guide to Learning Across Time and Space*. London: Chatham House.

# Part I

# Origins of the concept

The three chapters in Part I question where the concept of transnational organised crime (TOC) came from, why it came to dominate official discourse on the contemporary security of Western social orders and what the consequences have been for the emergence of a 'global' law enforcement regime or, more provocatively, a global 'protection racket'.

Mike Woodiwiss's chapter distinguishes between 'limited' and archaic conceptions of TOC. Whilst the latter has a long historical provenance, in terms of governmental concerns over the smuggling of contraband and consequent circumvention of customs and excise duties, the former has its origins in more recent policy discourse on the perceived threat from 'Mafia-type organisations' to the integrity of Western political-economies. Woodiwiss traces the frenetic policy-making activity on this threat, which occurred in international fora such as the United Nations, G7/P8 and European Union over the past decade, back to the domestic security concerns of the US Federal Government after the Second World War. In the context of the pre-war New Deal, Roosevelt's administration had emphasised the opportunities for organised crime that were generated by poor corporate governance and the connivance of 'respectable society' and had, consequently, implemented reforms to reduce these opportunities. Post-war federal administrations, however, eschewed this focus on the inter-dependencies of licit and illicit business. Thus, in the context of McCarthyism, the focus of governmental discourse shifted to the threat presented by ethnic, 'un-American', outsiders, in particular from the Italian community, poisoning an 'otherwise satisfactory' political economy. The official imprimatur for this 'alien conspiracy theory' of organised crime was first given in the Kefauver Commission of 1950–1 and reiterated in subsequent Presidential Commissions on organised crime under Lyndon Johnson (1967) and Ronald Reagan (1983). Reagan's Commission adapted this official discourse to acknowledge the increasing problem of drug trafficking as the principal basis for organised criminal activity and broadened the list of outsiders to include Asian and Latin American 'cartels'. Throughout, the conceptualisation of organised crime as a problem of ethnic outsiders remained the same, as did the promotion of law enforcement strategies as the most appropriate policy response. In addition to 'pluralising' the alien conception of organised crime, the Reagan Commission was notable for hypothecating US 'foreign assistance' policy to the control of organised crime and recommending that aid to drug producing and trans-shipment countries should be reviewed on an annual basis in terms of the extent to which these countries comply with US crime control strategy.

For Woodiwiss, the concept of transnational organised crime has its origins in this internationalisation of US law enforcement, a process that included the colloquium held at the Center for Strategic and International Studies in Washington, DC in September 1994 that included presentations from the Heads of the US Federal Bureau of Investigation, Central Intelligence Agency and Financial Crimes Enforcement Network (FinCEN) and gave birth to a 'new global pluralist' understanding of organised crime. Two months later this understanding underpinned the 'World Ministerial Conference on Organized Transnational Crime' convened by the United Nations in Naples, which propelled the threat of TOC to the forefront of the international and foreign policy agendas of Western liberal democracies. In these terms TOC is portrayed as a specifically American idea exported, with increasing global reach, by US law enforcement and intelligence agencies through the threat of reductions in foreign assistance to those countries failing to sign-up to the US agenda (see Nadelmann, 1993).

Yet, it was suggested in the ESRC seminar discussions provoked by this chapter and other contributions that the Naples conference represented a coincidence of interests between the US, the member states of the European Union and the internal politics of the United Nations itself. It was argued that, by 1994, EU member states had already been forging a common security agenda around the threat of TOC; in particular, concerns over cross-border crime were a key facet of the Third Pillar of the Maastricht Treaty on European Union, regarding issues of 'Justice and Home Affairs', including the establishment of the European Police Office (Europol), signed in 1992. The preoccupation of concerns over the threat of TOC to member states of the European Union was traced back further to debates over the criminogenic consequences of the removal of internal border controls in the Single Market; consequences that were anticipated in the establishment of the Shengen Group in June 1985, which, 'included measures on visa regime harmonization, hot pursuit and the establishment of a computerized data exchange system – the Shengen Information System (SIS)' (Benyon, 1996: 395). This 'Europeanisation of crime and police issues' has also been traced back further to the establishment of a number of 'security clubs' during the 1970s, such as Berne, Quantico, Vienna, Pompidou and TREVI, 'partly in response to American attempts to control Interpol', but also in response to 'fears about political violence and radical fundamentalism, tales of urban insecurity, and immigration issues fused with concerns about the so-called "fourth freedom": the freedom of movement' (Bigo, 2000: 69–70). Thus, although there was resistance amongst EU policy elites to the simple adoption of US law enforcement strategies, their own perceptions of security led to broadly the same outcome.

The evolution of policy responses to TOC in the European Union since the Naples conference is covered specifically in Martin Elvins's chapter. He traces this evolution from the Dublin European Council meeting of December 1996, at which the threat of TOC was first defined as a policy issue for the EU in its own right, through to the publication in December 2001 of a joint Commission–Europol report, 'Towards a European Strategy to Prevent Organised Crime'. The joint report built upon the EU's New Millennium strategy for the 'Prevention and Control of Organised Crime', announced in May 2000, which Elvins identifies as containing, 'the definitive account of how the threat from TOC is conceived at EU level'. Significantly the New Millennium strategy acknowledges an increasing threat from organised criminal groups 'outside the territory of the EU', but identifies EU nationals and residents as posing 'a significantly greater threat'. Organised crime is portrayed more in terms of an enemy within rather than as an alien conspiracy. Nonetheless, the strategy perpetuates the focus, common to official narratives of TOC, on groups of individuals who collaborate for prolonged periods of time and who threaten – whether from within or without – an otherwise satisfactory political economy, given their pursuit of profit and political power. The New Millennium Strategy makes this conception explicit in its depiction of groups that are, 'strengthening their international criminal contacts and targeting the social and business structure of European society'. In these terms organised crime is defined in *opposition to* 'legit' European society, rather than as *interdependent with* this society, thereby reproducing the dichotomy of licit and illicit corporations, or the 'underworld' and 'upperworld', that has been so deeply entrenched in popular and policy discourse on organised crime (Edwards and Gill, 2002b). The actual interdependencies between nominally licit and illicit entrepreneurs are examined in greater detail in subsequent parts of this text (see also Block, 1991; Edwards and Gill, 2002a; Ruggiero, 2000;) but what is of importance here is Elvins's suggestion that the threat of TOC is really the latest episode in a longer-running discourse on the security and definition of what the European Union stands for as an emerging social order. In this discourse, TOC is defined as both an internal and external threat to the project of European political and economic integration. Apropos Bigo's (1994) concept of the 'securitisation process', Elvins's chapter identifies how the threat of TOC has been used by European political elites to fortify their vision of European integration and how this vision has been advanced through a policy-making process that subordinates issues of transparency, accountability and open democratic deliberation over alternative conceptions of

European social order and, *ipso facto*, the threats to this order (see also the chapters by King and Bogusz, Rawlinson and Goodey in Part III).

An implication of Elvins's argument is that the promotion of concerns over TOC at the Naples conference coincided with, and suited the purposes of, the extant security discourse of EU policy elites. The chapter by Sheptycki expands this thesis further by drawing on Charles Tilley's theory of 'state-making as organised crime'. It is argued that the threat of TOC has increased in salience for Western policy elites over the past decade because it provided a useful device for legitimating their project of building institutions for governing the globe, post-Cold War, in accordance with their commitment to neo-liberal principles of political economy. Given their failure to provide substantive evidence on the scope and impact of this threat, Sheptycki argues that it is difficult to support official narratives on the 'reality' of TOC and the consequent argument that the development of transnational policing strategies is simply an enlightened and necessary response to security threats that cannot be addressed by nation-state authorities alone. For Sheptycki, the absence of such evidence, or even more sophisticated methodologies and research programmes that could illuminate the threat of TOC, justifies a more sceptical interpretation of the real factors that are driving policies for the co-ordination of international security and intelligence operations. He suggests that the real agenda is akin to a 'protection racket' in which the project of building a new, neo-liberal, world order is legitimated by law enforcement agencies that are 'self-replicating and self-guiding' in manufacturing various threats of TOC against which they can provide the necessary security. This agenda is discernible in the promotion of new technologies of control, such as 'intelligence-led policing', and new targets of control, such as the confiscation of criminal proceeds. In articulating the threat of TOC in this way, law enforcement agencies and their neo-liberal political masters establish themselves as the expert centres of authority on issues of global security. As a consequence, alternative conceptions of global security, which emphasise 'the underlying conditions that produce crime in the first place', are discredited or simply excluded from policy debates (see Edwards and Gill, 2000b).

Such exclusion is facilitated by the democratic deficit in global governance, wherein the transnational policing enterprise is left unfettered by politically accountable policy-making processes. Were these present, Sheptycki argues, it would be possible to shift the ethos of policy discourse on security away from the self-indulgent scaremongering of the protection racketeers towards a concern with the real causes of insecurity and social harm in the world, which he sees as the failure of political authorities to address questions of social justice, human rights, the rule of law and respect for the environment on a global scale. Whilst the prospects for this shift are even bleaker in the current, febrile, context of global security, following the attacks on the Pentagon and World Trade Center of 11 September 2001, the nascent 'War on Terrorism' should not be allowed to preclude a more imaginative debate over security in the new world order.

The contributions to Part I and the seminar discussions provoked by them differ in attributing the origins of TOC to: the hegemonic influence of US domestic and foreign policy concerns; the process of European political and economic integration; the construction of a new, neo-liberal, world order; and even the utility of this threat for key actors within the United Nations, who were seeking to advance their own bureaucratic interests in increasing the profile of crime control on the UN's policy agenda during the 1990s. Common to these interpretations, however, is scepticism about official narratives of the threat posed by TOC and the efficacy of those policing strategies entailed in these narratives. As Sheptycki argues, to be sceptical is not to deny the social harm that can be caused by the illicit activities that have been conflated into the idea of TOC, such as trafficking in drugs, people, nuclear materials and body parts. But we must also acknowledge the social harm caused by other practices, such as the dumping of toxic waste, insider dealing, tax evasion, fraud and the systematic corruption of state 'kleptocrats', that have, hitherto, been absent from policy discourse on the threat of TOC to global security. To recognise this broader repertoire of social harm and to acknowledge the possibility of governmental interventions that transcend the self-referential appeal for more refined law enforcement is to understand that global security is fundamentally a question of political deliberation, not technical expertise. Subsequent parts to this book examine the contribution that social scientific research on TOC can make to this deliberation.

## References

Benyon, J. (1996) 'The politics of police co-operation in the European Union', *International Journal of the Sociology of Law* 24: 353–79.

Bigo, D. (1994) 'The European internal security field: stakes and rivalries in a newly developing area of police intervention', in M. Anderson and M. den Boer (eds) *Policing Across National Boundaries*. London: Pinter.

—— (2000) 'Liaison officers in Europe: new officers in the European security field', in J. Sheptycki (ed.) *Issues in Transnational Policing*. London: Routledge.

Block, A. (1991) *Perspectives on Organised Crime: Essays in Opposition*. Dordrecht: Kluwer.

Edwards, A. and Gill, P. (2002a) 'Crime as enterprise? The case of "transnational organised crime"', *Crime, Law and Social Change* 37: 203–23.

—— (2002b) 'The politics of "transnational organised crime": discourse, reflexivity and the narration of "threat"', *British Journal of Politics and International Relations* 4, 2: 245–70.

Nadelmann, E. (1993) *Cops Across Borders: The Internationalization of U.S. Criminal Law Enforcement*. University Park, PN: Pennsylvania State University Press.

Ruggiero, V. (2000) *Crime and Markets: Essays in Anti-Criminology*. Oxford: Oxford University Press.

# 1 Transnational organised crime

## The global reach of an American concept

*Michael Woodiwiss*

Transnational organised crime, in a literal sense, has a history as old as national governments and international trade. Piracy, cross-border brigandage, smuggling, fraud and trading in stolen or forbidden goods and services are ancient occupations that increased in significance as nation states were taking shape. Piracy and cross-border brigandage have now been banished to parts of the world where state authority is weak. However, the other occupations have flourished in recent years in most parts of the world, irrespective of the strength or weakness of the authority of individual states or the collective efforts of the international community.

Transnational organised crime in the limited sense that most commentators and policy-makers use has a much more recent history. Since the early 1990s, it has usually been used as a synonym for international gangsterism in general or the 'Mafia' or Mafia-type organisations, in particular. In this sense, 'transnational organised crime' has become a term that is now an integral part of the vocabulary of criminal justice policy-makers across the world. Many governments are in a continuous process of devising new ways to combat what for most is a newly discovered problem. Multilateral treaties, United Nations conventions and transnational law enforcement institutions are proliferating and intelligence agencies once fully employed in Cold War activities now take on such presumed entities as the 'Mafia', the 'Camorra', the 'Yakusa', the 'Triads' or any others that may be given a Mafia label as identification. These groups, according to experts cited in a 1993 United Nations discussion guide, effectively constitute organised crime since it 'consists of tightly knit, highly organised networks of operatives that pursue common goals and objectives, within a hierarchical power structure that spans across countries and regions to cover the entire world' (United Nations, 1993).

This chapter presents a brief outline of American efforts to conceptualise organised crime and transnational organised crime. It argues that the USA has successfully exported its analysis of organised crime problems despite evidence of its inadequacy.

Organised crime first became the subject of academic and professional study in the 1920s and 1930s. It is important to note, however, that organised crime was not such a loaded term then as now. The phrase was usually understood literally as 'systematic criminal activity' or as being synonymous with 'racketeering' and was not chiefly associated with specific criminal groups. The word 'racket' was by then well established as meaning an illegal business or fraudulent scheme and it followed that racketeering was understood to refer to such activities as dealing in stolen property, insurance frauds, fraudulent bankruptcies, securities frauds, credit frauds, forgery, counterfeiting, illegal gambling, trafficking in drugs or liquor, or various forms of extortion. It was also generally understood that criminal networks could and often did include the active involvement of police, politicians, judges, professionals, such as lawyers and accountants, and ostensibly legitimate businessmen. Indeed, as an early definitional article by Alfred Lindesmith (1941: 119) put it, 'organised crime . . . requires the active and conscious co-operation of a number of elements of respectable society'. Most serious commentators also understood that fundamental political, legal and economic changes were necessary at local, state and national levels to reduce the damage done by organised crime.

The work of Raymond Moley, August Vollmer and most city or state crime surveys of the period made it clear that, as long as corruption and ineptitude existed in the law enforcement and criminal justice systems, organised criminal activity would flourish. For these commentators, therefore, successful organised crime control depended on the honest and efficient administration of justice (Moley, 1926; Vollmer, 1936).

Towards the end of the 1920s more commentators began to see Prohibition and other aspects of America's moral reform programme as significantly exacerbating the problem of organised crime. According to E.W. Burgess in the Illinois Crime Survey of 1929, there was 'no blinking the fact that liquor prohibition has introduced the most difficult problems of law enforcement in the field of organized crime' (Friedman, 1993: 340). Others extended the point to cover the anti-gambling, drugs and prostitution laws. The work of Frank Tannenbaum, Henry Barrett Chamberlin and many others made it clear that unenforceable laws governing personal behaviour provided the financial basis for much successful organised crime activity (Chamberlin, 1931–2; Tannenbaum, 1936).

Commentators such as Murray Gurfein, Walter Lippmann, Gordon Hofstetter and others suggested that organised crime was one of the unfortunate products of unfettered capitalism. They realised that more rigorous business regulation was necessary to lessen the opportunities for successful organised crime in legal markets. Gurfein's definitional essay in the 1931 edition of the *Encyclopaedia of the Social Sciences*, for example, listed the following characteristics of the American business system as key to the problem of organised crime: 'the pegged market in stocks, the manipulation of subsidiary companies, the reckless puffing of securities, the taking by corporate management of inordinately large bonuses, the rather widespread evasion of taxes, the easy connivance of politicians in grabs.' Had he added the shredding of documents, he might have been commenting on the recent Enron/Anderson scandal (Gurfein, 1967: 186–7; Woodiwiss, 2001: 150–2)!

During times of prosperity and complacency these insights about the nature and causes of organised criminal activity might have been lost, but they were made during America's Great Depression, aptly depicted as a time when capitalism faced its most serious crisis of the twentieth century. Franklin Roosevelt took office as President in 1933, informed by the expertise and judgement of many of the commentators mentioned already in this chapter and committed to take radical action to restore people's faith in the American system. During his first two administrations, government action at local and federal level not only ensured the conviction of large numbers of gangsters and at least some of their political and police protectors, but much more significantly it also reduced the opportunities for successful organised criminal activity. Roosevelt introduced a 'New Deal' for the American people and began an intense period of legislative and executive activity. Roosevelt's reforms saw a decline in the corporate employment of gangsters in labor-management disputes and made large-scale fraud, tax evasion and embezzlement more difficult and risky. To take the banking industry as an example, the pre-Roosevelt regulatory void allowed crooks to operate freely in many state systems, as indicated by the many scandals of the 1920s and early 1930s. Post-Roosevelt federal regulatory activity at least brought a measure of stability to American banking by reducing opportunities for fraud and protecting the savings of ordinary Americans (Dawley, 1991: 348).

US government wisdom about organised crime was short-lived, however. Instead of pursuing policies that reduced opportunities for successful organised crime activity, the USA redefined the problem and opted for an approach based on breaking up criminal conspiracies. The body of professional theory about organised crime became locked in an analysis that whitewashed a regulatory and criminal justice system that was still flawed and justified the retention of gambling and drug prohibition laws that were as easy to exploit as alcohol prohibition.

This new analysis de-emphasised the part played by 'respectable society' and suggested that a conspiracy of Italians known as the 'Mafia' dominated most organised crime in America. It was first given undeserved respectability by Estes Kefauver's Senate investigating committee in 1950 and 1951, which depicted the Mafia as a coherent and centralised international conspiracy of evil. In this view the Mafia had poisoned an otherwise satisfactory system – the Mafia was a threat to America's political, economic and legal systems and needed to be countered by any means necessary. The Mafia, according to this line, also dominated gambling and drug trafficking in the United States – it lurked behind every neighbourhood bookie and drug pusher and therefore weakened the 'vitality and strength of the nation'. And, as Robert Kennedy put it in a book called

*The Enemy Within* (1960), 'If we do not on a national scale attack organized criminals with weapons and techniques as effective as their own, they will destroy us' (Kennedy, 1960: 253; Woodiwiss, 2001: 227–312).

Politicians, public officials and journalists endlessly used the phrase 'organised crime' as a common noun with a meaning far removed from its earlier use. As President Johnson's Crime Commission defined it in 1967:

> Organized crime is a society that seeks to operate outside the control of the American people and their governments. It involves thousands of criminals, working within structures as complex as those of any large corporation, subject to laws more rigidly enforced than those of legitimate governments. Its actions are not impulsive but rather the result of intricate conspiracies carried on over many years and aimed at gaining control over whole fields of activity in order to amass huge profits . . .
>
> (President's Commission on Law Enforcement and the
> Administration of Justice, 1967: 187)

By the end of the 1960s, as a result of the constant repetition of the idea, most people understood organised crime as a hierarchical, centrally organised criminal conspiracy. This conspiracy threatened the integrity of local government. It infiltrated legitimate business. It corrupted police officers and lawyers. This new conceptualisation of 'organised crime' thus got officialdom and 'respectable society' off the hook.

In 1969 President Nixon added his weight to this line of analysis to support new legislation that increased federal jurisdiction over criminal activity to unprecedented levels. He warned that the Mafia's influence had 'deeply penetrated broad segments of American life' and announced a series of measures designed 'to relentlessly pursue the criminal syndicate'. In 1970 Congress supported this line and passed the Organized Crime Control Act. This and other legislation gave federal law enforcement and intelligence agencies an unprecedented array of powers – they could now more easily use wiretapping and eavesdropping devices, cultivate informants, secure convictions that would result in long sentences and seize the financial assets of their targets. This amounted to a major alteration in constitutional guarantees – it was compared to a grenade attack on the Bill of Rights – and it was all justified by the belief that organised crime was a massive, well-integrated, international conspiracy. The balance in America was tipped towards a much stronger, far richer and far less accountable policing presence.

The FBI's investigations of the twenty-plus Italian–American crime syndicates that undoubtedly existed has shown that many of them swear blood oaths of allegiance, form inter-state or regional alliances to try to regulate competition and use murder and intimidation to protect territory, markets and operations. But the evidence also showed the limits of

Mafia power. The trials of 'Fat Tony' Salerno and Tony 'Ducks' Corallo in the mid-1980s, for example, proved that these old men met in New York social clubs and could approve new Mafia members and try to resolve some of the conflicts amongst their associates. But the evidence also indicated that they could not direct or control criminal activity in New York, let alone nationally. They were certainly powerful gangsters but definitely not part of a tightly-knit, all-powerful national syndicate. FBI evidence has shown that these gangsters were only participating in an environment that was particularly conducive to crime, not controlling it.

In the 1980s the Reagan administration thought it necessary to appoint a Presidential Commission to investigate organised crime – a problem that had clearly not been solved despite a great deal of government expense and effort. At the Commission's first public hearing no doubts were expressed about the essential correctness of the law enforcement approach to organised crime control based on long-term investigation, undercover operations, informants, wiretaps and asset forfeiture. Successes against 'traditional organized crime' and the need to 'stay in front' of the emerging 'cartels' were emphasised throughout. Drug trafficking was identified as the most profitable organised crime activity and speakers stressed that this was the problem that most needed addressing (President's Commission on Organized Crime, 1983).

After three years' selective investigation of its identified problem areas of drugs, labour racketeering, money laundering and gambling, the Commission added very little to the government line outlined at the first hearing. Mafia mythology was adapted to a new age, through the assumption that, although the Mafia had once been the dominant force in US organised crime, it was now being challenged by several crime 'cartels', 'emerging' amongst Asian, Latin American and other groups. As Gary Potter argues in *Criminal Organizations*, this was an adaptation of the alien conspiracy interpretation rather than an overhaul in official thinking about organised crime. The argument remained the same: forces outside of mainstream American culture threaten otherwise morally sound American institutions. Potter describes the new official consensus as the 'Pluralist' revision of the alien conspiracy interpretation (1994: 7).

Despite the evidence of continuing failure, the Commission did not challenge the essential correctness of the law enforcement analysis and eventually concluded that the government's basic approach to the problem was sound but needed a harder line on all fronts: more wiretaps, informants and undercover agents in order to get more convictions which would require more prisons. Witnesses who might have pointed out the deficiencies of this approach were not consulted. The wisdom of prohibiting activities such as gambling and drugs was implicitly accepted throughout the hearings. Corruption within the law enforcement and criminal justice systems was scarcely considered during the three-year duration of the Commission.

Little noticed at the time were the Commission's recommendations on 'Foreign Assistance' which are worth quoting at length. They amount to a clear statement that the USA intended to internationalise drug prohibition as a response to its own organised crime problems. According to the Commission:

> Because drug trafficking and production are threats of such magnitude to the stability of existing democracies, a primary goal of the U.S. and its allies should be to enhance the security of drug producing and transshipment regions.
>
> As part of its international responsibilities, the National Drug Enforcement Policy Board should participate in the President's annual decision whether to suspend aid to drug producing or transshipment countries . . .
>
> The willingness of a country to engage in and actively implement drug-related extradition and mutual assistance treaties should be a primary consideration in the ultimate U.S. policy decision regarding foreign assistance to that country.
>
> The Departments of State and Defense should continue their programs of economic and security assistance with emphasis on assisting those foreign governments making concerted efforts to control their drug problems.
>
> The U.S. should continue to help producer and trafficking nations develop prevention and education programs aimed at drug abuse within these countries.
>
> (*Narcotics Control Digest*, 1986)

The Commission's understanding of organised crime was representative of a pervasive 'dumbing down' since the first conceptualisations of the problem. These had focused on defects in American laws and institutions and found them responsible for America's organised crime problems. Reagan's group focused on different groups of criminals and found them responsible for America's organised crime problems. The Reagan group's restricted understanding of organised crime allowed the Commission to avoid confronting faults in American laws and institutions, leaving only recommendations of tougher and more intrusive policing of unworkable laws. The implications of the Presidential Commission's recommendations on domestic and foreign policy responses to organised crime were clear: a harder line on all fronts at home combined with increasing efforts to spread the American gospel on drug control abroad.

The Commission's recommendations on 'Foreign Assistance' are clearly part of what Ethan Nadelmann has called the '"Americanization" of International Law Enforcement'. In *Cops Across Borders* (1993) he has traced the dominant part played by the United States in the harmonisation of national criminal justice systems in the past few decades. According to Nadelmann:

The modern era of international law enforcement is one in which U.S. criminal justice priorities and U.S. models of criminalization and criminal investigation have been exported abroad. Foreign governments have responded to U.S. pressures, inducements, and examples by enacting new criminal laws regarding drug trafficking, money laundering, insider trading, and organized crime and by changing financial and corporate secrecy laws as well as their codes of criminal procedure to better accommodate U.S. requests for assistance. Foreign police have adopted U.S. investigative techniques, and foreign courts and legislatures have followed up with the requisite legal authorizations. And foreign governments have devoted substantial police and even military resources to curtailing illicit drug production and trafficking. . . . By and large, the United States has provided the models, and other governments have done the accommodating . . .

(1993: 469–70)

Nadelmann also stresses the dominant role that drug enforcement has played in the evolution of US international law enforcement since the 1960s. Drug trafficking is only one of several illegal activities that transcend national boundaries, but the American war on drugs has 'provided the crucial impetuses for a host of actions and agreements that otherwise would never have occurred' (ibid.: 466–70).

Alongside the 'Americanisation' of national criminal justice systems, there has been an 'Americanisation' of the international community's response to drugs built around the framework established by United Nations conventions. The 1961 Single Convention on Narcotic Drugs was followed by the 1971 Convention on Psychotropic Substances and the 1988 Convention against Illicit Traffic in Narcotic Drugs and Psychotropic Substances. These were all established largely as a result of intense and long-term US pressure. The third Convention called on party states to take specific law enforcement measures to improve their ability to identify, arrest, prosecute and convict those who traffic in drugs across national boundaries. Such measures include the establishment of drug-related criminal offences and sanctions under domestic law, making such offences the basis for international extradition between party states, and providing for mutual legal assistance in the investigation and prosecution of covered offences, as well as the seizure and confiscation of proceeds from and instrumentalities used in illicit trafficking activities (ibid.: 389–91). All of these measures are clearly in line with American diplomatic objectives as outlined in the 'Foreign Assistance' recommendations of the Reagan Organized Crime Commission.

The war on drugs, however, was continuing to fail. In 1992 the UN itself noted that 'the illegal use of drugs has grown at an alarming rate over the past twenty years, crossing all social, economic, political and national boundaries' (United Nations, 1992: 7). Commenting on this legacy of the 1961 Convention, Anthony Henman asked, 'How is it that an instrument designed to reduce the use of illicit drugs can ultimately have ushered in an age when the consumption of these substances has increased beyond even the most alarmist projections?' 'Is it not obvious,' he continued, 'that the misconceived obsession with extirpating the use of certain drugs – those deemed illicit – greatly increases the profitability of their production?' (1985: 157–8). And, as money laundering scandals continue to show, the massive profits available from the distribution as well as production of illegal drugs has encouraged the development of significant international criminal associations and networks amongst professionals, such as lawyers and accountants, corrupt officials, career criminals and simple opportunists.

At the same time as the international war on drugs was being so comprehensively lost, American politicians, government officials, journalists and academics were seeking ways to reduce the world's complexities to the same type of 'good versus evil' propositions that served so well during the Cold War itself. In the immediate post-Cold War era, intelligence and national security agencies also needed to justify the high level of expenditures for their services. The menace of transnational or global organised crime not only helped explain away the failure in the drug war but was also as easy to communicate as Containment.

A Washington, DC conference of high-level American law enforcement and intelligence community personnel led the way in September 1994 by reflecting a new global pluralist understanding of organised crime. According to the executive summary of the conference:

> The dimensions of global organized crime present a greater international security challenge than anything Western democracies had to cope with during the Cold War. Worldwide alliances are being forged in every criminal field from money laundering and currency counterfeiting to trafficking in drugs and nuclear materials. Global organized crime is the world's fastest growing business, with profits estimated at $1 trillion.
>
> (Raine and Cilluffo, 1994: ix)

The keynote speaker at the conference, FBI Director Louis Freeh, stressed that 'the ravages of transnational crime' were the greatest long-term threat to the security of the United States and warned that the very fabric of democratic society was at risk everywhere. He was followed by CIA Director R. James Woolsey, who noted that 'the threats from organized crime transcend traditional law enforcement concerns. They affect critical national security interests ... some governments find their authority besieged at home and their foreign policy interests imperiled abroad' (ibid.). This new global threat of organised crime required a tougher and

more collaborative international response; more specifically it required more thorough information sharing between police and intelligence officials in different countries and improved methods of transcending jurisdictional frontiers in pursuing and prosecuting malefactors (Naylor, 1995: 38).

Two months after the Washington conference, the United Nations held the World Ministerial Conference on Organized Transnational Crime in Naples, which provided an international forum for the global pluralist theory of organised crime. The rhetoric and analysis at Naples was essentially the same as that employed by the representatives of the FBI and the CIA at the Washington Conference. According to the UN's press release, participants at the conference recognised the growing threat of organised crime, with its 'highly destabilizing and corrupting influence on fundamental social, economic and political institutions'. This represented a challenge demanding increased and more effective international co-operation. 'The challenge posed by transnational organized crime,' the document continued, 'can only be met if law enforcement authorities are able to display the same ingenuity and innovation, organizational flexibility and cooperation that characterize the criminal organizations themselves' (United Nations, 1994a). This was essentially the same line as that articulated by American politicians and federal officials from the middle of the twentieth century onwards and given presidential support by Richard Nixon in the early 1970s.

United Nations Secretary-General Boutros Boutros-Ghali set the tone of the conference when he told delegates:

> Organized crime has ... become a world phenomenon. In Europe, in Asia, in Africa and in America, the forces of darkness are at work and no society is spared ... [T]raditional crime organizations have, in a very short time, succeeded in adapting to the new international context to become veritable crime multinationals. Thus, illegality is gaining inexorably. It is corrupting entire sectors of international activity.... The danger is all the more pernicious because organized crime does not always confront the State directly. It becomes enmeshed in the institutional machinery. It infiltrates the State apparatus, so as to gain the indirect complicity of government officials ...
> (United Nations, 1994b)

Boutros-Ghali was followed by a series of speakers echoing similar themes: the threat posed by organised crime to societies and governmental institutions across the globe and the need for more international co-operation to meet this threat. The seriousness of the perceived threat was emphasised in the language of many of the speeches. For example, Elias Jassan, Secretary of Justice in Argentina, described organised crime as 'a new monster' and Silvio Berlusconi, Prime Minister of Italy, described crime

organisations as 'armies of evil' who could be defeated 'only by inter-national collaboration' (United Nations, 1994c).

Many speakers at Naples implicitly or explicitly emphasised the success of US-approved organised crime control strategies. This deferential con-sensus was most clearly reflected in a background document for this con-ference which singled out the 1970 Racketeer Influenced and Corrupt Organizations (RICO) statute as an example of 'dynamic' legislation able to 'adapt itself to ... developments.' The document then elaborated further:

> In the United States, the RICO statute is generally considered to be the starting point of a new process of awareness of organized crime by the United States Government and its criminal justice system. Its effec-tiveness has been demonstrated in the many indictments and convic-tions of members of organized crime groups that have resulted since the legislation was passed.
>
> (United Nations Economic and Social Council, 1994)

US Attorney-General Janet Reno reiterated this theme in her speech to the conference. She suggested that her fellow leaders should identify the strategies and tactics that contributed to recent successes against organ-ised crime. Other governments should, she continued, 'pledge to expand the implementation of such useful measures in their own legal systems and ensure that their recommendations were quickly put into place' (United Nations, 1994c). The language was carefully chosen to avoid sounding too arrogant but it can be safely assumed that she was mainly referring to American successes against such gangsters as 'Fat' Tony Salerno, Tony 'Ducks' Corrallo, John Gotti and others associated with America's Cosa Nostra crime families. It can also be assumed that the useful measures she was referring to included American organised crime control measures such as laws facilitating the use of covert methods to obtain evidence and the seizure of assets belonging to suspected or con-victed criminals.

The main result of the conference was to put the elaboration of an inter-national Convention against Transnational Organized Crime at the centre of discussion. In December 2000, representatives of more than a 100 coun-tries met in Palermo, Sicily, and signed the Convention. It is now going through the ratification process and it is hoped that it will come into force by the end of 2003. It took the relatively short time of two years to draft the Convention which indicates a high degree of consensus on the meaning of organised crime. The Convention defined an 'organized crime group', as 'a structured group of three or more persons existing for a period of time and having the aim of committing one or more serious crimes or offences established in accordance with this Convention in order to obtain, directly or indirectly, a financial or other material benefit ...' (United Nations,

2000). Top of the list of serious crimes, according to an attachment to a draft of the Convention, was the 'Illicit traffic in narcotic drugs or psychotropic substances and money-laundering, as defined in the United Nations Convention against Illicit Traffic in Narcotic Drugs and Psychotropic Substances of 1988' (United Nations, 1999: 52). When US Assistant Secretary of State Rand Beers announced that the convention would go to the Senate for review and ratification in February 2001, he also made it clear that the new convention was a 'follow-on' to the 1988 drug convention (US Department of State, 2001). Thus, among other things, it was hoped that the Convention would finally make global drug prohibition effective.

As in the case of the Mafia conspiracy theory and its American pluralist offspring, some evidence does support the new global pluralist theory articulated at the Washington, Naples and Palermo conferences. No one disputes the existence of gangster groups all over the world. Enough serious research has been conducted in the United States and elsewhere to reveal at least some of the ways various Triads, Mafiosi, Camorrista and other groups have survived and adapted to intermittent enforcement efforts and more frequent periods of internecine bloodshed. More recent groupings of Colombian and Mexican drug traffickers have proved just as likely to use violence and intimidation in the pursuit of business activities that are often damaging and destructive in themselves.

There are, however, problems with the global pluralist theory of organised crime. One of these is that Mafia-type groups only *participate* in illegal markets; they rarely, if ever, control them, despite countless claims to the contrary. Instead, as most conscientious researchers have confirmed, fragmentation and competition characterise drug and other illegal markets rather than monopolisation. Looking at the European situation, Vincenzo Ruggiero and Nigel South found, for example, that flux is the norm in illegal markets which 'seem populated by small firms, some of which are peripheral and ephemeral, in a highly mobile and active scenario' (Ruggiero and South, 1995: 86). Peter H. Smith's study of the Mexican situation found more rivalry than co-ordination among drug trafficking syndicates. Leaders in these syndicates 'have little connection with (or respect for) counterparts in other organisations – they are ruthless and relentless, and they readily resort to violence . . .' (Smith, 1999: 199).

Governments, whether individually or jointly, would have few problems combating organised crime if it really was dominated by a relatively small number of supercriminal organisations. They would eliminate the leadership of these organisations and that would be the end of the problem. However, as the Americans have found, orchestrating the downfalls of Al Capone, Lucky Luciano, Tony Salerno, John Gotti and the rest did not see the end of the messy reality of American gangsterism, let alone the much more pervasive and multifaceted problem of organised crime.

Another problem with the global pluralist theory is that, like the Mafia conspiracy theory, it uses semantics to camouflage the involvement of respectable institutions in organised criminal activity. Throughout Boutros-Ghali's speech in Naples, for example, the implication was always that respectable institutions were threatened by organised crime. Organised crime, he said, 'poisons the business climate', it 'corrupts political leaders', it 'infiltrates the State apparatus'. Understood in this way, the only response to the organised crime 'forces of darkness' is a harmonised international effort on behalf of 'legitimate society'. The history of organised crime in the United States has demonstrated the interest-serving inadequacy of this type of analysis. Organised criminal *activity* was never a serious threat to established or evolving economic and political power structures in the United States, but more often a fluid, variable and open-ended phenomenon that complemented rather than conflicted with those structures (Woodiwiss, 2001). Seen in this light, the wisdom of using the pretext of organised crime control to give extra powers to the officialdom that supports these structures should at least be questioned. The American concept of organised crime as a threat to legitimate society simply gives other governments ways of formulating organised crime control policy without fully examining past and current evidence of government, corporate or professional involvement in systematic criminal activity.

A final problem with the global pluralist theory is the oft-repeated corollary to it that suggests that American organised crime control methods are the answer to transnational organised crime. 'The United States,' according to Rensselaer W. Lee III, 'has largely contained or marginalised its organized crime problem' (Lee, 1999: 11). Although Lee is simply reflecting the conventional wisdom on US organised crime control, evidence continues to accumulate that contradicts such judgements. Undercover policing operations, witness protections programmes and asset forfeitures have made US organised crime problems more complex but they have not come close to solving them. As the Savings and Loans scandals of the 1980s and the more recent Enron/Anderson revelations have shown, high-level politicians and respectable members of business and professional communities gain more from criminal activity than other groups. Countless more localised scandals have indicated that the bribe and the fix are still features of the American criminal justice system, and the problem of police corruption is as acute as it ever was. Rackets of every variety continue to proliferate at every level of society and even inside the prisons, gangs compete for commercial dominance in systems based on corruption and brutality. After decades of intense effort against gangsters, US organised crime control measures have done little to control organised crime activity in either legal or illegal markets.

The US organised crime control strategy of targeting and immobilising specific criminals or criminal networks has already been successfully exported to many parts of the world and will continue to provide short-term successes for diligent policing and prosecuting agencies. This will certainly ensure sensational arrests and convictions of major international crime figures, but this strategy is hardly adequate to address the problems of international organised crime in the twenty-first century. These problems have not increased in recent years, because of 'some master plan by arch criminals'. Instead, as David Nelken has explained, the internationalisation of organised crime has been

> in response to technological advancements in communications and transportation; to market adaptations resulting from the internationalisation of investment capital, financial services and banking; to the internationalisation of manufacturing and increased segmentation and fragmentation of production; and, to the increased emphasis on unrestricted trade across borders.
>
> (Einstein and Amir, 1999: 469)

Today's illicit global economy involves trading in anything from hazardous waste to human body parts and the Internet has multiplied opportunities for fraud. Faced with the task of controlling organised crime in a world where opportunities are proliferating, governments might do better to limit the field of battle by replacing international drug prohibition policies with more pragmatic regulatory policies, aimed at taking the profit out of trafficking.

The world now needs a comprehensive and objective inquiry into criminal problems associated with both legal and illegal markets rather than the assurances of world leaders that the Transnational Organized Crime Convention is a thought-through framework for international cooperation. 'Intelligent action requires knowledge,' as an American Presidential Commission put it in 1931, 'not, as in too many cases, a mere redoubling of effort in the absence of adequate information and a definite plan' (Smith, 1991: 140). Urged by the Americans, however, world leaders are much more likely to follow the path of least resistance and help in the construction of a twenty-first century criminal justice equivalent of those labyrinthian traps for rats built by 1930s psychologists to learn whether and how soon the rats can escape from them.

## References

Chamberlin, H.B. (1931–2) 'Some observations concerning organized crime', *Journal of Criminal Law and Criminology* XXII: 652–70.

Dawley, A. (1991) *Struggles for Justice: Social Responsibility and the Liberal State.* Cambridge, MA: Bellnap Press.

Einstein, S. and Amir, M. (eds) (1999) *Organized Crime: Uncertainties and Dilemmas.* Chicago, IL: Office of International Criminal Justice.

Friedman, L.M. (1993) *Crime and Punishment in American History.* New York: Basic Books.

Gurfein, M. (1967) 'The racket defined', in G. Tyler (ed.) *Organized Crime in America.* Ann Arbor: University of Michigan Press.

Henman, A. (1985) 'Cocaine futures', in Anthony Henman *et al.* (eds) *Big Deal: The Politics of the Illicit Drugs Trade.* London: Pluto Press.

Kennedy, R. (1960) *The Enemy Within.* London: Popular Library.

Lee, R.W. (1999) 'Transnational organized crime: an overview', in Tom Farer (ed.) *Transnational Crime in the Americas.* London: Routledge.

Lindesmith, A. (1941) 'Organized crime', *The Annals of the American Academy of Political and Social Science* 217: 119–27.

Moley, R. (1926) 'Politics and crime', *The Annals of the American Academy of Political and Social Science* XXV, 214 (May): 78–84.

Nadelmann, E. (1993) *Cops Across Borders: The Internationalization of U.S. Criminal Law Enforcement.* University Park, PN: Pennsylvania State University Press.

*Narcotics Control Digest,* 19 March 1986.

Naylor, R.T. (1995) 'From Cold War to Crime war', *Transnational Organized Crime* 1, 4: 37–56.

Nelken, D. (1999) 'The most critical unresolved issue associated with contemporary organized crime'. Appendix 1 in Einstein, S. and Amir, M. (eds) *Organized Crime: Uncertainties and Dilemmas.* Chicago, IL: Office of International Criminal Justice.

Potter, G.W. (1994) *Criminal Organizations: Vice, Racketeering, and Politics in an American City.* Prospect Heights, IL: Waveland Press.

President's Commission on Law Enforcement and the Administration of Justice (1967) *The Challenge of Crime in a Free Society.* Washington, DC: Government Printing Office.

President's Commission On Organized Crime (1983) *Record of Hearing 1, Organized Crime: Federal Law Enforcement Perspective,* 29 November, Washington, DC: Government Printing Office.

Raine, L.P. and Cilluffo, F.J. (1994) *Global Organized Crime: The New Empire of Evil.* Washington, DC: Center for Strategic and International Studies.

Ruggiero, V. and South, N. (eds) (1995) *Eurodrugs: Drug Use, Markets and Trafficking in Europe.* London: UCL Press.

Smith, D.C. (1991) 'Wickersham to Sutherland to Katzenbach: evolving an "official" definition for organized crime', *Crime, Law and Social Change* 16, 2: 134–54.

Smith, P.H. (1999) 'Semiorganized international crime: drug trafficking in Mexico', in Tom Farer (ed.) *Transnational Crime in the Americas.* London: Routledge.

Tannenbaum, F. (1936) *Crime and the Community.* New York: Ginn and Company.

Tyler, G. (ed.) (1967) *Organized Crime in America.* Ann Arbor: University of Michigan Press.

United Nations (1992) *The United Nations and Drug Abuse Control.* United Nations International Drug Control Programme, United Nations Department of Public Information.

—— (1993) *Ninth United Nation Congress on the Prevention of Crime and the Treatment of Offenders,* Discussion Guide, 27 July.

—— (1994a) Background Release, 17 November 1994, *World Ministerial Conference on Organized Transnational Crime to be held in Naples, Italy, from 21 to 23 November.*

—— (1994b) Press Release, 21 November 1994, *Statement by the Secretary-General on the Occasion of the World Ministerial Conference on Organized Crime.*

—— (1994c) Press Releases SOC/CP/134–5, 22 November 1994.

—— (1999) General Assembly, Ad Hoc Committee on the Elaboration of a Convention against Transnational Organized Crime, *Revised Draft United Nations Convention Against Transnational Organized Crime* (A/AC.254/4/Rev4), 19 July 1999.

—— (2000) *United Nations Convention Against Transnational Organized Crime* (Document A/55/383) [online] available: http://www.odccp.org/palermo/theconvention.html

United Nations Economic and Social Council (1994) *Appropriate Modalities and Guidelines for the Prevention and Control of Organized Transnational Crime at the Regional and International Levels, Background Document,* E/CONF.88/5, 19 September.

US Department of State (2001) 'Crime convention will soon advance to U.S. Senate', *International Information Programs* [online] available: http://usinfo.state.gov/topical/global/traffic/01021401.htm [2001, Feb.].

Vollmer, A. (1936) *The Police and Modern Society.* Berkeley, CA: University of California Press.

Woodiwiss, M. (2001) *Organized Crime and American Power.* Toronto: University of Toronto Press.

# 2 Europe's response to transnational organised crime

*Martin Elvins*

With the publication of 'The prevention and control of organised crime: a European Union strategy for the beginning of the new millennium' in May 2000, the EU set itself the goal of developing an integrated strategy to prevent and control transnational organised crime (TOC). Although a number of policies and institutional arrangements were already in place at this time, the view from within the EU was that they 'do not constitute a clear and coherent strategy for the European Union in this field' (Council, 2000: 4). This chapter provides an overview of EU-level policy responses that have emerged since 1997, and gives an account of the policy-making process that has underpinned these developments. A number of concerns are raised with regard to the accountability of this process, given the far-reaching significance of a number of developments implemented in the name of 'reinforcing the fight against serious organised and transnational crime' (Commission, 1999: paragraph 40).

## Tampere and a new political consensus

The European Council meeting held in Tampere, Finland on 15 and 16 October 1999, was the first time an EU summit meeting was held specifically to discuss Justice and Home Affairs (JHA) issues.[1] Two broad themes emerged from this meeting: common EU asylum and migration policy, and a 'unionwide' fight against crime. Leaders of EU member states sought to associate this with the objective of maintaining and developing the Union as an area of 'freedom, security and justice', as set out under Article 2 of the revised Treaty on European Union (TEU) established by the Treaty of Amsterdam.[2] A previous European Council, held in Vienna in December 1998 had developed an 'Action Plan' to implement the changes brought about by the new treaty (Council, 1998). The 'Vienna Action Plan' aimed to build an integrated approach to prevent and combat crime, 'organised or otherwise'. The preamble accompanying the 'new millennium' strategy mentioned above contains the somewhat bald statement that the level of organised crime in the EU is increasing, without providing any objective data to substantiate this statement. It is suggested that, whilst the threat from organised crime groups *outside* the territory of the EU '*appears* to be increasing' [emphasis added] it is the groups that are composed predominantly of EU nationals and residents 'that appear to pose the significantly greater threat' (Council, 2000: 6). The description provided in the document is perhaps the definitive account of how the threat from TOC is conceived at EU level:

> These groups are strengthening their international criminal contacts and targeting the social and business structure of European society, for example, through money laundering, drug trafficking and economic crime. They appear to be able to respond easily and effectively both within the European arena and in other parts of the world, responding to illegal demand by acquiring and supplying commodities and services ranging from drugs and arms to stolen vehicles and money laundering. Their concerted efforts to seek to influence and hamper the work of law enforcement and the judicial system illustrate the extent and professional capability of these organisations.
>
> (ibid.)

The report stated that this assessment was based on annual reports submitted to Europol by member states describing the organised crime situation in their respective countries. After 1997, Europol produced a combined 'EU organised crime situation report' based on these submissions, but in March 2001 it was announced that, in future, it would produce two reports: a 'secret' version and a 'sanitised' version. It was decided that even the European Parliament should only have access to the latter, prompting the Chair of the Parliament's Citizens' Freedoms and Rights Committee to describe this as 'a step backwards for transparency' (Statewatch, 2001). In any case, the European Parliament has no right of initiative in policy-making in this most intergovernmental of EU policy areas. The current framework for TOC-related co-operation brings together the Council of the European Union (hereafter 'Council'), the European Commission, Europol, Eurojust, the European Judicial Network and the member states (via their home affairs ministries and policing and security agencies). Recent developments suggest that Europol is set to take on a more expansive role, as will be described later. First, however, it is important to place contemporary policy responses in context. The next section outlines the broader evolution of policies on organised crime at a European level.

## Drugs and borders: the nexus of European policy on organised crime

In the 1980s the notion of threat from organised crime was almost exclusively viewed as synonymous with an *external* threat from drug 'cartels'. This was also the period when the impact of globalisation was first seriously understood as a phenomenon that brought different policy challenges. Putting aside the question of how successful state defences have ever been against cross-border smuggling of unwanted or illegal items, it is clear that a more fluid transnational environment required a new set of policy responses, including cross-border police co-operation. The Single Act revising the Treaty of Rome was negotiated in 1985 and came into force as from February 1987, setting a timetable for the prospective abolition of internal border controls on 1 January 1993. Hebenton and Thomas (1995: 153) argue that the dominant discourse regarding European police co-operation has centred on the 'challenge posed' to law enforcement based on predicted expansion of crime in a border-free Europe (ibid.: see 160–1 for examples). Den Boer (1994: 184–92) has highlighted what she sees as the emergence of a 'reiterative pattern' in relation to this account, in which rhetoric was rarely supported by substantive arguments.

Estievenart (1995: 57) notes that in its White Paper on the completion of the Single Market (June 1985) the European Commission put forward a strategy that relied 'above all on the implementation of compensatory measures at the Community's *external* borders'. A corresponding logic underpinned the Schengen Agreement made between a sub-group of member states and covering a more limited geographical area from 1985 (for a full account see Anderson *et al.*, 1995: 56–63; den Boer, 1996: 396–401). This was on the basis of the more general principle that the overall threat to state security would be greater once border controls were removed, even though, as den Boer (1996: 393) again points out, 'few of these arguments were based on reliable statistics on the effectiveness of border controls for law-enforcement purposes.' A detailed account of Schengen cannot be provided here, but it is important to be aware of the groundbreaking nature of Schengen in that it allowed for various kinds of covert police action and cross-border police collaboration. Most significantly of all, the Schengen system made provision for the building of a data-based system of collaboration. The system was made up of two registration and surveillance databases: the Schengen Information System (SIS) and SIRENE (Supplément d'Information Requis a l'Entrée Nationale). Mathiesen (1999: 9) notes how, despite the avowed intention of Schengen to be at the forefront of fighting TOC, much of its work (and the information held in data files) has related to issues of immigration and more vaguely defined threats to public order and state security. The notion of 'internal' threat is thus elevated to a much greater level of significance. Both SIS and SIRENE have subsequently become part of a much broader plan for a European Information System (EIS), intrinsically linked to the development of Europol. The SIS contained more than ten million records by 2001, including 'alerts' on over one million individuals (Commission, 2001b: 6).

The Treaty on European Union formally established the principle that a European police office was needed to assist in meeting the challenge of TOC. Article K.1(9) of the original TEU covered police co-operation 'for the purposes of preventing and combating terrorism, unlawful drug trafficking and other serious forms of international crime, including if necessary certain aspects of customs co-operation, in connection with the organisation of a Union-wide system for exchanging information within a European Police Office (EUROPOL)' (Commission, 1992: 132). The idea for the creation of Europol predated the negotiation of the TEU, and discussion on an enabling Convention ran concurrently with the TEU ratification process.[3] In June 1993, Justice and Interior Ministers meeting in Copenhagen signed a Ministerial Agreement to set up the Europol Drugs Unit (EDU), for which no ratification (or debate) was required in national parliaments. This agreement signified a political compromise, allowing an embryonic Europol to begin operations on a limited basis whilst the implementing convention was prepared and then ratified, against the backdrop of the difficult passage of the TEU itself. Accountability concerns were raised concerning the minimal powers granted to the European Parliament under the draft Europol Convention, and the lack of consultation during the period of negotiation, as well as the apparent weakness of data protection controls and the absence of any definition of the term 'organised crime' in the Convention (see Bunyan, 1995: 1–2).[4]

Agreement on the draft text of the Convention proved difficult, even before the lengthy ratification process could begin, prompting Germany, which held the EU Presidency in the second half of 1994, to propose a Joint Action (under Title VI of the original TEU) extending the range of crimes under the EDU remit, adding illicit trafficking in radioactive and nuclear substances, crimes involving clandestine immigration networks and illicit vehicle trafficking to the original remit of drug trafficking alone. Once again, no national parliamentary agreement was required for this extension of the EDU role. The Europol Convention was finally signed in July 1995, although ratification proved a slow process, with the Convention entering force on 1 October 1998. Despite this, all implementing measures were not in place so Europol did not formally begin work until 1 July 1999 (after six years of de facto operation in the form of the EDU). Article 2 of the Europol Convention sets out the objective of Europol and provides an important illustration of the imprecise concept of organised crime that exists at the core of EU policy responses to TOC. Article 2, point 1, reads as follows:

The objective of Europol shall be, within the framework of co-operation between the Member States pursuant to Article K.1(9) of the Treaty on European Union, to improve, by means of the measures referred to in this Convention, the effectiveness and cooperation of the competent authorities in the Member States in preventing and combating terrorism, unlawful drug trafficking and other

serious forms of international crime where there are factual indications that an organized criminal structure is involved and two or more
Member States are affected by the forms of crime in question in such
a way as to require a common approach by the Member States owing
to the scale, significance and consequences of the offences concerned.

(*OJ* C 316, 27 November 1995: 3)

Understandably, critics have questioned the reasons for this loose definition, particularly the notion of 'factual indications'. As will be shown later,
the inclusion of an Annex to the Convention containing a list of 'potential' crimes that could fall under a future Europol remit proved to be a
ready-made means by which member states have been able to alter
Europol's mandate and competences without recourse to their national
democratic structures. The next section details the more specific TOC
measures that have emerged since 1997.

## Setting the TOC policy agenda

The decision of the Dublin European Council (13 and 14 December
1996) to establish a 'High-Level Group on Organised Crime' was significant for several reasons. First, it marked the first step towards the definition of organised crime as a policy arena for the EU in its own right.
Second, the sole responsibility for designing a strategy was given to
'expert' actors. This method has characterised JHA policy-making since
the 1970s in one form or another, although, until Dublin, organised
crime had generally been discussed 'in the round' with drug enforcement
policy. Specialist working groups existed under the pre-TEU Trevi system
(1976–93), whereby the Trevi III working group was tasked with matters
concerned with drugs and serious crime. The post-TEU structure
(1993–9) replicated this structure with 'Working Group 3' addressing
'drugs and organised crime'. The more limited Schengen arrangements
(1985–99) also mirrored this mode of working. Working groups are generally made up of representatives from ministries of home affairs and the
justice and police authorities of member states. Although no list of
participants is ever published, it can reasonably be assumed that the 'high
level' appellation implies that the group established at Dublin had a
slightly higher seniority level than the standard working party. A little over
four months (and six meetings) later, in April 1997, the High Level Group
submitted an 'Action Plan to combat organised crime' to Council, with
the intention of seeking endorsement by the Amsterdam European
Council meeting (16 and 17 June 1997). The Action Plan contained 15
'political guidelines' and 30 specific recommendations in the form of a
work plan ranging from prevention, legal instruments for combating
organised crime, practical co-operation between police, judicial author-

ities and customs, the scope of Europol's remit and the combating of money laundering and confiscation of the profits of crime.

Under the political guidelines, point 9 recommended that a 'permanent multidisciplinary Working Party on organised crime' should be established within Council. In effect, the group was giving itself a mandate to continue. Another important recommendation advocated that Europol should be given 'operative powers' working together with national authorities, whereby representatives of Europol would act in a support capacity in investigating cases of organised crime. This recommendation was made at a time when the Europol Convention had not yet been ratified (in fact it would be two years before Europol became 'officially' operational). Council recommended that the European Council approve the proposed action plan, and that heads of state should adopt the recommendations contained in Part II of the report as their 'own political guidelines'. The Amsterdam European Council approved the report and agreed that it should be made public (*OJ* C 251, 15 August 1997: 1–16). As well as endorsing the action plan, the setting up of a 'Multidisciplinary Group on Organised Crime' (MDG) was also agreed. The recent development of EU policy on TOC has thus been promulgated by law enforcement 'experts', even to the extent that political priorities for heads of state were specified (and subsequently adopted) through the report of the High Level Group. Post-Amsterdam, the MDG appears to have become the principal source of EU policy ideas in relation to TOC, and it is charged with both implementing and evaluating the efficiency of its own strategy.[5] At this time it was suggested that the MDG meet at least once a month to work on the implementation of the 30 recommendations contained in the Action Plan.

In May 1998, ministers responsible for JHA matters in EU applicant countries signed a Pre-Accession Pact (adopted in May 1998), committing them to parallel legislative measures (i.e. adoption of the *acquis*, the body of existing hard and soft law of the EU) and crime prevention projects as a condition of their future membership. The MDG (via a specialist Pre-Accession Pact Expert Group, PAPEG) played a key role in this and, as a Council press release revealed, 'has promoted co-operation with key countries and bodies outside the EU: in the margins of its meetings discussions took place with representatives of the USA, Canada and the Council of Europe' (Council Press Release No. 8856, Presse 170, 29 May 1998). Both of these actions reveal the influential and wide-ranging nature of the role played by the MDG, despite having an ostensibly 'technical' remit.

The Vienna European Council (11 and 12 December 1998) sought to define a set of objectives in the form of an Action Plan on 'how best to implement the provisions of the Amsterdam Treaty establishing an area of freedom, security and justice'. Organised crime is discussed *inter alia* in the plan, especially within the police and criminal law section, and it is clear that the 1997 Action Plan on organised crime informed a large part of its content. Adding to the growing profile of the TOC issue, a Council

Resolution was passed on 21 December 1998 'on the prevention of organised crime with reference to a comprehensive strategy for combating it' (*OJ* C 408, 29 December 1998: 1–4). This Council resolution makes reference to a European Parliament resolution of 20 November 1997 on the 1997 Action Plan, which had called for closer consideration of the prevention aspect. The resolution gave responsibility to the Commission and Europol for the preparation of a comprehensive report by the end of 2000 addressing the issue of prevention and organised crime. The Commission–Europol joint report eventually came out in December 2001 and is interesting for the fact that it revealed the working definition of organised crime used within the EU. The document reveals that 'in order to speak about organised crime' at least six out of a set of 11 characteristics need to be present, four of which must be those numbered 1, 3, 5 and 11 (italicised) out of the following list:

1   *Collaboration of more than two people;*
2   Each with own appointed tasks;
3   *For a prolonged or indefinite period of time;*
4   Using some form of discipline or control;
5   *Suspected of the commission of serious criminal offences;*
6   Operating at an international level;
7   Using violence or other means suitable for intimidation;
8   Using commercial or businesslike structures;
9   Engaged in money laundering;
10   Exerting influence on politics, the media, public administration, judicial authorities or the economy;
11   *Determined by the pursuit of profit and/or power.*

(Commission, 2001a: 41)

The report notes that this definition is used in the context of the annual EU organised crime situation report co-ordinated by Europol and in the Joint Action 'on making it a criminal offence to participate in a criminal organisation in the member states of the European Union' (*OJ* L 351, 29 December 1998: 1–2).

The 1998 Vienna action plan had called for the development of a new action plan on organised crime, and the MDG submitted a first draft of this document to Council in June 1999. The Article 36 Committee eventually approved this 'new millennium strategy' on 28/29 February 2000, subsequently endorsed by a Justice and Home Affairs Council meeting on 27 March 2000. Note once again that national democratic oversight was entirely absent from this decision – JHA ministers essentially 'rubber stamped' the strategy. The delay in finalising the strategy appears to have been in order for the conclusions from the Tampere summit to be incorporated. Reading the document, it soon becomes apparent that it is a comprehensive restatement and broadening of the 1997 Action Plan. It contains 39 detailed recommendations and sets a priority for each recommendation, using a scale of 1–5 with 1 as the highest priority. Amongst the measures given the highest priority was the establishment of an 'evaluation mechanism' with the goal of establishing a 'uniform, EU concept of topics and phenomena relating to organised crime' (Council, 2000: 9). The Tampere meeting had called for the establishment of a 'European Police Chiefs Operational Task Force' to be established, on the basis that it would exchange experience and best practices with Europol on current trends in cross-border crime and contribute to the planning of 'operative actions' (Council, 2000: 23). Recommendation 10 included this point, alongside a call for combating illegal immigration networks to be given the highest priority.[6] Perhaps the most significant area to be given highest priority relates to the strengthening of Europol. Recommendations 12 and 13 call for Europol to be given a prominent role, the latter promoting the idea of involving Europol in joint investigative teams.

Chapter 2.11 of the Action Plan sets out the mandate and role of the MDG itself, noting that this includes 'the designing of EU strategies and policies in the prevention and control of organised crime' (Council, 2000: 55). Amidst a comprehensive statement of the MDG remit, recommendation 39 sets a timetable for the MDG to continue its work, with June 2003 set as a deadline for reporting on the implementation of the overall plan, with a more comprehensive report to follow in June 2005. The action plan thus marked a significant reassertion of the EU commitment to extend the mandate of various agencies dealing with criminal matters (including Europol), introduce new legal instruments and build co-operation with third states and bodies. One of the most striking features of the report is the extent to which 'existing mandates and initiatives' are presented as if debate has taken place around them. A good example is found in Chapter 2.6 ('Strengthening Europol'), calling for 'an examination of Europol access to SIS or EIS investigation data'. This point was previously included under the Vienna Action Plan, and is included without acknowledgement of the significance of such a step.

A significant partnership agreement in the form of an EU 'Action Plan on common action for the Russian Federation on combating organised crime' arose from initial discussion at the Cologne European Council in June 1999 (*OJ* C 106, 13 April 2000: 5–16). A draft strategy emerged in March 2000 and it is likely that the MDG was consulted on its content and future operation. By the time a review of the Tampere conclusions was held in December 2001 (Council, 2001) it was noted that 'work is underway' to identify those articles of the Europol Convention that most need to be amended. In fact, changes to Europol had been taking place in parallel with the work of the MDG. Let us now consider those changes. The mandate of Europol has been extended several times in the post-Tampere period, most recently to include all of 'the serious forms of international crime listed in the Annex to the Europol Convention' (*OJ* C 362,

18 December 2001: 1). This extension, which took effect on 1 January 2002, in common with previous extensions of the Europol mandate, took place 'without any prior objective assessment of [Europol's] efforts and achievements' (Hayes, 2002: 8). This most recent extension of the Europol mandate – effected via a binding Council Decision – gave Europol the widest possible interpretation of organised crime. This is despite the aforementioned ambiguity in the definition contained in the original convention. In February 2002, under the incumbent Spanish presidency of the EU, member states were asked to consider two issues with far-reaching implications concerning the future shape and remit of Europol (Council, 2002). The first called for amendment of the Europol Convention in order to allow 'joint operational teams' involving Europol and police authorities in individual member states, in practice adding operational powers to Europol. This development far exceeds original claims that Europol would only ever be a 'clearing house' for intelligence data. Second, the proposal advocated the use of instruments to circumvent the delays typical of Protocols (under Article 43, the only means of amending the Convention). Both measures reflect the culmination of a process whereby Europol has become the fulcrum of EU policy responses to TOC, with some critics seeing a trend towards making Europol the equivalent of the US Federal Bureau of Investigation. However, the final section will now draw together the concerns that relate to this process.

## EU policy responses to TOC: observations and concerns

The aim of this chapter has been to provide an overview of EU policy responses to TOC and to examine the ethics and accountability of this process. It has been shown that the EU is developing an interlocking set of policy responses to TOC with a significant expansion apparent since 1997. The most striking feature of this process is the extent to which the expansion has occurred with minimal transparency in the policy-making process, within which democratic accountability has, at best, been marginalised. The legitimisation of 'security measures' in the name of fighting TOC, along with a requisite secrecy, has been successfully propagated by EU political elites. The primary question raised in this chapter is not whether or not there is a need for measures to control TOC within the EU, but whether the policy responses in place meet the standards of ethics and accountability that all EU citizens (as well as non-EU citizens) have a right to expect. Certain measures – notably the expanding mandate and competence of Europol and the growth of computerised databases – clearly fulfil broader political priorities in relation to EU security.

Policy-making on TOC at EU level has increasingly become a 'technical' process whereby decisions are de-politicised through being placed in the hands of law enforcement 'experts' to develop ideas and legitimising discourse for political elites. Such bodies do not have to justify either the basis of those decisions, or their implications, to national democratic structures. Neither the deliberations of such experts nor the evidential base on which they make recommendations is subject to national demo-cratic oversight, due to the secretive nature of the intergovernmental JHA policy-making process. The sheer volume and complexity of decision-making in this field adds a further practical problem for effective demo-cratic scrutiny. All of this raises a series of concerns about the ease with which measures put in place to combat TOC are then used for other pur-poses related to protecting 'state security'.

At the Amsterdam European Council, EU leaders decided to incorpor-ate the Schengen *acquis* into the EU institutional framework. In doing so, measures that were highly secret and subject to no effective parliamentary scrutiny have simply been accepted without an assessment of the implica-tions. The two Schengen databases, SIS and SIRENE, have become a de facto EIS: the embryonic police co-operation, internal security and border control database for the EU.[7] This raises a series of important issues about the protection of data and systems of redress. Mathiesen (1999: 24) notes how the High Level Group on Organised Crime made a secret recommen-dation that Europol should have access to the SIS database in April 1997. Since then, this process has gathered considerable momentum, illustrat-ing the influential role of unaccountable experts on policy. When this is set alongside the range of legislative tools that allow 'soft law' measures to be passed without ratification by national parliaments (or even debate in many cases), then there are serious grounds for concern.[8] The question for further research is the degree to which a European system of surveil-lance and registration of individuals has been built and legitimised in the name of fighting TOC. Recent indications suggest that two new dedicated databases are to be created on the SIS, the first covering public order and protests, the second building a register of third country nationals.

Mathiesen (1999: 20–5) provides a full account of the concerns raised by the data-related matters associated with Europol, including the exchange of data with third parties outside of the EU. This is a further illustration of the disregard for democratic standards inherent to JHA policy-making: JHA Council (ministerial level) meetings frequently pass points without debate (so-called 'A' points), one example being the decision taken on 19 March 1998 to allow Europol to request and accept information from non-EU sources. Data protection safeguards were not debated by elected officials, but taken to be satisfactory based solely on expert advice. The more recent example, cited above, of the attempt to circumvent the ratification process on changing the Europol Convention offers another insight into the prioritisation of expediency over demo-cratic standards that exist at EU level where TOC policy responses are con-cerned. Europol has been assigned an increasingly prominent role in fighting TOC and is now tasked with fighting almost all forms of crime. Hayes (2002: 8) notes that a proposal to cover public order offences as

part of Europol's mandate was made in June 2001 at a special meeting of
EU Justice and Home Affairs Ministers. Such decisions appear to heighten
the sense that organised crime has begun to mean 'any crime' defined as
a threat to the state. The failure to provide a definition of organised crime
in the Europol Convention and the very general set of 11 criteria
described above illustrate the flexible interpretation of the meaning of
TOC on which policy responses are and have been justified.

A report prepared for the European Parliament makes the observation
that the action plan on how best to implement the provisions of the Amsterdam Treaty on an area of freedom, security and justice states that
freedom includes 'freedom to live in a law-abiding environment in the
knowledge that public authorities are using everything in their collective
power (nationally at the level of the Union and beyond) to combat and
contain those who seek to deny or abuse that freedom' (European Parliament, 2000: 24). Concern is expressed at this definition of freedom as it
'would appear to indicate that there is no tension between freedom and
security measures. While security and freedom may be compatible, state
security measures and freedom will not necessarily be. The idea of security
is not coterminous with the practice of state security measures' (ibid.).
This reservation highlights the tension between the secretive, rarely evaluated 'security' approach to TOC and fears that it provides a basis on which
state security can be evoked to target particular groups or individuals that
engage in activities that run counter to 'state interests'. The signs of the
EU commitment to freedom, security and justice are less than encouraging. In the Presidency conclusions from Tampere, it was stated that:

> The area of freedom, security and justice should be based on the prin-
> ciples of transparency and democratic control. We must develop an
> open dialogue with civil society on the aims and principles in order to
> strengthen citizens' acceptance and support.
>
> (Commission, 1999: 2)

As critics point out, this statement leaves out *participation* in the decision-
making process, implying that citizens must be persuaded of the desirability of actions taken on their behalf. The difficulties of acquiring
information on the policy-making process (witness the 'sanitised' Europol
report) mean that the opportunities to evaluate the ethics (and efficacy)
of EU policy responses to TOC are highly problematic for parliamen-
tarians, let alone citizens.

# Notes

References in the text to the *Official Journal of the European Communities* are cited as '*OJ*', with a 'C' suffix referring to the 'Information and Notices' series, and an 'L' suffix referring to the 'Legislation' series.

1 For readers unfamiliar with the structure of the European Union, the Treaty on European Union (TEU) that brought the EU into being entered force on 1 November 1993. Under the TEU three policy-making areas or 'pillars' were created, the third of which covered the policy-making area of Justice and Home Affairs, with the right of initiative and approval resting solely with member states developing policy solely on the basis of intergovernmental decision-making, primarily through the Council of the European Union.

2 The Treaty of Amsterdam was agreed on 17 June 1997 and entered force on 1 May 1999. It transferred issues concerning internal and external borders, visa, asylum, and immigration policies and judicial co-operation on civil matters to a new Title IV under the EC 'pillar' of the TEU. Police co-operation and judicial co-operation on criminal matters remained in a revised third, or JHA, 'pillar'. The treaty itself contains no definition of the concept of an area of 'freedom, security and justice'.

3 See Woodward (1993: 11–14) for an account of this process.

4 United Kingdom constitutional procedure offers limited powers of scrutiny for measures of international law (the legal status of third-pillar instruments), requiring only that a measure be 'laid before' Parliament for a prescribed period, based on the Ponsonby Rule of 1924. The Europol Convention was passed in this way, without debate in Parliament. See 'MPs denied their say on Europol law', the *Guardian*, 8 December 1995.

5 The post-Amsterdam JHA policy-making structure is headed by the 'Article 36 Committee', a co-ordinating committee comprised of senior officials responsible for police, customs and criminal matters. The MDG, which is often described as a 'strategic working party', reports directly to the Article 36 Committee. A number of specialist working parties are responsible for more detailed policy development that relates to MDG proposals: Working party on Co-operation in Criminal Matters, Working party on Substantive Criminal Law, Working party on Police Co-operation and the Working party on Europol. There are also two working parties covering SIS and another for Sirene. The secretive nature of working parties makes it extremely difficult to verify their precise role in relation to TOC policy development.

6 By December 2001, the Police Chiefs Task Force had met on four occasions. In reviewing the conclusions from Tampere at this time it was noted, in a Council document, that it would be better if in future the Task Force 'focussed to a greater extent on the planning and execution of actual police operations at Union level' (Council, 2001: 10).

7 The entry into force of the Treaty of Amsterdam brought in several new legislative instruments to replace joint actions. Decisions are more binding and are intended for any purpose other than approximating the laws and regulations of the member states. National parliaments are unlikely to have an opportunity to debate or challenge Council Decisions before they take effect.

8 See Mathiesen (1999: 20). Yet another component of EIS will be the CIS, or Customs Information System, under development by EU customs authorities.

9 For example, an embryonic European public prosecutions unit, Eurojust, began operating solely on the basis of a Council Decision, pending future enabling legislation. The so-called pro-Eurojust began operational work in early 2001, working with the existing European Judicial Network (which links mutual legal

assistance units in member states) and with Europol officers to build prosecution cases related to those offences within the competence of Europol, handling 180 cases by November 2001. Eurojust was not formally established until a Council Decision on 28 February 2002 (*OJ* L 63, 6 March 2002).

# References

Anderson, M., Boer, M. den, Cullen, P. and Gilmore, W. (1995) *Policing the European Union*. Oxford: Clarendon Press.

Boer, M. den (1994) 'The quest for European policing: rhetoric and justification in disorderly debate', in M. Anderson and M. den Boer (eds) *Policing Across National Boundaries*. London: Pinter.

—— (1996) 'Justice and home affairs: cooperation without integration', in H. Wallace and W. Wallace (eds) *Policy-Making in the European Union*, 3rd edn. Oxford: Oxford University Press.

Bunyan, T. (1995) *The Europol Convention*. London: Statewatch.

—— (ed.) (1997) *Key Texts on Justice and Home Affairs in the European Union. Volume 1 (1976–1993) From Trevi to Maastricht.* London: Statewatch.

Commission of the European Communities (1992) *Treaty on European Union*. Luxembourg: Office for Official Publications of the European Communities.

—— (1999) *Tampere European Council: Presidency Conclusions*, SN 200/99 (Brussels, 16 October).

—— (2001a) 'Joint report from Commission services and EUROPOL "Towards a European strategy to prevent organised crime"', *Commission Staff Working Paper*, SEC (2001) 433 (Brussels, 13 March).

—— (2001b) 'Communication from the Commission to the Council and the European Parliament. Development of the Schengen Information System II', COM (2001) 720 final (Brussels, 18 December).

Council of the European Union (1998) 'Action Plan of the Council and Commission on how best to implement the provisions of the Amsterdam Treaty establishing an area of freedom, security and justice', *Note from Council to European Council*, 13844/98 LIMITE (Brussels, 4 December).

—— (2000) 'The prevention and control of organised crime – a European Union strategy for the beginning of the new millennium', *Note from Article 36 Committee to COREPER/Council*, 6611/00 LIMITE (Brussels, 3 March).

—— (2001) 'Evaluation of the conclusions of the Tampere European Council', *Note from Presidency to General Affairs Council/European Council*, 14926/01 (Brussels, 6 December).

—— (2002) 'Amendments to the Europol Convention', *Note from Presidency to COREPER/Council*, 6579/1/02 REV 1 (Brussels, 25 February).

Estievenart, G. (1995) 'The European Community and the global drug phenomenon', in G. Estievenart (ed.) *Policies and Strategies to Combat Drugs in Europe. The Treaty on European Union: Framework for a New European Strategy to Combat Drugs?* Dordrecht: Martinus Nijhoff, pp. 50–97.

European Parliament (2000) 'The impact of The Amsterdam Treaty on justice and home affairs issues', *Working Paper Vol. 1, Civil Liberties Series*, LIBE 110 EN.

Hayes, B. (2002) *The Activities and Development of Europol – Towards an Unaccountable 'FBI' in Europe.* London: Statewatch.

Hebenton, B. and Thomas, T. (1995) *Policing Europe. Co-operation, Conflict and Control.* Basingstoke: Macmillan.

Mathiesen, T. (1999) *On Globalisation of Control: Towards an Integrated Surveillance System in Europe.* London: Statewatch.

Statewatch (2001) *Where Now for Accountability in the EU?* London: Statewatch. Online: available: http://www.statewatch.org/news/2001/mar/07accountab.htm (accessed May 2002).

Woodward, R. (1993) 'Establishing Europol', *European Journal on Criminal Policy and Research* 1, 4: 7–33.

# 3  Global law enforcement as a protection racket
## Some sceptical notes on transnational organised crime as an object of global governance

*James Sheptycki*

### Introduction: the threat of TOC

In the 1990s the concept of transnational organised crime (TOC) emerged as a relatively new one in academic criminology and popular discourse. Other chapters in this book reveal that TOC remains something of a contested term. As Adam Edwards and Pete Gill explain in the Introduction, the terminology of TOC emerged at a specific historical conjuncture where a confluence of salient factors, foremost among which was the end of the Cold War and its replacement by a seemingly more fragile and tentative 'new world order', gave rise to a new security discourse predicated on *combating* TOC. The insecurity that TOC describes has its roots in two phenomena, the global movement of peoples and of commodities, which are interrelated in complex ways. Those interrelationships can be related back to contradictions in the neo-liberal underpinnings of the new world order itself, for that order has established two realms of trade and movement. In brief, there is both illicit and licit trade in the globalising economy and, while both may engender human misery even while they offer up opportunities, only some illicit market practices attract concerted efforts at control via the attentions of law enforcement. It is the practices so targeted that define the real official parameters of TOC.

This chapter will not attempt to comprehend broad questions about transnational policing and TOC (see Sheptycki, 1998a, 2002). The aim of this chapter is more narrow. I want to explore an idea suggested by the American political scientist Charles Tilley; that state-making is analogous to a protection racket (1985), although I must caution at the outset that I have somewhat different ends in mind. In his contribution, Tilley aimed to cast light on the processes associated with state-building and war-making that attended the historical emergence of the state system in Europe and, latterly, more globally. Here I am concerned to look at the emergence of transnational crime control on the agenda for 'global governance' in the contemporary period. I reason that, just as the analogy between state-making and organised crime could be used to cast light on the historical conditions of modern governance, it can be pressed into use to illuminate some of the contradictions of global governmental institution-building in the contemporary period.

Governance is the development and implementation of policy for the management of populations and territory. Democratic governance implies that this is undertaken with regard to the general interests of society, wherever the boundaries of such can be said to lie. Global governance suggests that policy development and implementation for the management of populations and territory is undertaken with regard to world-wide issues, and there are real questions about the extent to which such is undertaken within a democratic framework and under the rule of law (Marks, 2000). Issues of governance are often linked in fundamental ways to questions about the (in)stability of the social and political order generally, and in the contemporary period this has given rise to criminological speculation about the crisis of insecurity in high-crime societies (Garland, 2000). It seems obvious that a world enthralled by Globalisation-crisis-talk will produce a globalised version of the 'crisis of crime control'. What we are concerned to understand here is TOC as an object for global governance. In order to do so we need to look at the institutions that seek to govern TOC, their practices and how they are legitimated.

The basic task of this chapter is to provide a short descriptive overview of changes in the architecture of policing common to a number of OECD countries and to characterise the emergent architecture of transnational policing. The chapter is an attempt to show this institution-building in a more sceptical light than the engineers of the transnational policing complex would normally entertain. These institutional developments can be understood as both a product of, and productive of, a wide and continuously emergent assortment of identified TOC 'threats'. This reciprocal relationship between controller and controlled raises questions about how much latitude law enforcement 'experts' should be given in defining the transnational agenda for crime control and how it might be rendered accountable to the global community. In other words, TOC discourse is related to more general questions about the political complexion of the global system. A sceptical view will serve to show that political ideals about transparency of government, human and civil rights, and a host of others are all affected by changes in social control practice, changes which are increasingly being led from a transnational domain that lies above the strictures of democratic accountability and the rule of law as it has been traditionally understood. In the world after 9–11 (when the United States suffered a catastrophic terrorist attack and subsequently set about creating a transnational alliance which, however frail, declared a world-wide war on terrorism), such questions might seem academic. However, it should be made plain that many of the developmental trends in transnational policing that became headline news after 9–11 were already well underway prior to that time. The terrorist attacks on the World Trade Center and the Pentagon in September 2001 were horrific and consequently lent a seemingly unassailable aura of legitimacy to an already established project of institution-building. Despite the present circumstances, it is well to be vigilant and ask some sceptical questions. This is so because the awesome power of law enforcement institutions lies in their capacity to orchestrate surveillance and muster coercive force in the maintenance of a social order. In a world that has gone global we must ask: whose order and how is it sustained?

## The protection analogy

Let us examine Tilley's analogy in a little more detail. It is well to recall that his contribution to political theory was not made in an expressly criminological vein. Rather, Tilley's essay was part of a long running dialogue about state formation in Western Europe (Evans *et al.*, 1985; Tilley, 1975). At the risk of great oversimplification, that problematic might be reduced to four core questions: how states establish themselves against other states (the military question); how states establish an administrative monopoly of coercive force over their territory (the police question); how states maintain a system of resource extraction in order to pay for it all (the tax question); and how they did so with at least a minimal degree of legitimacy (the political question). The essay, 'War making and state making as organised crime' (1985) brings all of these concerns together. Therein Tilley examines the way in which European states incrementally built up their capacities of resource extraction in order to fund war abroad and how this process required a system of domestic police. Political sociologists broadly concurred with his outline (Mann, 1993) as did historians of the police (Bayley, 1975; Liang, 1992; Mazower, 1997).

In sketching the parameters of this paradigm, we might begin by noting that there is a uniqueness to each state's institutional development and, hence, each enclave of governance has its own policing history (Bayley, 1975). Further, each state has had different political traditions, hence different ways of legitimating its governance of the social body defined as 'the nation'. Policing was a set of practices intended to assure domestic tranquillity and boost resource extraction so as to be able to amass the resources to engage in military ventures abroad in defence of 'the nation's interests'. At a high level of abstraction, we could say that the nation state system that grew up in Europe was, *mutatis mutandis*, akin to the competitive interplay of neighbourhood protection rackets found in some large cities.

What makes this analogy so interesting in the contemporary period is that it can be applied in the context of *global* governmental institution-building. Robert Keohane (1989) explained this institution-building with reference to what he termed 'neo-liberal institutionalism', wherein interstate relations are governed, albeit only partially and imperfectly, by established transnational rules, norms and conventions. According to Keohane, in order to understand state behaviour in the contemporary period 'we must not only take account of the relative physical power capabilities of states and recognise the absence of hierarchical authority [between them], we must also comprehend world political institutions – regardless of whether they are formally organised and explicitly codified' (1989: 2). According to this perspective, foreign policy personnel who pursue a given state's interests are constrained by transnational regimes of which they are only part authors. Some time in the recent past the United Nations and a host of other supranational bodies including, but not limited to, the OECD, the IMF, the GATT (the fore-runner of the WTO), NATO, the WEU, the EU and the Commonwealth Secretariat, became important global institutions in their own right. The sometimes explicitly codified, but more often informal network of transnational policing that is part of this complex of 'world political institutions', should not escape the criminologist's attention. The protection analogy that Tilley used to cast light on nation state building in an earlier period of modernity must be modified in order to take account of these transnational institutions of governance. The protection racket is being extended up to the transnational level where global institutions also lay claim to the responsibility to 'govern' crime.

## Policing with global intelligence

There have been many fads and fashions in policing since 'Police Studies' was established as an area of academic inquiry. Problem-oriented policing, community policing, police 'management by objectives': all have had their moments. Towards the end of the 1990s, the policing idea that gained world-wide currency was 'intelligence-led policing' (Sheptycki, 2000a). Intelligence-led policing (ILP) rests on a technological revolution aimed directly at controlling crime and criminals. It has thus manifested itself around the world on the back of transnational police technology transfer (Sheptycki, 1998b). It is in keeping with the police occupation's self-perception of 'real police work' (Reiner, 2000). Intelligence-led policing is strategic, future oriented and targeted. It focuses on the identification, analysis and management of criminal threats. At the organisational level it requires policing institutions to allocate more resources to the computer-aided collection, collation and analysis of 'criminal intelligence'. It is information dependent and the (inter)connectivity of its information environment holds the key to its success.

Echoing Mike Maguire (2000: 333), the ILP revolution brought about a shift in the language of policing, introducing new terms such as 'strategic' and 'pro-active', 'risk-based' policing. The approaches implied by these terms aim to target suspect populations and individuals in a highly systematic way. Kevin Haggerty and Richard Ericson (2000) coined the term 'surveillant assemblage' to describe the repertoire of techniques, including electronic surveillance, participating informants, database matching and CCTV surveillance which so changed the performance of policing. In the contemporary period the state apparatus is highly complexified, with a multiplicity of state institutions (Departments for Health, Work, Environment, Revenue, etc.) sharing responsibility for different aspects of the maintenance of the health of the social body. Public police institutions (the 'state' police) are loosely coupled to these other institutions via an apparatus of information exchange for the management of suspect populations and territory (Broder, 2000; Ericson and Haggerty, 1997; Johnston, 2000). In Pete Gill's (2000) estimation, the ILP project is merely the technologically enhanced 'rounding up of the usual suspects'. As will be shown, this process is extending transnationally.

The ILP approach took root in the United Kingdom following the Audit Commission's report *Helping with Enquiries* (1993), but it was developed first in the United States. Early work there laid down the precedent for prioritising the intelligence function in policing (Godfrey and Harris, 1971; Dintino and Martens, 1983). Subsequently the United States invested heavily in building a cross-agency intelligence sharing capacity. At the turn of the twenty-first century, knowledge gained from the electronic surveillance by the FBI could be combined with information from undercover DEA agents, financial intelligence held by the Internal Revenue Service as well as knowledge held by Customs, the Coast Guard and other agencies on a routine basis. The USA had created a nationwide surveillant assemblage that was almost inconceivable only a short time before (Sheptycki, 2002). These changes were evident further afield. Another instance is the pattern of development that took place in South Africa in the post-apartheid years. According to Elrena van der Spuy (2000), overseas assistance to the South African Police Service (SAPS) moved through three distinct phases during this time. At first the focus was on integrating the police service there and reorienting it around the philosophy of 'community policing'. In the second phase, the emphasis was on developing basic policing capacities 'on the ground'. Previously policing in South Africa had been bent to the task of enforcing racial segregation and thus the practical task was to develop the ability to deliver basic policing services (see also Brogden and Shearing, 1993). This development project remained incomplete when the emphasis of overseas aid to the SAPS shifted towards controlling organised crime. Integral to this, and in common with developments elsewhere, was an increased emphasis on orchestrating regional criminal intelligence capacity. The aim was to network the communications function across the entire region of southern Africa. No small task. Similar developments can be seen in a variety of regions (Sheptycki, 1995, 1998b). There was no escaping the fact that in the early years of the twenty-first century, the techno-cops were in global pursuit of organised crime.

Perhaps the 1997 annual report of the Criminal Intelligence Service of Canada (CISC) put it best. The report noted that while 'transnational crime' had become part of the police lexicon, policing had been undergoing its own evolution. The CISC applauded the move from old-style reactive policing to future oriented, multi-agency law enforcement as a necessary response to the challenges of organised crime. Intelligence-led policing and the image of (transnational) organised crime went hand-in-hand. A similar set of observations were put forward by Jürgen Storbeck, Director of Europol, in his 1999 Police Foundation Lecture in London. He welcomed the furtherance of police intelligence capabilities in the member countries of the European Union because clandestine trade and associated money laundering activities were 'undermining the security and well-being of our citizens at every level and in every community' (1999: 5). In his view, this necessitated some transference of resources from the local level up to the national and transnational level. He argued that, by doing so, 'we might stand a real chance to challenge the continuing growth of international crime and help preserve the security, not just of nations, but of local communities and of every citizen' (ibid.: 13).

In many places around the world, albeit to greater or lesser extents, policing agencies changed in fundamental ways towards the end of the twentieth century. The ILP approach, propelled by transnational police technology transfer, heralded a renewed emphasis on controlling crime, especially 'serious and organised crime'. This dove-tailed well with rising concerns to police transnational clandestine markets and, when it came to it, could be pressed into service against terrorism as well. As a result, the variety of styles exhibited by different national policing systems began to blur into one another. Such blurring makes possible the orchestration of transnational policing under the rubric of 'risk forecasting'. International 'liaison officers' (Bigo, 2000) may be tasked according to risk-based logic, but it should not escape our attention that the strategic analysis produced by these transnational agents affects the framing of police priorities in local communities. It is thus that the transnational capacities of police agencies grow and are fused into a transnational police 'intelligence pyramid' (Report of Her Majesty's Inspectorate of Constabulary on the National Criminal Intelligence Service, 1997: 7). Policies for the governance of TOC are set at the apex of this pyramid, in the transnational domain (see Peter Stelfox's chapter, this volume, pp. 114–26).

## Strategies of 'police protection' in the contemporary period

Along with the rise in intelligence-led-policing approaches to these forms of crime, we can note a significant shift in enforcement strategy away from the criminals towards going after the proceeds of crime (Sheptycki, 2000b). This strategy is justified on five counts (OCDETF, 1984). The first is an argument that seizing the proceeds of crime will disrupt criminal enterprises. It is reasoned that the removal of criminal assets will deprive criminal groups of some of the necessary resources to carry out criminal activity. The second is that it will deter crime. Since the crimes of the illicit market are undertaken on the basis of cost/benefit calculations made by reasoning criminals, threat of asset seizure is in accord with traditional deterrence theories. The third is closely allied to the first and suggests that taking away criminal assets undermines the criminal opportunity structure. Since the proceeds of crime can be used to finance future crime, it makes sense to confiscate it when possible on the grounds that it will avert future ills. The fourth is that, with enough attention to detail, the extra administrative costs to the criminal justice system for the management of asset freezing and forfeiture could be offset by monies seized. The fifth is that 'dirty money' is a threat to the well-being of the financial system and, as such, any police action to weed it out is of utmost necessity.

Of course, subsequent to 9–11, the idea that 'suspicious transactions' ought to be policed in order to protect society from the clear and present danger of 'narco-terrorism' made this project virtually unassailable politically. Actually this was a crucial transformation in the global anti-money-laundering movement. Up to that point, money laundering was understood to be about taking 'dirty money' and making it clean, hence the metaphor of 'laundering' (Sheptycki, 2000b). Suspicions that the terrorists attacks of September 11, 2001 had been financed by monies coming from legitimate sources, that 'clean money' had been made 'dirty', meant that logic of financial surveillance was no longer restricted to that of 'anti-money-laundering'. All transactions could be considered suspicious. Narco-terrorism, the practices of financing political violence through the clandestine trade in drugs, gave a legitimacy basis for total global financial surveillance that transcended all but the staunchest libertarian objections (Rahn, 2001).

We shall return to the issue of terrorism in the conclusion, but it should not escape our attention at this point that the trend towards ever-greater law enforcement watchfulness over the money-movers was already well established prior to September 11, 2001, and that it had a logic of its own. The new enforcement strategy of going after the proceeds of crime accompanied the shift to ILP, indeed in some instances it helped to finance it. This prompted some critical reflection about the perverse effects of civil asset forfeiture as a budgetary supplement to law enforcement (see, for example, Blumenson and Nilsen, 1997; Hawkins and Payne, 1999; Jensen and Gerber, 1996). The shift towards going after the proceeds of crime makes policing into a system of resource extraction. That system of extraction may be rationalised and legitimated on the basis of the above-mentioned criteria, but any such system of evaluation would be fatally flawed.

First, the suggestion that seizing the proceeds of crime disrupts criminal enterprises may be correct but, from a strictly criminological point of view, this is not necessarily a good thing. Cash and illicit commodities are linked in a complex chain of exchange lubricated by debt and credit. When law enforcement operations take money out of a debt–credit chain, indebted criminal entrepreneurs may feel forced to adopt alternative ways of raising funds (such as armed robbery) or risk the wrath of their debtors. The unintended and therefore unpredictable consequences of law enforcement action on criminal networks may outweigh the benefits. Tallying criminal assets seized has all of the same problems that traditional measures of police performance, such as arrest or clear-up rates, do. They do not signal a change in the underlying conditions that produced the crime in the first place. Announcing in press releases quantities of illegal commodities or cash seized is no more a measure of police success than arrest statistics or other police recorded crime measures.

Second, the idea that asset forfeiture will act as a significant deterrent to enterprise criminals who operate on the basis of a profit and loss balance sheet is contradictory. Apart from the rather obvious point that general deterrence has long been attempted, using a range of disciplinary techniques from capital punishment to the fine, without measurable success, the idea falls down on its own terms. Rational, calculating criminals trading in the illicit market, if indeed they are rational and calculating, will seek to predict their percentage loss due to these administrative efforts. Seeing that their enterprise risks the threat of asset confiscation, such rationally calculating criminals would obviously seek to ensure that the profits from successful transactions will compensate for the losses incurred. The cost of such losses can be passed on to the customer, or squeezed out of the primary producer, thereby compounding the miseries symptomatic of illicit markets. It is not certain that there are actually rationally calculating criminals totting up a balance sheet in strict accountancy terms, but it seems undeniable that threats to confiscate or freeze assets are merely another cost of doing business.

Opportunity reduction theory may be viewed as an extension of the deterrent argument. This suggests, among other things, that criminal assets are an essential part of the criminal opportunity structure. Removal of these assets therefore does not so much deter as it reduces the opportunities to commit crime. This gives rise to insuperable measurement difficulties, since the stated goal is to reduce potential future offending. While criminologists have produced a raft of research showing the utility of crime prevention in a host of contexts (see Pease, 1997 for an overview), it has not been demonstrated that this way of thinking can be applied to the illicit market. This is because market offences are committed with the aim to supply an illegal service or product to willing buyers and there is no accurate means of measuring the extent of either. While it may be plausible that confiscating criminal assets to some extent denies the tools necessary to trade in the criminal market, there is no way to measure the effect of this with confidence. Further, what little evidence criminologists have accumulated about the functioning of criminal markets does not indicate that they are particularly vulnerable to this tactic of disablement (Hobbs, 1995, 1998; van Duyne, 1998; Ruggiero, 1997). Periodically the level of asset confiscation may be truly catastrophic for a *particular* criminal enterprise, but for the market as a whole it is merely part of the cost of 'doing business'. Asset confiscation tactics against illicit markets *generally* amount to a form of taxation.

Fourth, it is often suggested that, by going after the proceeds of crime, the mission against transnational organised crime can be achieved in a cost-effective manner. This might be re-stated as a hope that asset forfeiture will impact on criminal enterprise as *excessive* taxation does on legitimate business. If levels of resource extraction from the criminal market are sufficient, so this line of reasoning goes, it cuts into profits, reduces the availability of working capital for existing ventures, and dries up reserves which might otherwise be used to start up new ones. This assumption fails to recognise that, just as legitimate capital is displaced offshore when it is threatened by 'excessive taxation', so too may 'dirty money' be displaced. It is possible to expand the enforcement regime transnationally in order to compensate for this displacement, but that may only serve to further spread the circulation of 'dirty money' within the circuits of global capital. It has been documented how anti-money-laundering initiatives that began in the banking sector later moved on to other parts of the financial system, including insurance companies and credit card companies, because the 'dirty-money' had moved (Gilmore, 1995, 1999; Sheptycki, 2000b). This somewhat undermines the logic of the fifth reason for going after the proceeds of crime, since the ironic and unintended consequence of anti-money-laundering has been to spread the 'contamination' around the financial system. If 'dirty money' is a systemic risk to the financial system, displacing it across the institutional field is not a good thing.

These issues beg questions about the size of the global illicit market. This is a difficult matter and estimates of the amount of global illicit capital circulating in the late 1990s ranged from between US$100 billion and US$500 billion (Sheptycki, 2000b), paltry beside the estimated US$175 billion *a day* of financial transactions and money movements taking place in the legitimate circuits of capital (Nelken, 1997). The proceeds of crime which are also flowing through the veins of the transnational financial system are difficult to distinguish, isolate and fix on. As a result, successful confiscation can be no more than a random occurrence, a far off probability which potentially poses great inconvenience (akin to bankruptcy) to particular participants in illicit trade. However, systemically it accomplishes little more than modest resource extraction from the market as a whole.

## A global protection racket?

We have seen how many different national policing systems have begun to harmonise as a result of several transnational trends. In particular we have observed that policing resources are being re-deployed at the local, national and transnational levels as a result of concerns about TOC, and that policing is increasingly 'intelligence-led'. We have also observed that these structural changes have been accompanied by the rise of a new enforcement strategy that is being pursued globally, a strategy predicated ongoing after the proceeds of crime. Valsamis Mitsilegas has shown in his contribution to this book (Chapter 12, pp. 195–211), that the adoption of anti-money-laundering tactics has differed in important respects between jurisdictions. However, as was observed in an earlier part of this chapter, the apex of the police intelligence pyramid lies in the transnational domain. It is here that we encounter what Robert Reiner has described as 'the new International of technocratic police experts' (1997: 1007). It is policies and practices established at a level above national states that are shaping the outcomes of transnational policing.

The flagship of the 'police international' is Interpol. The historical development of this institution is a story well told (Anderson, 1989) but the details of that history need not detain us here. What is important to note is that Interpol is one small but important 'piece of the machinery' comprising the transnational policing complex (Sheptycki, 1995, 1997). Like transnational policing generally, Interpol was never constituted by any formal treaty. In the words of Fenton Bresler (1992), it is more of a 'policeman's club'. It is often said that Interpol is an 'inter-governmental organisation' (IGO). If this is taken in its formal sense, as defined by Article 57 of the United Nations Charter, this is erroneous. This is evidenced by the answer to a written question put by MP Brian Gould to the UK Home office in 1977. Mr Gould asked 'whether there is any formal signed agreement under which the United Kingdom is a member of Interpol'. The reply was that since 'membership of the International Criminal Police Organisation (Interpol) is not obtained by an intergovernmental treaty or agreement ... the question of a formal signed agreement by the United Kingdom does not therefore arise' (House of Commons, 1977). In 1949, the organisation was granted category 'B' status as a non-governmental organisation with consultative status at the UN. NGOs are non-profit citizens' organisations which may be national or international. These are in contrast to IGOs which are a variety of specialised agencies established by intergovernmental agreement. Interpol cannot be described as a non-profit citizens' voluntary organisation, neither is it an IGO properly speaking, it is merely treated *as if* it were an IGO. Its ambiguous status vis-à-vis the United Nations is reinforced by its own Constitution which has long served to guard the organisation from outside political control (Swallow, 1999).

Here we have an actually existing transnational policing platform which, like the transnational police enterprise generally, is only loosely coupled to the transnational state system. The nature of Interpol's autonomy is difficult to grasp since its personnel are police officers (sub-state actors) on temporary secondment from member police forces and its budget has historically been limited to what member *police forces* have been willing and able to supply. Therein lies the significance of the developments analysed here. Interpol is ideally situated to participate in the transnational orchestration of intelligence-led policing operations that draw on the resources of national states. At the same time, the organisation might expect to benefit financially from the sharing of assets confiscated, thereby fuelling itself for the next ILP initiative against global clandestine trade. Such a pattern might be repeated endlessly, accompanied by performance indicators that relate the assets frozen and seized, the number of criminal enterprises broken up through arrest and ever darker prognostications about transnational organised crime and the need to take stronger enforcement action. Protection racket indeed.

Interpol enthusiasts might protest that this unfairly labels the organisation and it is perhaps too easy to target this one particular institution. This does nothing to alter the fact that the transnational policing enterprise *generally* lacks any framework for political accountability. Prior to the ILP revolution this was less consequential, because transnational policing was only sporadic and *ad hoc*. The advent of techno-policing capacities at the same historical moment when a new enforcement strategy (going after the proceeds of crime) was advanced contributed to propitious conditions for the emergence of transnational policing as a self-replicating and self-guided enterprise. This raises urgent questions about the nature and character of policing as an aspect of global governance in the contemporary period.

## Holding transnational policing to account

It is possible to ask sceptical questions about the character of global governance with regard to a whole range of policy areas. When it comes to transnational policing, it is especially important to do so because the awesome power of police institutions lies in their surveillance capacity and the ability to muster coercive force in the maintenance of social order. This is not an attempt to side-step the issue of the social harms caused by TOC or terrorism, but if global governance is to be undertaken with regard to the general interests of the global commons, it is well to enquire as to who and what is being policed against and with what results. In the decade prior to 2001, transnational policing was almost exclusively deployed against 'transnational organised crime'. But a close look at what was defined as TOC revealed that it was not all that TOC could be. Transnational organised crime consists of illicit trade. A range of commodities can be brought to the transnational illicit market place. Drugs, nuclear and radioactive substances, human body parts and human beings, endangered species and products distilled from them, stolen goods or 'counterfeit goods' (i.e. intellectual property theft), weapons, precious gems and other high value commodities, pornography and toxic waste have all been bought and sold illegally. Further, the illegal dumping of toxic waste, insider dealing, tax evasion, fraudulent business practices and the corruption of state-based kleptocrats might also be described as crimes of the illicit market, or at least as economic crimes. The concept of transnational organised crime as it has been deployed by the transnational police has never stretched to all of these commodities and practices, although the UN Convention Against Transnational Crime is general enough in scope that most of these may come under its purview.[1] From the point of view of transnational governance, the issue is how priorities are set for the policing of this diverse range of issues so that selective law enforcement is in the best interests of the global commonweal.

Seen from the perspective of global governance, what is required is an agreed calculus by which to allocate policing resources in order for them to be efficiently and effectively targeted on criminal activities that cause social harm. It is not contentious to suggest that scarce policing resources should be targeted where they can be expected to do the most good, or at least cause the least harm. And yet it is not an easy matter to decide if the illegal dumping of toxic waste on the high seas is more or less harmful than any other type of economic crime, or if law enforcement against drugs markets does more good than harm, or if the exploitation associated with human smuggling or trafficking might be better answered by more concerted efforts at peacekeeping and development-aid rather than border maintenance and the restriction of asylum policies. These are not technical questions, they are political ones. What is required, therefore, is an open platform where the questions of global justice and legitimacy can be discussed and debated so that the transnational police enterprise does not become insensitive in its partiality and selectivity.

A precondition for such dialogue is to sweep away the police-centred criteria for judging the success of the transnational policing mission. It is not impossible in principle to develop methods for measuring social harm using a diverse range of indicators and, on that basis, develop a set of systematic competences for formally established and accountable transnational policing. Sadly, at present, that is not how things go. Instead, transnational policing is a more, rather than less, self-directed set of surveillance and enforcement practices that randomly impact on some sectors of the transnational illicit market. These impacts are justified and legitimated on the basis of process indicators – the number of arrests, assets seized, criminal groups disrupted – not on the basis of concrete outcomes, such as the harm averted, or the enhanced quality of life and justice. More worrying still, in recent years, as police surveillance capacity has grown, legal innovations making it possible for 'asset confiscation' have potentially created an inexhaustible source of revenue for this capricious enterprise. It does not stretch credulity to suggest that, financed by the confiscated proceeds of crime, transnational ILP may indeed become something akin to a protection racket.

In the wake of the 9–11 catastrophe, there is a danger that our ability to sceptically analyse the contradictions in transnational policing will be undermined. It has been possible, up until now, to mount criminological criticisms about this venture. Criticism regarding the self-reinforcing criteria of agency success (arrest figures, illicit goods seized, monies confiscated) and demands that some external criteria of success based on minimising the social harms due to clandestine trade could be articulated, perhaps with some success. The observation that 'going after the proceeds of crime' amounted to nothing more than a tax on criminal markets and nothing less than a perpetual source of funding for a politically unaccountable transnational policing enterprise might have been expected to hold some force when the putative target was TOC. But the rhetorical stakes have been raised. The target for the transnational police over the coming years will shift to narco-terrorism. Although it may be difficult to do so, it is well to remember that the transnational organised crime discourse that unfolded during the 1990s helped to dis-embed policing from national states and local communities with negative effects for democratic police accountability and, in many places, community safety. In such circumstances the sceptical power of the 'protection analogy' had the potential to expose some of the contradictions inherent in transnational policing and might have contributed pressure towards democratising this central feature of global governance. There is, as yet, no clue as to how the success of the transnational police effort against transnational terrorism will be evaluated nor how its practices legitimated. All the indications are that it will be a long campaign. If it is not to be a permanent condition, it is well to remain sceptical in order that we may stand a chance of tipping the balance in global governance towards democracy and freedom and away from the tyranny of self-replicating and self-financing 'global-cops'.

## Conclusion

Not all that is policing lies with the police. The only possible alternative to a global protection racket is a transnational policing enterprise predicated not on fear of crime and gross feelings of insecurity, but rather on global justice and legitimacy. What is required is a commitment not to a war on crime, or a war on terror, but rather a commitment to the rule of law and upholding standards of human rights. Transnational terrorists and criminals should be pursued and brought before an International Criminal Court so that such action can be seen to be not merely a robust form of policing, but above all one that aims to protect people of all faiths and nationalities, in every region, as well as the global commons generally. This will require a massive effort to create a new form of global political legitimacy, one which does not credit the self-interested, partial, selective and insensitive practices of institutions that have long since parted company with the general interests of global civil society. Above all, the project of global governance will require an acknowledgement that the ethical and justice issues posed by the global polarisation of wealth and power need to be resolved. Those who are poor and vulnerable because they are locked into geo-political situations which have neglected their economic, social and political claims for generations will always provide fertile grounds for the recruitment of criminals and terrorists. In order that transnational policing does not become a mere protection racket, the project of global governance must open up to include the principles of social justice, which must also include an awareness of new welfare and environmental rules and conditions. Echoing Robert Reiner (2000: xi), and updating him for the transnational age, it is possible to say that, to the extent that the underlying global culture and political economy provides meaningful and rewarding lives, social conflict and crime are diminished. Only then can police agents, transnational and otherwise, realise their highest ideals and appear as 'knights errant'. At the heart of the project of global governance, including perhaps especially the governance of crime, must lie a concern with justice and legitimacy predicated on the values of multi-culturalism, human rights, the rule of law and respect for the environment. Everyone, in every country has a role to play in policing the transnational world order. It cannot be left to the experts alone. A new global project aimed at justice and peace has to displace the practices of the protection racketeers who promise security, but merely compound collective insecurity in order that they may better profit from it.

## Note

1 This convention is essentially an instrument of international co-operation. Its purpose is to promote inter-state co-operation in order to combat TOC. Five offences, whether committed by individuals or corporate entities, are covered: participation in an organised crime group; corruption; money laundering; obstruction of justice; and 'serious crime'. There are two essential prerequisites for application: the relevant offence must have a transnational aspect and the offence must be committed by an organised criminal group. These terms are defined very broadly; 'serious crime' in particular is defined in such a way as to include all significant criminal offences 'punishable by a maximum deprivation of liberty of at least four years or a more serious penalty'. The United Nations Convention Against Transnational Organised Crime, opened for signature 12 December 2000, UN GAOR, 55th Sess. Annex 1 Agenda Item 105, at 25 UN Doc. A55/383 (2000). A vast range of activity is encompassed by this legal frame, far beyond the capacities of all the national and transnational police-type agencies combined. It is therefore inevitable that some sort of selection in law enforcement will take place, whether by random probability, ideological bias, or a mixture of the two.

## References

Anderson, M. (1989) *Policing the World*. Oxford: Clarendon.

Audit Commission (1993) *Helping With Enquiries: Tackling Crime Effectively*. London: Audit Commission.

Bayley, D. (1975) 'The police and political development in Europe', in C. Tilley (ed.) *The Formation of National States in Western Europe*. Princeton, NJ: Princeton University Press.

Bigo, D. (2000) 'Liaison officers in Europe; new officers of the European security field', in J. Sheptycki (ed.) *Issues in Transnational Policing*. London: Routledge.

Blumenson, E. and Nilsen, E. (1997) 'Policing for profit: the drug war's hidden economic agenda', *University of Chicago Law Review* 65: 35–114.

Bresler, F. (1992) *Interpol*. London: Mandarine.

Broder, J. (2000) *Risk Analysis and the Security Survey*, 2nd edn. Boston, MA: Butterworth Heinemann.

Brogden, M. and Shearing, C. (1993) *Policing for a New South Africa*. London: Routledge.

Dintino, J.J. and Martens, F. (1983) *Police Intelligence Systems in Crime Control*. Springfield, IL: Charles C. Thomas.

van Duyne, P. (1998) 'Money laundering, Pavlov's dog and beyond', *The Howard Journal* 37, 4: 359–74.

Ericson, R.V. and Haggerty, K.D. (1997) *Policing the Risk Society*. Toronto: University of Toronto Press.

Evans, P., Rueschemeyer, D. and Scocpol, T. (1985) *Bringing the State Back In*. Cambridge: Cambridge University Press.

Garland, D. (2000) 'The culture of high crime societies: some preconditions of recent "law and order" policies', *The British Journal of Criminology* 40, 3: 347–75.

Gill, P. (2000) *Rounding Up the Usual Suspects? Developments in Contemporary Law Enforcement Intelligence*. Aldershot: Ashgate.

Gilmore, W.C. (1995) *Dirty Money: the Evolution of Money Laundering Counter Measures*. Strasbourg: Council of Europe Press.

—— (1999) *Dirty Money: the Evolution of Money Laundering Counter Measures*, 2nd edn. Strasbourg: Council of Europe Press.

Godfrey, D.E. and Harris, D. (1971) *Basic Elements of Intelligence*. Washington, DC: US Government Printing Office.

Haggerty, K.D. and Ericson, R.V. (2000) 'The surveillant assemblage', *The British Journal of Sociology* 51, 4: 605–22.

Hawkins, C.W. and Payne, T.E. (1999) 'Civil forfeiture in law enforcement: an effective tool or cash register justice?', in J.D. Sewell (ed.) *Controversial Issues in Policing*. Boston, MA: Allyn and Bacon.

Her Majesty's Inspectorate of Constabulary (1997) *The National Criminal Intelligence Service*. London: HMSO.

Hobbs, D. (1995) *Bad Business*. Oxford: Clarendon.

—— (1998) 'Going down the glocal: the local context of organised crime', *The Howard Journal* 37, 4: 407–22.

House of Commons (1977) Vol. 924, Column 344, 21 Jan. 1977.

Jensen, E.L. and Gerber, J. (1996) 'The civil Forfeiture of assets and the war on drugs: expanding criminal sanctions while reducing Due Process protections', *Crime and Delinquency* 42: 421–34.

Johnston, L. (2000) *Policing Britain: Risk, Security and Governance.* Harrow: Longman.

Keohane, R.O. (1989) *International Institutions and State Power.* Boulder, CO: Westview Press.

Liang, H.-H. (1992) *The Rise of the Modern Police and the European State System from Metternich to the Second World War.* Cambridge: Cambridge University Press.

Maguire, M. (2000) 'Policing by risks and targets: some dimensions and implications of intelligence-led crime control', *Policing and Society – Special Issue on Surveillance and Intelligence-Led Policing* (J. Sheptycki (ed.)) 9, 4: 315–36.

Mann, M. (1993) *The Sources of Social Power Vol. 2, The Rise of Classes and Nation-States, 1760–1914.* Cambridge: Cambridge University Press.

Marks, S. (2000) *The Riddle of All Constitutions: International Law, Democracy and the Critique of Ideology.* Oxford: Oxford University Press.

Mazower, M. (ed.) (1997) *The Policing of Politics in the 20th Century.* Providence, RI: Berghahn.

Nelken. D. (1997) 'The globalisation of crime and criminal justice', in M.D.A. Freeman and A.D.E. Lewis (eds) *Law and Opinion at the End of the Twentieth Century, Current Legal Problems,* Vol. 50. Oxford: Oxford Clarendon.

OCDETF (1984) *Annual Report of the Organized Crime Drug Enforcement Task Force Program, March 1984.* Washington, DC: US Government Printing Office.

Pease, K. (1997) 'Crime prevention', in the *Oxford Handbook of Criminology.* Oxford: Clarendon.

Rahn, R.W. (2001) 'Taxation, money-laundering and liberty', a presentation to the 19th *Cambridge Symposium on Economic Crime,* Jesus College, Cambridge, Sept. 13 (unpublished manuscript).

Reiner, R. (1997) 'Policing and the police', in M. Maguire, R. Morgan and R. Reiner (eds) *Oxford Handbook of Criminology,* 2nd edn. Oxford: Clarendon.

—— (2000) *The Politics of the Police,* 3rd edn. Oxford: Oxford University Press.

Ruggiero, V. (1997) 'Criminals and service providers: cross-national dirty economies', *Crime, Law and Social Change* 28, 1: 27–38.

Sheptycki, J.W.E. (1995) 'Transnational policing and the makings of a postmodern state', *The British Journal of Criminology* 35, 4: 613–35.

—— (1997) 'Transnationalisation, crime control and the European state system', *International Criminal Justice Review* 7: 130–40.

—— (1998a) 'Policing, postmodernism and transnationalisation', *The British Journal of Criminology* 38, 3: 485–503.

—— (1998b) 'Reflections on the transnationalisation of policing: the case of the RCMP and serial killers', *International Journal of the Sociology of Law* 26: 17–34.

—— (2000a) 'Editorial reflections on surveillance and intelligence-led policing', *Policing and Society: Special Issue on Intelligence-Led Policing* 9, 4, Winter: 311–15.

—— (2000b) 'Policing the virtual launderette', in J. Sheptycki (ed.) *Issues in Transnational Policing.* London: Routledge.

—— (2002) *In Search of Transnational Policing: Towards a Sociology of Global Policing.* Aldershot: Ashgate.

Storbeck, J. (1999) *Organised Crime in the European Union – the Role of Europol in International Law Enforcement Co-operation.* London: the Police Foundation.

Swallow, P. (1999) *European Police Co-operation,* unpublished Ph.D. Dissertation, University of Southampton.

Tilley, C. (ed.) (1975) *The Formation of National States in Western Europe.* Princeton, NJ: Princeton University Press.
—— (1985) 'War making and state making as organized crime', in P. Evans, D. Rueschemeger and T. Skocpol (eds) *Bringing the State Back In.* Cambridge: Cambridge University Press.
van der Spuy, E. (2000) 'Foreign donor assistance and policing reform in South Africa', *Policing and Society* 10: 343–66.

# Part II

# Measurements and interpretations

If, as Sheptycki argues in Part I, it is necessary to question how scarce policing resources can be targeted, 'where they can be expected to do the most good, or at least cause the least harm', then a more reflexive and democratic dialogue over the substantive content of TOC threats is needed. As we have argued elsewhere (Edwards and Gill, 1998, 2002), social science has a key role to play in the facilitation of this dialogue, in eliciting the unintended consequences of policy responses to these threats and in shaping the knowledge-base for policy change and learning. The chapters in this section of the book address the frequent refrain that policy responses to TOC have been predicated more on assertion than rigorous research. They debate the insights and limitations of different research methods and how these can be used to interest policy-makers in different conceptualisations of TOC.

Burnham discusses a research project he is conducting on the possibility of quantifying the threat of TOC. This project, which is funded by the United States National Institute of Justice (NIJ), has its origins in an NIJ seminar on the need to measure TOC. Whereas some participants insisted that quantification was a necessary prerequisite of designing (and evaluating the impact of) rational control strategies, others argued that it would never be possible to accurately measure TOC and therefore alternative approaches to evidence-based policy-making must be considered, for example the use of social network analysis. It was suggested at this seminar that, before a particular research method was dismissed, it would be useful to know exactly what data sets already exist and how different national authorities and intergovernmental organisations (IGOs) collect and interpret data on TOC. Burnham presents interim findings from the NIJ project and considers the problems associated with developing a common recording method that could facilitate international comparisons of the incidence, prevalence and concentration of TOC.

Gregory explores the challenges of quantifying TOC further, through reference to the design and implementation of the Organised Crime Notification Scheme (OCNS) in the United Kingdom. He notes that problems of 'activity identification' in criminological research per se are accentuated in the particular case of measuring organised crime in the UK, given that there is no specific offence category of 'organised crime'. The OCNS was initiated in 1997 as a response to this problem. The OCNS is based on data collected through a survey questionnaire distributed to all local police forces plus national policing agencies, such as the British Transport Police, and other national government agencies thought to be relevant, such as Her Majesty's Customs and Excise (HMCE), the Immigration and Nationality Department Intelligence Service (INDIS), the Benefits Agency Strategic Intelligence Service (BASIS), the Serious Fraud Office (SFO) and Inland Revenue. The questionnaire has been refined through each of its annual sweeps since 1997 and currently asks each of the responding agencies to quantify the number of Organised Criminal Groups (OCGs) they are aware of, the specific activities of these groups (in terms of drug trafficking, fraud, money laundering, alcohol and tobacco smuggling and the facilitation of illegal immigration and human trafficking), their ethnicity, the extent to which particular OCGs network with one another to share expertise and resources, the geographical location of these groups, their penetration of the legitimate economy, the extent to which they display so-called 'Mafia-type' behavioural characteristics (such as the use of violence to maintain internal discipline and the corruption of public officials). Finally the OCNS questions respondents on the outcomes of law enforcement operations against OCGs.

Gregory notes that 1999 was the first annual sweep for which comprehensive responses to these questions were provided and discusses the findings from this. These findings provide interesting insights into some of the basic theses about organised crime discussed in Part I. Contrary to the 'alien conspiracy theory', the overwhelming majority of the 965 OCGs identified in the UK are staffed by white European nationals, whilst it is estimated that only 7 per cent of these groups originate from the former states of the Soviet Bloc, which have been a major factor driving EU concerns over TOC (see chapters by Rawlinson, Bogusz and King and Goodey in Part III). The transnational scope of these groups' activities is also limited relative to their principal focus on local markets, as 42.8 per cent are known to be active outside of the UK, principally in other EU countries, whereas only 7.4 per cent are known to be active in at least three continents. Findings from the OCNS support the argument that organised crime remains a primarily local activity (Hobbs, 1998). The OCNS also suggests that there is a significant interrelationship between nominally licit and illicit markets, as 43 per cent of the OCGs identified were known to have established 'cover' companies for their illicit enterprises and 20 per cent were known to have invested in legitimate companies. This finding supports the increasingly popular thesis that there is no strict dichotomy between the 'upperworld' of legitimate economic enterprise and the 'underworld' of racketeering; rather, there are strong interdependencies between licit and illicit economies (Block, 1991; Ruggiero,

2000). The OCNS is more equivocal on the 'Mafia-like' characteristics of OCGs in Britain, such as the use of violence to maintain internal discipline and the attempted corruption of public officials. Given the lack of 'cross-matching data', Gregory argues that it is only possible to draw tentative conclusions. Knowledge about corruption is undeveloped and this is identified as a key issue for future research, although 12.7 per cent of OCGs reported to the OCNS in 1999 were known to have attempted to corrupt public officials. The 1999 return also reported 36 per cent of OCGs were known to have used violence to discipline their members.

Gregory acknowledges certain limitations to the OCNS survey, such as low reporting thresholds, poor methods for assuring the quality of intelligence data on OCGs and the absence of a standardised data collection model, although he notes how this is currently being addressed by the UK National Criminal Intelligence Service (NCIS). The National Intelligence Model developed by NCIS will also be used to generate measurable outcomes and performance indicators for law enforcement operations against organised crime, including the target of disrupting 10 per cent of organised crime activity by 2004 that is specified in the Home Office's service agreement with NCIS, and more detailed targets for reducing the flow of class A narcotics into the UK and controlling organised illegal immigration.

As discussed in Part I, however, the use of such intelligence-led policing techniques as the OCNS can be criticised for limiting policy change and learning to a refinement of the usual, law enforcement-oriented strategies aimed at the usual suspects. In his chapter, Klerks argues for the need to experiment with alternative research methods that are capable of revealing certain qualities of organised crime hitherto obscured by taking groups as the basic denominator of organised criminal activity. Klerks discusses the adoption of social network analysis by policy-makers in the Netherlands following the report of the Van Traa Commission in 1995, convened to investigate the conduct of covert policing operations. The Commission found that these operations had resulted in police officers facilitating the importation of 285 tonnes of soft drugs and 100 kilos of cocaine into the Netherlands as part of a strategy to build up informants as a precursor to prosecuting the traffickers, but the informants became major drug traffickers in their own right acting with de facto police protection. A group of senior criminologists, known as the 'Fijnaut Group', were invited to submit evidence to the Van Traa Commission on alternative control strategies premised on innovative conceptions of how organised crime is conducted. In a later report to the Dutch Ministry of Justice research centre (WODC), the Fijnaut Group criticised the Mafia image of semi-stable structures with fixed leaders who systematically co-ordinate subordinate members. It was argued that this image obfuscates the fluid, protean (see Dorn's chapter in Part IV) character of criminal 'co-operatives' (a concept preferred by the Fijnaut Group to the more immutable image of criminal 'organisations').

The concept of criminal co-operatives emphasises the importance of focusing on informal social ties of friendship, kinship, even amorous liaisons, rather than formal business structures of command management, in order to understand how criminal enterprises are enabled and, by implication, how they can be disabled. Within these social ties, certain individuals act as intermediaries who establish contacts, and reinforce mutual bonds, between criminal entrepreneurs (notwithstanding the male-dominated imagery of organised crime, Klerks notes the crucial role that is often performed by women acting as intermediaries). These intermediaries, invariably obscured by the preoccupation with 'kingpins' or mob bosses, are crucial to ensuring the continuity of criminal co-operatives after the removal of purported leaders. They enable co-operatives to adapt to, and exploit the opportunities for, more contemporary modes of collaboration, trading and communication than traditional hierarchically structured organisations. If this is recognised as important for the sustainability of licit businesses, it is even more pertinent for illicit enterprises operating in the hostile climate of law enforcement and intelligence operations.

Klerks argues that social network analysis has further benefits beyond explaining the effective resistance of criminal co-operatives to law enforcement and intelligence strategies. It enables an understanding of processes of recruitment into co-operatives, the way in which criminal expertise is transferred within and between these co-operatives and a means of tracing the impact of control strategies on their functioning. Social network analysis also provides a method of researching the real extent of infiltration by criminal actors into licit enterprises and public authorities, thereby addressing the lacunae in knowledge about corruption identified by Gregory. As a consequence, social network analysis reveals alternative points of intervention for control strategies. To generate this practical knowledge, however, Klerks argues:

> it is useless to explain human behaviour or social processes solely through categorical properties and norms of individual actors. Instead, the emphasis is on their functioning within structured social relations. Individual behaviour is always seen in relation to the behaviour of the groups which a person is part of. In brief, a person manifests himself or herself in a socially relevant way primarily in his or her relationship to others, and therefore these relations deserve careful and systematic scrutiny.
>
> (See also Coles, 2001: 1)

In his contribution, Stelfox examines the relationship of academic research on organised crime to the nature of policy responses by the police in England and Wales. This chapter complements Klerks argument in so far as it is critical of the preoccupation of policing strategies with kingpins or, in the argot of British law enforcement, 'core nominals'. The focus on core nominals has been used to justify both the increasing centralisation of policy responses, including the establishment of the National Criminal Intelligence Service and National Crime Squad, and a concern with 'an ever narrowing band of the criminal spectrum'. In addition to the opportunity costs of targeting limited policing resources on this narrow band of individuals and activities, this strategy ignores cumulative evidence on the limited effect of law enforcement. Stelfox contests the argument that this limited effect can be attributed to the absence of adequate resources or enabling legislation. Conversely, law enforcement has intrinsic flaws as a mechanism for controlling crime because, while it is powerful enough to make the exchange of illicit goods and services a hazardous and expensive business, it is insufficiently capable of choking-off the flow of such goods and services altogether. The unintended consequence is that:

> this merely ensures that prices remain high, particularly where there are a group of dependent customers, as in the market for controlled drugs. This in turn makes it attractive to criminal entrepreneurs who provide a steady flow of replacements to those arrested by the enforcement activity.

Given these inherent limitations, Stelfox argues for a shift in emphasis wherein control strategies should employ insights from the criminologies of everyday life, such as opportunity reduction and the manipulation of routine activities. He identifies Sutton's (1998) idea of reducing the markets for illicit goods and services as an exemplary instance of an innovative theoretical model that can be 'actioned on the ground' in police operations. The broader salience of theories of opportunity reduction and routine activity is in their capacity to reveal the overwhelmingly local qualities of crime. In turn, these theories have important implications for devolving policy-making to local policing agencies where both the knowledge-base and techniques of policing are tailored to the diverse local contexts in which all crime, whether organised or not, actually occurs. Whereas, 'formal structures which seek to funnel all activity through a central [national or supra-national] controlling point are likely to be overloaded at some point', such devolution will enable policy-makers to better manage, interpret and apply intelligence on organised crime. It will also enable important connections between organised crime and issues of community safety in particular localities to be recognised and acted upon. To this end, Stelfox advocates encompassing strategies for reducing organised crime within the ambit of local partnerships for crime and disorder reduction, such as those established in England and Wales by the Crime and Disorder Act 1998. To realise the full potential of such devolved policy-making, however, there is a need for 'toolkits' that translate the insights of criminological research and theory into more practically adequate knowledge (see chapters by Dorn and Ekblom in Part IV).

In the ESRC seminar discussions provoked by these papers it was noted that, if law enforcement strategies premised on knowledge of the categorical properties and individual norms of criminal organisations have certain limitations, then control strategies premised on social network analysis and theories of opportunity reduction can also be subjected to criticism for failing to adequately consider the social, political and economic conditions that facilitate and engender organised criminality (Hobbs, 1998, 2001). These conditions are considered in Part III of this book through case studies of the policy response to transnational organised crime in Europe.

# References

Block, A. (1991) *Perspectives on Organized Crime: Essays in Opposition.* Dordrecht: Kluwer.

Coles, N. (2001) 'It's not what you know – it's who you know that counts: analysing serious crime groups as social networks', *British Journal of Criminology* 41, 4: 580–94.

Edwards, A. and Gill, P. (1998) 'Coming to terms with transnational organised crime', *International Journal of Risk, Security and Crime Prevention* 3, 2: 87–90.

—— (2002) 'The politics of "transnational organized crime": discourse, reflexivity and the narration of "threat"', *British Journal of Politics and International Relations* 4, 2: 245–70.

Hobbs, D. (1998) 'Going down the glocal: the local context of organised crime', *The Howard Journal* 37, 4: 407–22.

—— (2001) 'The firm: organizational logic and criminal culture on a shifting terrain', *British Journal of Criminology* 41, 4: 549–60.

Ruggerio, V. (2000) *Crime and Markets: Essays in Anti-Criminology.* Oxford: Oxford University Press.

Sutton, M. (1998) *Handling Stolen Goods and Theft: A Market Reduction Approach.* London: Home Office.

# 4 Measuring transnational organised crime

## An empirical study of existing data sets on TOC with particular reference to intergovernmental organisations

*Bill Burnham[1]*

## Introduction

Transnational organised crime (TOC) has moved higher up the agenda of some governments and intergovernmental organisations. This chapter is based on an ongoing project for the National Institute of Justice (NIJ), the Research Arm of the Department of Justice of the Government of the USA in Washington, DC. It outlines some of the issues involved in measuring TOC statistically, with a case study of one country, and the specific issues raised in respect of the three intergovernmental organisations (IGOs) that may reasonably be expected to play a leading role in the fight against TOC. A more detailed analytical description of the main features of these IGOs as regards statistical data on TOC forms the second part of the chapter.

## Statistical data on TOC

Some time ago I attended an expert group meeting funded by NIJ in Washington on the question of whether it is feasible to measure TOC, and how it should be attempted, if at all. The meeting divided, psychologically and epistemologically, into two groups. The first argued that, unless and until some sort of quantitative measure of TOC can be developed, it will not be possible to construct rational strategies and policies to counter it; and, above all, it would not be possible to evaluate the effectiveness of such strategies and policies. The second group argued that it will never be possible to measure TOC accurately enough for orthodox evaluation methods to be used, and that a quite different approach based on, for instance, network analysis, will have to be developed.

The suggestion was made that the first step could be to find out what sets of data already exist in different parts of the offices of governments, primarily but not necessarily restricted to, in Ministries of Justice and Statistical Offices. The funding of this project by NIJ was the result of that proposal.

### The epistemology and methodology of the project

The epistemology of the project is more important, both with regard to the output of the project and to the theme of this book, than the methodology. The latter is conceptually very simple, and consists of identifying a contact official in an appropriate agency in national government or an intergovernmental agency, discussing the topic with him or her and then being guided to other officials, in an open-ended sequence. It can be called, somewhat pompously, a 'heuristic methodology'. As we progress through agencies and countries, we will attempt to develop a template of known methods of recording TOC statistically, and be able to demonstrate the extent to which a given country or agency conforms to or differs from that template. The template will represent the most common forms of recording TOC, and these may not be the best. Deviation from the template may prove to be a good strategy or a poor strategy, but that judgement can only be made much later. Our current concern is to describe, not to evaluate.

The mention of description leads naturally to an account of the epistemology. The term is used here in its basic sense of what theory of knowledge and development of knowledge underlies the practical activities, and what the scientific status of the output and outcome of the project is. The underlying logic of the study is the progressive reduction of uncertainty. From a starting point of identifying what is not known, the goal is to build a foundation of what would be known if all the data that actually exists could be assembled in some kind of structure. That, in turn, would allow the clear identification of the next layer, or category, of what is unknown, and possibly, though not certainly, provide guidance as to how to conduct research into that second layer.

The primary objective of the project, therefore, is to provide a structured account of what sets of statistical data on TOC are held by different agencies of government in six countries and three intergovernmental organisations. The six countries are divided into two groups of three: those that are centrally governed and those that have a federal structure. The three centrally governed countries are Denmark, the Netherlands and the UK. The three federated countries are Canada, Germany and the USA. The three intergovernmental agencies are the International Criminal Police Organisation (INTERPOL), the World Customs Organisation (WCO) and the United Nations International Drug Control Programme (UNDCP).

The UK Home Office has provided funds for the study to be extended to include France and Italy. At the time of writing (late August 2002) the fieldwork has been carried out in the three IGOs and in Germany, and is in progress in Canada, the USA and the UK. It will be completed by the spring of 2003, with the report scheduled for publication in the second half of 2003.

Countries with these different characteristics were chosen to allow examination along two parameters. The first is the governmental structure; whether countries that are centrally governed show differences from countries that have a federal system. Countries with a federal structure will undertake most of the data collection at the state level. The way in which the data are passed on to and recorded at the central (federal) level may affect the form in which the data sets are kept and the details of what data is and is not included. The second parameter is the legal structure. Three of the countries have a common law legal system, and three have a codified legal system, and it is possible that the form of legal structure may affect the manner and detail of statistical recording.

It is a basic assumption of the study that official criminal statistics are a record primarily of the decisions made by one or more officials, in this case in one of the law enforcement agencies. Although the numbers of cases or people recorded is not an accurate picture of the number of cases that have occurred, these numbers may bear some relationship to the actual prevalence and incidence. To obtain a statistical record that has been captured and assembled with care and consistency, therefore, provides one 'handle' on the scope of the phenomenon, albeit a decidedly incomplete one.

In 'orthodox' criminology the relationship between official statistics and 'reality' has been illuminated over the last 30 or 40 years by the science of victimology, specifically surveys of rates of victimisation. These can be compared with the official statistics and, over time, for a given crime type in a given community, some sort of picture of the degree to which the official numbers record what actually happened can be built up. The development of alternative indicators in the case of different crime types of TOC, parallel to victim surveys, would be a major development in the study of TOC. As yet, to the best of my knowledge, little progress has been made in this regard.

With the qualifications given above, the results of the study are expected to throw light on some specific questions. In particular, it is expected that the different categories of crime that make up TOC can be classified into three categories, namely those the prevalence and incidence of which, as measured by official statistics (but with the reservation noted above):

a    can be measured with some confidence at present;
b    could be measured with some confidence if certain identifiable modifications were made in data capture and recording;
c    will not be measurable in the foreseeable future.

The output of the project will consist of a first inventory of data sets relevant to TOC held in the different countries and agencies, with a commentary as to how they are constructed. The term 'first' inventory is important. It is axiomatic in the heuristic logic of the work that other sources and sets of data will come to light after the first inventory is published. The output of the project is intended to stimulate such an outcome, and the inventories can be updated and expanded periodically.

One question to be considered in the output is that of the feasibility of countries using an agreed common system of recording TOC statistically. This project does not have the remit or status to recommend for or against countries developing and using a common recording method. It will, however, be able to provide knowledge of what some of the main parameters should be, what some of the main obstacles will be, and what would be entailed if countries were to decide to follow that course of action.

### The fieldwork to date

The provisional findings of the research are that the three federated countries (Canada, Germany and the USA) use noticeably different systems. The example of Germany is perhaps of most interest and value here, because of the way the *Bundeskriminalamt* (*BKA*) set up their system. Around 1990, the problem of organised crime had begun to attract regular attention in the media, and gave a higher profile to the senior management of criminal justice in Germany, which is organised primarily at the level of the state (in the American sense). The *BKA* only become involved when there is a case of national concern that crosses state boundaries or in helping to co-ordinate the activities of the states. Organised crime is an instance in both respects.

The *BKA* held a series of meetings involving police officers of different ranks from the different states, with two objectives. The first was to create a definition of organised crime that was meaningful to and usable by operational police officers. The second was to create a system of reporting that would not be too onerous for the operational officers dealing with the actual crime but would make possible the production of an accurate statistical summary for the country as a whole. Thus the case officer, having decided that he/she is dealing with a case of organised crime, starts a report of the case that allows for the recording of all aspects. That report, in hard copy, is sent at specified intervals to the *Landeskriminalamt* (*LKA*), the headquarters of the state police force.

At the *LKA* the report is automated, by being entered into a software application already set up for this specific purpose. That application can then be used for comparison with other cases, in the normal operational manner; but it can also have the identifiers of the individuals removed, along with some other data not needed centrally. It is then forwarded electronically to the *BKA*. By receiving data in this way from all the states, the *BKA* can easily generate an accurate and homogeneous report on recorded organised crime across the country.

Two features of this procedure are noteworthy in the context of this chapter. The first is that the system being introduced was built on the professional knowledge of a range of experts in specific fields. The primary group was operational police officers, but statisticians, criminal lawyers and information technology experts in software applications were also involved from the start. It was a 'bottom-up' operation. The second is that the system was designed, on the one hand, to satisfy several different audiences or constituencies, and it was accepted that several years would pass before it would begin to yield results that would otherwise have been unobtainable.

The other lesson to be learned from the experience in the three countries is that each country records TOC in its own way. One of the basic principles of database research is that a data set cannot be properly analysed unless the way in which it was compiled is understood. This is not the case currently with national data sets on TOC, as the ways in which they are compiled differ between countries, in ways not yet documented. The chapter by Gregory (this volume, Chapter 5) illustrates in detail some of the complexities to be met when 'deconstructing' statistical data sets on this topic.

## The intergovernmental organisations

All three of the IGOs have been visited, and the remainder of this chapter is concerned with the activities and roles of these agencies in relation to issues of data and measurement. The assumption that these three IGOs, with their international character and remit, will play an important and increasing role in the fight against TOC seems simply to be common sense. However, there are important differences between them, and each of them is faced with specific problems that require resolution before the progress that might be expected actually occurs.

One aspect of the workings of intergovernmental organisations that is often not appreciated by those unfamiliar with them is that the Secretariat of each organisation has very little formal room for initiative in, or control over, much of their work programme. They each have a governing body that is made up of delegates sent by the governments of member states. In the case of ICPO/INTERPOL and the World Customs Organisation (WCO) the delegations are normally composed of senior police and customs officers respectively, in each case often accompanied by an official from the appropriate ministry in central government. The composition of delegations at United Nations meetings is more unpredictable and less easy to describe. The UN is, in general, a much more complex organisation than INTERPOL or WCO. The role that it seems to envisage for itself in future work in this respect is equally more complex, which is the reason why the UN is therefore discussed at greater length than the other two IGOs.

The complexity and uncertainty of the data issue between the three IGOs can be illustrated by the situation relating to statistical data on what is probably the most common and profitable form of TOC – drug trafficking. In the early 1990s, I was one of the UNDCP officials responsible for comparing and combining the records on drug seizures across the three main intergovernmental bodies concerned – INTERPOL, WCO and UNDCP – each of which kept their own records in this respect. We expected to find only a moderate overlap between INTERPOL and WCO, because the former receives data from police forces responsible for criminal activity inside the border of a country, and WCO for data on offences and offenders who cross national boundaries. UNDCP receives its data from the offices in national governments responsible for monitoring the drug situation within their country. A large overlap with the data from both the other sources was therefore expected.

We were surprised to discover that all three data sets contained, very roughly, one-third of that held by one of the other agencies and rather less than one-third of that held by both, while somewhat over one-third was held by just the one agency. The relatively low overlap between INTERPOL and WCO was to be expected, but the other discrepancies gave rise to greater concerns, including one specific question relevant here. If collecting data on the most visible and discussed form of TOC is characterised by such uncertainties, how much more complex may collecting data on other types of TOC be? This is not an argument against trying, because many of these problems can be resolved with contemporary statistical expertise and information technology. It is an argument, however, against expecting quick results that are valid and reliable.

### The United Nations Programme for International Crime Prevention

The economic and social aspects of the work of the UN are handled, for the most important sectors, by functional commissions, including Drug Control and Crime Prevention and Criminal Justice. The primary product of a given Commission is a set of draft resolutions that mandate the Secretariat to undertake a course of action. For the resources that are necessary to carry out the activity to be made available, the resolutions of the Commissions have to be formally passed by the ECOSOC, because the ECOSOC has the authority to spend money, which the Commissions do not.

UN policy documents often take the form, at least in the field of criminal justice, of long annexes or appendices attached to relatively short resolutions. The Convention on Transnational Organised Crime and the Vienna Declaration, a product of the Tenth Congress in April 2000, are annexes to resolutions. They form the substantive statements on the obligations of states under the Convention and courses of action by which these obligations may be discharged and objectives met.

The UN has taken an interest in TOC since the eighth of the quinquennial Congresses on the Prevention of Crime and the Treatment of Offenders, held in Havana, Cuba in 1990. That Congress passed a large range of resolutions on topics across the spectrum of crime and justice. There was criticism from governments of the programme trying to be all things to all people, and it was clearly necessary to set priorities. The government of Italy took the initiative in putting the issue of TOC at the top of the agenda by convening an inter-ministerial meeting at Naples in 1994, which culminated in the Naples Declaration on TOC.

At the same time, within the Secretariat, the International Drug Control Programme and the (as was then) Crime Prevention and Criminal Justice Programme were being brought closer together, and have subsequently become one office. The Executive Director of UNDCP and the Director of CPCJP were both Italian nationals. The leading role played by Italian nationals in both intergovernmental activity and in the Secretariat was later enhanced by the appointment of Pino Arlacchi as head of the joint crime and drugs programmes. Arlacchi had apparently made his name in opposing the Mafia, and it is quite understandable that he and his compatriots assumed without question that the Mafia is the paradigm model for organised crime.

If it is a reasonable assumption that the people responsible for policy in respect of a given phenomenon will have some kind of model of the phenomenon in their mind, although it may be unarticulated, the apparent dominance of the Mafia model in UN thinking and instruments is not surprising. The American acceptance of the Mafia model is documented in Chapter 1 of this volume, and the support of the USA for the Italian approach has been a theme of informal but informed speculation for some years.

In the view of many of those contacted via the NIJ project, the Mafia model is increasingly inappropriate. A significant amount of TOC is carried out by fluid networks whose personnel constantly change, and in which authority is a devolved and shifting phenomenon. The Mafia model is, of course, of a monolithic formal organisation, or group of organisations ('families'), with a clear-cut structure of command and of line management similar to a sizeable corporation in the world of legitimate business. Against such an organisation, strategies of 'taking out' the CEO and a few key departmental managers form a rational policy. Against fluid networks, the outcomes of such strategies give less ground for optimism (see Peter Klerks, this volume, Chapter 6).

The UN Convention against Transnational Organised Crime is the first major attempt by governments in the forum of an intergovernmental body to address the issue of TOC as a whole, and on an interregional basis. The term 'interregional' is used in UN parlance as a synonym for 'global'. Thus, for instance, the development of strategies against TOC by the European Union is excluded from this analysis, except for one mention later as a possible role model.

The GA adopted the Convention in its resolution 55/25 of 15 November 2000. It is a detailed document, written, inevitably, in legalistic language. Its main purpose is to provide a platform on which international co-operation and collective action against TOC can be built. It has, I believe, been well accepted as a significant achievement, and will be of value for a long time. It will assist in questions of the harmonisation of legislation, cross-national prosecution and all aspects of making the legal process efficient. However, there are two main components of crime prevention. The first is the traditionally legal, in essence how to process villains when they are caught, in which respect the Convention seems to be a real advance; and the operational aspect, how to forestall or catch the villains in the first place. My comments on the Convention focus only on matters of operational concern and of expected scope.

There is considerable emphasis on international co-operation, but with two strange features. It is written as if INTERPOL were merely a specialised marginal body to deal with one category of urgent matters (Article 18 paragraph 13) and there is no mention of WCO at all. It may be that there are technical, legal problems involved in naming other intergovernmental bodies in such conventions, but if that is the case, some of the consequences might be counter productive. My impression that the UN does not include INTERPOL and WCO in its thinking, and vice versa, was strengthened when I attended the meeting of the UN Commission in April 2002, and could find no representative of either of the law enforcement IGOs.

The omission of WCO seems particularly strange in respect of Article 29, *Training and mutual assistance.* The Article has nine sub-paragraphs on specific tasks, most of which seem to require the expertise of national customs services, and therefore the concern of WCO. Paragraph 1(b) of the Article urges States Parties to the Convention to develop programmes to deal with 'Routes and techniques used by persons suspected of involvement in offences covered by this Convention, including in transit States, and appropriate counter measures.' This presumably comes close to the main objectives of WCO.

There are several other paragraphs or sub-paragraphs in which the Convention (including its Annexes) seems to be calling for activities already undertaken by the other two interregional intergovernmental organisations. It may be that a considerable extension of these activities is envisaged by the Convention, but by which bodies or under whose aegis is not stated.

A review of the activities that States Parties to the Convention are called upon to undertake introduces the second pragmatic point to be made about the Convention. The type of work entailed in its implementation is that usually known as 'bottom-up', whereas the whole tradition of working in the UN Crime and Justice programme is 'top-down'. Article 26, *Measures to enhance cooperation with law enforcement authorities*, Paragraph 1, gives a list of activities, all of which depend on the expertise of front line operational law enforcement officials. It therefore raises the issue of how this knowledge is to be gathered and structured in a manner that makes it usable for policy analysis, a task that is the essence of the bottom-up approach.

The dichotomy between the work, primarily legal, that went into framing the Convention and the operational work that is entailed by much of it is shown more clearly in a more recent document, the report of the Commission on Crime Prevention and Criminal Justice on its resumed tenth session, in Vienna, September 2001. One of the agenda items of that session was the drafting of *Plans of action for the implementation of the Vienna Declaration on Crime and Justice: meeting the challenges of the twenty-first century*. Section 1 is 'Action against transnational organised crime'. The section on 'International Actions', setting out the activities to be undertaken by the Centre for International Crime Prevention, states that it will, in co-operation with other relevant international and regional organisations:

c   assist states in the establishment or intensification of bilateral and multilateral co-operation in those areas covered by the Convention, in particular those involving the use of modern communications technologies, on request;
d   carry out the regular collection and analysis of data on transnational and organised crime, in consultation with interested states;
e   maintain a database to permit a more comprehensive in-depth analysis of patterns and trends and geographical mapping of the strategies and activities carried out by organised criminal groups, and of best practices to combat transnational organised crime, in consultation with interested states.

For all of these activities, the most appropriate places to start seem to be INTERPOL and WCO, who have substantial data and expertise on these matters already. The data and practical experience of these two organisations may well prove to be no more than a foundation on which other, more specific advances can be made; but to start from anywhere else would seem strange. 'Best practices' (on which more later) will be provided primarily, and overwhelmingly, from law enforcement officials who are represented at the intergovernmental level by these two organisations, rather than from some other source linked to the UN.

Finally there is a question concerning the level of generality in the Plan of Action. To operational law enforcement officers it would read as vague aspirations, except for the data and best practice parts. These are already catered for in other intergovernmental organisations, or could be so with relatively little investment of resources and effort. The shortage of practical proposals is perhaps best illustrated in the section on National Actions, Paragraph 3: 'States will also endeavour, as appropriate: (c) promoting growth and sustainable development and eradicating poverty and unemployment.' The vagueness and unfeasibility of this clause raises doubts as to how useful UN initiatives will be, and could be interpreted as a desperate bid to say something when the body in question has nothing else more concrete to say.

### INTERPOL and WCO

To go from the UN to one of the other intergovernmental criminal justice organisations at the global level, or vice versa, is to experience quite different worlds. These two organisations are operational law enforcement bodies, and their primary concern is to assist national police or customs forces to track and apprehend specific suspects in specific cases. Their governing bodies are made up of senior officials from the service in question, and do not have to report to some higher body. Importantly, their budgets are self-contained rather than in permanent competition with other parts of the same organisation. The range and scope of their deliberations, prioritising and decisions are therefore much narrower and more precise. The organisational culture of INTERPOL/WCO is that of an operational law enforcement agency, while the organisation culture of the UN is that of an agency of negotiation.

There are significant differences between INTERPOL and WCO in the way in which they conduct their work; not least that there is historically a significant level of antipathy and distrust. Several officials in both organisations with whom I discussed this issue assured me that the level of antagonism between customs and police services has declined markedly in the last 10 to 20 years, but they all agreed that it used to be quite high. Some years ago I remember being told by a senior French customs officer that when a colleague was responsible for a controlled delivery, the main decision the officer had to make was which he or she distrusted less, the French police or the customs service of the other country.

As mentioned, both INTERPOL and WCO are seen by the member governments, and see themselves as, primarily being operational organisations focused at the level of individual cases. There are staff members who are charged with development of strategy, but this task seemed to be again in the context of individual cases, and groups of individuals. In informal conversation, when the question of why more attention was not paid to 'the bigger picture', the answer was that such activities are not given priority in their terms of reference, and that therefore resources were not allocated to them.

Both INTERPOL and WCO are focused on individual current cases, and do not put many resources into the analysis of patterns and other inferences to be drawn from data collected in the past. This is not in any way a criticism. The job that these organisations were set up to do was to assist national police and customs services to track and arrest suspects who had moved to another country; and that is, properly, still their priority. They have built up, over the years, a collection of data on what is now called TOC, but it is fragmented and largely archived. It seems that this could be an excellent resource for research work, but some work would be needed to utilise it to the full. However, this is not work the organisations can be expected to do unless they are mandated to do so by their govern- ing (member state) council, and resourced accordingly. There is, there- fore, a potentially productive source of data on the patterns of recorded TOC in the past 20 years or more, which has yet to be used strategically to its full potential.

## Conclusion

In reviewing the problem of attempting to measure TOC, this chapter has inevitably discussed different aspects of the main intergovernmental organisations involved. How these different aspects come together with the scientific questions entailed, and possible implications for future inter- governmental activity, is the theme of this last section.

The nature of work to be done is normally one of the main defining dimensions of the organisation set up to do it. Political parties have one way of behaving, scientific institutions another. Such concepts as 'loyalty' or 'disagreement' can be interpreted very differently in each. Politics is concerned with making things possible and getting things done. Science is concerned with finding things out. The UN is primarily a political organisa- tion, enabling governments to relate to each other in a way that would not be possible if the organisation were not there. Its way of handling even those questions that have a strong scientific (that is, factual enquiry) component is still in essence political; and politics is usually a top-down process. The other two interregional intergovernmental organisations in this context are both operational, enquiring organisations; they are, essen- tially, bottom-up. It is unlikely that any special new intergovernmental organisation will be created specifically to deal with TOC so that whatever is done at the global level will have to be done by these three organisations.

There has been one development, at least, of real significance in crim- inology, or criminal justice science, in the last 10 or 20 years; namely, the coming to maturity in this context of the science of evaluation. 'Evalu- ation', as a specialist sub-division of social science has, of course, been developing for several decades, but in recent years its use has transformed the practice of crime prevention and criminal justice policy development. Some governments have adopted a formal philosophy of supporting 'what works' and 'evidence-based strategies'.

One characteristic of such an approach is that the indicators required for good evaluation are identified, and if necessary built into the given strategy, before the strategy is launched. Evaluation is the core of identifying 'best practice', as identified in the UN Plan of Action; and the core of contemporary evaluation is quantitative methods. Evaluation is possible without numbers, but it is vague and can never demonstrate the definitive nature of its conclusions. Quantifying is not always possible, and attempts to pretend that it is when it is not feasible or appropriate are counter-productive.

Measuring the immeasurable and claiming validity for the product cannot be defended, but assessments of 'best practice' without some sort of strong, i.e. rigorous, evidence cannot be relied upon. Evaluating 'best practice' is another archetypal bottom-up exercise. The situation is, in fact, even more complicated. Some of my university colleagues have recently been involved in the evaluation of 'what works' in burglary prevention. One key finding is that what works in one context may not work in another, even within roughly similar contexts in the culture of northern England. If the UN, or any other body, is to identify 'best practice' in countering TOC, it will need to plan for the long term and demonstrate the logic and detailed stages of that research planning before much expectation can be invested in it.

The situation with regard to the statistical measurement of TOC at the moment might be summed up as follows.

1   Some good work in the form of case studies of TOC has been done in various centres, although this chapter has not touched on these activities, and the quantitative aspects thereof tend to be estimates, not records.
2   Relatively little is known about the phenomenon on a broad scale, including the question of whether 'one model for all' is a feasible and achievable objective; but the evidence at this time suggests that this is not the case.
3   Different countries compile such databases as they have on TOC by different methods, and these data sets are not directly comparable at present.
4   The objective of compiling a cross-national database on TOC might or might not be feasible; but it will take some considerable time and careful detailed work to achieve, even if it is feasible.
5   The problem of 'top-down' in contrast to 'bottom-up' is significant in this context, both in terms of the intellectual traditions of the inter-governmental organisations involved and the types of task to be undertaken in the immediate future.
6   There is a potentially serious problem of the co-ordination of the work of different intergovernmental agencies in law enforcement and crime prevention and criminal justice that will have to be resolved before much progress can be made.

# Note

1 All views expressed in this chapter are the personal views of the author, and do not represent in any way the official position of the organisations referred to. This chapter draws on material provided by the different organisations named above that have been visited in the course of the NIJ study, and materials made available at UN meetings. It also draws on personal conversations with officials of all organisations.

# 5 Classify, report and measure

## The UK Organised Crime Notification Scheme

*Frank Gregory**

## Introduction

Knowledge is a key element in devising responses to policy problems. In the field of criminal justice policy an obvious problem is the natural desire of the perpetrators of crimes to conceal their activities. This problem of activity identification is compounded in the UK, in the case of organised crime, by the fact that there is no separate organised crime offence category. Therefore organised crime appears neither in recorded crime statistics nor in statistics on convictions. This chapter focuses on the problems of knowledge acquisition, at the official level, on organised crime in the period from 1996–2002. It draws upon hitherto unpublished Home Office sources and locates the raw data gathering process within the context of national, global and regional (EU) crime control agendas. The chapter addresses the topic by examining the general issues related to crime data collection, the origins of the UK's Organised Crime Notification Scheme (OCNS), the method selected for OCNS data collection, the quantitative and qualitative problems encountered in the management of the OCNS and the problems of evaluating the collected data.

Organised crime is a good example of a high profile political issue, whose existence as a policy problem area has been asserted by political leaders and law enforcement practitioners *before* the collection of comprehensive, reliable and comparable data. Moreover, once on the political agenda, there tends to be a need to produce policy responses notwithstanding the inadequacies of the data on the problem area. For example, both the National Criminal Intelligence Service (NCIS) and the National Crime Squad (NCS) were established prior to the existence of the UK's first comprehensive organised crime data collection in 1999. It is also a

* The author is grateful to the Home Office Policing and Reducing Crime Unit for permission to use materials from his Year 2000 Review of the OCN Scheme. He alone is responsible for the interpretations and commentary contained in this chapter. The author also wishes to acknowledge the research support provided by the ESRC under Award No. L213252013 (with Rawlinson and Brooke) for 'Crime, Borders and Law Enforcement: a European "Dialogue" for improving security', a project in the ESRC's *One Europe or Several?* programme.

policy area whose definitional problems are openly acknowledged. The 1999 Summary Report on the UK's Organised Crime Notification Scheme clearly stated that: 'Achieving a universally accepted definition of organised crime has, so far, defeated all experts working on national and international levels.' However, this problem can be side-stepped, as the EU has done, by having very broad criteria with a low (2–3 person) membership reporting threshold for organised crime groups (OCGs), thus embracing organised crime groups ranging from a two-person counterfeiting group to one of the Sicilian Mafia families (see further in Elvins, this volume, Chapter 2). The Home Office justified its scheme on two grounds. First, so that 'policy decisions ... are based on the best possible knowledge of the actual (OC) position'; and, second, 'to enable us to co-ordinate effectively our efforts to combat organised crime with our neighbours, the other member states of the European Union.'

Any system of data collection and reporting on crime is a problematic activity. The related issues are expertly presented in Walker (1995) and in the recent Home Office Research Series Paper (Burrows *et al.*, 2000). The main concerns with the more widely known data sources on crime are the gaps that exist between the figures generated by victim reports in the British Crime Survey and those recorded by the police.

Regarding the OCNS, it is unlikely that public reporting of 'crimes' had any marked significance, except perhaps in helping to identify clusters of car thefts or drug dealing by geographical location. However, variations in police and other agencies' recording practices are a common problem. A factor which can be affected by the police and other law enforcement agencies now being part of a 'performance culture' (Burrows *et al.*, 2000: 5). Thus, whilst reporting increasing numbers of OCGs identified may be seen as delivering 'proactive' law enforcement, any decline in the number of OCGs reported as being dismantled could be seen as evidence of less effective law enforcement.

This chapter provides the first public consideration of detail and data from the hitherto unpublished annual official analyses of the data reported in the returns to the UK's OCNS which was managed by the Home Office RDS Directorate between 1997–2000 but whose product was mainly used by NCIS.

Sheptycki has provided a useful background commentary by reference to NCIS reflections on organised crime, tracing these from the 1993 NCIS 'Threat Assessment Conference'. Noting the contested nature of organised crime, Sheptycki nevertheless offers a useful way of understanding how the concept has been applied in official use in the UK. The applications Sheptycki notes offer a helpful, conceptual underpinning to the rationale for the OCNS:

> The definition of organised crime used in British Police circles has two levels of meaning: denotative and connotative. At the denotative

level, organised crime has been constructed so as to point to crimes associated with the 'illicit economy' and the drug market is the *sine qua non* of this. At the connotative level, organised crime has come to be associated with foreign contagion. The denotative and connotative levels of meaning act in combination promoting a powerful control response.

(2000: 32)

This latter point can be further illustrated by the recent decision to tackle what is seen as the emerging threat of 'hi-tech crime' by the establishment of a new multi-agency law enforcement body, the National Hi-Tech Crime Unit.

In the UK, some information on OCGs is publicly available from sources such as the annual reports of NCIS, NCS, HM Customs and Excise and the Immigration and Nationality Department (IND). Useful data and commentary are also to be found in the appropriate reports of HM Inspectorate of Constabulary, the National Audit Office and the linked reports of the Commons Public Accounts Committee. Occasionally, the Commons Home Affairs Select Committee also publishes reports related to this area. The NCIS annual 'Threat Assessment Report' is a classified document as is the EU organised crime assessment contained in the annual Presidency and Europol 'Situation Report'. However, in the case of both of these documents, unclassified versions are available and commentary on the EU reports is to be found in the reports of the Commons European Scrutiny Committee.

Despite the problems of restricted access to some of the data sources, this chapter can offer insights into the methodologies of data collection on organised crime at a national level in the UK between 1997–2000, and to some extent, on the methodologies of certain other EU states based on research from a Falcone Project (Gregory, 1999). A basic problem is that, under the EU and national schemes, a large number of OCGs can be recorded simply on the basis of the low reporting threshold, increasing law enforcement agency awareness of the OCN Scheme's requirements and more agencies reporting to the Scheme.

With reference to the OCNS, this chapter will address the following issues: the Scheme and its relationship to Home Office responsibilities and law enforcement agency service delivery goals, the method of data collection, qualitative and quantitative issues related to agency response level, OCG activity in the UK as shown by the OCNS annual data summaries and the development and use of the Scheme from 2000 onwards.

## The OCN Scheme and its institutional location

The UK's OCNS was a response to a requirement for the collection of data on organised crime groups (OCGs) and their criminal activities. At the EU level, the JHA Council highlighted member states' common concerns about organised crime from 1993 onward. Specific obligations in this area were summarised in the Action Plan to Combat Organised Crime adopted by the JHA Council in July 1997 (*OJ* No. C251 of 15/8/97). Among these obligations member states agreed to provide, on an annual basis and against common criteria, a situation report on organised crime activity in their countries (see EU Council, 1995, 1996).

At the national level, the UK moved from a position of 'no data because we don't have a problem' in the early 1990s, to an 'awareness of the issue' stage in the mid-1990s, to the current stage of trying to understand what policy and institutional responses are required by reference to the data gathered on OCG activity. As mentioned earlier, not all the relevant sources are in the public domain. For the mid-1990s the most important public sources of data are provided by: the Commons Home Affairs Select Committee Report on 'Organised Crime' (1995) and the Home Office Research Series Paper by Mike Porter (1996). An important, unpublished source is the 1996 ACPO Report known as the Phillips Report (1996), after the Chairman of the Inquiry. Although not widely available outside official circles, its assessment of what was known about the UK situation in the mid-1990s can be quite well understood by reference to Stelfox (1998) and Hobbs (1998).

In 1997, as issues surrounding measurement and definition of organised crime became increasingly recognised, there was a significant institutional change through the establishment of the NCIS, which had been a Home Office department since 1992. The core role of NCIS is 'to develop intelligence to combat serious and organised crime' (HMIC, 1999). Whilst NCIS does target OCG groups, much effort is also directed towards individual criminals via its 'core' and 'current' nominals scheme (Stelfox, 1998).

In order to improve UK knowledge of the nature and extent of OCG activity and to fulfil the national obligation to the EU, NCIS was 'tasked with the production of a survey instrument which would gather data enabling the production of a more accurate and factual based assessment of such crime in the UK' (Dunnighan and Hobbs, 1996). The NCIS Organised Crime Unit designed and distributed a pilot questionnaire in 1996. This questionnaire process and its results were the subject of an external review for the Home Office by Dunnighan and Hobbs. They concluded that there was 'merit in a national survey ... [and] that with further reflection and modifications, the data could become a 'successful, pragmatic addition to our knowledge of the perplexing, and at times, elusive phenomena [of organised crime]' (1996: 16).

After the 1996 review, the Home Office decided to proceed with a full national data collection exercise, but to reassign the project away from NCIS to the Home Office Research, Development and Statistics Directorate (RDS). At the time, the decision reflected judgements about the optimum location of the scheme in terms of criminal justice survey research expertise and the location of the requisite level of authority to ensure the co-operation of all the target reporting agencies. In the mid-1990s, NCIS was still establishing its credibility and developing its own identity. Earlier research into the predecessor of NCIS, the NDIU (National Drugs Intelligence Unit), had revealed that such new national bodies can experience mixed perceptions of their status and function from the longer established law enforcement agencies (see Wright, Waymont and Gregory, 1993). However, despite this reassignment of the OCN Scheme from NCIS to the Home Office RDS Directorate, it was still necessary for NCIS to utilise additional means of data collection on organised crime among the various law enforcement agencies in order to fulfil its operational tasks, and so it developed a parallel data collection scheme, the Strategic Intelligence Requirement (SIR).

Thus, data acquisition on organised crime in the UK can serve several purposes:

- a simple data source on which primary and rigorous research can be carried out and from which policy relevant conclusions may be drawn;
- it may provide real-time information on crime patterns and trends that can be used in reordering operational priorities;
- data from the questions on arrests or disruptions may be usable as a basis for performance indicators.

Each of these purposes has different implications for a scheme such as OCN (see Bottomley and Coleman and also Copas in Walker, 1995).

There are two major points of relevance to be drawn from the discussion on the institutional location of the responsibility for the OCN Scheme. First, the reputation of the data collecting processing agency must be such that those agencies sending in the data can feel that sensitive information will be adequately safeguarded. Second, it is necessary for the rationale of such a scheme to be adequately understood by the reporting agencies. Government departments are increasingly calling for a variety of data to be recorded and reported. This can raise problems of data collection overload and suspicions about how the information may be used from the perspective of the reporting agencies.

Notwithstanding the high policy status assigned to organised crime by the EU, this has not yet been accompanied by the development of a uniform data collection methodology across the EU. The following examples serve to illustrate this point. Germany, which perceives itself to be mainly facing very loosely organised criminal groupings, bases its annual reports around particular yearly cohorts of 'suspects' (BKA, 2000). The Netherlands uses the EU criteria but introduces a financial threshold, so that only OCG activities believed to create illegal turnovers above a particular amount are analysed and reported through their OCG reporting system. France uses a two-tier system: offences notified against sections of the Criminal Code are analysed by the appropriate specialist police units and an overall trends assessment is then produced (Gregory, 1999). The country that appears closest to Britain in the methodology of its organised crime data collection scheme is Belgium. This member state is able to provide very local level details of OC activity and a detailed presentation of its data, plus some discussions of methodological problems is to be found in a Report to the Belgian Senate (Senat de Belgique, 1998).

## The method of data collection

The data required from 1996 for EU and UK purposes had not previously been collected in any regular or systematic way. Moreover, this data did not fit in with the existing collection of national crime statistics. Thus, the only feasible method of data collection was one that recorded linkages between criminals which met at least the qualifying criteria and characteristics. Once such sets of linkages were deemed by the reporting agencies to be returnable, more detailed information on membership, geography, range of criminal activities and criminal methods could also be requested as part of the OCG data collection process. Thus, respondents were being asked to give both classificatory and explanatory details.

The aim was to obtain national coverage from all relevant public sector agencies in the UK: police forces (including British Transport Police (BTP), Royal Ulster Constabulary (RUC, now the Police Service of Northern Ireland), NCIS and NCS, Customs and Excise, the Immigration and Nationality Department Intelligence Service (INDIS), the Benefits Agency Strategic Intelligence Service (BASIS), the Serious Fraud Office (SFO) and Inland Revenue. Counting each police force as a separate reporting agency, the total number of potential reporting agencies is 60 and all of these were included in the 1999 returns. However, in the 1997 collection, only 23 such agencies made OCN returns.

Given the geographical dispersion of the reporting agencies and the fact that a return had to be completed for each OCG identified, a questionnaire-based process was the only feasible data collection method. The OCN questionnaire was mostly transmitted and returned in hard copy format, although now electronic means are increasingly utilised. The questionnaire was subject to some developmental changes after the 1996 review of the NCIS pilot scheme. The Home Office RDS and the reporting agencies had agreed that the 1997 and 1998 OCN collections would take the form of a post-pilot development period with the aim of achieving a comprehensive coverage of agencies and known OCGs in the 1999 collection and maintaining that level of response thereafter.

The questionnaire was mainly of the 'tick box' format with spaces for brief qualitative comments. Respondents were not asked to 'score' any

answers. OCGs could even be reported if they did not meet all four qualifying criteria. The Home Office Research and Development Directorate
assigned relatively limited personnel and technical resources to this
scheme. In the period from 1997 to 1999, most of the OCN Scheme management effort went into increasing agency participation, chasing up late
returns and checking for double counting.

Although considerable effort was put into 'selling' the importance of
the OCN Scheme to the responding agencies by the Scheme manager and
NCIS, the review of the Scheme in 2000 (Gregory, 2000a) found, as did
the 1996 Pilot Review, that more still needed to be done. All such questionnaire processes require underpinning to ensure that respondents feel
a sense of shared ownership of the activity, particularly in the form of
analytical outputs from the data that are usable in meeting agencies
operational needs.

## Quantitative and qualitative issues related to agency responses

Both quantitative and qualitative issues are crucial to the development of a
comprehensive and reliable OCN Scheme. For quantitative reliability, it is
necessary for reporting agencies to have their own collection, monitoring
and validation system. Qualitative reliability requires agency systems in
place that provide quality assurance tests to support the data submitted on
OCGs. Whilst these may seem obvious points, they are based on presump-
tions about organisational capacity and behaviour which may not be completely valid in all circumstances. The OCN Scheme had to assume the
following:

1    that OCN reporting agencies can receive the full co-operation of all
     their sections in terms of knowledge of OCGs operating in their func-
     tional and geographical areas of responsibility.
2    that the data used has been the subject of internal organisational reli-
     ability and validity checks.

On the first point, although completion of the OCN returns was a Home
Office requirement and, as such, endorsed to police forces by the Association of Chief Police Officers (ACPO) Crime Committee, it took a little
while to receive returns from all the police forces. Moreover, the OCN
2000 review still found some evidence of residual problems in respect of
whether all relevant parts of particular police forces had either received
the OCN questionnaires for completion or completed as many returns as
their actual knowledge of OCG activity might necessitate.

At the root of both of these issues is the capacity of police forces (or,
indeed, other law enforcement agencies) to provide proactive law enforcement or, as it is termed in the police service, 'intelligence-led policing'.

The police service has recognised the contemporary importance of this strategy since the Baumber Report of 1975 (HMIC, 1997a). However, the HMI thematic inspection *Policing with Intelligence* had to note that: 'despite the best efforts of ACPO, a structure comprising 43 individual forces is bound to result in diversity in procedures ...' (HMIC, 1997b: 6) and 'A greater proportion are reviewing their practices and tactics while others still have some way to go to match the performance of their peers' (ibid.: 1). In the early years there was, as with the police, a clear problem of obtaining a fully comprehensive return from the other national agencies on all the OCGs of which they were aware in each year. In part, this was due to problems of internal agency communications and also with uncertainties about when it was or was not appropriate to complete an OCN return. For example, the Customs and Excise returns for 1997 were felt by that agency to only account for about half of the OCGs that they knew to be active. Similarly, in 1997, the returns from BASIS were small and reflected about a 10 per cent sample of the groups known to the agency. BASIS did, however, feel that the returns were at least a representative sample of the OCGs' criminal activities in the area of their responsibility. For INDIS, its return of only four OCGs in 1997 was a function of the fact that it was not then structured in such a way as to provide a full response. By 1999 all the agencies were reporting a near complete coverage of the OCGs of which they were aware.

There are two main interrelated qualitative problems underlying the 1997–9 OCNS. These are the reliability and validity of the data submitted and, hence, the reliability and validity of conclusions drawn from the data. Both of these problems relate to the degree of possible comprehensive coverage achieved and the nature of the quality assurance procedures that may have been applied to the content of individual returns. It was argued in the 1997 OCG report that, up to then, 'UK annual reports on organised crime have provided a detailed description of the threat from organised crime and the measures that are taken to combat it [and that they] contained an informative account of the nature of organised crime in the UK *but* have been able to say little about its extent.' However, in its 1997–8 Report, NCIS was able to make statements such as: 'A report on Turkish organised crime in the UK identified this group as responsible for the importation of between 80 per cent and 90 per cent of the heroin seized in this country' (NCIS, 1999b: 9).

This, at first glance, was an important development and parallels the availability of new information through the OCNS. Moreover, in 1998 NCIS produced its first strategic assessment: *The Threat from Serious and Organised Crime to UK Security and Interests.* This document was described in the 1998 HMIC NCIS Inspection as 'a foundation document of fundamental importance to the NCIS and the wider UK law enforcement efforts, and will inform government policy and practice in the area of crime and criminality' (HMIC, 1999: para. 6.3). However, in the previous paragraph,

HMIC (para. 6.2) had pointed out that 'the quality of the analysis of serious and organised crime relies heavily upon the quality of the information passed to the NCIS from police forces and other law enforcement agencies'. The OCNS data was one of the major sources for the NCIS Threat Assessment document up to 2000, and any data unreliability in the former would be reflected in any analyses based upon it at the time.

## The OCNS data

The data from the OCN collections, between 1997 and 1999, were subject to an annual analysis within the Home Office and a yearly report, *Organised Crime Groups*, was produced for circulation to responding agencies and other relevant officials. Because of the caveats concerning the OCN data collection process, the following selected presentation of data has been chosen to minimise the possible impact of data collection 'gaps'. Naturally, completed OCN returns are closed sources of information, available only for official purposes. However, NCIS press releases provide illustrative examples of criminal groups that could meet the qualifying criteria and which were, in all probability, cited in an actual return. In November 1998 (NCIS Press Release, 20/98, 13/11/98), NCIS gave details of the arrest of 26 persons connected with the illicit production and supply of amphetamines. The group's amphetamine production capacity was estimated to have a street value equivalent of £5 million and NCIS claimed that the 'intelligence led operation ... has greatly disrupted illegal drug production in the North West of England'. Another report, published in February 1999 (NCIS Press Release 04/99, 11/2/99), referred to five men being convicted for conspiracy to produce counterfeit £20 notes. In the related raids on the suspects' premises, over 1,600 sheets of counterfeit notes were found. In terms of OCG activity disruption, it was claimed that the success of the operation 'lay in the arrest of individuals involved in all levels of the counterfeiting process as well as the large quantity of material seized'.

Neither group fits in with the popular conception of OCGs in terms of Mafia imagery. Indeed, that was acknowledged during the OCN review (Gregory, 2000a) by the law enforcement agencies to be an important problem in the OCNS. The returns do cover groups as diverse as Chinese Triads, armed robbery 'specialists' and crime groups with only a very local geographical significance.

In the data available on the OCN Scheme, as set out in the annual internal *Organised Crime Groups* reports, the only means of identifying the more significant OCGs is by reference to the number of returns from NCIS, NCS and Customs and Excise. In the case of both NCIS and NCS, the criteria for deploying their resources means that both intelligence and investigation activities are only directed at the more serious criminal threats. In the case of Customs and Excise, the criminal organisational

*Table 5.1* The upper level of OCG groups

|  | 1999[1] |
|---|---|
| Total number of OCGs reported | 965 |
| of which NCIS reported | 51 |
| of which NCS reported | 153 |
| of which Customs and Excise reported | 211 |

Note
1 Only 1999 data presented because of the incomplete nature of returns for 1997 and 1998.

requirements generally needed for illicit commodity trafficking are such that the term 'significant' can probably be applied to the majority of their OCN returns. Applying these considerations to the data, one can suggest that the number of OCGs shown in Table 5.1 may represent those likely to have the most impact in terms of criminal activities.

In general, the annual internal reports produced on the OCN returns for the period 1997–9 were based largely on a process of 'totalling-up' the answers given for the various question categories. However, some useful qualitative analyses were carried out which help to provide a more detailed picture of organised crime, according to the specified criteria, in the UK. The following aspects of the phenomenon have been selected for OCN data illustration (mostly using the 1999 collection), criminal activities (Table 5.2), ethnicity (Tables 5.4 and 5.5), geographical locations (Table 5.6), criminal group networking (Tables 5.7 and 5.8), penetration of the legitimate economy (Table 5.9), presence of Mafia-like behavioural characteristics (Table 5.10) and the 'outcomes' of law enforcement responses (Table 5.11).

The data in Table 5.2 has been selected to reflect what is *reported* about the principal criminal activities of OCGs. The number of groups said to be involved in money laundering shows what might have been anticipated and has some degree of correlation with the principal OCG activity of drug trafficking.

*Table 5.2* Selected OCN criminal activity picture

| Percentages of OCGs involved in specified criminal activities | 1997 | 1998 | 1999 |
|---|---|---|---|
| Drug trafficking | 57.9 | 60.0 | 41.1 |
| Fraud | 18.5 | 17.4 | 18.0 |
| Money laundering | 53.0 | 51.0 | 46.0 |
| Alcohol and tobacco smuggling | 4.2 | 2.0 | –[1] |
| Illegal immigration and human trafficking | –[2] | 4.5 | 12.0 |

Notes
1 Not separately identified in the 1999 Report.
2 The 1997 Report gives no figures for human trafficking.

It is interesting to note that, despite the widespread public information on the rise in alcohol and tobacco smuggling, by both volume and value (see, for example, the report in the *Independent on Sunday*, 24 July 2000), the OCG involvement does not show an increase in numbers of groups active in this area but this may simply reflect the nature of that criminal activity. It may encompass a very few OCGs and many independent 'black market' traders. The figures do show a rise in the number of OCGs whose principal activity is illegal immigration and/or human trafficking which, again, is a crime area that is alleged to show a rising involvement of OCGs. However, this may also be more to do with greater OCG awareness within INDIS, because their number of returns, shown in Table 5.3, has risen quite significantly.

A common way of describing OCGs is by reference to the ethnic origins of the majority of a group's membership, especially the core or principal members. The responses in the section on 'Ethnicity' show that the dominant ethnic group involved in crime in the UK is 'white European' – see Table 5.4. This is a confirmation of general predictions.

Not surprisingly, given the ethnic composition of British society, the next two dominant ethnic groups, in terms of numbers and power in the groups, in the 1999 data, are Afro-Caribbean (12 per cent of groups) and Asians from the Indian subcontinent (10 per cent of the groups). Allowing for geographical distance, one would not expect a high presence of OCGs comprising nationals of the former USSR or CEE States but press reports and pronouncements by some EU governments have suggested a spreading out of OCG activity from the former Eastern Bloc. Yet, are these perceptions reflected in the OCN Scheme?

Clearly, the figures in Table 5.5 do not reflect a large amount of OCG activity by nationals from the former Soviet Union and the central and eastern European states, but they do suggest a small rising trend.

From Chief Constables' Annual Reports, NCIS and NCS reports and trial details, it can be shown that 'gang' activity tends to be concentrated in metropolitan areas. This is not necessarily the same as OCG activity

*Table 5.3* INDIS annual OCN returns

| 1997 | 1998 | 1999 |
|------|------|------|
| 4 | 23 | 53 |

*Table 5.4* Ethnic origin – 'white European'

| Percentages | 1997 | 1998 | 1999 |
|-------------|------|------|------|
| In terms of numbers of OCGs | 71.0 | 70.0 | 64.5 |
| In terms of power | 68.0 | 65.5 | 61.0 |

*Table 5.5* Percentages of OCGs containing former USSR and East European
nationals

| 1997 | 1998 | 1999 |
|------|------|------|
| 4.0 | 5.3 | 7.0 |

under the OCN classification criteria. However, one could expect there to
be a correlation in terms of the geographical concentration of significant
numbers of OCGs reported from metropolitan areas being recorded by
the OCN data. Because of the problem of low returns in 1997 and 1998,
the data presented on this point is again only taken from the 1999 OCN
collection.

The OCN questionnaire asked respondents, first, if they have knowledge of an identifiable base for an OCG. Second, if the respondents have
answered 'yes' to the previous question, they are then asked to identify the
base area. In respect of the 965 groups identified in 1999, 85 per cent
were known to have an identifiable base in the UK. The location of these
787 groups is shown in Table 5.6.

Thus, 75.5 per cent of the OCGs with an identified base were located in
or near major metropolitan areas.

Another common assertion on the geographical aspects of OCG activity
is that organised crime is an increasingly transnational phenomenon. The
OCN questionnaire tried to gather information on this point. A problem
here is that some responding agencies did not include their knowledge of
OCGs operating from outside the UK into the UK, or UK-based OCGs
operating outside the UK, so there may be an underreporting issue
related to this question. Of the 787 groups with known bases, 14 (1.7 per
cent) were based outside the UK and of these, 11 were based in another
European country. Another question asks about the geographical scope of
the activities of OCGs based in the UK. Information on this point was
available for 851 groups (91.5 per cent). Of these, 42.8 per cent were
known to be active outside the UK and 7.4 per cent were known to be
active in at least three continents. If this information is taken to indicate a
globalisation trend of OCG activity, then, on the known information, it
only relates to 6.7 per cent of all OCGs reported in 1999. However, as
pointed out earlier, at present the available OCN data has not been fully

*Table 5.6* Geographical base of OCGs

|  | 1999 ( figures in percentages) |
|------|------|
| London | 29.5 |
| Midlands and East Anglia | 19.6 |
| North West | 14.6 |
| North East and Yorkshire | 11.8 |

cross-matched. Therefore it is not possible to give any indication of the volume or value of the activities of particular subsets of the OCGs such as those operating sub-globally and globally.

Both academic and practitioner analyses are making increasing use of the concept of 'criminal networks' as a conceptual tool that may help to produce a more accurate picture of OCGs as being actually less formally and hierarchically structured and permanent in the real world. The 1999 OCN data provides some interesting material on this point – see Table 5.7.

Of the 633 groups with known linkages, the types of linkages identified are shown in Table 5.8.

Whilst no precise figures were available in the 1999 OCG report, it was suggested, from the data, that 'Links frequently involved co-operation in two or more of the four ways (identified in Table 5.8)'. It is not possible to give any accurate figures of the number of criminals or criminal suspects involved in these networks. However, some indications of 'membership parameters' can be estimated by reference to the fact that in 1999, 92 per cent of the groups had between three and nine central/principal members and varying numbers of fringe members. Additionally, in 77.2 per cent of the groups, each member was believed to have a particular task.

Van Duyne (1993), among others, has identified the problem of criminal groups merging illegal activities and profits within the legitimate economy. On this issue, the OCN data has provided some relevant indicators (identified in Table 5.9).

*Table 5.7* Intergroup linkages

|  | Number of groups | Total no. of groups (%) |
| --- | --- | --- |
| Groups known to have UK links | 633 | 66 |
| Groups known to have links with other groups internationally | 448 | 46 |
| Most common external link – to Europe | 234 | 24 |
| Next most common external link – Asia | 48 | 5 |

*Table 5.8* Types of intergroup linkage

| Type of linkage | Number of groups |
| --- | --- |
| Use of others' expertise | 246 |
| Use of others' facilities | 289 |
| Use of others' personnel | 203 |
| Co-operation in buying and selling commodities (e.g. drugs) | 480 |

*Table 5.9* Penetration of legitimate economy[1]

|  | 1997 | 1998 | 1999 |
|---|---|---|---|
| Formal establishment of 'cover' companies | 39.0 | 43.0 | 43.0 |
| Investment in existing legitimate companies | n/a | 18.0 | 20.0 |

Note
1 All the figures are percentages of the groups for whom the information was reported.

The information on cover companies is much as would be expected in terms of activities that could support criminal activities or be used for proceeds laundering. Responses link OCG activity to companies being involved in transportation (of various types), garages, leisure services (pubs and clubs), IT retail outlets, security firms and employment agencies. In terms of OCG structures it was also found, in the 1999 returns, that 59.2 per cent of the groups used commercial or business-like structures. This correlates with the dominant position that the responses give to activities associated with illicit commodity trafficking, for example, stolen vehicles, electrical goods, and alcohol and tobacco smuggling.

The popular image of OCGs is often linked to the portrayals of the Italian Mafia or the US Cosa Nostra. Here, as is well known, the image is of a numerically large, hierarchically structured group, which uses violence to maintain internal discipline, and violence and corruption to put the group itself 'beyond the reach of the law' (UN, 1980, in Gregory, 2000b). The OCN data provides some indications of this form of OCG but, because of the lack of data cross matching, conclusions must be very tentative. For example, although the annual analysis of the OCN returns tell us how many groups were believed to exhibit a high number of possible OCG characteristics, it is not yet possible to say how many of these groups actively used discipline and control over members *and* attempted to corrupt outsiders, whose positions might threaten the continuance of OCG activities. A major preoccupation of the European Union and the United Nations is the use of corruption by organised crime (Gregory, 2000b; see also Williams and Beare, 1999) and it may be important for the UK to be informed about the nature and extent of corrupting activities by criminal groups in this country. At present, the OCN analysis only reveals relative information by separate clusters of answers, as shown in Table 5.10.

*Table 5.10* Mafia-like characteristics

| Figures are percentages | 1997 | 1998 | 1999 |
|---|---|---|---|
| OCGs with highest number of characteristics | 4.2 | 3.0 | 4.1 |
| OCGs using violence for internal discipline | 37.0 | 36.0 | 36.0 |
| OCGs known to use corruption | 16.0 | 13.8 | 12.7 |

What would be interesting to derive from the OCN data in respect of the OCGs in Table 5.10 is the cross matching of data on ethnic composition, principal crime activity, geographical location of base and scope of activity. This might help to clarify our understanding of the composition of the top level of serious crime activity.

The establishment of both NCIS and NCS is evidence that there has been a shift in resource allocation and redistribution towards serious and organised crime. In addition, in terms of both public accountability and government policy priorities, the OCN data can be investigated for 'outcomes' in terms of law enforcement activity. The Scheme asks five questions that can be said to relate to 'outcome':

- Investigative output?
- Arrests of OCG members?
- Prosecution of OCG members?
- OCG groups disrupted?
- OCG groups dismantled?

The first of these 'outcomes' is of little value because, although an OCG can be returned as either known via 'intelligence only' or from 'investigation', in all three years (1997–9), a very high percentage always related to investigations (range 84–94 per cent). The problem, however, is that the OCNS did not require 'investigation' to meet any minimum level of qualifying resource allocation.

These four outcome measures also need to be treated with some care. Arrests can be for very minor offences such as non-payment of a statutory fine. Data is also not always available to indicate if prosecutions actually resulted in convictions. In the case of 'disruptions', the agencies were not using any rigorous common criteria for assessing and determining disruptions. Both HMIC and the Commons Public Accounts Committee (PAC) have commented on this point.

In its 1998 Report on NCIS, HMIC noted (1999: para. 4.9) that, with regard to the NCIS performance indicator on disruption, members 'of the directorate considered that the current method of assessing performance

*Table 5.11* Measurement of outcomes of law enforcement activities[1]

|  | 1997 | 1998 | 1999 |
| --- | --- | --- | --- |
| Arrests | 60.0 | 56.0 | 56.0 |
| Prosecutions | 37.0 | 36.0 | 41.0 |
| Disruptions | n/a | 48.0 | 59.0 |
| Dismantling | 26.0 | 23.0 | 18.0 |

Note
1 Figures are percentages of OCGs subject to outcomes.

did not adequately reflect what was being achieved and there was concern regarding the quality of disruption'. Similarly, when reviewing the Comptroller and Auditors General 1998 Report on 'Customs & Excise – Drugs Prevention', the House of Commons Public Accounts Committee (1999: para. 26) noted that the Customs and Excise performance indicator of organisations disrupted depended 'to a significant degree on the subjectivity of the investigating staff involved in individual cases'. Moreover, the PAC drew attention to the fact that, although Customs and Excise claimed to have dismantled or disrupted 130 OCGs in 1997–8, 'they were unable to place this result in context against the number of organisations smuggling drugs into the UK ... because of the constantly shifting nature of the organisations themselves and the clandestine nature of the activity' (1999: para. 9).

## Looking to the future

This chapter has presented some of the problems and outcomes that resulted from seeking data against very broad qualifying characteristics with low reporting thresholds and a lack of insistence on evidence of adequate quality assurance procedures to back-up claims being made in terms of outcomes. Nonetheless, the commitment to carry out this type of data gathering exercise will remain a priority for both national and EU policy purposes. The current UK official concerns about organised crime activity and the need for optimum responses from the law enforcement agencies are well known. In August 2000, NCIS released an unclassified version of its report on 'The Threat from Serious and Organised Crime' which estimated that crime cost the country around £50 billion per year and that the 930 crime families and gangs posed 'a serious threat to the economy and justice system' with 56 per cent of the gangs involved in drug trafficking and many also involved in money laundering (the *Guardian*, 3 August 2000).

An important development from the national scheme for data reliability and utility is the attempt by NCIS to get all police forces and law enforcement agencies, such as Customs and Excise, to use its new national intelligence data collection and evaluation model, the National Intelligence Model (NIM) (NCIS, 1999a; see also Home Office, 2001: 44–5) as a common national system. What is called 'intelligence-led' law enforcement is supposed to contribute to measurable outcomes in terms of performance indicators related to organised crime such as achieving certain annual levels of disruption of OCG activities.

With regard to the OCNS, the current position is that, following the year 2000 OCN Review, it was decided, through consultations between the Home Office and NCIS, to transfer responsibility for the management of the OCN Scheme to NCIS with effect from summer 2000. This decision was based on available resources, locational advantages and the option of controlling the data collection demands being made on responding agencies. Currently, OCN data is being collected on a quarterly updated basis by NCIS, using a single data collection questionnaire. The new questionnaire combines the old OCN format, revised in response to the year 2000 OCN Review Recommendations, with the addition of more operationally related and trends-related questions from the NCIS SIR (Strategic Intelligence Requirement) scheme. The new questionnaire format includes quality assurance reporting requirements that will improve the quantitative and qualitative results that may be derived through data analysis. The intelligence products are also subject to quality assurance procedures through peer review by user agencies.

The NCIS Service Plan 2002–2003 (NCIS, 2002) demonstrates two ways in which the value of the official collection of knowledge on organised crime can be audited: first, there is the intelligence product requirement laid upon NCIS; second, by reference to whether or not the Home Office's Public Service Agreement (PSA) objective to increase disruptions of organised crime enterprises by 10 per cent by 2004 (base line 2001–2) is met.

With reference to the first point, NCIS, in 2002–3 has to provide 'high quality and actionable intelligence' to support the Government's inter-agency strategy (CIDA) to reduce the flow of Class A drugs in the UK and the Government's strategy for combating organised immigration crime. In order to try to meet these nationally set objectives, the NCIS Service Authority has set its own performance targets. For example, 90 per cent of all intelligence reports on Class A drugs and 85 per cent of the illegal immigration reports must meet the two highest levels of the NIM quality matrix. In numerical terms, NCIS must produce 29 assessments covering drugs (15) and organised immigration crime (14). It is also possible to examine the problem priority and extent–agency resource allocation relationship through the data provided. Thus NCIS will be devoting 49 per cent of its dedicated resources to Class A drugs and 9 per cent of its dedicated resources to organised immigration crime. These resource allocations also correlate quite well with last OCNS report on the 1999 data (see Table 5.2) that showed drug-related crime as the main OCG activity (at 41 per cent) and immigration related crime involving 12 per cent of OCG activity. With reference to the value of 'disruption' as a performance indicator, this is crucially dependent on, first, qualitative knowledge about the impact of target OCGs and, second, on the accuracy of disruption measurement and its demonstrable linkage to reductions in OCG activity.

# References

## Unpublished reports

*Annual Reports on the OCNS*, Home Office, RDS.
Dunnighan, C. and Hobbs, D. (1996) *A Report on the NCIS Pilot Organised Crime Notification Survey.* University of Durham, November, for the Home Office.
EU Council (1995) *Elaboration of a Common Mechanism for the Collection and Systematic Analysis of Information on International Organised Crime.* ENFOPOL 161, 28/2/1995, LIMITE.
—— (1996) *Revision of the Directives referred to in Annexes B and C to 12247/1/94 ENFOPOL 161 REV 1.* ENFOPOL 35, 19/2/1996, LIMITE.
Gregory, F. (1999) Falcone Project Report contribution to the Cross-Channel Intelligence Conference (CCIC).
—— (2000a) *Year 2000 OCN Review.* University of Southampton, February, for the Home Office.
Phillips, K. (1996) *International, National and InterForce Crime* (Report), ACPO, April.

## Published reports

BKA (2000) *Situation Report Organised Crime in the Federal Republic of Germany.* BKA: Wiesbaden, May.
Bottomley, K. and Coleman, C. (1995) 'The role of the police', in M.A. Walker (ed.) *Interpreting Crime Statistics.* Oxford: Clarendon Press, pp. 61–90.
Burrows, J., Tarling, R., Mackie, A., Lewis, R. and Taylor, G. (2000) *Review of Police Forces' Crime Recording Practices.* Home Office Research Paper (HORS) No. 204.
Copas, J. (1995) 'On using crime statistics', in M.A. Walker (ed.) *Interpreting Crime Statistics.* Oxford: Clarendon Press, pp. 207–28.
Gregory, F. (2000b) 'Private criminality as a matter of international concern', in J. Sheptycki (ed.) *Issues in Transnational Policing.* London: Routledge, p. 117.
HMIC (1997a) *1997 Inspection, National Criminal Intelligence Service.* London: HM Inspectorate of Constabulary.
—— (1997b) *Policing with Intelligence – Criminal Intelligence: a Thematic Inspection on Good Practice.* London: HM Inspectorate of Constabulary.
—— (1999) *1998 Inspection, National Criminal Intelligence Service.* London: HM Inspectorate of Constabulary.
Hobbs, D. (1998) 'Going down the glocal: the local context of organised crime', *The Howard Journal*, 37: 407–22.
Home Office (2001) *Policing a New Century: A Blueprint for Reform*, Cm.5326.
House of Commons Public Accounts Committee (1999) *15th Report 'Customs & Excise – Drugs prevention'* (Session 1998–9).
House of Commons Select Committee on Home Affairs (1995) *Organised Crime*, Report by the (HC 18-I). London: HMSO.
NCIS (1999a) *NCIS and the National Intelligence Model.* London: NCIS.
—— (1999b) *NCIS Annual Report 1997–98.* London: NCIS.
—— (2001) *UK Threat Assessment 2001.* London: NCIS.
NCIS Service Authority (2002) *NCIS Service Plans 2002–2003.* London: National Criminal Intelligence Service Authority.

NCS (1999) *NCS Annual Report 1998–99.* London: NCIS.

Porter, M. (1996) *Tackling Cross Border Crime,* Police Research Paper 79. London: Home Office.

*Report of the Comptroller and Auditor General 1997–1998 Vote 12 Class xii DSS* (HC1–xii, Jan. 2000).

*Report of the Comptroller and Auditor General 1997–1998 'Customs & Excise – Drugs Prevention'* (HC854 1997–98).

Senat de Belgique (1998) *Commission Parlementaire chargée d'enquêter sur la Criminalité organisée en Belgique – RAPPORT FINAL FAIT PAR MM. COVELIERS ET DESMEDT.* Session De 1998–1999, 1-326/9, 8 Décembre.

Sheptycki, J. (2000) 'Organisational changes in the UK police and prosecution services of Great Britain as a result of policy considerations in organised crime', *Falcone Research Project,* 1998/TFJHA–FAL/145.

Stelfox, P. (1998) 'Policing lower levels of organized crime in England and Wales', *The Howard Journal* 37: 393–406.

van Duyne, P. (1993) 'Organised crime and business crime-enterprises in The Netherlands', *Crime, Law and Social Change* 19, 103–42.

Walker, M.A. (ed.) (1995) *Interpreting Crime Statistics.* Oxford: OUP, chapters by Walker, Bottomley & Coleman and Copas.

Williams, J. and Beare, M. (1999) 'The business of bribery: globalization, economic liberalization, and the problem of corruption', *Crime, Law and Social Change* 32: 115–46.

Wright, A., Waymont, A. and Gregory, F. (1993) *Drug Law Enforcement and Intelligence Gathering.* London: The Police Foundation.

# 6 The network paradigm applied to criminal organisations

## Theoretical nitpicking or a relevant doctrine for investigators? Recent developments in the Netherlands

*Peter Klerks*

### Egghead meets gumshoe

Does it matter at all what criminologists think crime looks like? Is there any relation between criminological theories as they develop in academic surroundings and the daily practice of those whose job it is to catch criminals? We criminologists like to think that the stuff we say and write has some relevance to the real world. When I first started to work as an academic in a law enforcement intelligence department back in 1993, the question that puzzled me most was whether my mostly theoretical knowledge would be of any use to the sceptical practitioners who would become my colleagues.[1] In a way, this 'reality test' to me was of more importance than the recognition I received from my peers at university. I had invested a lot in gaining what I thought was not only interesting, but also useful knowledge. Now I was longing for an appreciative remark, a pat on the back from a detective with a modest formal training but substantial 'street wisdom'.

The appreciation was there soon enough, although it was gained mostly by displaying research skills I picked up in journalism instead of university. My ability to locate information on companies, persons, laws and tools from open sources and odd contacts did earn me some reputation, but did it matter to anyone that I read a pile of books on criminology and organised crime? Not in day-to-day work perhaps, but it did prove useful when I was asked to help think out wider strategies of crime control. This chapter explores some of the possibilities and pitfalls when thinking about new ways to understand and deal with organised crime.

## A brief history of organised crime paradigms

In the criminology classes I teach to mid-level police officers, the module on organised crime begins with a sheet picturing Joe Barbara's estate in Apalachin, NY, where, back in 1957, the police broke up what is believed to be one of the rare meetings of top Mafioso representing crime families from all over the United States.[2] The stereotypical faces of Vito Genovese, Joe 'Bananas' and other infamous Mafia hoodlums seem all too familiar to my Dutch students: many of them immediately start to hum the *Godfather* theme. Now why is this relevant? Because to many Western people, organised crime until about a decade ago was something that only existed in the USA or Italy. The archetypal images and ideas of what organised crime was all about originated from Hollywood: images of Al Capone, the fictitious Don Vito Corleone, and more recently the Colombian coke barons aiming to poison America. The influence of all this is not limited to the general public: in more than one way, the idea of La Cosa Nostra as the primordial criminal conspiracy has shaped the thinking of generations of law enforcement officers, in the USA but also, through them, in many other parts of the Western world (e.g. Nadelmann, 1993). This knowledgeable audience doesn't need an extensive treatise on the core elements of this orthodox doctrine: serious crime results from an elaborate, nation-wide conspiracy, operating through ethnically monolithic and pyramid-like, strictly hierarchical structures led by 'godfathers' and 'capi' that somewhat resemble military or corporate organisations. While this representation of Italian organised crime may or may not have been true in a distant past, it is certainly far too simplistic to explain most of the recent varieties of organised crime that have sprung up in various countries. It originates from a rigid crime-fighting doctrine that thinks in hierarchical terms, and the law enforcement efforts that such thinking produces concentrate on repression, going for the 'big catch' and 'dismantling' supposedly stable organisations by arresting the major 'bosses'.[3]

Now of course, I am oversimplifying and in a way misrepresenting the orthodox organisation-oriented crime-fighting doctrines: their rigidness of the 1970s and 1980s has not remained untouched by more modern insights. Also new and more sophisticated paradigms of organised crime, such as the enterprise metaphor, have entered the field.[4] Some other scholars and researchers have suggested alternative views, such as the anthropologically-oriented Ianni's, whose ideas hold the potential of coming up with a more empirically based and fine-grained image of organised crime (Ianni and Reuss-Ianni, 1972). However, they have shown themselves susceptible to the reproach that they are naïve, since they seem to have largely ignored the more hideous (and hidden) elements of the social phenomenon they have been studying.

But be all that as it may, my conclusion is still that many law enforcement practitioners I have encountered, and whose reports I have read both at home and abroad, appear to hold rather simplistic views of their adversaries: they often think in rigid terms of leaders, chains of command, bag carriers and stable criminal infrastructures, where I observe mostly improvisation, fluid networks and *ad hoc* coalitions, opportunistic and very flexible individual entrepreneurs, criminal omni-vores and organisational chaos. To some extent this no doubt has to do with our differing objectives: officers of the law are paid to come up with proof of concrete criminal acts and responsibilities, and (if possible) with conspiracies, since a good criminal scheme with a leader and members adds a firm percentage on the final verdict in terms of years behind bars. Social scientists such as myself, on the other hand, are more interested in the motives, choices, causes and relationships behind the acts. The question is whether this curiosity can contribute anything to an effective controlling of criminal phenomena such as the ones we are dealing with here.

## Some consequences of the way we look at organised crime

The preconceived ideas that we hold about social phenomena shape the things we see, and subsequently what we perceive influences what we do about it.[5] No perception is possible without a theory behind it. This holds true for detectives investigating a group of drug smugglers, but it also applies to policy-makers who design the strategies in which society deals with forms of organised crime. To once again put it in simple terms: for far more than a decade, detectives in Holland have explained organised crime to their superiors and later to concerned policy-makers in terms of conspiracies, ring leaders, more or less stable and familiar organisations, and mega-profits. This process has decisively influenced the way in which counterstrategies took shape, and it has, in particular, created the nearly unlimited leeway that covert policing until recently was allowed to operate in. All this came to an abrupt end in the period 1994 to 1996, when the heat finally came down and the largest scandal ever to affect the Dutch judicial system struck fear in every covert investigator's heart. Under the 'Delta method', the police were found to have turned a blind eye to enormous quantities of drugs under their surveillance in an attempt to build an informer's credibility among his co-conspirers. But apart from this dramatic climax, the conventional wisdom about serious crime also precluded the introduction of all sorts of more prudent, preventive meas-ures that could have limited the opportunities for such crime to expand in the first place.

Thinking about crime more in terms of opportunity, of risk mechan-isms, of personal motives, co-optation and seduction demands a willing-ness to depart from the familiar paths and usual suspects. This is not an easy thing to promote in a world that has more than enough crime to keep all the coppers busy all day long. No wonder put-offs abound: 'We have no time to contemplate ethical niceties and come up with subtle theories of why criminals behave the way they do: there's virtually a war going on, and if we don't catch the bad guys soon they become invulnerable and we will have lost for good.'[6] It took a confidence crisis of unprecedented magnitude to produce the organisational and intellectual space for more elaborate approaches to organised crime to arise. Over the last five years, at least two dozen academics have started working in Dutch law enforcement in some capacity, many of them with a direct involvement in operational matters. One can expect tactics and strategies to benefit from this, in spite of the much more rigid system of legal checks and balances that has recently been set up and which, in itself, seriously restricts the operational capabilities of investigative squads.

## What does it mean when we refer to organised crime in terms of 'social networks'?

The paradigm of organised crime as social networks has become widely accepted among Dutch criminologists within just a few years. This in itself is remarkable, because until the early 1990s there was hardly anyone in academia who gave any serious attention to organised crime: such shady domains belonged exclusively to dangerous crooks and secretive police operatives, and almost no-one else felt the need to get involved or ask questions. The usefulness of the network approach in studying serious crime is, by now, not only appreciated among researchers in Holland, but also in the UK (where Dr Dick Hobbs has recently done interesting ethnographic work on serious crime networks) and in the US (where Professor Phil Williams among others has applied the concept to transnational drug trafficking).

In 1995, a group of four leading criminologists referred to as the 'Fijnaut Group' worked for a year to draw up an extensive panorama and threat analysis of organised crime in the Netherlands.[7] On the whole, they criticised the orthodox idea of semi-stable criminal structures with fixed leaders and some form of co-ordination between gangs. Instead they emphasised the fluidity of organised crime, the importance of improvisation and the fact that the drug trade especially allows for relatively small operators to expand dramatically on the basis of a few successful drug imports and thus become criminal 'top dogs' almost overnight.[8] This unprecedented study of organised crime in the Netherlands was based on a detailed analysis of many hundreds of confidential police intelligence reports from all over the country, and its conclusions gained authoritative status overnight. Policy-makers, investigating magistrates and police chiefs were forced to reconsider their strategies and refocus their efforts. This new criminological orthodoxy, together with the introduction of a much stricter set of judicial controls on intrusive police methods, drastically changed the atmosphere in Dutch law enforcement in the second half of the 1990s.

The Fijnaut Group's findings were more or less confirmed by a later report by the Ministry of Justice Research Centre (the WODC), which again looked into the dossiers of over a hundred organised crime cases and confidential investigations dating between roughly 1995 and 1998 (Kleemans *et al.*, 1998). However, this study emphasised even more the need to look at 'criminal co-operatives' (the term they propose instead of 'organisation', 'group' or 'structure') in terms of fluid network relations with occasional 'nodes' representing the more successful and enterprising operators. The WODC researchers point out that, while extensive and prolonged investigations will remain necessary, their observations need to result in a substantial retargeting of law enforcement intervention efforts towards more 'short strike' missions intended to take out 'facilitators' and clandestine service providers, as these form essential elements in the networks that allow many others to successfully perform their criminal acts. So far, such 'small-time' service providers nearly always remained at the fringes of criminal investigations, with detectives often not being aware that these 'minor' characters surfaced in many of the supposedly different criminal organisations that they attempted to investigate. Another interesting observation is that the supposed ethnic homogeneity of criminal groups that supposedly caused the participating individuals to co-operate and obey is, in fact, now largely a thing of the past. Also, specific groups are much less likely to restrict themselves solely to one particular drug or criminal activity. Opportunism and *ad hoc* coalitions, but also relationships based on friendship and even amorous ties now much more than before form the basis for criminal projects. Women too, it seems, play a very important role in establishing contacts and reinforcing mutual bonds. In short, social ties much more than business relations of formal command structures form the basis for criminal co-operation. Pyramid-like criminal authority structures are increasingly rare, although within separate, smaller cells such as nuclear families, the more traditional father–son-like authority relations can still be found. (Semi-)independent criminal operators often work in pairs, teaming up with several different 'criminal co-operations' instead of belonging to only one group. The WODC researchers and other criminologists have now retrospectively demonstrated that the 'conspiracies' and mega-hierarchies that the police had identified in the past among Dutch and Turkish organised crime were in fact constructions that cannot stand up to close scrutiny. What seemed like awesome mammoth organisations were, in fact, strings of interlinked smaller groups that lacked a central leader but co-ordinated their activities along logistic trails and through bonds of friendship.

The common thread in all of these recent studies is that the network mode of organisation between people and functional entities has proven to be far better adapted to modern modes of collaboration, trading and communication than the traditional hierarchic structures. This is quite obvious to anyone familiar with 1990s economics, but it is even truer for present-day sub-legal activities such as producing and trafficking illicit products and delivering clandestine services. Such activities exist in a hostile environment and thus they need the capacity of rapid innovation, adaptation and avoidance in response to possible law enforcement interventions. According to simple Darwinist reasoning, in a continuously changing world the more flexible 'social life-forms' stand the best chance of survival.

Looking at criminal structures in terms of networks means that certain questions need to be asked, such as: what constitutes the bonding mechanisms that tie people together in different constellations? Greed is perhaps the most common motivator among criminals, but the lust for money certainly cannot explain all the activities that we observe. Other social mechanisms are equally important, such as ethnic or tribal ties, family relations or common backgrounds in a geographical (neighbourhood) or institutional (prison) sense. A common interest in certain cultural or consumer habits (music, consumption, cars) can also form the fabric for co-operation. The social network perspective allows for a greater or lesser concentration on the importance of such social mechanisms, as we shall see later on.

Another typical trait of network structures that makes them rather hard to dismantle is their resilience against damage. The term 'dismantling' used to be quite popular among law enforcement officials in Holland in reference to criminal structures. The way to put an end to a criminal organisation traditionally was to arrest the leaders, thereby incapacitating the remaining bad guys that did most of the leg work. These were somehow considered to be too stupid to initiate any substantial criminal activities by themselves. The official working programmes of many police organisations until recently had a target, for a given year of 'dismantling' at least an *x* number of criminal organisations. Nowadays, the awareness that a compromised network can often limit the damage by developing other latent functional connections in a short timescale and thus rebuild most of its original operational potential before long, has made the police a lot more modest in its claims.[9]

## Varieties in network analysis

In itself, the application of the social network paradigm is not altogether unproblematic. Originating from a long tradition in ethnography and sociometrics, the idea to use the network metaphor to describe and explain social structures has been put into practice by a number of different scholars in a variety of ways. This implies that there isn't such a thing as *the* social network analysis approach: about the only common element among the different varieties is the conviction that it is useless to explain human behaviour or social processes solely through categorical properties and norms of individual actors. Instead, the emphasis is on their functioning within structured social relations. Individual behaviour is always seen in relation to the behaviour of the groups which a person is part of. In brief, a person is manifested in a socially relevant way primarily in his or her relationship to others, and therefore these relations deserve careful and systematic scrutiny.

In social network studies, first there are those who work in the 'strictly sociometric' tradition: they are the mathematically oriented sociologists who revel in the prospect of being able to calculate the exact 'denseness' and 'centrality' of human network relations in any given empirical setting. Researchers of this breed will approach an empirical situation armed with questionnaires for participants to fill out, in which respondents are asked to state exactly who they favour, appreciate or detest and under what circumstances. The results are entered in a computer, which then produces a detailed map representing the entire set of social relations and mutual feelings. This research tradition has spawned a number of quite interesting studies on school classes, hospital settings and so on, which provided new insights into how people co-operate and realise certain goals, how they resolve conflicts and how they, for instance, find a new job. Unfortunately, criminals in their natural habitat seldom fill in researchers' questionnaires.

It will be clear that, although such methods can offer certain insights in social structures, there are obvious limits to what can be achieved. Measuring and counting presupposes that there is something to be counted, and people who prefer to operate in surreptitious ways seldom expose themselves voluntarily to a sociologist's curious gaze. One can, of course, attempt to use other ways of collecting data, such as analysing telephone taps and surveillance logs, but in such cases it should be realised that data collection is very partial and certainly biased, since not every actor is exposed to an equal extent and therefore some of those observed (perhaps the 'usual suspects') contribute far more to the data set than others. Any calculations, diagrams and conclusions that are subsequently drawn from such incomplete data sets are, by definition, unreliable. To perform a network analysis in the traditional way, one needs to know the boundaries of the 'data universe' under study. Empirical experience shows that, in the real world of serious criminality, it is all but impossible to agree on a static boundary which includes some while excluding all others.[10]

Crime analysts using mapping tools to depict relationships between suspects usually do not bother too much about the exact mathematical density and proportions. Their aim is mainly to visualise who does what to whom, and with what frequency. In spite of all the visual gimmicks, the basic technique behind such link analysis software is quite straightforward: one counts the number of established contacts, and based on that figure, a stronger or weaker link is assumed. The data thus assembled can be entered in a data matrix such as that shown in Figure 6.1.

Based on these data, a drawing can be made of the various entities and their contacts, as is shown in Figure 6.2.[11]

The use of analytic linking software in making sense of massive amounts of data is now common among practitioners around the world. In spite of the theoretical and methodological problems with creating sociodiagrams of criminal structures that are outlined above, the availability of such rather sophisticated network analysis software such as i2's Analyst's Notebook package and Active Analysis's Netmap has motivated some to attempt experiments with 'traditional' network analysis tools. Based on these practices, the use of less familiar analytical techniques such as cluster analysis and the smallest space algorithm is being pioneered by academics and law enforcement analysts alike.[12]

The usefulness of second-generation analytical tools (the first generation being the hand-drawn Anacapa charts and maps with coloured pins) such as i2's Analyst's Notebook software is also widely accepted in Dutch law enforcement, with many dozens of analysts trained in their operational use. The level of sophistication, however, remains modest, as many analysts use such network mapping software merely to provide graphic representations of the simple raw data obtained from phone taps and

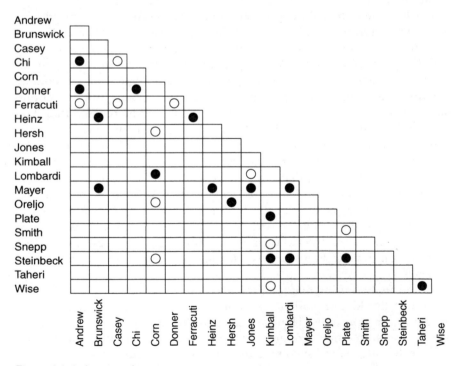

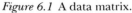

*Figure 6.1* A data matrix.

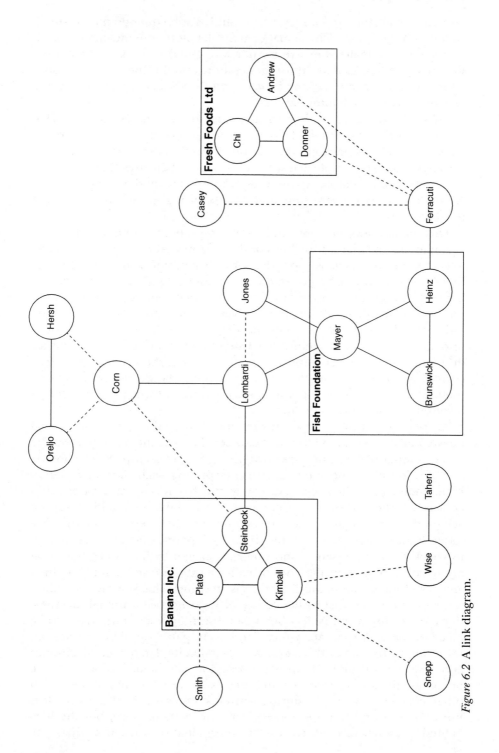

*Figure 6.2* A link diagram.

physical surveillance reports: A calls B, and B subsequently meets with C an *x* number of times. The actual content, let alone the meaning of such contacts is only analysed in a very crude way. *Social* network analysis of the sort that we could call 'third generation' would focus much more intensely on the content of the contacts, on the social context, and on the interpretation of such information.

My first experiences with such mapping software dates back to 1994, when I had the opportunity to re-examine the raw data that formed the basis of several link diagrams. I soon found out that the almost completely automated generation of such maps disguises certain risks that are inherent to using any data set drawn up by relatively inexperienced personnel. A number of errors were sometimes made in registering and encoding the data.

First of all, specific individuals were registered multiple times, for example under different spellings of their names. Also, phone calls made to certain persons such as bartenders or girlfriends of suspects were sometimes encoded with the name of that bartender or girlfriend at the receiving end, and on other occasions the suspect who soon after came on the phone was identified as being the receiver. In short, the data proved to be rather unreliable. I decided to re-encode a part of the enormous amount of data, and the link diagrams that I subsequently produced were rather different from the original ones. Strictly speaking, the original data were correct when it came to the technical contact between certain phone numbers, but in a sociographic sense, different people were often involved on both sides of the wire.

My objective at the time was to attempt to use 'third generation' social network analysis on an operational data set. That meant going beyond the mere drawing of links, to registering the more subtle aspects of contacts and relationships, and ultimately to interpreting such data in order to better understand in a qualitative way the behaviour, motivations and choices of the individuals concerned. This ambition could never be achieved by merely using the encoded data as they were originally registered. It meant going back to the original telephone and surveillance logs to check each conversation and observation line by line, encoding what occurred there and, in the end, bringing all those insights into the final analysis of the crime network that I was studying. This is a quite cumbersome exercise, one that in the course of most normal criminal investigations would simply not be feasible. I had drawn up a set of questions to be asked of the data I was analysing. Those were partly simple questions on, for example, the use of threatening or intimidating language, the amount and direction of authority in a conversation and similar aspects. Some other questions were more complicated, such as who talks about which other persons in what way during conversations with third persons. It is not possible to go into too much detail on methods here, but the idea behind it is that, through such forms of qualitative content analysis, the study of social networks can contribute to a better understanding of vital social processes, power and affinity structures. It would, of course, be a gross waste of time and resources to go through so much trouble to unravel a simple heroin transport, but considering that the Dutch police has spent tens of millions of guilders during seven or more years of extensive investigations on certain major criminal networks, it could be worthwhile to get to know such persons in a structured way and by tested methods that do not depend on the skills or biases of individual detectives or analysts.

Third generation social network analysis is intended to enable investigators to identify positions of power and to attribute them to specific individual traits or to structural roles that these individuals fulfil. A unique position of intermediate contacts, for example, can allow someone to monopolise the connection between two networks. Such a position is worth guarding, as it brings possibilities of selective information management, blackmail and so on. Being the sole supplier of certain goods or services, or the unique channel into a supplier country (perhaps because of language skills) makes one a very interesting person, to fellow criminals but certainly to investigators as well. Social network mapping can show what material resources someone can mobilise and what information s/he has access to. Such access and power is highly relevant in manipulating social structures, as any manager can testify. Social network analysis can also introduce dynamics into the rigid and 'frozen' understanding of social structures that traditional organisational diagrams convey. Processes of recruitment become clearer by looking at previous connections, and the transfer of knowledge and criminal innovations can also be traced.

A traditional crime analysis can fail to identify the informal 'cliques' by limiting itself to relationships between individuals and 'hard' organisations. Thus it may seem that, in a certain field, only few enduring structures exist, when a more intense analysis may indicate that among the seemingly transient contacts, indirect links exist when people from certain 'pools' (such as sporting schools, coffee shops or neighbourhoods) are shown to be working together. Social network analysis not only draws attention to established contacts, but also to relationships that appear not to exist and are oddly missing. Conflicts, for example, may never result in actual contacts and thus never show up in traditional diagrams, but third generation social network analysis will register adversaries and their hostilities, and will thus also visualise 'silent' conflicts. By paying attention to 'structural holes' (remarkable white spots and hard-to-fill positions in a network), hypothesis building can be supported. Blind spots in a 'social floor plan' are soon noticed. By looking at a criminal structure from the angle of social network analysis, certain persons and roles draw attention that otherwise would easily go unnoticed. In the case of the specific group I was analysing, it became apparent that a number of seemingly insignificant characters always showed up at the right moment and at the right spot to help in establishing crucial contacts. Those usually independently operating 'social bridge builders' I refer to as 'criminal contact brokers'.

From the annals of organised crime it is quite easy to illustrate the value of social network analysis over the simplistic 'focusing on the leaders'. Interesting figures who by themselves are no 'heavyweights', but who have access to much vital information through their social functioning, quickly draw the analysist's attention. One good example from the US Cosa Nostra literature is Willie Boy Johnson, at one time an FBI informant from Queens, New York, who for personal reasons would play a key role in the demise of Gambino family chief John Gotti (Cummings and Volkman, 1992: 148). Johnson was a much-wanted 'strong-arm man', who could never formally become a mafioso because he was only half-Italian. He was what both the FBI and Cosa Nostra refer to as a 'floater', someone who is assigned to a specific crew, yet loaned out to other crews for various assignments because of a particular speciality. As a consequence, Johnson had a panoramic view of the entire New York Cosa Nostra. In Holland, such floaters have, on occasion, also been identified.

It will by no means be easy to develop the 'third generation' social network analysis into an established methodology that can be taught and applied uniformly. Although some progress has been made, a lot more empirical work based on 'learning by doing' needs to be done. Preferably, those doing such analysis must be thoroughly familiar with both regular criminal analysis and social science methodologies, which means that such method development costs a lot of time and money. The more ambitious and sophisticated criminal intelligence analysts could probably contribute a lot as well, but the problem here is that Dutch analysts are often merely used as administrators for the investigative teams and as *post hoc* presenters of complex criminal cases to the public prosecutor and the top brass in order to secure funds and continuity of the investigation. This is now improving somewhat, but the analyst's role is still seen by many LE managers as a supporting one, used to interpret data after they have been collected instead of a proactive involvement in setting out investigative and control strategies.

## The current situation in the Netherlands

With all the new insights available to them, have the prosecutors' strategies changed, do investigators now go about their daily work in a different way, have their aims and tactics been adapted to new insights and, if so, how and with what results? As the lessons learned are still quite recent, it is not that easy to identify a trend. In Holland, running investigations against organised crime networks is a demanding job at the best of times. At the moment, according to many investigators, it is all but impossible. Most prosecutors now maintain a hands-on management role in keeping police investigators on a very short leash and, under new laws, permission has to be given by a national oversight body for every application of many of the more intrusive and all innovative tactics and techniques. If, for example, a telephone intercept records information on an upcoming drug transport, chances are high that the police have to intervene without hesitation to avoid the drugs coming on the market. Allowing any 'harmful goods' to go through with the police knowing about it is nearly unthinkable these days. The result is often a 'blown case', since all operational details as well as the immediate cause of the intervention have to be disclosed in court. All this makes it much more difficult to run major investigations over a prolonged period. In a way, this almost forces police teams to adapt their strategies and focus on more intermediate goals instead, an approach favoured by many advocates of the social network approach. On the negative side, the new legal restrictions seem to have a 'chilling effect' that, to some extent, paralyses those investigators, for example, who have to operate in a region where an over-cautious district attorney refuses to allow even mildly intrepid initiatives.

After van Traa, we saw an increasing number of cases in which the police target supposedly major narcotics networks through 'short strike' tactics rather than through the 'long haul' approach, waiting for the 'ultimate catch' of a large shipment of drugs. To some extent, this is no doubt the result of the new judicial doctrine that requires the police to intervene almost immediately once a drug shipment is traced. But insiders claim that police managers are really beginning to realise that waiting for the major catch is not all that efficient in terms of return on investment. After all, arrests for transporting a modest amount of cocaine can already result in many years' imprisonment, and the extra 400 kilos that you could perhaps catch one day do not justify allowing the criminals to carry on with all their endeavours for many months or even years, building up a reputation of invulnerability in the process and thus presenting a bad example to those susceptible to the seemingly profitable lurings of crime.

Perhaps one could say that an increasing number of analysts began to see the utility of social network analysis and 'short strikes'. Many tactical investigators, however, are still hesitant. Perhaps understandably so: they do see bosses and hierarchies as they are conditioned to see them because of the legal requirements of proving that a (semi-)formal organisation exists and that there are identifiable leaders. Besides, criminal structures differ. There is certainly authority in the smaller groups, and occasionally an investigation may even run into 'Mr Big', the genuine 'Man with the Plan'. So some doubts about the omnipresence of fluid social networks are justified. The concept of the 'criminal broker' and the facilitator is more readily accepted among investigators, especially in the context of 'upper world' contacts in relation to, for example, synthetic drugs and financial and juridical services.

The council of chiefs of police (a body somewhat similar to the UK's ACPO) has recently decided to endorse the 'short strikes' strategy, but several leading public prosecutors are not at all happy with this new policy. They claim that the social network paradigm may hold true for Dutch and Western European criminal operators in general, but, in their opinion, the much tougher Turkish, Kurdish and Pakistani heroin traders are of a different breed entirely: dealing with these groups requires a more prolonged and fierce approach. This scepticism regarding the new strategies and even the network perspective in general is not limited to some gung-ho prosecutors. A follow-up enquiry by a second parliamentary commission looking into the implementation of the Van Traa recommendations during 1998–9 concluded that the 'short strikes' strategy was generally not supported in the police and the judiciary.[13] It is widely interpreted as 'catching the small fry while allowing the big guys to walk'. The concept of affecting networks by targeting crucial facilitators has not been explored in any detail, and the commission found that apart from some individual creativity among the ranks of law enforcement, there is very little in the way of systematic thinking about new investigative strategies. It therefore recommended the establishment of a new centre of expertise for the development of investigative strategies.

Meanwhile, in the field, some creative detectives are already experimenting with applying the new insights. Over coffee, this author heard several recent examples of relatively 'heavy' and notorious criminals who were lured from their relative insulation because they felt they had to become involved once a relatively small drug shipment had been intercepted. The necessary maintenance of their reputation, but also the urge to 'help out their friends' simply didn't allow them to keep a low profile and avoid all risks. They used their (supposedly safe) anonymous cell phones, and showed up on the scene to check what happened and/or to provide comfort. This allowed the police to tie them to the narcotics trafficking and thus, via an indirect tactic, brought them to the dock. Once such tales of success find their way to more police canteens, they will provide the best word-of-mouth advertisement for such innovations. And, of course, introducing them into formal courses and establishing a centre of expertise helps as well.

## Some thoughts on the future

Where does all of this lead us? Do police investigators suddenly need to become trained social scientists with a keen eye for affinity bonds? Not really: the majority of criminal investigations will continue to be run largely as they are now, without much more sophisticated analysis support than the familiar link diagrams. It is only the most complicated, prolonged and sensitive kind of projects that could use these new insights. Meanwhile, criminologists still need to ask the deeper question about the usefulness of theory for practical applications: *if* we as researchers come up with 'better' knowledge and explanations of empirical phenomena, does this have consequences for the practitioners? Does such criminological research have any relevance and influence on the 'real' world?

Closer involvement of trained social scientists and economists in the investigative process will benefit both domains: the police gain more understanding and the academics become more realistic about what can be achieved. In Holland, for example, the process of establishing priorities for the allocation of the many hundreds of specialised organised crime investigators working in large permanent teams has been overhauled with the input of universities and consultants' expertise. Periodical and more objective monitoring 'scans' of the magnitude and nature of organised crime have replaced the old back channels through which gloomy detective chiefs indoctrinated ministers and politicians. In this sense, criminologists certainly can play a role by interpreting information as objectively and intelligently as possible.

Realistic assessments of criminal threats are needed to avoid overkill and unwanted invasions of privacy. In the recent past, the threat of organised crime have, in some ways, been exaggerated, especially when the alarm was sounded over the 'immediate threat' that organised crime was said to pose to democratic institutions such as the courts, local councils and parliament. Any substantial infiltration attempts in 'upper-world' power structures have yet to be proven, and the criminals are not out to take over state power in Western Europe. But, on the other hand, failing to appreciate organised crime for what it is, a social phenomenon closely tied in to our society's structure and profiting from its inherent weaknesses such as greed and ignorance, can in the longer run result in serious problems.

All in all, it is quite likely that law enforcement in the next century can only hope to remain successful in controlling organised crime if it can transform itself into more flexible modes of organisation and operation. It will probably take a lot more networking to effectively deal with criminal networks.

## Notes

1 From late 1993 to mid-1996, I worked as a researcher in the Research and Analysis department of The Hague regional police force on a project involving social network analysis of an organised crime group. After a brief period at the Nederlands Politie Instituut (Dutch national police institute) I joined Eysink Smeets & Etman, Holland's leading specialised security and crime control consultancy firm where most of my work involved research for police organisations. After obtaining my Ph.D. in 2000, I started working as a researcher at the Netherlands Police Academy in Apeldoorn.

2 This event is immortalised in several Hollywood movies, most recently in *Analyze This* featuring Robert DeNiro as a 1990s Godfather suffering from anxieties and depression.

3 In the intelligence literature, this phenomenon of thinking about the adversary in terms of similarity to your own culture and form of organisation is referred to as 'mirror imaging' (cf. Bathurst, 1993).

4  Limited space does not allow me to go into the virtues and pitfalls of the criminal enterprise paradigm, which I dealt with in more detail in my dissertation ('Groot in de hasj. Theorie en praktijk van de georganiseerde criminaliteit', *Alphen aan den Rijn.* Antwerpen: Samsom Kluwer, 2000).

5  One of the first things many students of sociology are taught is the so-called 'Thomas theorem': 'If men define situations as real, they are real in their consequences.'

6  This idea of being involved in a 'war on drugs' is what in the end caused the 'Van Traa crisis', named after the chairman who presided over the parliamentary commission that, in 1995, investigated covert policing practices. During the preceding decade, police operatives at the lowest levels had been allowed to operate in a judicial and command vacuum, applying all sorts of intrusive tactics at will and making decisions almost entirely on their own. Individual detectives had been called upon to do the dirty work, while senior officers and public prosecutors either pretended not to know anything, in order to avoid responsibility, or joined in the fight with even more cowboyish eagerness, ignoring a good part of the penal code in the process. At one point, the Van Traa commission established that the police had been instrumental in bringing 285 tonnes of soft drugs and 100 kilos of cocaine onto the market. Such incredible decisions had been made in naïve attempts to 'build up informants' who had to establish credibility with major criminal organisations but who later turned out to have been 'double agents' who became major traffickers on their own account under police protection.

7  Their report to the parliamentary Van Traa commission was later translated and published as C. Fijnaut, F. Bovenkerk, G. Bruinsma and H. van de Bunt (1998) *Organized Crime in the Netherlands.* The Hague: Kluwer Law International).

8  The Fijnaut Group defined organised crime as: 'If and when groups of individuals join for financial reasons to sytematically commit crimes that can adversely affect society. And are capable of relatively effectively shielding these crimes from targeted intervention of the authorities, in particular by way of their willingness to use physical violence or eliminate individuals by means of corruption.'

9  The very existence of the Internet is a result of the awareness of the US Department of Defense in the 1960s that the redundancy of a network would be needed to allow for strategic communications after a major nuclear attack.

10  There are only a few examples to be found in the open literature of analysts who have attempted to describe criminal networks using the regular set of instruments (methodology, algorithms and software). A Dutch Ph.D. student with full access to police resources and data and support from leading experts in the network analysis field gave up the project within a year for lack of prospects (J. Herbrink (1995) 'Netwerkanalyse. Nieuw vangnet voor de politie?' *Modus* 4, 3: 2–6). Since then, no serious attempt has been made to apply such sociometric techniques in crime analysis.

11  Of course, newer generations of analysis software can make all sorts of distinctions between, for example, command links, financial links and logistical (such as drug transport) links. The direction of the relation can also be indicated by arrowheads, and the reliability of specific pieces of information can be taken into account by drawing unconfirmed relations with a dotted link.

12  Two examples: Dr Malcolm K. Sparrow of Harvard University explored several analytical techniques in relation to social network analysis in a number of open and closed publications (e.g. (1991) 'Network vulnerabilities and strategic intelligence in law enforcement', *International Journal of Intelligence and Counterintelligence* 5, 3); more recently and closer to home, Detective Superintendent

Andrew Rennison presented a 'smallest space' analysis based on itemised telephone bills in his paper, *Social Network Analysis of a Group of Criminals* (Manuscript, 1999).
13  Handelingen Tweede Kamer 1998–1999, Bijlagen 26269 Nrs 4–5: 201.

## References

Bathurst, R.B. (1993) *Intelligence and the Mirror.* Oslo: PRIO.

Cummings, J. and Volkman, E. (1992) *Goombata: The Improbable Rise and Fall of John Gotti and His Gang.* New York: Avon Books.

Ianni, F.A.J. and Reuss-Ianni, E. (1972) *A Family Business: Kinship and Social Control in Organized Crime.* London: Routledge and Kegan Paul.

Kleemans, E.R., van den Berg, E.A.I.M. and van de Bunt, H.G. (1998) *Georganiseerde criminaliteit in Nederland. Rapportage op basis van de WODC-monitor.* The Hague: WODC.

Nadelmann, E. (1993) *Cops Across Borders: the Internationalization of U.S. Law Enforcement.* Pennsylvania: Penn State Press.

# 7 Transnational organised crime

## A police perspective

*Peter Stelfox*

This chapter explores the nature of the response made by the police in England and Wales[1] to transnational organised crime. In doing so it focuses on policing activity in this area rather than formal police structures or the legal provisions which support transnational policing. The justification for this approach is that these formal organisational and legal structures do not in themselves adequately reveal the nature of the strategies that the police use. Policing is defined not by how the police are organised or by what they could or should do but rather by their actions, or as Manning (2000: 182) has put it: 'Without analysis of dynamic policing transactions, one is left with stark formalism and typologies with are intellectually impoverished.'

The strategic response made by the police service to transnational organised crime has not been explicit but has been embedded in two wider strategic developments; the transnationalisation of policing, much of which has occurred independently of any development which specifically relates to organised crime, and developments in the policing of organised crime, many of which have been unconnected to any transnational dimension it may have.

The transnationalisation of policing predates present concerns about organised crime and has been directed as much towards the wider social role of the police as it has towards a strictly law enforcement agenda (Sheptycki, 1998: 492). This has led to the establishment of a multitude of formal transnational policing organisations, from those concerned with the management of policing, such as the International Association of Chiefs of Police, those with an explicit law enforcement function, such as Europol and Interpol, to those with exclusively fraternal aims, such as the International Police Association. Underlying these formal organisations is an extensive network of informal contacts which have been built up as a result of joint operations, training courses, seminars and peace-keeping missions. While policing may not be the most exclusive club in the world, it is arguably one of the largest.

The nature of organised crime in the UK, and the most appropriate means of policing it, is as much a contested area amongst police officers as it is amongst academics and policy-makers. Such debate as there has been within the service has been characterised as occurring at a 'superficial level' (Penrose, 2000: 13), where it has centred on a battle for resources between local and national levels of policing, or has become stalled on the question of the nature, or even the existence, of the organised crime threat to the UK (Levi, 1998: 341). It is not intended to add further to the spoil heap from that particular mine here. It is sufficient to note that developments specifically related to the policing of organised crime have tended to be most noticeable within the National Criminal Intelligence Service (NCIS) and the National Crime Squad (NCS), both of which have national and international remits. Local police forces have tended to concentrate on specific types of policing such as drugs, vehicle crime, fraud, and so on, which, whilst often discussed in the literature as forming part of the generic organised crime problem, continue to be treated as separate policing domains within the service. It is tempting to speculate that this distinction reflects a real difference between the various levels of policing along the lines that Edwards and Gill (1999: 4) have termed the 'attribute' and the 'process' narratives of organised crime. The 'attribute narrative' focuses on the characteristics of the individuals or groups involved, such as their internal structure, the type of crime they are involved in, the level they operate at or perhaps their country of origin or ethnic group. The 'process narrative' concentrates on the way in which certain processes of crime are organised, such as 'organised vehicle crime', 'organised fraud', and so on. But to characterise the differences between NCIS/NCS and local police forces along these lines would be too simplistic. A closer examination of the work carried out at each level reveals that both concentrate heavily on an enforcement approach based on the 'attribute narrative'; it is simply that local forces tend to organise themselves into domain-specific units to apply this approach, whilst national-level units are organised more generically. To all intents and purposes both levels are applying the same approach to the same types of people.

Clearly the points at which the transnationalisation of policing and the policing of organised crime overlap constitute the domain which is of particular interest in this chapter. But this is not a well-mapped area and, in the messy world of operational policing, it is impossible to make fine distinctions between policing applied to organised crime in general and that applied specifically to transnational organised crime. This difficulty is not eased by the lack of any commonly accepted definition of transnational organised crime amongst academics. As a consequence, the unit of analysis for this chapter will be the policing of organised crime in its entirety on the assumption that much, if not all, of this will involve some transnational aspect.

In the UK, the policing of organised crime finds its most obvious expression in the work of the NCIS and the NCS. These agencies are the product of the gradual amalgamation of crime squads that started in the 1960s with the creation of the Regional Crime Squads. This reached its present state of evolution in 1992 when NCIS was formed from the National Drugs Intelligence Unit and the Regional Criminal Intelligence Offices, and in 1998 when the National Crime Squad was formed by bringing the various Regional Crime Squads into a single unit.

The NCIS collates intelligence from police forces and other agencies in the UK and abroad and provides the official gateway for UK police forces to access an international network of policing agencies through Interpol and Europol. The intelligence network to which the NCIS gives access can be thought of as consisting of a vertical axis representing international police agencies, including Interpol and Europol as well as the policing agencies of individual countries, and a horizontal axis representing the various internal UK police forces and other agencies which have an interest in transnational organised crime, such as Her Majesty's Customs and Excise and the Immigration Service.

Whilst this evolution towards a more centralised capacity to address organised crime has improved co-ordination, it has been accompanied by a concentration of their operational focus on an ever-narrowing band of the criminal spectrum. As Her Majesty's Inspector of Constabulary noted in relation to the NCIS:

> There was a clear commitment to target serious crime and major criminals, but originally it was hoped that wider levels of service could be provided, continuing in effect the role of the defunct Regional Criminal Intelligence Offices (RCIO). It soon became clear that there were simply too few resources to meet such wide ranging objectives. If NCIS was to succeed, it was vital to prioritise and resources were refocused on gathering intelligence to support operations against top tier criminality.
>
> (HMIC, 1997)

The NCS has followed a similar pattern of concentrating their resources on a narrower band of 'quality' targets. During their first year, they had a target of carrying out 819 operations (set by the Service Authority on previous RCS performance) but only actually carried out 497. The Director General explained that:

> figures don't always tell the whole story. We are more interested in high quality work rather than in quantity. That is why the operations undertaken did not meet our target. As a new national organisation we are able to take a much more strategic view, taking on more major criminals, many of whom have been regarded as too difficult to tackle.
>
> (Fogg, 1999: 9)

By the end of the financial year 2000/2001, the number of operations carried out by the NCS had fallen to 247 (The Service Authority for the National Crime Squad, 2001: 15). Again, this was held to represent improved quality. The concentration on fewer operations had enabled the NCS to increase to 45 the number of 'core nominals'[2] they arrested, which represented an improvement of 25 per cent on the previous year.

The policing activity carried out by the two UK agencies with the clearest mandate for addressing organised crime is concentrated quite deliberately on a relatively small number of 'higher quality' targets, and whilst it is not entirely clear from publicly available documents what criteria is being used to make this judgement, it is assumed that the majority of them will fall within most definitions of what constitutes organised crime.[3]

At the local level of policing, the strategy for addressing organised crime is less clearly defined. England and Wales have 43 individual police forces, each of which has a chief constable with a high level of operational autonomy. As a consequence, both transnational policing and the policing of organised crime have developed more idiosyncratically than at the national level.

The geographical location of some forces has led to the development of formal transnational policing arrangements with specific foreign police agencies, such as, the European Liaison Unit (ELU) which is based near the entrance to the Channel Tunnel in Kent and acts as a communications centre for south coast forces who need to liaise with their counterparts across the Channel (Sheptycki, 2002). But for most forces, transnational policing is something that is conducted either through formal mechanisms such as Europol or Interpol, or through informal networks.

The total volume of work channelled through formal and informal transnational networks at the local level is unknown. However, some idea of the extent of the transnational co-operation between forces is provided by the number of messages passing through the UK National Central Bureau of Interpol, which is located in the International Division of the NCIS. During 2000/2001 the Bureau processed 100,000 messages to or from foreign police agencies on behalf of UK forces. During the same period it was notified of 213 extradition applications (Service Authority for the National Criminal Intelligence Service, 2001: 10). Given that the option of using Interpol as a method of communication is often chosen only as a last resort by officers who believe it is slow and bureaucratic (Lavers and Chu, 1997: 127, for the US experience and personal communication between senior detectives and the author in the UK), messages routed through Interpol are likely to represent only a small portion of all contact between UK police forces and their foreign counterparts.

In relation to the strategy for addressing organised crime, most forces have at least some resources in central squads who police specific domains which encompass organised crime, such as drugs, fraud, vehicle crime, and so on, and these have tended to adopt a specific enforcement approach involving the proactive methods of intelligence and evidence gathering used by the NCIS and the NCS (Phillips Report, 1996).

As with the level of transnational policing, the volume of work carried out by local forces in connection with organised crime is impossible to quantify. However, the NCIS provide a service to UK police forces and HMCE that enables them to 'flag' an individual. A flag is a means of registering force or agency interest in a particular individual, usually because they are carrying out an intelligence- or evidence-gathering operation in relation to them. Flags are only accepted for major criminals and are intended to prevent duplication of effort by encouraging intelligence sharing and preventing multiple operations against the same person or group. In the year 2000/2001, 12,221 such flagging applications were received by the NCIS (Service Authority for the National Criminal Intelligence Service, 2001a: 62). The NCIS also disseminated 37,895 intelligence logs during 2000/2001 (ibid.: 58). There are no published figures showing the agencies from which these flagging applications and intelligence logs originated. However, it is understood that the majority originated from police forces, either directly as a consequence of operations they were carrying out themselves or indirectly as a consequence of them passing information to the National Crime Squad which was later transmitted to NCIS as either a flagging application or an intelligence log.

These figures, incomplete though they are, suggest that the majority of work in relation to transnational policing and organised crime is carried out by local police forces. This follows from the deliberate policy of having a highly focused central intelligence function in the NCIS, which collates intelligence nationally on a narrow band of organised crime, the NCS which focuses almost exclusively in dealing with a small number of what are perceived to be the 'top tier' criminals and local forces addressing the main body of those involved through the activities of force central squads and command units.

These figures have important implications for the debate on the nature of organised crime. In 1996, the Association of Chief Police Officers of England and Wales (ACPO) Working Group into International, National and Inter-force Crime found that local managers had little incentive to undertake cross-border operations against organised criminals because they were subject to performance management regimes that focused them exclusively on achieving local results (Phillips Report, 1996). Since then, the focus of the performance management regime on achieving local results has been strengthened by the passing of the Crime and Disorder Act 1998. Under the Act, local policing priorities are defined by local Crime and Disorder Reduction Partnerships, underpinned by national performance measurements. During 2000/2001 these were:

• total recorded crimes per 1,000 population and percentage detected;
• domestic burglaries per 1,000 households and percentage detected;

- violent crimes per 1,000 population and percentage detected;
- vehicle crimes per 1,000 population and percentage detected;
- number of offenders dealt with for supply offences in respect of Class A drugs per 10,000 population (some of those would have fallen within the flagging criteria, but most would not);
- number of public disorder incidents per 1,000 population.

Despite this emphasis on local performance, NCIS figures on the volume of flagging applications and intelligence logs show that a great deal of local attention was focused on organised crime. This suggests that local police forces have either identified connections between organised crime and local performance management figures which make it worthwhile for them to target it, or alternatively, organised crime is impacting at the local level in such a way as to justify targeting it, irrespective of its impact on local performance management figures, for example as the result of shootings related to drugs markets. It seems plausible that both of these will be true, to some extent, in any given location.

However, what this shows is that the majority of organised crime that is known in England and Wales, and it is accepted that much of it will remain unknown, manifests itself in such a way as to enable local police to target it, even when their primary focus is on responding to local crime figures. This lends support to those who argue that organised crime is primarily a consequence of locally based criminals exploiting the opportunities created by globalisation (Hobbs, 1998). The debate over the nature and definition of organised crime is complex and multi-faceted and so it would be unwise to over-interpret the meaning of a couple of statistics. For example, it may well be the case that certain types of organised crime are more amenable to this explanation than others and that the individuals targeted locally represent only a particular sub-set of organised crime. The fact remains, though, that most organised crime known about in England and Wales is not occurring in some virtual transnational domain which remains un-policed in the absence of the sort of international treaties, legal instruments, data sharing protocols and cross-border policing structures which feature large in the literature. It is occurring, and being policed, locally.

Whatever level it is being addressed at, the dominant approach to organised crime in England and Wales has been enforcement. Unlike reported crime, such as theft or personal violence, the police rarely have a report from a member of the public as a starting point for enforcement activity in relation to organised crime. As a consequence, enforcement activity relies heavily on the techniques of intelligence gathering and surveillance. The techniques described by Dorn, Murji and South (1992) as being used by the (then) Regional Crime Squads in the early 1990s remain pretty much state of the art today. A few electronic gismos have made life a bit easier for surveillance officers, but the essentials of intelligence-led policing on the ground remain much as they always have. The most significant changes have occurred at the organisational level, described earlier in the chapter.

The overall effectiveness of the enforcement approach has been questioned in the literature. It is not possible in a short chapter such as this to rehearse all of the arguments for and against, but it is undeniable that despite all the effort over the years, enforcement does not seem to have led to any appreciable reduction in the one area of organised crime where it has been applied most consistently and with most vigour, the market for controlled drugs (for recent views on this market in the UK, see May *et al.*, 2000; Pearson and Hobbs, 2001).

These limitations appear not to be connected to the resources made available or the determination of policy-makers to support the enforcement approach. Few countries have invested more talent and money into this approach than the USA where, since 1954, the Organised Crime and Racketeering Section of the US Department of Justice has co-ordinated a national law enforcement drive against organised crime. Viano, in his review of recent legislative developments in the USA, which has 'been in the forefront of fighting both domestic and international organised crime using criminal law and justice systems as major tools', concluded that 'the government's approach to apprehend and prosecute as many crime bosses (particularly Italian-American) as possible has had little impact on the overall activities and strength of organised crime' (2000: 203).

The reasons for the apparent failure of the enforcement approach to deliver significant changes in levels of organised crime may lie in the fact that it can have unforeseen effects in favour of the illegal market. Enforcement activity is often sufficient to make the operating environment of organised crime hostile to those who seek to operate in it, but not efficient enough to choke off the flow of goods altogether; this merely ensures that prices remain high, particularly where there are a group of dependent customers, as in the market for controlled drugs. This, in turn, makes it attractive to criminal entrepreneurs who provide a steady flow of replacements to those arrested by the enforcement activity (May *et al.*, 2000: 9).

This is not to say that the law enforcement approach is entirely misguided. There is, after all, a good case to be made for the state to maintain a credible capacity to bring to justice those who are causing significant harm by breaking the law. Even though enforcement operations against organised crime are always likely to be difficult, expensive and to have uncertain outcomes, they at least mark the boundaries of society's intolerance of criminal behaviour. The argument for enforcement does not therefore rest entirely on its contribution to the reduction of organised crime. However, acknowledging the limitations of the enforcement approach should lead to greater consideration of the role that crime reduction measures could play in this area.

It is something of a cliché to state that the first responsibility of the police is to prevent crimes occurring, but a great deal of current thinking within the police service is returning to this tradition. There has been widespread adoption of the principles of problem solving policing within the service, although full and effective implementation may be some way off (Read and Tilley, 2000: 35), and the Crime and Disorder Act 1998 has provided a statutory framework within which the police must work with partner agencies to reduce crime in their area. If, as is argued above (p. 119), a great deal of organised crime occurs and is policed locally, then there is a compelling rationale for using the problem solving and crime reduction structures currently being developed locally to address it.

In some areas of organised crime, reduction measures have already played a significant role in reducing the range of criminal opportunities, particularly where significant stakeholders have an incentive such as with fraud and vehicle crime (Pease, 1998: 11). But, taken overall, problem solving and Crime and Disorder partnerships have concentrated on the ' "sharp end" of operational policing and tended to focus on the offender' (Read and Tilley, 2000: 36) rather than on the more strategic level, such as reducing criminal opportunities through interventions in the processes of organised crime. However, Levi (1998: 343) has noted that 'criminologists have begun to see "the causes of crime" as including an analysis of how crime is organised socially and technically' and the Home Office have sponsored a number of studies with the specific intention of informing the police and policy-makers about criminal processes. Amongst these are: vehicle theft (Hinchliffe, 1994); counterfeiting credit cards (Newton, 1994); the distribution of stolen electrical goods (Kock, Kemp and Rix, 1996); the theft of heavy goods and plant (Brown, 1995); and middle market drug distribution (Pearson and Hobbs, 2001). In addition to these, the NCIS have produced a number of process-specific threat assessments. However, the potential of such work has not always been exploited to the full due to the difficulty of operationalising the findings so that they have a practical effect. It is insufficient for the police to obtain a general overview of how crime processes work; what is required are toolkits which turn theoretical models into useful information that can be actioned on the ground.

Such an approach was taken in Sutton's (1998) examination of the market for stolen goods that proposed a model by which the police could understand the nature of these markets in their area. It also included a methodology for gathering data to map out the nature and extent of the market. This was linked to recommendations about the type of multi-agency interventions that might prove effective in reducing the market. The Home Office are currently funding pilot projects to assess the viability of Sutton's approach and, although not yet finally evaluated, those involved believe the results achieved to date are promising for the wider application of these methods (personal communication from the project team in one of the two pilot sites).

Another recent development that lends itself to the greater use of a crime reduction approach is the National Intelligence Model. This provides an operating framework within which officers are encouraged to make greater use of analysis to identify problems affecting the area they police. The methodology involves the use of standard analytical products, such as crime pattern analysis, market profiles, demographic/social trend analysis, criminal business profiles, network analysis and risk analysis, all of which can be used to map out organised criminal processes for the crime reduction approach (NCIS, 2000: 29).

Whether in the future the police adopt a more 'crime reduction approach' or continue to rely heavily on enforcement, it seems likely that they will continue to be faced by ever-evolving challenges. As Pease, following Felson, has noted: 'the necessary elements of crime, namely the conjunction of motivated offender and suitable victim, in the absence of a capable guardian, dance to the tune of a society's routine activities' (Pease, 1998: 3). It seems to follow that, as these routine activities become ever more transnational, then so too will the criminal opportunities that they give rise to. This is likely to lead to innovations in criminal processes which the police and their partners will have to address. Whatever approach they take in any given instance, there are two measures which need to be taken to ensure that the local level of policing is able to respond to organised crime.

The first of these measures is the development of an effective means by which local officers can communicate with others who have a stake in a transnational policing problem. Given the scale of organised crime and the policing response to it, formal structures that seek to funnel all activity through a central controlling point are likely to be overloaded at some point. Indeed, the view that formal structures of transnational communication are slow and bureaucratic, the existence of informal policing networks and the concentration of NCIS and NCS resources on a narrow band of the criminal spectrum all suggest that the limited capacity of the central structures designed to police organised crime have already been exceeded.

One response to this is to increase the resources of these structures to improve their capacity to cope, and to some extent this has been done already. Over the four year period to 2002, the NCIS's budget rose from 38 million pounds to over 90 million pounds (Service Authority for the National Criminal Intelligence Service, 2001b: 3), which is generous when judged against rises in other public service budgets during the same period. Although this increase in budget undoubtedly enabled the NCIS to improve its service, this was not to the extent where it could even begin to cope with the volume of all policing directed towards organised crime and it is highly likely that its current narrow focus will continue.

The alternative to greater capacity at the centre is to embrace the formal and informal peer-to-peer networks that have already been developed by officers. If globalisation has freed up criminals from the constraints of time and space through cheap and frequent international travel and the Internet, could it not also do the same for the police service and others involved in the policing of organised crime? This may require little more than the development of a website that enables officers to contact those who share a common problem with a view to establishing co-operation. If linked to problem-solving toolkits, knowledge databases, central agencies such as the NCIS, Europol, Interpol and the NCS, local authorities and other non-police agencies that may have a stake in transnational organised crime problems, then so much the better. The Crime Reduction Website (http://www.crimereduction.gov.uk/cpindex.htm) developed by the Home Office, though still not fully developed, offers a model for such a network.

Enforcement operations arising out of such a peer-to-peer network would have to be underpinned by the legislative instruments covering transnational policing as at present, but as has already been noted, there is a large volume of such work being carried out already. The introduction of a peer-to-peer network would require no new legislation. However, the main benefit of such a network is likely to be in the area of crime reduction where greater transnational co-operation is unlikely to require a legal foundation. For example, a city which found that some of its sex workers were illegal immigrants who may have been trafficked to the UK for this purpose could quickly tap into the latest Home Office, UN and NCIS research on the subject, could contact the Immigration Service for advice on the legal procedures that apply, contact NGOs who may be able to provide advice and services to the women and make contact with the police from the country of origin to establish the extent to which they were able to share information and take action at their end of the problem. This could lead to enforcement action within the supply chain or at either end of it, or it could lead to other crime reduction measures, such as the provision of information to women in the country of origin with a view to better informing them of the reality of the arrangements they may be entering into and assisting those at the other end of the chain to disengage from the networks that are exploiting them (see Goodey, this volume, Chapter 10).

At present, none of this is actually impossible using present systems, but it could hardly be described as easy or common. If, as seems likely, the extent of transnational crime is set to grow, then peer-to-peer policing arrangements that enable those with a stake in a particular problem to address it independently of central structures may offer the only way of coping with demand.

The second measure required to enable local police officers to address organised crime is the introduction of incentives to do so. As noted above, the government has successfully encouraged police forces to concentrate effort in particular areas through the use of performance measures. These do not cover all areas of policing but, on the basis of 'what gets measured gets done', they have been influential in determining the type of activity the police undertake. At present these measures are focused only on local issues and there is a danger that this will mean that action to address organised crime will be given a lower priority. If the framework for applying a crime reduction approach to organised crime is to be used effectively, it will be essential to ensure that officers have an incentive to use it. Providing local forces with performance measures similar to those used by the NCIS and the NCS would give them such an incentive.

This review of policing activity shows that the majority of organised crime in England and Wales occurs at a level where it is visible to local police forces, who are able to take action against it in so much as they identify offenders for enforcement activity and flag them to the NCIS. There were 12,221 applications for such flagging in the financial year 2000/2001. Because only those who are considered to fall into the category of 'major criminal' are flagged, it is probable that a much larger number of individuals who were involved in organised crime were actually targeted during this period, but that the majority of them were not subject to flagging applications. The extent of policing activity against organised crime at the local level lends support to those who argue that transnational organised crime consists predominantly of local criminals taking advantage of the opportunities created by globalisation.

The implication taken from this is that the present structure for policing organised crime in England and Wales, whereby the NCIS provide national collation of intelligence, the NCS targets a small number of 'top tier' organised criminals and local forces address the bulk of organised crime, is probably the most appropriate because it ensures that strategies are developed to take account of local conditions, including community views, and in conjunction with local partner agencies.

However, the realisation that organised crime may best be addressed at the local level of policing opens up opportunities to make more use of crime reduction approaches. This would supplement the enforcement approach that currently dominates the policing of organised crime but which has been found to be limited. It is often successful in dealing with individual criminals or groups and provides a symbolic response to criminality, but there is little evidence that it has been successful in reducing organised crime.

The mechanisms for making more use of a crime reduction approach are already largely in place as a consequence of the adoption of a problem-solving approach to policing, the establishment of Crime and Disorder Reduction Partnerships under the Crime and Disorder Act 1998, and the introduction of the National Intelligence Model. To be effective these measures need to be linked to incentives to encourage local managers to use them and to peer-to-peer policing networks that enable officers to co-operate with others who have a stake in a particular organised crime problem.

## Notes

1 England and Wales are treated as a single jurisdiction within the United Kingdom.
2 'Core Nominal' is the term the NCIS use to describe the individuals they believe pose the greatest criminal threat. The Service Authority for the NCS state that 'core nominals' are the Squad's key area of business (Service Authority for the National Crime Squad, 2001: 5).
3 [Editors' note] The 'National Operations Evaluation Formula' developed initially in the South East Regional Crime Squad and subsequently adopted by the National Crime Squad is reproduced in Gill, 2000: 142–3.

## References

ACPO (1996) 'Report of the working group on international, national and inter-force crime' (The Phillips Report). Unpublished ACPO report.

Brown, R. (1995) *The Nature and Extent of Heavy Goods Vehicle Theft*. London: Home Office PRG.

Dorn, N., Murji, K. and South, N. (1992) *Traffickers*. London: Routledge.

Edwards, A. and Gill, P. (1999) 'Coming to terms with transnational organised crime'. Paper presented to the ESRC Seminar Series Policy Responses to Transnational Organised Crime, University of Leicester, September.

Fogg, E. (1999) 'NCS fails to reach operations target', *Police Review*, July.

Gill, P. (2000) *Rounding Up the Usual Suspects*. Aldershot: Ashgate.

Her Majesty's Inspector of Constabulary (1997) *Inspection Report: The National Criminal Intelligence Service*. London: HMSO.

Hinchliffe, M. (1994) *Professional Car Thieves: Their Knowledge and Social Structure*. London: Home Office PRG.

Hobbs, D. (1998) 'Going down the glocal: the local context of organised crime', *The Howard Journal of Criminal Justice* 37: 407–22.

Kock, E., Kemp, T. and Rix, B. (1996) *Disrupting the Distribution of Stolen Electrical Goods*. London: Home Office PRG.

Lavers, J. and Chu, Y. (1997) 'Informal police cooperation: the fight against international crime', *The Police Journal*, April, 127–34.

Levi, M. (1998) 'Perspectives on organised crime: an overview', *The Howard Journal of Criminal Justice* 37: 335–45.

Manning, P. (2000) 'Policing new social spaces', in J. Sheptycki (ed.) *Issues in Transnational Policing*. London: Routledge.

May, T., Harocopos, A., Turnbull, P.J. and Hough, M. (2000) *Serving Up: The Impact of Low-Level Enforcement on Drugs Markets*. London: Home Office.

National Criminal Intelligence Service (2000) *The National Intelligence Model*. London: NCIS.

Newton, J. (1994) *Organised Plastic Counterfeiting*. London: Home Office PRG.

Pearson, G. and Hobbs, D. (2001) *Middle Market Drugs Distribution*. London: Home Office.

Pease, K. (1998) 'The future of crime and crimes of the future'. Unpublished paper presented at Home Office seminar, November.

Penrose, R. (2000) 'Clear and present danger', *Policing Today* 6: 12–13.

Read, T. and Tilley, N. (2000) *Not Rocket Science? Problem Solving and Crime Reduction.* London: Home Office.

Service Authority for the National Crime Squad (2001) *The National Crime Squad Annual Report.* London: Service Authority for the National Crime Squad.

Service Authority for the National Criminal Intelligence Service (2001a) *The National Criminal Intelligence Service Annual Report.* London: Service Authority for the National Criminal Intelligence Service.

—— (2001b) *The National Criminal Intelligence Service: Service Plan for 2002/2003.* London: Service Authority for the National Criminal Intelligence Service.

Sheptycki, J. (1998) 'Policing, postmodernism and transnationalization', *British Journal of Criminology* 38: 485–503.

—— (2002) *In Search of Transnational Policing: Towards a Sociology of Global Policing.* Aldershot: Ashgate.

Sutton, M. (1998) *Handling Stolen Goods and Theft: A Market Reduction Approach.* London: Home Office PRG.

Viano, E.C. (2000) 'The criminal justice system facing the challenges of organised crime', in E.C. Viano (ed.) *Global Organised Crime and International Security.* Aldershot: Ashgate.

# Part III

# Case studies

If, as argued by Klerks and Stelfox in Part II, it is accepted that responses to TOC need to be questioned in terms of their sensitivity to the specific social contexts in which they are implemented, then qualitative case study research has much to offer policy change and learning. The contributions to Part III discuss the findings of case study research into European Union responses to the perceived threat from organised criminality originating in Central and Eastern European (CEE) states.

The chapters by Rawlinson and Bogusz and King argue that the very notion of TOC has been defined by the European Union in relation to the key objective of the third pillar of the Treaty of European Union, on Justice and Home Affairs, which calls for the creation of a 'high level of safety within an area of freedom, security and justice'. It is clear from the panoply of action plans, directives and other policy instruments developed by the European Union over the past decade that organised criminality originating in CEE states is regarded as a principle threat to this objective (see also Chapter 2 by Elvins in Part I). As such, the EU has made improvements in the policing and judicial capacity of CEE states a key criterion for their accession to the EU. Specifically, the Commission of the EU has identified the need for improvements in mutual judicial assistance, joint policing operations, greater law enforcement and judicial co-operation in the fight against organised crime and in tackling money laundering, terrorism and transnational offences. The basic instrument for compelling candidate states for accession to comply with these improvements is the *acquis communautaire* (the entire body of law to which EU member states are subject), especially those laws specified in the Justice and Home Affairs pillar. Progress in complying with the *acquis* is monitored by the Commission through the Regular (annual) Country Reports on each candidate state's performance which, in turn, inform bilateral Accession Partnership Agreements between the EU and these states. The Country Reports are also used to identify priority areas for action to be undertaken by candidate states and, since 1998, these have specified action on illicit drugs trafficking, illegal immigration and organised crime more generally.

Bogusz and King argue that, whilst such accession criteria seek to ensure a basic level of governing competence within candidate states, it does not take into account the 'respective histories or cultural and socio-economic contexts' of CEE countries. Their case studies of responses to illicit drug trafficking in Hungary, Lithuania and the Czech Republic identify a basic contradiction between the EU's accession criteria, which attribute problems of organised criminality primarily to the efficacy of law enforcement strategies, and public authorities within these candidate states who emphasise the 'liberalisation of society' and 'the transition from a command economy to a market economy' post-Cold War as the real causes of organised crime in CEE states. This contradiction, they suggest, reveals the real agenda behind the accession criteria: to secure the external borders of the EU rather than to assist CEE states in amelior-ating the transition to market societies.

Rawlinson discusses this contradiction between the domestic priorities of CEE states and their subordination to the priorities of the EU through a focus on responses to organised crime in the Baltic states of Latvia, Lithuania and Estonia and argues that 'the effect of misjudged risk assess-ments, of external agendas which are ill-conceived or in conflict with domestic concerns threaten not only to stymie reform but could prove to be positively detrimental to the development of good governance'. It is argued that the escalation of anti-crime legislation in the Baltic states, at the behest of the EU, has been based on a profound misreading of the evidence about the actual nature and functioning of illicit markets. Crim-inal organisations have evolved in these states primarily to provide services demanded by individuals excluded from opportunities to gain access to legitimate goods and services. In ignoring this and other social causes of crime, narratives on TOC have been used by EU member states for two specific purposes: first, to legitimate more exclusive policies on migration from Eastern to Western European countries and, second, to enable state institutions to abnegate their responsibility for implementing more effect-ive welfare and security policies on problems in their jurisdiction. There are also severe opportunity costs attached to prioritising action on organ-ised crime, whether transnational or not, in taking scarce resources away from local welfare and control agencies. Evidence from the Baltic case studies substantiates this concern over the opportunity costs of alternative crime control strategies and of the broader project of EU enlargement. Whereas there is no comparative research evidence on trends in organ-ised crime in member states and accession states, and therefore no eviden-tial basis for arguing that CEE states present a greater threat of cross-border crime than their Western counterparts, there is evidence to suggest that, as in Western European societies, crime is an overwhelmingly local phenomenon. Crime is woven into and generated out of the milieu of local political, economic and cultural relations and, if this is accepted, then the policy response should also be local.

A key insight of Rawlinson's chapter is that citizens of CEE states should be considered as victims of organised criminality and not just the source of threats to the EU. Goodey develops this argument further by shifting the debate over TOC away from the relationship between public authorities and the perpetrators of organised criminality towards a concern with the victims of organised crime. Taking the trafficking of women for the purposes of sexual exploitation as a focus, Goodey argues that, in its drive to enhance the Justice and Home Affairs *acquis* across member states of the EU, the Commission has introduced additional security measures to protect EU citizens from a perceived 'enemy without', specifically the threat of organised crime and illegal immigration from CEE states. As a consequence, 'the "victim" of trafficking has traditionally fallen into a "no man's land" between criminal and victim status because of four important factors: (i) their association with criminal elements; (ii) their illegal entry into the EU; (iii) their "work" as prostitutes; and (iv) the unequal distribution of victim's rights in the EU.' If it is accepted that the victim status of those who are illegally trafficked across borders should be recognised then there are important implications for policy change and learning about the response to TOC. Goodey discusses recent policy initiatives by the EU and by non-governmental organisations, notes the limitations of criminal justice reforms and witness protection schemes and emphasises the need for a re-orientation of policy priorities towards the prevention of forms of organised crime such as human trafficking.

In broadening debates over TOC to encompass the social and political conditions and causes of crime, the contributions to Part III reflect current controversies in criminological thought over the limits of law enforcement and the need for a broader spectrum of policy responses entailing the prevention as well as reduction of crime. Part IV considers current and prospective developments in the response to TOC in the light of these controversies.

# 8 Bad boys in the Baltics[1]

*Paddy Rawlinson*

## Introduction

The term 'transnational organised crime' (TOC) evokes images of a world without frontiers assaulted by the trans-border activities of criminal groups indigenous to states in transition or Third World countries. It is an attack on civilised states by the 'forces of incivility', the price we must pay for the benefits globalisation has bequeathed (or will bequeath) on those invited to participate in the free market and the development of democracy. The imminent enlargement of the European Union, to include ten former communist states in Eastern and Central Europe, brings these security fears into focus; that is, a vulnerability to the expanding presence of organised crime, particularly from Russia and other CIS countries. Full membership of the EU will entail the automatic ratification of the Schengen *acquis*, which guarantees the free movement of persons and goods within the EU, thereby providing plentiful opportunities for criminal networks to expand their business activities westwards.

The Baltic States – Estonia, Latvia and Lithuania – lie at the Eastern frontier of this expansion and will effectively become crime control sentinels for the new Europe. Their ability to fulfil the task of stemming the flow of TOC from Russia and beyond makes them strategically vital for maintaining the Treaty of Amsterdam's stated objective to create an 'area of freedom, security and justice' within the EU. This threat from TOC from the East has prompted the initiation of objectives and policies by Brussels aimed at helping accession states fulfil their role in reducing this risk. These include the Pre-Accession Pact on Organised Crime and other programmes, not all confined to the EU, such as the Task Force on Organised Crime in the Baltic Sea Region and the Northern Dimension Action Plan 2000–2003 (CEU, 2000) which collectively make provisions for *inter alia* mutual judicial assistance, joint police operations, greater law enforcement and judicial co-operation in the fight against organised crime, money laundering, terrorism and transnational offences currently outside the EU, including Russia and its European exclave, the Kaliningrad oblast.

Acquiescence to the stipulations set out in the Justice and Home Affairs *acquis*, based on security priorities set by member states, is essential for full membership of the EU. The impact of these priorities on domestic reforms of the criminal justice systems in the Baltic States, particularly during this crucial formative stage in their transition from the old authoritarian system to democratic governance, will be of huge significance. Unlike member states, whose legislation and law enforcement institutions developed over a period of time in response to internal demands, accession states such as the Baltics are faced with the dilemma of simultaneously having to attend to *external* as well as domestic priorities, the former having an impact on the latter. Further, they have had to do this over a relatively short period and under conditions of sometimes-draconian change. Therefore the effect of misjudged risk assessments, of external agendas which are ill-conceived or in conflict with domestic concerns threaten not only to stymie reform but could prove to be positively detrimental to the development of good governance.

The majority of these Brussels-directed justice and home affairs priorities are based on the assumption of threat from transnational organised crime from the East. But how far does this assumption reflect reality? And to what extent are these agendas, as prescriptions for reforms within the accession states, part of a supranational strategy for the creation of what has been termed 'Fortress Europe'?

The chapter presents findings from the ESRC project 'Crime Borders and Law Enforcement: A European Dialogue for Improving Security', the aim of which was to discover the nature and extent of the threat of Russian-speaking organised crime in and across the Baltic States. The findings challenge the orthodoxy that the presence of transnational organised crime from Russia and its southern neighbours constitutes a security risk for an enlarged Europe. Such a convention, it argues, promoting this 'Fortress Europe' mentality, has encouraged strategies for law enforcement reforms in accession states, which fail to give sufficient emphasis to the impact of organised crime at a local level. In distracting from those tangible causes and consequences of organised crime, which reflect regional social and economic activities, the 'transnational' agenda engages accession states in the struggle against what Dick Hobbs has described as 'abstract fields devoid of relations' (Hobbs, 1998), a type of virtual criminality. Nor are the dangers of misplaced threats confined to transition countries. In the definitional minefield within which the term 'organised crime' per se sits, perceptions of the nature and extent of its dangerousness within countries with long histories of dealing with the problem have been challenged by academics such as Naylor who claims that, in the case of the US fight against organised crime: 'there is a possibility the entire escalation of anti-crime legislation has been based on a profound misreading of the evidence about the nature and functioning of the criminal marketplace' (1997: 1).

## Reluctant ties

Given the recent history of the Baltics' relations with Russia, it is hardly surprising that they are seen as targets of and transit for Russian organised crime. Even as republics of the Soviet Union, the Baltic States served as a corridor for the movement of illegal goods. During 1987–8 the KGB reported the confiscation of just fewer than one million roubles' worth of contraband and 22 million dollars of hashish in transit from Latvia alone (ITAR–TASS, 1988). But it was after the break-up of the USSR and the huge burgeoning of organised crime that the Baltic corridor became a route for frenetic cross-border illegal trade. Contraband alcohol and tobacco, stolen vehicles, illegal arts and antiques, guns and computer parts comprised some of the inexhaustible list of trade along the golden corridor. The trafficking of heroin from areas such as Tajikistan and Afghanistan intensified as the more traditional route through the Balkans became hazardous during the civil war. Human misery as a commodity was also on the increase as growing numbers of illegal immigrants, many escaping civil conflict and dire poverty, travelled a hopeful path through the Baltics to the Nordic countries where asylum and refugee legislation was, at the time, some of the most moderate in Europe. In 1994, approximately 40,000 illegal persons entered Latvia, the population of which is just under two-and-a-half million (Ulrich, 1994).

Russian-speaking criminal networks were undoubtedly well established in Estonia and Latvia during the early 1990s. Many of these had been formed as a consequence of the practice of sending all felons in the Soviet Union convicted of serious crimes to camps East of the Urals. But it was the Russian *vory-v-zakone*, or elite 'thieves-in-law' who dominated the camps and controlled the networks (Rawlinson, 1997). The Russian influence on the criminal underworlds of Estonia and Latvia was also encouraged by their demographies, a result of Stalin's brutal Russification policy, which deported thousands of the population from all three Baltic countries to Siberian gulags in 1944 and replaced them with ethnic Russians. Of the three, Lithuania managed to maintain its national identity most successfully, as reflected in the low ratio of Russians to indigenes, which in 1999 stood at 8 per cent and 82 per cent respectively, compared with Estonia's 28 per cent ethnic Russian population and Latvia's even higher 32 per cent (in the capital, Riga, approximately half the population are ethnic Russian) (Statistical Office of Estonia, 1999).

These links were most manifest in the chaotic early years of transition. Estonia's bloody 'Metal Wars', which in 1993 endowed Tallinn with the sobriquet of the 'world's most violent capital', were fought around the trade in non-ferrous metals exported from Russia. Russian crime groups, such as St Petersburg's Tambov gang, worked with and against other non-Estonian gangs from Perm, Novosibirsk, Krasnodar and Chechnya, many of them engaged in the profitable sale of anabolic steroids to Scandinavia which were transported on the regular ferry crossings from Estonia and Finland. The only powerful Estonian group known to operate at this time was the Saha-Loo gang (Baltic News Service, October 9, 1998).

In Latvia the picture was much the same, but close links between the Russian and Latvian underworld were also established at the more sophisticated level of banking and finance. When two of the country's leading banks – Banka Baltiya and Olympia – collapsed in the mid-1990s, it was common knowledge that the respective directors, Alexander Lavents and Vladimir Leskov, had been *tsekhoviki* (underground entrepreneurs) and had maintained links with Russian criminal counterparts.[2] Even Lithuania experienced the incursion of the Russian-speaking underworld, albeit in limited form. Its most feared and violent group of the early 1990s, the Vilnius Brigade, was led by a Russian–Georgian, Boris Denakidze, who was executed in 1995 for his involvement in the murder of one of the country's most respected journalists, Vytautus Lingys. Lingys had exposed an illegal arms deal, which drew in a complex network of individuals including Lavents and Denakidze (Lase, 2000). But by 1996 the then-Estonian Prime Minister Tiut Vahi was able to announce at an EU summit in Dublin that 'almost all criminal groups of the Russian Mafia type have been eliminated in Estonia', progress he attributed to the improvement in law enforcement and legislation. The days of Russian criminal dominance in and across the Baltics were very much on the decline. What did persist, according to a study of Estonian organised crime by Anna Markina, were relations between Russian and Estonian criminal groups which 'rather resemble business co-operation between partners ... In other words, the locally organised criminal groups could not be treated as an Estonian Division of the Russian Mafia' (Markina, 1998). This trend also applied in Latvia, the Head of Riga's Organised Crime Unit claimed, where Russian-speaking criminal groups comprised of disaffected and marginalised youths engaged in low levels of extortion.[3]

More realistically, it was nationalist rather than crime control strategies which saw off the Russian influenced underworld. Embittered by years of oppression and encouraged to look west after the 1993 Copenhagen European Council invited Central and Eastern European states to apply for accession, Estonia, Latvia and Lithuania embarked on an intensive reconstruction of national and cultural identity. A series of citizenship and language laws were implemented, designed to purge high-level and strategically important positions in government and other state institutions of Russian influence. This helped to stem the incursion of non-indigenous criminal influence on public-sector employees. The gradual stabilisation of the economies in each state further curtailed the influence of Russian-speaking organised crime, excluded as many were from high-profile business links.

**Russians as anti-heroes**

Backman (2002) has criticised the Finnish obsession with Russian crime as verging on racism: 'Finns regard all Russian women as prostitutes and all Russian men as thieves and gangsters.' He also points out the discrepancies between perception and reality, which inform this attitude:

> Cases resembling organised crime have included the illegal trade in alcohol and tobacco and prostitution, as well as the more severe cases of organised automobile theft, international drug-trafficking and economic crime over the Finnish–Russian border. Although such cases receive wide public attention they are not numerous in comparison with Finnish domestic crimes.
>
> (Backman, 1998)

This focus on the threat posed by ROC as a transnational phenomenon is a common view world-wide, given substance by the enduring Cold War mentality that remains impressed in the consciousness of Western policy-makers. In the UK the media obsession with all things criminal in and from Russia during the mid-1990s (and, admittedly, supported at that time by the author) did little more than grab the headlines and help label all Russian businessman as mafiosi. A report in 2000 by the UK National Criminal Intelligence Service pours cold water over the notion that Britain is facing 'an "invasion" by a "red mafiya"' (NCIS, 2000). Near hysteria over the presence of the Russian Mafia in the US has also been criticised by a study of the impact of ROC on American society. It concludes:

> the actual and potential illegal markets available do not lend themselves to domination and monopolization by these Russians. Indeed, in the most lucrative of the illegal markets – drugs and gambling – there is considerable competition from a variety of criminal organizations that are sufficiently powerful to make it impossible for Russian criminals to force them out . . . It is our judgement that there is no Russian Mafia in the United States.
>
> (Finckenauer and Waring, 1998: 252)

Interestingly, the 'alien conspiracy view' so favoured by the Western media and many policy-makers, the notion that it is ethnicity which demarcates and defines our understanding of organised crime, was markedly absent in the interviews we conducted in the Baltic States from the people most likely to express anti-Russian feelings. Indeed, Andres Anvelt from the Estonian Organised Crime Unit commented on the 'romantic' notion so prevalent in the West of the ubiquitous presence of the Russian Mafia. This blinkered view of Estonia's susceptibility to ROC, as expressed by Western specialists, distracted attention from local 'mafias', giving them time to develop relatively unchecked.[4] Beyond the concerns of specific Russian-speaking crime, however, the dominant discourse of law enforcement agendas encouraged in accession states is that of fighting *transnational* organised crime.

## TOC: targeting other criminalities?

Hobbs states that the experience of organised crime occurs at a local level. While the concept of transnational organised crime is concerned with the movement and co-ordination of illegal activities across borders and cultures, the opportunities, needs and responses to those needs are contained within a definable, local space. The demand for any number of illicit commodities and services is met by organised crime, as exploitative provider. Users of these services and commodities are invariably marginalised sections of the 'world' economy, individuals excluded from legitimate opportunities or those who are caught in the poverty trap of having the minimum to survive but not enough to fully partake, a chain of human misery which provides lucrative outcomes for the criminal opportunist. From the opium poppy crops of impoverished farmers in Central Asia, the customs officers and border guards in the transit countries, supplementing meagre incomes from bribes (we constantly fail to distinguish the various motivations behind corruption. There is a world of difference, in terms of moral choice, between corruption from need and corruption from greed), to the heroin addict in the netherworld of social and economic exclusion in urban (and increasingly rural) areas of no opportunity, no employment, no hope, transnational organised crime is criminal entrepreneurship working the spaces that link the fixed loci at which different human needs, failing to be satisfied legitimately, seek fulfilment.

Interpreting local problems as transnational concerns has two distinct advantages. First, it allows voices from the legitimate world to erect barriers to keep out undesirables from the home space. In her work on responses to human trafficking within the EU, Jo Goodey highlights the contradictory stances towards migrants in the Union; they are regarded both as victims and as part of the security 'problem'. She writes:

> the central onus of both the Treaty of Amsterdam and the Tampere Summit is to combat the latest EU 'folk devils' of TOC and illegal immigration. Justification for ever more stringent border controls and the policing of the least desirable immigrants (the poor) is made in the name of providing a safe environment for EU *citizens*, who are depicted as the potential victims of these threats from outside.
>
> (Goodey, 2002 and see also Chapter 10, this volume)

With this inverse logic of security defined walls, now designed to keep people out rather than in, controlling the expanding terrain granted to first-class members of our global society becomes even more pressing as an increasing number of the world's population seek to leave civil conflicts and economic deprivations within their own region (often a consequence of first-class citizen policies) and gain access to 'ours'. In Bauman's (1998) words, we are a world of 'tourists and vagabonds', a two-tier global society comprising those who choose to move freely with visas and hand luggage and those who are forced to move, visa less, baggage less and stateless. Dependent on criminal services to gain this access, the concept of illegal migrant becomes a 'fusion of "migration–crime–security", under a continuum of insecurity issues'. In an enlarged Europe, it falls to the Baltic sentinels to patrol the Eastern frontier of 'Fortress Europe'.

Second, the concept of TOC removes the point of threat away from the local, where there is a higher expectation that state institutions can and should respond more efficiently and effectively to the problem. By prioritising threats that lie within these 'abstract fields devoid of relations' to a transnational space, to which everyone has access but where no-one exerts control, it becomes possible to abnegate responsibility for ineffective responses to the problem at a local level. The problem of crack cocaine in London or heroin addiction in Glasgow becomes a problem of Jamaican Yardies and Afghan warlords, targets based outside the jurisdictions of member states or other developed countries. The task of policing these targets lies with diverse domestic and supranational agencies, which diffuses responsibility for failure to respond effectively. This, in turn, perpetuates the notion of organised crime as something 'out there', a subcultural phenomenon existing and working against the acceptable norms and moralities of 'good' societies. These are the very societies, after all, which stand as examples to those states climbing out of the ruins of communism. To admit that Jamaican Yardies and Afghan warlords feed off the dysfunctionalities of democratic societies and the inequalities of the free market would entail the transformation of many aspects of crime control to that of social care. It would require acknowledging the injustices and inconsistencies of the dominant global ideology. Transnational organised crime moves the gaze away from social breakdown at local levels by blinding us to the propinquity of failure.

For the Baltic States, however, as prospective members of and gatekeepers for an enlarged Europe, there is a convergence of transnational and domestic crime issues. Their role in maintaining 'an area of freedom and security' places them within that transnational space, whereby domestic priorities are inextricably bound up with transnational agendas of the EU. Hence, instead of abnegating responsibility to an 'abstract field', they need to respond at a domestic level to its possible presence. Theirs then is a double responsibility – the policing of domestic and transnational organised crime.

## Local problems, local solutions?

What, then, are these 'local problems of organised crime'? As with member states, the Baltics have seen an increase in the trafficking and use of illegal drugs, such as heroin. In Tallinn the street price of heroin has seen a steady decrease from $70 per gram in 1996 to $20–$30 in June 2000. The picture repeats itself in Latvia and Lithuania. According to the Drug Trade Investigation Division (DTID) in Vilnius, poppy straw, opium, heroin, marijuana and ephedrine hydrochloride come into Lithuania from Kazakhstan, Tajikistan, Afghanistan and other opiate-producing republics in the CIS to provide for an increasing number of users within the country (Vilnius Drug Control Division, 2000). Nor is the traffic one-way. Cocaine, LSD, marijuana and amphetamines are imported from the West, often along the same routes used by second-hand car dealers (a lucrative trade in Eastern Europe) where vehicles bought in the Netherlands and Germany are used as transportation for illegal drugs.

However, the extent to which 'organised' as opposed to other crime should be regarded as a priority remains debatable. According to official data from Lithuania only every eighteenth crime linked with illegal drug circulation involved a criminal group. A study carried out by Markina and Tabur (1999) on corruption in the Estonian road haulage sector showed little evidence of organised crime involvement in overland transport structures, an area seen as particularly vulnerable to criminal groups. (Bucking the trend are events in Latvia, which have seen a recent increase in contract killings.) There has been no recent comparative study (to the author's knowledge) between organised crime rates and trends in member states and those in accession states, raising the question as to whether, if placed in context with other countries, the Baltics experience a greater problem of organised cross-border crime than their developed counterparts. Nonetheless, policing organised crime remains a priority for EU accession.

The dangers of macro policy responses to organised crime, as Edwards and Gill state, result in:

> a failure to tailor policy responses to the locally specific contexts of organised crime [that] is likely to promote a 'naïve' emulation of crime control strategies and techniques. At best this will fail to address the real causal dynamics of crime in these different contexts, and at worst, prove counter productive in taking scarce resources away from local welfare and crime control agencies.
>
> (Edwards and Gill, 2002)

Even if organised crime in the Baltic States were to remain at the level of the early 1990s, which is definitely not the case, the requirements of the JHA *acquis* and its attendant programmes such as the Pre-Accession Pact on Organised Crime continue to put pressure on crime control agencies to prioritise areas such as money laundering, international drugs and arms trafficking and other related TOC activities. In many cases the emphasis on these areas, as opposed to the policing of ordinary crimes, has exacerbated the already significant problems facing newly founded organisations trying to come to grips with the fundamental principles of policing in a democracy, and in which initiatives such as community policing have barely taken hold. Strategies for policing organised crime differ from those of ordinary crime. Intelligence-led policing, including the use of informants and technological surveillance, remains politically sensitive in these emergent democracies where the memory of totalitarian policing, in which such strategies were employed as a regular component of social control, remains acutely fresh. This is especially the case in Latvia and Lithuania where relations between law enforcement agencies and the public remain strained, if not hostile. People still expect to pay bribes both to the police and the judiciary, from the 'obligatory' handouts to the traffic police to the 'purchase' of a verdict in court. Despite the use of dedicated air time on local TV for police promotion programmes, the viewing public regard these as little more than a propaganda exercise and remain unconvinced of the role of the members of the criminal justice system as public servants.

Responding to the Pre-Accession Pact on Organised Crime, law enforcement reforms have attempted to make sense of the largely ambiguous perceptions of organised crime by creating units, which reflect the 'meaning' of this term. Hence the creation, in one of the states, of two departments to deal with corruption, one of which was attached to the organised crime unit, and an economic crimes department which appeared to be a catch-all for those crimes that failed to fit into other categories. This involved a continuous shifting around of personnel between the units, lack of communication and duplication of effort and resources (not unknown to law enforcement in member states) in a public sector already suffering severe budgetary constraints. Some of the EU initiatives have put further strain on finances which have meant difficult choices for management between resourcing crime reduction at a national level and satisfying those parts of the JHA *acquis* which provide for international-based policing. One finance officer from the state police confided that he doubted whether funds would be able to pay pensions to police officers due for retirement within the next couple of years. It is hardly surprising that, under these conditions, less than orthodox methods of fund raising are employed. The problem of scarce resources for international policing is not confined to the Baltics. EU policies towards the accession states depend on the use of expertise from member states, such as in the area of money laundering, which tap equally constrained budgets, meaning that often conflicting priorities determine needs on the one hand, and responses to those needs on the other.

Many of the bi- and multilateral programmes set up in response to the JHA criteria are based on assumptions, which Frank Gregory (2001) has identified as follows. First, the 'resource assumption'. Some of the broader issues are described above, but more direct problems emerge when expectations are laid on counterparts to employ methods of policing which are not, as yet, economically or culturally viable. The Witness Protection Programme, which all accession states must have in place, is a case in point. As the three countries are so small, any effective witness protection needs to either relocate those under the programme abroad, or at the very least, provide a new identity and relocation within the country, both of which are prohibitively costly. Further, the notion of offering protection to a suspect in return for intelligence does not fit into the current cultural framework for relations between the police and offenders. Second, the 'retention assumption', refers to those beneficiaries of training programmes provided by member states that are expected to pass on learned skills and expertise to the appropriate departments within the police. With such skills at a premium, some of the beneficiaries are able to seek work in the private sector, which offers significantly higher pay and better conditions of service. Third, the 'change agent' assumption presumes a political will 'to deliver the system changes necessary to meet the JHA *acquis* requirements "gaps"'. This also involves ensuring that the trained trainers are given long-term managerial positions, which will allow them to make maximum use of the technical assistance provided. And, finally, the 'accession date assumption', which implies that, by achieving the stated objectives, accession will be achieved quickly. The closing of the JHA chapter for all three states earlier this year would denote that these objectives have been fulfilled, but as one critic of the accession process has pointed out, 'to reach a positive conclusion, the [2001 state of negotiation] report minimized, in quite a systematic way, the difficulties of implementing the famous European *acquis* in the candidate countries' (Dehousse, 2002). If the JHA chapter is anything to go by, implementation difficulties are far from over.

## Unsocial security

Expectations and assumptions arise from both sides. It is not just member states expecting the delivery of a certain level of security from the accession states of the Baltic region. In turn, Estonia, Latvia and Lithuania are anticipating (perhaps over-optimistically) a large degree of security after membership. Their biggest priority is economic security, an aspiration the Soviet system failed miserably to provide. However, beneath the rhetoric and gestures of goodwill to accession states, there lie deeply entrenched problems which the member states themselves continue to struggle with, from the minefield of agricultural policies, the new security 'threat of terrorism' to the ever-present asylum issues which appear to be favouring a swing towards the right in European politics. Security is no guarantee from either side.

In what we now term a post-September 11 world, the word 'security' has greater implications than ever before. Political concerns and economic interests of the strongest countries and supranational decision-makers, however, direct the articulation of these implications and responses to them. Local issues are prioritised according to the status of the territory in which they occur. Hence the terms 'transnational' or 'global' become politically useful when they allow intrusion by the stronger states into the weaker ones in the interests of protecting the local securities and interests of the former. If the interests converge, there is a win–win situation, but this rarely happens. So far, the Baltic States have reaped many benefits from the assistance provided by member states, from the initiatives and policies issued from Brussels aimed at reforming their criminal justice systems and fighting organised crime. But strategies of inclusion come at a price. If, as Jorg Monar (2000) states, 'the Union has been drifting more and more towards a "fortress" rationale', then the Baltic States need to consider what price they are paying for inclusion into an enlarged Europe and whether the security role expected of them can be fulfilled. The difficulties they face in engaging with this so-called phenomenon of TOC is not only indicative of their own limitations but also reflects the limitations of member states to understand the complexities and realities of organised crime and what its growing presence actually signifies in the broader context of the economic, social and political health of the Union. That is a responsibility well beyond the remit of the Baltic sentinels.

## Notes

1 This chapter has been produced within the framework of ESRC project No. L21325 2013 'Crime, Borders and Law Enforcement: A European Dialogue for Improving Security', as part of the 'One Europe or Several?' programme.
2 Conversations with local journalists, foreign liaison and intelligence officers in Riga, 1999.
3 Interview given to author, November 1999.
4 Interview and informal conversation with the author in Tallinn and the UK 2000–1.

## References

Backman, J. (1998) *The Inflation of Crime in Russia: Paradoxes of a Threat Around the Baltic Sea*. Paper given at a seminar organised by the Scandinavian Research Council for Criminology, Espoo, Finland.
—— (2002) *Finlandia bez maski*, Communication via Police–Post Soc List 12/05/02.
Bauman, Z. (1998) *Globalization*. New York: Columbia University Press.
Council of the European Union (2000) *Action Plan for the Northern Dimension with External and Cross-Border Policies of the European Union 2000–2003*. 14 June (9401/00).
Dehousse, F. (2002) 'The EU's "one-eyed" enlargement strategy', *Challenge Europe*

(on-line journal) The European Policy Centre (21 May) http://www.theepc.be/challenge.

Edwards, A. and Gill, P. (2002) 'Crime as enterprise? The case of "transnational organised crime"', *Crime, Law and Social Change* 37, 3: 203–33.

Finckenauer, J. and Waring, E. (1998) *Russian Mafia in Amercia*. Boston: Northeastern University Press.

Goodey, J. (2002) 'Whose insecurity? Organised crime, its victims and the EU', in A. Crawford (ed.) *Crime and Insecurity*. Cullompton: Willan Publishing, pp. 135–58.

Gregory, F. (2001) 'Good cops': issues related to EU enlargement and the 'policing' requirements of the justice and home affairs *acquis*. *One Europe or Several?*, Working Paper 24/01.

Hobbs, D. (1998) 'Going down the glocal: the local context of organised crime', *Howard Journal* 37, 4: 407–22.

ITAR–TASS (1988) Soviet Baltic Panorama, November (4686).

Lase, I. (2000) 'The bankruptcy of Banka Baltiya', in E.K. Stern and D. Hansen (eds) *Crisis Management in a Transitional Society: The Latvia Experience*. Stockholm: Crismart, Vol. 12.

Markina, A. (1998) 'Organised crime in Estonia: a national and international issue', in Aromaa, K. (ed.) *The Baltic Region: Insights in Crime and Control*, Scandinavian Studies in Criminology, Vol. 15. Oslo: Pax Forlag A/S, p. 186.

Markina, A. and Tabur, L. (1999) 'Vulnerability to corruption in Estonian road haulage sector'. Interim report for Falcone Research Project, Tallinn.

Monar, J. (2000) 'Justice and home affairs in a wider Europe: the dynamics of inclusion and exclusion', *One Europe or Several?*, Working Paper 07/00, http://www.one-europe.ac.uk/cgi-bin/esrc/world/db.cgi/publications.htm.

Naylor, R.T. (1997) 'Mafias, myths, and markets: on the theory and practice of enterprise crime', *Transnational Organized Crime* 3, 3: 1–45.

National Criminal Intelligence Service (NCIS) (2001) *UK Threat Assessment 2001*, www.ncis.co.uk.

Rawlinson, P. (1997) 'Russian organized crime: a brief history', in P. Williams (ed.) *Transnational Organised Crime*. London: Frank Cass.

Statistical Office of Estonia (1999) *Statistical Yearbook of Estonia 1999*. Tallinn.

Ulrich, C.J. (1994) *The Growth of Crime in Russia and the Baltic Region*. RFE/RL Research Report, Vol. 3, No. 23, 10 June.

Vilnius Drug Control Division (2000) 'Situation related to illegal drug and psychotropic substance circulation in Lithuania', Lietuvos Kriminaline Policija.

# 9 Controlling drug trafficking in Central Europe

## The impact of EU policies in the Czech Republic, Hungary and Lithuania

*Barbara Bogusz and Mike King*

## Introduction

The main focus of this chapter is on the European Union's approach towards combating illicit drug trafficking, and how this affects Central European Countries (CECs) in their preparations for accession into the EU. To this end we draw from the findings of a research project funded by the European Commission as part of the INCO–Copernicus programme.[1] This examined the impact of EU illicit drug trafficking control policies in three Central European countries, namely the Czech Republic, Hungary and Lithuania. We begin with an overview of the wider context of apparent EU concerns, drawing attention to recent EU developments in drug trafficking control strategies. We then critically consider some of the inconsistencies, realities and impacts in the case-study countries. The chapter concludes by asserting that, whilst there is demonstrably political will in all three countries to conform (even to some extent in excess) to EU direction given the promise of accession, there is largely a mismatch between this and feasible practical implementation.

## The regulation of prospective enlargement

In the immediate post-Cold War period, the prospect of CEC accession into the European Economic Community was inconceivable. Not only were they fledging democracies but economically they were considerably weaker than the poorest member state in the EU (Dinan, 1999: 185). However, in 1993, the Copenhagen Council devised a strategy whereby countries seeking membership of the European Union would have to fulfil certain criteria covering areas that are seen as being compatible with a 'liberal–democratic' state and functioning market economy. Further, they would be required to have the necessary capability to adhere and incorporate the Community *acquis communautaire* (body of established legal measures) (European Commission, 2000a). These are universal criteria, not only applicable to CEC candidate states, but all countries seeking membership into the EU. This uniform approach on the one hand provides the minimum requirements for entry, but on the other does not take into account CEC candidate states' respective histories or cultural and socio-economic contexts.

In 1997 the EU formulated the Agenda 2000 programme aimed at providing an accession plan which prospective member states were to follow. This also acted as an impact assessment of EU enlargement for the EU member states. Association Agreements (known as Europe Agreements) had already been signed by the new CEC candidate states in the early 1990s, and Agenda 2000 enabled the Commission to evaluate the progress towards implementation of the *acquis* in those candidate countries. The implementation of the *acquis* is monitored through Regular (annual) Country Reports produced by the Commission (and published since 1998) on the progress made by candidate states in their preparations for accession (King and Koci, 1999), and these, in turn, inform the Accession Partnership agreements.

These Regular Country Reports identify areas of concern to be tackled by the candidate state and provide a new framework of priority areas for each of the countries to address. Following the 1999 reports (European Commission, 1999b, c and d), amendments were made to the Accession Partnership agreements. These, in turn, not only identified priority areas for action, but also suggested how the PHARE programme might provide targeted assistance to the individual candidate state using the Regular Country Reports as the basis for their assessment. The Commission in conjunction with the individual candidate states set an agenda and a framework of action to be incorporated in the Accession Partnership agreements. The priority areas cover various themes for each of the candidates to address in their preparation for accession, such as the internal market, agriculture, employment and social affairs, and justice and home affairs, divided into short-term and long-term goals. The respective Accession Partnership agreement, together with the candidate state's own national programme for adopting the *acquis*, form part of their commitment to fulfilling the accession criteria and joining the EU.

In other words, the EU stipulates universal criteria for membership, but recognises that individual candidate countries have, to some extent, different needs within these universal accession criteria and time-frame priorities in order to comply. This would seem to be an important point for our research, in that although the case study countries are recognisably working, within separate time frames, towards compliance of the EU illicit drug trafficking mandate, as indicated earlier, ultimately no allowance is made for individual histories, cultures, socio-economic conditions, geographical location, and so on.

## EU drug policy

The EU's approach to combating drug trafficking in and through Central Europe is one of combining and developing its policy on a broader strategy of preparing the first and second round countries for their accession to the EU (King and Koci, 1999); and also, under the Justice and Home Affairs pillar, creating a 'high level of safety within an area of freedom, security and justice' (Article 29 Treaty on European Union (TEU), 1993).

The 'high level of safety' objective is to be achieved by working within a framework of closer police and judicial co-operation, and achieving approximation on criminal matters in member states, targeting *inter alia* illicit drug trafficking. The perceived threat to the internal security of the EU from 'organised crime', drug trafficking and illegal immigration, particularly from the CECs, stems from what would seem to be the feared porous nature of Western Europe's eastern borders. In its attempt to combat these challenges and maintain a high level of security within its borders, the EU introduced certain controls on the four 'freedoms' of movement, namely capital, labour, goods and services, and also formulated an Action Plan to Combat Drugs (1999a).

### EU Action Plan to Combat Drugs

The aim of the EU Action Plan to Combat Drugs (1999a) is to achieve a concerted action amongst member states to develop a global, multi-disciplinary and integrated approach in combating drugs, *inter alia*, fighting illicit drug trafficking. The current strategy is based on three main elements, namely demand reduction, supply reduction and international co-operation (European Commission, 1999a). The Action Plan further recognises that there are new challenges that must receive immediate attention, one of which is the preparation for enlargement. The Commission also envisages candidate states having greater participation in collaborative programmes under Title VI (Justice and Home Affairs), although currently, as this is an intergovernmental pillar, participation is restricted to EU member states.

Many of the developments in drug-trafficking policies have been made since the entry into force of the TEU. The European Monitoring Centre for Drugs and Drug Addiction (EMCDDA) was established under the TEU to provide reliable comparable information concerning drugs and drug addiction at a European level. In their annual report for 1998, concern was expressed over the increase in trade, traffic and transit of illicit drugs through Central and Eastern Europe and the inability of these countries to combat the problem (EMCDDA, 1998: 21). This would seem to have been a primary concern influencing the development of EU drug policy. Indeed, it is suggested by Dorn (1996) that EU drug policy is shaped by the EU's external policies, where issues of crime and drug control are important issues in the light of enlargement. Cohen (1993) also argues that 'Western powers' strong interests in making the Eastern Republics adopt drug control policies are based not upon the analysis and evaluation of options in the field of drug control alone, but on other political priorities.' These political priorities, he suggests, do not lie in creating a drug control policy per se, indeed they 'may be immaterial' (Cohen, 1993). The focus, according to Cohen, rests on developing effective border control policies aimed at preventing mass immigration into Western European countries. Further, he argues that it is this perceived threat of mass immigration (which has no basis in reality) that would seem to be a major force in driving the EU's drug policy (ibid.).

## Critical observations of EU drug control policy from Central Europe

The external pressure put on the CECs by the EU in order to accede into the European Union has played a dominant role in speeding-up the process of change undergone by the case study countries. As mentioned earlier, in accordance with the accession process, each candidate state must adopt the *acquis* in the realm of drug control. However, the apparent rises in drug consumption and trafficking in these countries have also acted as catalysts in the drive by the governments in these countries to institute measures in an attempt to deal with the problem. A tendency to inflate the problem could also be created, though, as a consequence of over-emphasis on (and resources for) drug control per se by the EU.

Our research has found that EU drug policy and the Commission's Regular Country Reports do not necessarily reflect or take into account the current state of affairs in these countries. The comments and criticisms given in these reports merely 'scratch the surface', if that, of how these countries are attempting to meet their accession criteria. The following sections will consider the difficulties encountered by the case study countries, and highlight contradictions between the findings from the Commission's Regular Country Reports and the actual situation in these countries.

### The European Commission's critical assessment of CECs

The European Commission's Regular Country Reports describe the Commission's assessment of how the CECs are progressing in their preparations for accession. The reports highlight both achievements and areas of concern to be addressed by the candidate country. Although Lithuania had a positive assessment with regard to drugs in the 1999 Regular Country Report, and the Commission concluded that drugs were not a serious problem, the Commission did suggest that the fight against drugs should remain high on the political agenda and more attention was required on demand reduction measures (European Commission, 1999c: 44). We have found that there is some contradiction between the Commission's findings and other research findings. For example, Bukauskas (1999) notes that, between 1990 and 1998, there was an eight-fold increase in 'drug-related offences' (although details of these are not specified). Further, a report published by the Lithuanian Ministry of Health indicates that there appears to be an annual increase in drug abuse amongst 15–16 year olds (Grimalauskiene, 1999). According to Bukauskas (1999), drugs are used across the whole range of social strata. The primary reason identified by Bukauskas for the increasing drug problem is that, initially at least, Lithuania did not have sufficient legal measures in force to control the circulation of drugs (1999: 12). Clearly, the assessment made by the Commission, particularly in its 1999 Regular Country Reports, failed to take these points into account in its assertion that Lithuania does not have a serious drug problem. In contrast, the Lithuanian 2000 Report (2000c) does not make such an assertion but focuses on the ability to implement measures in this field and makes suggestions for further improvements. For example, the Commission was somewhat critical of Lithuania's National Programme for Control of Drugs and Prevention of Drug Addiction for 1999–2003 because it 'lacks an overall operational action plan to define priorities both in demand and supply reduction activities' (European Commission, 2000c: 86). The Commission's 2001 Report does, however, note that an Action Plan for implementation was approved by the government in January 2001; also, that in 2000, 'crimes related to illegal trade in narcotics and psychotropic substances' increased by 33 per cent compared with 1999 (European Commission, 2001c: 92). In order to combat illicit drug trafficking, the Commission urges greater co-operation with law enforcement agencies, particularly in neighbouring countries.

Both the Commission's 2000 and 2001 Regular Country Reports on Hungary (2000b; 2001b) note that a National Strategy to Combat the Drug Problem, where special emphasis is placed on preventive measures, has been adopted. However, Benke (1999; 2000) is critical of the lack of commitment on behalf of the Hungarian government in implementing the national drug prevention programme. In theory, a national programme dealing with medical and social care should have been implemented and in operation but, from his research, he found that drug control was actually left solely to the criminal law, where prohibition and punishment were the only means of deterrence (Benke, 1999: 13). This position may, of course, change given that the National Strategy stipulates a 'long-term task' of 'strengthening means of criminal law, prevention, and social action ... and reinforcing prevention, rehabilitation and medical institutions' (European Commission, 2001b: 85).

The Commission's assessment of the Czech Republic's move towards police reform in their October 1999 Regular Country Report (European Commission, 1999d) was described by King and Koci (1999) as 'rather bleak'. In the light of the Commission's criticisms, this became one of the priority areas in the Accession Partnership (European Commission, 2000e). The Commission's 1999 Regular Country Report (1999d) suggested that the problem especially lies with the bureaucratic obstacles which affect the efficiency of the police, including a dual system for investigating crimes. It also highlighted the lack of career policy and poor pay that lead to difficulties in recruitment and the development of ethical behaviour (European Commission, 1999d: 45). It is important that these issues be addressed in the restructuring of the police, where higher levels of pay may make the police less susceptible to corruption and less inclined to abuse their authority. Despite the Commission's findings, from their interviews, King and Koci (1999) suggested there was a positive move to change, and this is now shown in an amendment to the Police Act incorporating measures contributing to the Schengen *acquis* (European Commission, 2001a: 88) and the creation of a unified Criminal and Investigation Police Service (European Commission, 2001a: 89).

In its 2000 Regular Country Report (2000d), the Commission is highly critical of the general progress made by the Czech Republic in the area of Justice and Home Affairs, except in asylum and alien legislation. In particular, the police structures were regarded as 'too weak to effectively combat illegal immigration, corruption and organized and economic crime' (European Commission, 2000d: 90). However, in its 2001 Report, the Commission does recognise the 'encouraging progress' that the Czech Republic has made in 'substantially reorganising its law enforcement authorities' (European Commisssion, 2001a: 89). With regard to the issue of border controls, problems of understaffing, insufficient equipment and inadequate training continued to cause concern, despite the creation of a new integrated Alien and Border Police (2001a: 88, 90). Hence, the Commission appears to have found little change in this regard since the 1999 Report.

There appears to be a serious lack of development in this area by the Czech government. However, the Czech economy has had its share of problems: it has been in recession since 1996 through to mid-1999, during which there was a growth in unemployment and inflation (European Commission, 2000d: 29), and the banking sector suffered considerably in 1999–2000 due to financial irregularities, the impact of which has led to the Commission severely criticising the inefficiency and weakness of the legal system (European Commission, 2000d: 34–5). The downturn in the economy and scandals in the banking sector have been prominent on the political agenda, and it appears that law enforcement issues have, to some extent, been set aside. However, adequate resources, training and salaries are essential for the efficiency and effectiveness of the police, and the maintenance of the integrity of law and order.

### Growth in drug traffic and trade

The post-1989 period saw the development of a drugs market in Central Europe, which is now comparable to that found in Western Europe. Several factors have contributed to this. Bilateral agreements signed by individual CECs with individual Western European countries in the early 1990s have, for example, enabled greater and less restrictive movement between the CECs and Western European countries. It must be noted, however, as Dufkova asserts, that drug trafficking through the Czech Republic (and indeed other CECs) existed even before the end of the Cold War, despite the strict conditions applied to cross-border travel through socialist states (Dufkova, 1999: 2). The convertibility of the Central European currencies has, Ruggiero and South (1995: 54) suggest, in some way contributed to the growth of the illicit drugs market, where previously their non-convertibility would have acted as a barrier to the import of goods and drugs.

The development of the drugs market in the Czech Republic appears to have grown more rapidly than in the EU member states (Dufkova, 1999: 5). According to Dufkova (1999), there are several reasons for this. She suggests that, on the supply side, this is exacerbated by the following: light penalties being imposed for drug offences; the willingness of Czech citizens to participate in drug trafficking for low wages; the ease in which it is possible to establish bogus firms, and hence engage in risk-free laundering of drug money and, finally, those involved in the drugs market may initially have gained experience in (and from) Western countries (Dufkova, 1999: 8). Dufkova also notes that there has been 'a permanent increase' in problems relating to drug use, production and trafficking since 1989 and suggests that the reasons for this are the opening of borders which has led to increased traffic in goods and persons and the more general liberalisation and transformation from a command economy to a market economy (ibid.: 23). It is apparent from our research that all the case study countries share this view. Undoubtedly, there is a greater flow of illicit drugs across the borders – perhaps, too, in the post-1989 situation, it is more overt.

The attitude adopted in Hungary to the rise in drug consumption from the late 1960s was dismissive; drug abuse was a sign of the decline in Western culture, and did not formally exist in socialist states (Benke, 2000: 1). This attitude of denial was, to some extent, carried through to the early 1990s, where the control of illicit drugs and trafficking appeared to have a low priority in comparison to economic and political reform.

Currently, rather than dealing with the increasing social problems that drug consumption creates, the candidate states appear to be focusing their efforts on simply fulfilling the accession criteria as quickly as possible, and thereby securing a date for accession.

The Czech government has attempted to develop more positive strategies and policies to combat the proliferation of the drugs market and trafficking, by setting an objective which incorporates a more balanced approach by using both punitive and preventative measures. The Czech National Drug Commission described 1999 as a 'watershed year from the point of view of drug policy', the reason being the entry into force of the 'Drug Act' (National Drug Commission, 2000: 4). This piece of legislation provides for stricter punishments for the smuggling, sale and distribution of illicit drugs; further, possession of drugs for personal use is now subject to punitive sanctions. Provisions in the 'Drug Act' include additional intrusive surveillance methods for detection. According to Dufkova (1999) the new 'Drug Act' has, to some extent, strengthened the position for law enforcement agencies.

An apparent effect of the new legislation led to a change in the illicit drug market. For example, drug dealers have retreated to selling their drugs in a covert and less open way, deals are increasingly made using mobile phones (National Drug Commission, 2000). Part of the government's strategy was to penalise the possession of drugs for personal use in an amendment to the Criminal Code and the Act of Transgressions (140/1961 Dig and 200/1990 Dig respectively). The level of punishment depends on the quantity of the substance in possession rather than its designated use; if someone is in possession of a small quantity of drugs this would be dealt with under administrative procedures, larger quantities would invoke criminal sanctions (Dufkova, 1999: 29). According to Dorn (1999) the use of administrative measures is a tactical alternative to using the criminal law, and one that is found in a number of member states in the EU (1999: 24–6). The definition of what constitutes a small quantity has been defined by the Czech Supreme State Attorney's office but this is not publicly available (Czech News Agency, 2000).

The approach taken by the Czech government towards controlling illicit drugs has been severely criticised by the US Bureau for International Narcotics and Law Enforcement Affairs in their 1999 'International Narcotics Control Strategy Report' for having a more repressive than preventative orientation (Bureau for International Narcotics and Law Enforcement Affairs, 2000). However, in a statement made to the United Nations in 1999, the Czech Republic's representative stated that this amendment to the Penal Code is part of the harmonisation of Czech drug legislation towards international legal norms (Holikova, 1999). Many of the countries seeking entry into the EU are faced with bringing their countries 'up to speed' with EU member states and, at the same time, dealing with 'new problems' such as the rise in drug abuse, trafficking and trade of drugs. These countries find themselves seeking to adopt a working model used by their Western counterparts in order to deal effectively with their 'new challenges'. The effect of this is that, on the one hand, on the supply side, tighter laws have been introduced to stem the growth in the traffic, trade and consumption of drugs. On the other hand, programmes dealing with demand reduction have also been implemented to achieve a more balanced approach towards combating illicit drug trafficking and trade. The Czech government has also now adopted a National Drug Policy for 2001–4, with the aim of fulfilling the requirements of the 2000–4 EU Action Plan (European Commission, 2001a: 89).

### Obstacles to implementing national drug programmes

Both Bukauskas (1999) and Grimalauskiene (1999, 2000) criticise the severe shortage of funds which has hampered the implementation of the Lithuanian government's programme on drug prevention and combating illicit drug trafficking. The political will is present to the extent of designing and developing a strategy; however, the financial aspect has not been resolved. Bukauskas (2000: 5), in his observations of the drug situation in Lithuania, criticises the inadequacy of the institutions dealing with drug prevention and control, the lack of education and expertise in this area. Only limited funds have been made available by the government for their drug programmes, however, suggesting that these programmes have a low priority.

A Hungarian national drug programme does exist, as mentioned earlier (p. 147), but in reality, controlling the problem associated with drugs had predominantly been left to punitive measures up until the late 1990s. A change in the approach towards drug abuse is evident in an amendment to the Penal Code (1993) where medical treatment was offered as an alternative to punitive measures in certain cases. Although this alternative therapy was provided in the legislation, the underlying approach continued to be one of punitive control (Fridli, Pelle and Racz, 1994). Even an amendment made to the Penal Code in 1998, according to Benke (2000), dealt with drug-related problems by punitive means; for example, imposing higher penalties for drug trafficking, but not enough attention was paid to prevention. Benke (2000) is highly critical of the lack of government debate surrounding the prevention and treatment of drug abuse. From his interviews, he found that, in the process leading up to the enactment of the 1998 amendment to the Penal Code, little consultation had taken place with experts in this area. It is suggested that such a lack of debate can negatively impact on the political will to implement drug prevention programmes. However, recently, there would seem to be a more concerted action to implement the National Drug Prevention

Programme (Association of European Police Colleges, 2001: 55, 57; European Commission, 2001b).

### Co-operation amongst enforcement agencies

As a part of the *acquis* in combating drug trafficking, the EU stipulates co-operation between the police forces and customs services at a national level. To ensure efficiency and effectiveness of their collaborative efforts, a number of provisions must be met, *inter alia*, precise delineation of the competencies of each of the two services, and agreed police–customs procedures for operational matters (European Council, 1996).

In the Lithuanian 2000 Regular Country Report (2000c), the Commission criticises the lack of co-operation and co-ordination amongst law enforcement structures not only at a national level but also with neighbouring member states. This weakness has also been reported by the Supporting European Integration in Lithuania (SEIL) project, which prepared an analysis of Lithuania's deficiencies under the third pillar (SEIL, 2000). Their analysis showed that there was no clear delineation of competencies and responsibilities between the police and customs. Further, Bukauskas (2000) argues that there is a lack of co-operation between the respective enforcement agencies. Whilst the Commission's 2001 Report acknowledges that an inter-institutional co-operation agreement between the State Border Guard Service, the Customs Department and the Police Department was signed in November 2000, it still finds there is need of significant development in this area (European Commission, 2001c: 91). Similar to Bukauskas's (1999) and Grimalauskiene's (1999, 2000) criticisms concerning the lack of implementation of the drug prevention programme referred to above (p. 151), the Commission asserts that 'severe budgetary constraints have had a clear impact on the development of a modern, efficient and professional police service' (European Commission, 2001c: 94).

Both Benke (2000) and the Hungarian 2000 Regular Country Report (2000b) argue that co-operation between the police and customs works effectively. The Commission in its assessment of the Czech Republic, on the other hand, is critical of a lack of co-ordination between the police, border guards and customs (European Commission, 2000d: 105; 2001a: 91, 94). In contrast, however, Dufkova (2000: 5) suggests that there is actually a high level of co-operation between the police and customs officials, facilitated by an agreement between the Ministry of Interior and Ministry of Finance which has enabled joint groups from the police and customs to work together on a day-to-day operational basis.

## Conclusion

There are apparent difficulties experienced by the candidate states in fulfilling their obligations under the accession process, particularly as they
are in a weaker position economically. The EU is not averse to enlargement (this was clearly apparent at the Nice meeting 7–9 December 2000)
and, arguably, there are benefits to be gained by the individual member
states and the EU as a whole: the EU would become a major player on the
global stage; political stability in Europe would be enhanced and this, in
turn, would reinforce peace; it would also open up the prospect of greater
economic development and easier access to emerging markets (Dinan,
1999). However, enlargement does bring other problems to the fore.
Illicit drug trafficking is an ongoing problem that has not even been
tackled successfully by Western European countries. Gregory (1995: 130),
for example, mentions that the 'west has, seemingly, forgotten that it too
is unable to effectively regulate criminality in the market place and that
our transnational crime problems were in existence before 1989.'

The European Commission's 2000–4 Action Plan on Combating Drugs
(1999a) may represent a way forward in that it does not simply blame 'the
other', but rather attempts to recognise and deal with a 'common threat',
thus requiring both an 'integrated approach' and 'intense co-operation at
all levels' (European Commission, 1999a: 6). However, from our research
findings, it is evident that there are differences and contradictions,
particularly with the Commission's assessment of the state of affairs in the
candidate states according to the accession criteria. Furthermore, there
also appear to be discrepancies in the policies adopted by the candidate
states and their implementation. Whilst the governments in the case study
countries are showing a high level of political will in creating these policies, even to the extent of instituting over-compensatory measures, such
policies would seem to be stricter than the enforcement agencies can actually deliver. Further, the Commission, by focusing primarily on policy
achievements of the candidate states, fails to fully evaluate the practice.
This position is serious in that the potential effectiveness of these policies
towards combating drug trafficking and consumption is thereby compromised.

Moreover, it appears that the EU's drug control policy is concentrating
its efforts on securing its borders against the perceived potential threat
coming particularly from the CECs and further East, rather than tackling
environmental conditions by focusing more specifically on the causes of
traffic, trade and drug abuse within these countries. This, in turn, raises
the question of whether the policy is, in fact, aimed primarily at combating drug trafficking or adopting a more general exclusionary policy
towards countries outside the EU.

## Note

1 The authors were research associate and project co-ordinator respectively.

## References

Association of European Police Colleges (2001) *Hungary on its Way to the EU: Report on the PHARE Project 'European Curriculum for Police Training in Central and Eastern European Countries'.* Warnsveld: AEPC.

Benke, M. (1999) *Illicit-drug Trafficking in Hungary.* Unpublished report to the EC INCO–Copernicus Programme.

—— (2000) *Country Report 2000: Hungary.* Unpublished report to the EC INCO–Copernicus Programme.

Bukauskas, A. (1999) *Country Report 1999: Republic of Lithuania.* Unpublished report to the EC INCO–Copernicus Programme.

—— (2000) 'Drug trafficking control in Lithuania'. Unpublished paper presented at a Workshop on Illicit drug trafficking controls in Central Europe, Barcelona, 2–4 June.

Bureau for International Narcotics and Law Enforcement Affairs (2000) *International Narcotics Control Strategy Report, 1999,* Washington, DC: Bureau for International Narcotics and Law Enforcement Affairs, http://www.state.gov/www/global/narcotics_law/1999_narc_report/europ99_part2.html.

Cohen, P.D.A. (1993) 'Future drug policy in the countries of the former Eastern Bloc: the difficult choice to be non-Western'. Paper presented to the European Colloquium on the Crisis of Normative Systems, Paris, 25 February. http://www.cedro-uva.org/lib/cohen.future.html.

Czech News Agency (2000) *State Defines Legal Amounts for Drugs, Keeps them Secret.* http://www.centraleurope.com/news.php3?id=172879 [27 June 2000].

Dinan, D. (1999) *Ever Closer Union: An Introduction to European Integration,* 2nd edn. Basingstoke: Macmillan.

Dorn, N. (1996) 'The EU, home affairs and 1996: intergovernmental convergence or co-federal diversity?', in N. Dorn, J. Jepsen and E. Savona (eds) *European Drug Policies and Enforcement.* Basingstoke: Macmillan.

—— (ed.) (1999) *Regulating European Drug Problems: Administrative Measures and Civil Law in the Control of Drug Trafficking, Nuisance and Use.* London, The Hague: Kluwer International.

Dufkova, I. (1999) *Country Report 1999: Czech Republic.* Unpublished report to the EC INCO–Copernicus Programme.

—— (2000) *Developments in Drug Trafficking Control Strategy.* Unpublished paper presented at a Workshop on Drug Trafficking Controls in Central Europe, Barcelona, June.

EMCDDA (1998) *Summary and Highlights: Annual Report on the State of the Drugs Problem in the European Union.* Luxembourg: OOPEC.

European Commission (1999a) *Communication from the Commission to the Council and the European Parliament on a European Union Action Plan to Combat Drugs (2000–2004).* COM (1999) 239 Final.

—— (1999b) *Regular Report from the Commission on Hungary's Progress Towards Accession.* http://europa.eu.int/comm/enlargement/dwn/report_10_99/en/word/hungary.doc.

—— (1999c) *Regular Report from the Commission on Lithuania's Progress Towards Accession.* http://europa.eu.int/comm/enlargement/dwn/report_10_99/en/word/lithuania.doc.

—— (1999d) *Regular Report from the Commission on the Czech Republic's Progress Towards Accession.* http://europa.eu.int/comm/enlargement/dwn/report_10_99/en/word/czech.doc.

—— (2000a) *Quoted in Enlargement.* http://europa.eu.int/comm/enlargement/pas/phare/wip/copenhagen.htm.

—— (2000b) *Regular Report from the Commission on Hungary's Progress Towards Accession,* 8 November. http://europa.eu.int/comm/enlargement/dwn/report_11_00/pdf/en/hu_en.pdf.

—— (2000c) *Regular Report from the Commission on Lithuania's Progress Towards Accession,* 8 November. http://europa.eu.int/comm/enlargement/dwn/report_11_00/pdf/en/lt_en.pdf.

—— (2000d) *Regular Report from the Commission on the Czech Republic's Progress Towards Accession,* 8 November. http://europa.eu.int/comm/enlargement/dwn/report_11_00/pdf/en/cz_en.pdf.

—— (2000e) *Accession Partnership 1999, Czech Republic.* http://europa.eu.int/comm/enlargement/dwn/ap_02_00/en/ap_cz_99.pdf.

—— (2001a) *Regular Report from the Commission on the Czech Republic's Progress Towards Accession,* 13 November. http://europa.eu.int/comm/enlargement/report2001/cz_en.pdf.

—— (2001b) *Regular Report from the Commission on Hungary's Progress Towards Accession,* 13 November. http://europa.eu.int/comm/enlargement/report2001/hu_en.pdf.

—— (2001c) *Regular Report from the Commission on Lithuania's Progress Towards Accession,* 13 November. http://europa.eu.int/comm/enlargement/report2001/lt_en.pdf.

European Council (1996) Council Resolution of 29 November 1996 on the drawing up of police/customs agreements in the fight against drugs. *OJ* C 375.

Fridli, J., Pelle, A. and Racz, J. (1994) *Drug Police Before and After the Regime: A Study of Criminal Proceedings in Budapest between 1990 and 1992 in Cases of Drug Abuse and Inducement of Pathological Addiction,* Political Science Working Paper No. 4. Budapest: Central European University.

Gregory, F. (1995) 'Transnational crime and law enforcement cooperation: problems and processes between East and West in Europe', *Transnational Organized Crime* 1, 4: 105–33.

Grimalauskiene, O. (1999) *Drug Abuse Problems in Lithuania, 1999: Short Analysis, Political Developments.* Vilnius: Ministry of Health.

—— (2000) *National Report on the Drugs Situation in Lithuania 2000.* Vilnius: European Commission.

Holikova, N. (1999) Statement by Ms. Nadezda Holikova, Second Secretary of the Permanent Mission of the Czech Republic to the United Nations, on Agenda Item 107 and 108. http://www.un.int/czechrepublic/PAGEDATA/czc3ga54.htm#Agenda.

King, M. and Koci, A. (1999) *Drugs Trafficking Controls in Central Europe: a Preliminary Appraisal of the European Commission's Findings Concerning the Czech Republic, Hungary and Lithuania.* Unpublished report to the EC INCO–Copernicus Programme.

National Drug Commission (2000) *Annual Report on the Situation and Development in Drug-Related Issues in the Czech Republic for 1999.* Prague: National Drug Commission, Office of the Government of the Czech Republic.

Ruggiero, V. and South, N. (1995) *Eurodrugs: Drug Use, Markets and Trafficking in Europe.* London: University College of London Press.

Supporting European Integration in Lithuania (SEIL) (2000) *Strategy for Justice and Home Affairs: 'the third pillar'.* Vilnius: SEIL.

Treaty on European Union (1993) Maastricht.

# 10 Recognising organised crime's victims

## The case of sex trafficking in the EU

*Jo Goodey[1]*

Sex traffic is Europe's shame

(Guardian, 9 March 2001)

Italy's sexual slave trade

(BBC News Online, 2 August 2000)

Headlines such as these have become regular features of British and international media reports. Trafficking in women for sexual exploitation is now 'big business' for the criminals who profit from these activities, for the 'clients' who use trafficked prostitutes and for the news organisations who benefit from the public's appetite for titillating human interest stories. The only people not to benefit are the women who end up as victims of human trafficking in what has been described, in the worst case scenarios, as virtual 'slavery-like' conditions.

The recent high profile given by the media to cases of human trafficking for the sex industry is reflected in the national and international response to this problem from governmental and non-governmental organisations. Within Europe, sex trafficking has been on the political agenda since the 1990s with an array of recommendations and guidelines promoted, from the European Commission (EC) through to the Council of Europe,[2] to tackle the problem. The European Commission has also made funding available, through the STOP and DAPHNE programmes, for a range of initiatives that can be utilised for victims of sex trafficking. While there are European recommendations, guidelines and funds to combat the problem of sex trafficking, there has been, as Kelly and Regan state (2000: 12), a sense of 'much talk but limited action'. The *Guardian* report of 9 March proceeds to outline an 'open article' by the European Commission's social affairs commissioner which berates the EU's lack of progress in combating, and supporting the victims of, trafficking for the sex industry. As the remarks of the commissioner illustrate, there is little sense of progress and, as non-governmental and police intelligence sources indicate,[3] the problem of sex trafficking, if anything, appears to be on the increase.

In the light of this book's focus on (transnational) organised crime, this chapter engages with the problem of, and responses to, trafficking in women for the sex industry as a product of organised criminal activity; with the European Union forming the political and geographical backdrop through which evidence is presented. Trafficking serves as a means of addressing the under-researched 'flipside' of organised crime; that is, organised crime's victims as opposed to its perpetrators. First, the chapter introduces the 'problem' of trafficking with respect to its definition, nature and extent, and origins. From here, the chapter examines legislative and practical 'responses' to trafficking. Finally, the 'victimhood' of trafficked women is contextualised with regard to the status of victims, more generally, in the EU.

## The 'problem' of sex trafficking

### *Defining the problem*

Trafficking in women for the purpose of sexual exploitation, or 'sex trafficking', is an activity that has gained in prominence and, arguably, extent and scope, over the last few years. In common with smuggling of illegal immigrants, sex trafficking is an international enterprise perpetrated by organised criminal groups. However, smuggling and trafficking are distinct activities that can be differentiated by several factors; namely, in the case of trafficking for the sex industry: (i) the trafficked victim, unlike the smuggled person, does not buy a criminal organisation's services to assist her entry into a country; and (ii) the criminal organisation exploits the trafficked victim, against her will, to satisfy the demands of the sex market. Here, the United Nations's Convention Against Transnational Organised Crime, signed by member states in 2000, which is supplemented by two protocols on trafficking and smuggling, provides the latest and most comprehensive definition and distinction between the activities of 'trafficking' and 'smuggling'.[4] Other international organisations and non-governmental organisations, from Europol through to the Coalition to Abolish Slavery and Trafficking (CAST),[5] provide various definitions of 'trafficking' which generally comply with the UN definition.

Trafficking, as the UN protocol illustrates, can also encompass the exploitation of people for non-sexual activities, such as indentured domestic service. Similarly, the UN protocol incorporates children as 'persons' vulnerable to trafficking which can entail sexual exploitation. However, in light of this chapter's limited scope, and the wealth of evidence to date on women's experiences, I will concentrate on trafficking for sexual exploitation as it, primarily, impacts on women. Given the chapter's focus on the European Union, the European Commission's definition of 'trafficking for the purpose of sexual exploitation', from 1996, provides a useful summary of the problem:

the transport of women from third countries into the European Union (including perhaps subsequent movements between Member States) for the purpose of sexual exploitation ... Trafficking for the purpose of sexual exploitation covers women who have suffered intimidation and/or violence through the trafficking. Initial consent may not be relevant, as some enter the trafficking chain knowing they will work as prostitutes, but who are then deprived of their basic human rights, in conditions which are akin to slavery.[6]

Undeniably, some trafficked women are aware they are being recruited for prostitution and may initially consent to this. However, they are not fully prepared for the extent of abuse they are likely to receive from traffickers, pimps, brothel owners and clients, either in transit or at their destination. The issue, as both the EC communication from 1996 and the UN protocol on trafficking clearly illustrate, is not one of initial 'consent'. Rather, it is one of persistent exploitation. Smuggled persons may be exploited with regard to the amount they pay criminal organisations, and the abysmal means of transport used to get them, hopefully, to their desired destination. However, once at their final destination, smuggled persons are generally left to their own devices. In comparison, the trafficked woman is often held in slavery-like conditions of debt bondage, to the brothel owner or pimp who has paid for her delivery, which she has to re-pay through prostitution. In turn, the extent and nature of coercion and violence used against trafficked women, as a means of control and subjugation into a state of submission, tends to exceed the level of abuse received by smuggled persons. An industry which exists on the basis of sexual exploitation of women is, understandably, not shy when it comes to using violence against women.

### The extent and nature of the problem

While definitions of 'trafficking' variously comply with the UN protocol on trafficking, the 'problem' itself is a difficult activity to quantify with any accuracy. As with most organised criminal activities, one can pick a number and times it by a factor of ten in order to come up with a rough 'guesstimate' of its extent. Figures are frequently inserted in policy papers, often with no reference to their source, which attempt to impart the scale of the problem. As trafficking in women for sexual exploitation is only part of the trafficking problem, there is often a need to differentiate between the evidence presented in order to determine 'what' is being counted.

In the EU, and looking specifically at trafficking in women for sexual exploitation, official criminal justice statistics provide only a limited account of the extent of the problem. The German *Bundeskriminalamt* (*BKA*; German Federal Criminal Police Office) produces annual situation reports on trafficking. In 1999, the *BKA* recorded 801 victims of trafficking; two of whom were men. In England and Wales, Kelly and Regan (2000) have produced the most comprehensive report, to date, on trafficking in women. The report was commissioned by the Home Office and found that, of the five police forces in England and Wales handling trafficking cases in 1998, the number of women victims totalled a mere 71. These figures, culled as they are from officially recorded police data, represent the tip of the iceberg when it comes to the true extent of the problem. Kelly and Regan proceed to estimate the 'real' extent of the problem in England and Wales as anywhere from two to twenty-times greater than their official research findings suggest. In comparison, the International Organization for Migration (IOM, 1995), an international non-governmental organisation (NGO) with field offices throughout much of Europe, has provided an oft-quoted estimate of the number of women trafficked into the EU; the figure being 500,000 for the early 1990s. Given this range of 'guesstimates', research is in danger of either over-estimating or under-estimating the extent of sex trafficking. However, what is abundantly clear, regardless of scale, is the shared nature of this problem, and its origins, between various EU member states.

The *BKA* report usefully outlines the nature of trafficking as it relates to the supply and demand of women for the German sex industry. Women originate, overwhelmingly, from Central and East Europe; with German nationals and non-EU nationals, notably from Turkey and Central and East European countries, variously employed in the exploitation of women. Central and East European women, alongside women from Thailand, also feature predominantly in Kelly and Regan's report on England and Wales. The pattern of sex trafficking in the EU that emerges from police sources, and evidence gathered from various NGOs, is a familiar one. Women originate from poor non-EU countries and are trafficked, predominantly, to rich EU countries or countries that border the EU. Having acknowledged this simple but important fact, one can begin to outline a number of issues that point to the origins of the problem and, in turn, some of the problematic responses to it.

### The origins of the problem

Trafficking for the sex industry predominantly impacts on women as victims. A root cause of this gendered phenomenon is the feminisation of poverty. As cases of trafficking in Europe illustrate, women originate from poor countries in transition, the former communist countries of Central and East Europe, and developing countries, such as Nigeria and Thailand. While, arguably, it is not useful to speak in terms of countries of 'origin', 'transit' and 'destination', as trafficked women can be found in any country where there is a thriving sex industry, we can acknowledge the overall consistency in women's backgrounds with respect to their experience of poverty.

Economic instability, in combination with and as a reflection of civil conflict, as in the Balkans, has exacerbated women's slide into poverty in these regions. Where cultures of lawlessness thrive, and there is an absence of adequate criminal justice response, traffickers are able to exploit the needs of women against a cultural background of instability, economic uncertainty, and gendered inequality (OSCE, 1999). Traffickers, through adverts in newspapers and word-of-mouth, trick women with offers of lucrative employment in the EU as waitresses, dancers or au-pairs. As already stated, some women may suspect the legitimacy of gainful offers of employment, but what they are not able to foresee is the exploitation they will suffer at the hands of the criminal networks that organise trafficking. There have been various NGO and government-based campaigns in countries of 'origin' to alert young women, as the main targets of traffickers, to the dangers of apparently lucrative employment offers.[7] However, these campaigns are limited to a few places in each country and are not able to combat the root causes of trafficking's success which lie with poverty and the attractiveness of seemingly legitimate employment.

In turn, the origins of the sex trafficking problem cannot be attributed simply to gendered poverty and the tactics of traffickers which have, so far, outwitted the police and the campaigns of various NGOs. If there is to be a supply of trafficked women there has to be a demand for their services. As evidenced by Europol, it appears that trafficked women are beginning to outnumber, under-price and, 'out perform' EU-nationals as prostitutes; in other words, trafficked women, in conditions of bondage, are having to submit to conditions and services which would not normally be tolerated by prostitutes who are EU nationals.[8] Not only are traffickers and brothel owners answerable to this, but so are the clients who use the services of trafficked prostitutes. While it may be the case that most male clients are unaware that a woman has been trafficked, perhaps the EU should also consider campaigns that target clients to consider the 'legitimacy' of the women they visit. Without entering into the territory of abolitionist debates concerning the legitimacy of prostitution itself, one can assist attempts to distinguish between legitimate and exploitative practices. In this respect, recent Dutch legislation (1/10/01), which lifts the ban on brothels in an attempt to register their activities, can be cautiously offered as a means of filtering out unlawful practices with regard to the exploitation of under-age minors and trafficked women. However, it is unlikely that the worst case scenarios, given the underground nature of trafficking, will be altered through such attempts at new legislative and registration practices.[9]

Finally, the EU itself must be assigned some 'blame' with respect to the existence of trafficked women within its borders. In enforcing ever more stringent border controls, in the name of controlling external security threats and unwanted immigration, the EU has opened up a lucrative business for traffickers. To date, traffickers in human beings have bene-fited from legislative gaps in different EU states that have not prioritised human trafficking as a criminal activity worthy of stiff punishment. In this respect, traffickers have made considerable profits, at low risk, from their human goods. Individual EU member states have introduced measures that attempt to deal with the problem of human trafficking as cases come to light, but we are currently on the cusp of new EU-level legislative agree-ments that seek to deal more effectively with the problem of trafficking.

## Responding to the problem of sex trafficking

### Combating crime

The Organization for Security and Co-operation in Europe (OSCE) has commented in one of its reports on 'Trafficking in Human Beings':

> most States have not integrated human rights concerns or strategies into their laws or policies relating to trafficking. The 'human rights approach' to trafficking defines trafficking first and foremost as a vio-lation of individual human rights, and only secondarily as a violation of state interests ... Advocates stress the need to integrate a 'human rights analysis' into anti-trafficking legislation, strategies, and initi-atives, which have historically focused solely on controlling illegal immigration, prostitution and organized crime.
>
> (1999: 24–5)

To date, the OSCE's statement has rung true. In the EU's desire to create an 'area of freedom, security and justice' within the EU, the focus has been on external threats posed to the freedom and security of EU citizens by outside elements. Transnational organised criminal groups have come to personify these outside threats. However, the 'security threat' posed to the EU by organised criminal networks has been confused with the 'human security problem' of trafficking in human beings as it impacts on the victims of trafficking (Goodey, 2001). In this respect, the 'human rights approach' to sex trafficking has been subsumed by concerns to control and combat organised criminal activities as they impact on the EU.

The British Government's White Paper 'Fairer, Faster and Firmer – A Modern Approach to Immigration and Asylum' (July 1998), which fed into the 1999 Immigration and Asylum Act,[10] personifies this failure to distinguish between unwanted immigration and asylum, criminal actors and an external security threat. In the merging of an 'immigration–crime–security' problem, legislation and criminal justice practice have, largely, been ineffectual in recognising the victim status of trafficked women. Immigration and criminal justice authorities, in their efforts to crack down on illegal immigration and crime, have not, until recently, been given the remit to respond to the other side of organised criminal activity as it impacts on victims. On discovering foreign prostitutes who are possible victims of trafficking by organised criminal networks, the most common response within the EU has been to arrest and deport the women (Beare, 1997). Without a legislative and practical foundation to alert criminal justice authorities to alternative responses, the effective criminalisation of trafficking's victims has been the easiest route to follow. While Turnbill (1997: 203) gives the example of trafficking in women and children as an area of 'significant success' in the EU's move towards co-operation in the area of justice and home affairs, I am not inclined to agree with her merit award. If 'success' is measured with due regard for criminal convictions and victim assistance, rather than the volume of recommendations and guidelines for co-operation between member states, then 'success' in this area is not a foregone conclusion. Having said this, one cannot dismiss the considerable efforts, at the level of the EU and individual member states, to recognise and respond to the problem of sex trafficking.

### Responses at the level of the EU and individual states

The Council of the European Union's announcement, in 1996, of a comprehensive joint action plan to combat trafficking in women and children for sexual exploitation, has been reflected in a number of parallel joint actions which directly or indirectly address sex trafficking in the EU, and beyond. Notable amongst these are the European Commission funded STOP and DAPHNE programmes.

The STOP programme began in 1996 and ended in December 2000, having co-financed, to the sum of 6.5 million ECU, 85 projects variously working against trafficking and sexual exploitation of women and children. While STOP was primarily aimed at criminal justice agencies, immigration and other public services, NGOs participated in a number of STOP financed projects. The involvement of candidate EU countries was also central to the STOP programme, with nearly 50 per cent of funded projects, in the years 1999 and 2000, working with candidate states. Following the end of the STOP programme, further funds have been made available for the launch of STOP II which will run for two years from 2001. Complementing the STOP programme, but with a broader remit to combat violence against women, children, and other vulnerable groups (such as disabled, minority and migrant people), the DAPHNE initiative ran from 1997–9. In total, the DAPHNE initiative funded 149 projects, for 11.8 million ECU, and was open to NGO and multi-agency partnerships. The second phase of DAPHNE, the DAPHNE programme, has already started and is due to end in 2003, with funding available for 5 million ECU-worth of projects for each year of the programme.

Extended funding for both STOP and DAPHNE would appear to indicate their ongoing success. However, as with the various trafficking recommendations and guidelines that have flooded the EU in the 1990s, 'success' has to be cautiously inferred at a number of levels. First, there are the practical problems of running a project under these programmes which, in turn, impacts on the nature and the final outcome of a project that, ultimately, has implications for the people the project sets out to assist. As is the case with the majority of EC-funded projects, particularly those based with NGOs, there is the problem of raising 'matched funding' in order to secure EC funds. Coupled with this is the uncertainty of having to work to short-term funding on projects with a limited duration. Again, this poses a particular problem for NGOs which are reliant on external funds for their staffing and their very survival. While the latest DAPHNE programme has extended its original remit to fund projects with a scheduled duration of more than one year, this serves to illustrate the short-term nature of most funding which does not allow for long-term consistency in planning, staffing and operating a project. In this respect, it is hardly surprising that a significant number of projects foresee the need for further funding in order, not only to secure their own future but, also, to allow for long-term projects that pursue ongoing goals of prevention and assistance for victims of trafficking.

While it is relatively easy to criticise funding and implementation aspects of the STOP and DAPHNE programmes, as they impact on victims of trafficking, they need to be read for their practical input alongside the bulk of EC-based initiatives which are 'paper-driven'. In this respect, 'The Hague Ministerial Declaration on European Guidelines for Effective Measures to Prevent and Combat Trafficking in Women for the Purpose of Sexual Exploitation', launched in April 1997, is a classic example of the limited impact of many EC initiatives. Emphasising and encouraging international criminal justice co-operation in the fight against sex trafficking, alongside the needs and rights of victims, the Hague Declaration did much to recognise the human rights element of sex trafficking as a gendered phenomenon. However, the Hague Declaration could only encourage and not enforce its suggestions. In this respect it is noteworthy that the Declaration's suggestions for the appointment of national EU rapporteurs to report to governments on trafficking, originating as the Declaration did under the Dutch Presidency of the EU, has only resulted, at the time of writing, with the establishment of a Dutch rapporteur's office. There has been no coherent follow-up to the Hague Declaration.

Besides EC-based recommendations and guidelines, or the practical efforts of STOP and DAPHNE, one can turn to laudable developments in individual EU member states that serve to highlight a diversity of responses to the problem of sex trafficking. While the Hague Declaration may have only resulted in one official *Rapporteur*'s Office for trafficking, in the Netherlands, the function of *rapporteur* is currently being fulfilled in a number of EU member states. Multi-agency partnerships, or 'expert groups', have been established to highlight, and respond to, the problems of sex trafficking, notably in Belgium, Germany and Sweden. For example, in February 1997, prior to the Hague Declaration, Germany set up a *Bundesarbeitsgruppe fuer Frauenhandel* (Federal Working Group for Trafficked Women), which has, to date, included the police, NGOs and various government departments in the development of a multi-agency response to sex trafficking. With such working partnerships, the practical problems of different agencies can be shared in order to establish some level of understanding and co-operation in combating and assisting victims of trafficking. In this respect, the German working group is currently looking at practical aspects of provision for, and funding of, prolonged periods of residence for women wishing to testify against organised criminal groups.[11]

In contrast with some member states' internalised efforts at organised partnership responses, the majority of states have responded in an *ad hoc* way to sex trafficking as and when law enforcement problems arise. So, for example, while negotiations, at the time of writing, are currently underway in Italy to approve a new law specifically aimed at trafficking, the Italian government introduced, in 1998, the possibility of an extended permit of stay for victims of trafficking willing to give evidence against traffickers. In turn, this has been facilitated against a background where there is no police unit with a special remit to combat trafficking. Likewise, the Danish government, in 2000, initiated a police database to monitor trafficking that requires local police forces to inform the Danish national crime squad with respect to all cases of trafficking.[12]

Aside from individual initiatives by member states to combat and respond to the problem of sex trafficking, or cross-national projects funded by the STOP and DAPHNE programmes, there is a pressing need for the organised exchange of 'good practice' and co-operative action at a cross-national level within, and beyond, the EU. While the police in one member state may individually team-up with the police in another member state, or an applicant EU country, there is, undoubtedly, more scope for information exchange and practical co-operation at the level of the EU. Arguably, Europol, with the extension of its remit to include trafficking in human beings, fills this role with respect to developments in policing. Europol's information exchange network, alongside its expert group meetings and police training initiatives, do provide the EU's police, as the 'frontline' criminal justice agency tackling organised crime and trafficking, with a level of co-ordinated cross-national action against traffickers. The feasibility of establishing a European database on 'good practice' in organised crime reduction, through the application of certain crime prevention principles, has been explored by the Home Office and

Britain's National Criminal Intelligence Squad, along with Europol and the Swedish Crime Prevention Council, in an EU-wide project. The results reveal some interesting critiques of cross-national applications of crime prevention in the fight against organised crime. Whether crime prevention principles can be successfully moulded for a broad range of organised crime problems, such as sex trafficking, across different member states, has yet to be established.

While the efforts and success stories of individual governments and international organisations against sex trafficking, often with due regard for victims, are laudable, it is only with binding legislative initiatives, at the level of the EU, that, arguably, co-ordinated action can be effectively introduced. In this respect, the January 2001 Communication from the Commission on a Proposal for a Council Framework Decision on 'Combating Trafficking in Human Beings',[13] is a benchmark development for concerted co-operative criminal justice responses to trafficking, including sex trafficking, in the EU. The Commission's proposal aims to establish commonly adopted definitions and penalties against trafficking in individual member state's legislation. If adopted, the Commission's proposal will have far-reaching consequences against traffickers that will also be to the benefit of 'victims'.

The impetus for this latest proposal can be traced to a variety of recommendations, guidelines and actions at the level of the EU and other European organisations, such as the Council of Europe and the OSCE. More recently, the Treaty of Amsterdam (May 1999) and the Tampere Summit (October 1999) made reference to trafficking in human beings within their main agenda's focus on EU efforts to combat transnational organised crime and illegal immigration. Aside from these European-based developments, one can argue that the latest UN Convention Against Transnational Organised Crime, with its Protocol on Trafficking in Persons, to which the European Commission was a signatory on behalf of its member states, has played a significant role in pushing the Commission's latest proposal for a Framework Decision on Trafficking. With the UN having taken the initiative in standardising responses to sex trafficking, the European Commission has had to follow suit.

## The 'victimhood' of sex trafficking

### Recognising victims in the EU

In recent decades there have been a number of significant developments in consideration of victims' rights, and standards of service provision for victims, across the EU (Brienen and Hoegen, 2000; Wergens, 1999). The Council of Europe, which extends its focus beyond EU member states, has taken a lead in promoting the issue of victims and human rights in Europe. The Council's Recommendation (85)11, on the 'Position of the

Victim in the Framework of Criminal Law and Procedure' (Brienen and Hoegen, 2000), introduced at the same time as the UN 'Declaration of Basic Principles of Justice for Victims of Crime and Abuse of Power', exemplified the mid-1980s push towards enhancing victims' status. Yet, given this encouraging background, an individual's eligibility for 'victim' status within the EU is often confined, both implicitly and explicitly, to certain categories of victimhood. While recommendations may purport to speak for 'all' victims this, in reality, tends to mean a distinction between different types of victim. One of the most important distinctions, at the level of the EU, is the victim's status as citizen or non-citizen and, in turn, their legal status within the EU.

The European Commission, through its latest Proposal for a Council Framework Decision on 'Combating Trafficking in Human Beings', is making significant progress towards standardisation of criminal justice responses against the perpetrators of trafficking and, in turn, its victims. However, this development, like the work of previous recommendations, guidelines and funding initiatives in the field of trafficking, is undertaken without sufficient insight and reference to the work of the Commission, and other European organisations, more broadly, in the area of 'victims'. In this respect, different Commission communications, and even the same communications, can appear to be in conflict with regard to the status that should be afforded victims of trafficking, including sex trafficking, as some of the most vulnerable victims in the EU.

The Commission's 1999 communication on 'Crime Victims in the European Union: Reflections on Standards and Actions', typifies some of the problems encountered when attempting to 'place' the victim of sex trafficking within a general victim framework. The 1999 communication focuses on the problems of victims in an EU member state 'other than their own'. This would appear to indicate that the onus is on EU citizens. However, the same communication adds: 'Although the Commission will occasionally refer to victims as "European citizens", this will, where applicable, also include third country nationals who are legally residing in the European Union' (1999: 3). In turn, the reference to 'legally residing' would appear to exclude illegal immigrants and, therefore, the majority of those trafficked for the sex industry. However, this clarification of eligibility for 'victim' status is further confused, on the same page in the communication, with the statement: 'The importance of victim support has also been demonstrated in respect of women trafficked for the purpose of sexual exploitation' (ibid.).

This 1999 communication, which fed into Portugal's initiative in April 2000, under the terms of its EU Presidency, for a Framework Decision on 'The Standing of Victims in Criminal Procedure in the EU',[14] reflects an essential conflict of interest in the European Commission's work in the area of justice and home affairs. In the Commission's drive to strengthen the arm of justice and home affairs across the EU's member states, in the name of European Union citizens, so compensatory measures are introduced to 'protect' EU citizens against the 'enemy without': that is, those real and 'folk devil' incarnations of organised crime and illegal immigration. In this respect, the 'victim' of trafficking has traditionally fallen into a 'no man's land' between criminal and victim status because of four important factors: their association with criminal elements; their illegal entry into the EU; their 'work' as prostitutes; and the unequal distribution of victims' rights in the EU.

It has to be seen whether the 2001 Council Framework Decision on 'Combating Trafficking in Human Beings' can be aligned with the 2000 Council Framework Decision on 'The Standing of Victims in Criminal Procedure'. Both Framework Decisions illustrate the EU's move towards enforceable legislation and standardised criminal justice responses to crime and, more importantly, victims of crime. However, the extent to which the Union is prepared to assist all victims of crime in practice, such as women trafficked for the sex industry, has yet to be seen. While children and 'little old ladies' command sympathy as 'victims', prostitutes, whether trafficked or not, have traditionally been awarded little sympathy as vulnerable victims. In this respect, the true test of the Council's latest Framework Decision on 'Combating Trafficking in Human Beings' will be in the extent to which individual member states promote criminal justice responses on behalf of victims of trafficking.

### Responding to victims' needs

Having recognised that victims of trafficking should receive recognition as designated 'victims', there are a number of practical solutions that can be forwarded in response to their specific needs.

Witness protection is frequently held up as a desirable goal in the effort to secure victim testimonies in the fight against organised crime (Pearson, 2001). Given the nature of organised crime, which employs violence against those who speak against it, there is an obvious need for protection to be offered to women who are willing to testify against traffickers. In securing a testimony, while offering protection, witness protection appears to provide a pay-off in the balance of interests between criminal justice agencies, who need a conviction, and victims, who need some level of security. However, while the provision of witness protection might be offered as a central goal of any legislation and practice concerning trafficking, it has its limitations both for victims and criminal justice.

As a recent Council of Europe report on witness protection states:

> The use of witness protection in cases of human trafficking is seen as less effective [than in other cases], at least from a prosecutorial viewpoint. This is due to the fact that the illegal immigrants involved usually only have information on one or two traffickers and

therefore their testimony is not sufficient to dismantle the criminal organisation.

(1999: 12)

In other words, from the standpoint of the prosecution, witness protection, in the majority of sex trafficking cases, does not produce testimonies that can provide convictions. However, in serious cases, the police do see the benefits of witness testimonies in their efforts to secure convictions. But the benefits to victims are generally limited to the duration of a case and their own protection in the country in which they testify. A significant disincentive to testifying lies with a woman's knowledge that traffickers can use violence against her family in her country of origin. If violence is not threatened, women can also fear that their 'work' as prostitutes might be revealed to unsuspecting family members which, in the context of certain cultures, can mean the difference between re-acceptance back into the home community or rejection.

In turn, if a woman decides to testify, she should be given recourse to an extended residence permit for the country in which she will testify. Many EU countries currently offer some form of extended stay. However, this is usually limited to cases where women are willing to testify. Given the push for a human rights response to trafficking, one could argue that trafficked women, regardless of their willingness to testify, should be offered the opportunity to remain in their 'host' country; particularly given the dangers they might face on return to their home country. While extended residence permits for trafficking victims might be considered an incentive for illegal immigrants to falsely claim their 'victim' status, there are the more pressing needs of eligible victims to consider, in offering residence permits, with respect to employment, housing and social provisions. The rehabilitation of trafficking victims requires that a range of services are provided for them. If assistance, from governmental offices and NGOs, is not available, trafficking victims are vulnerable to revictimisation at the hands of criminal networks. While lists of 'good practice' initiatives for trafficked victims can be drawn up, a number of practical questions remain; for example: which government services will shoulder the responsibility for providing funds to assist victims? If a woman is repatriated after a period of witness protection, will her 'host' country take some responsibility for her ongoing protection and assistance in the country of origin?

Given the statement above by the Council of Europe with respect to the feasibility of witness protection for cases of human trafficking, there are alternatives that must be considered by the police in their attempt to secure convictions of traffickers. Phone tapping and tracing of laundered assets are two of the alternative means by which prosecutions might be secured. However, these methods do not have a higher success rate than efforts at securing witness testimonies and, in many cases, can lead to the infringement of suspects' human rights. Perhaps the 'real' alternative to the continued focus on securing convictions lies with a re-focusing of attention towards prevention of sex trafficking. In this respect, the forthcoming Falcone-sponsored Home Office report on the feasibility of crime prevention initiatives against organised crime should be read with a mind to the limitations of witness protection.

The German *BKA* prefer the term 'victim protection' rather than 'witness protection' when referring to their work with victims of sex trafficking.[15] What this reflects is a shift in perspective away from the limited perception of a trafficked woman simply as a possible witness for the state, towards the idea of her as a victim who is in need of assistance and protection from the state. The *BKA* is not alone amongst the EU's police forces in thinking this way as, increasingly, the 'victim' status of trafficked women is being incorporated into police responses to the problem of trafficking.[16] This shift in police emphasis towards recognition of the victim status of trafficked women can be said to reflect two important factors: first, the increasing push from governmental and non-governmental organisations for recognition of 'victims' in the trafficking process; and, second, the practical benefits that are accrued by the police in women's willingness to co-operate when they are able to offer trafficked women a service that recognises their needs as victims. The *BKA*'s trafficking unit, which is distinct from the German police's work in the area of smuggling, goes so far as to distinguish between the 'victimhood' of trafficking and smuggling. In this respect, the *BKA* recognises the victim status of a person in cases of sex trafficking; while, in the case of smuggling, the state is seen as the primary victim.

Finally, one has cautiously to critique legislative and criminal justice developments for victims of trafficking in the light of what victims, in general, are eligible for in different EU member states. In other words, it might not be practical to promote the rights and needs of victims of trafficking in a policy 'vacuum' which does not give due regard to existing provisions for all victims. This consideration returns us to an earlier critique of calls for enhanced legislation and 'service' provision for trafficking victims which, frequently, are made irrespective of current provisions for other vulnerable victims. 'Listing' victims' needs can aspire to 'best practice' goals, but should also reflect the reality of current provisions and what is obtainable in light of funding, current provisions for victims and, ultimately, what victims themselves want and can be reasonably expected to receive.

## Concluding comments

This chapter set out to highlight the 'flipside' of organised crime with respect to its victims. Sex trafficking provides a notable example of exploitation of 'human goods' at the hands of traffickers. Having outlined the nature, extent and origins of the problem, in the context of the EU, the chapter provided a critique of EU responses to sex trafficking with respect to the neglect of the victim in the continued focus on perpetrators and the criminalisation of unwanted immigrants. In turn, the chapter questioned the 'victimhood' of trafficked persons in light of inadequate cross-reference between, primarily, the European Commission's work on victims, in general, and its more recent focus on victims of trafficking. However, in light of encouraging developments at the legislative and practical level, from the Commission through to national police initiatives, the chapter pointed to noteworthy developments 'for' victims of sex trafficking which focus on the human rights approach to their needs. To this end, it is hoped that the chapter has provided a general introduction to some of the problems and promises of current responses, within the EU, to victims of sex trafficking as one aspect of organised criminal activities.

## Notes

1 The author is in receipt of an EC-funded research fellowship and is based at the UN Office on Drugs and Crime in Vienna. Her research is examining criminal justice responses to 'vulnerable' and 'at risk' victims in the EU, including victims of sex trafficking. The opinions expressed in this chapter are those of the author and do not represent the UN.

2 For example: Council of Europe (1994) 'Final Report of the Group of Specialists on action against traffic in women and forced prostitution as violations of human rights and human dignity', Strasbourg: CDEG, European Commission (1996) Communication from the Commission to the Council and the European Parliament on trafficking in women for the purposes of sexual exploitation, COM(96) 567 final, Brussels (20.11.96); European Parliament (1996) Resolution on trafficking in human beings, *OJ* C 32 (5.2.96).

3 See International Organisation for Migration (IOM) (1995) *Trafficking and Prostitution: The Growing Exploitation of Migrant Women from Central and Eastern Europe.* Geneva: IOM; plus IOM's regular news bulletins. Also Europol's (1999) *General Situation Report on 'Trafficking in Human Beings'.* The Hague: Europol.

4 The UN definition of 'trafficking', under the terms of the Protocol to Prevent, Suppress and Punish Trafficking in Persons, Especially Women and Children (supplementing the 2000 UN Convention against Transnational Organized Crime), Article 3(a) states:

> 'Trafficking in persons' shall mean the recruitment, transportation, transfer, harbouring or receipt of persons, by means of the threat or use of force or other forms of coercion, of abduction, of fraud, of deception, of the abuse of power or of a position of vulnerability or of the giving or receiving of payments or benefits to achieve the consent of a person having control over another person, for the purpose of exploitation. Exploitation shall include, at a minimum, the exploitation of the prostitution of others or other forms of sexual exploitation, forced labour or services, slavery or practices similar to slavery, servitude or the removal of organs.

(A/55/383)

In comparison, the UN Protocol against the Smuggling of Migrants by Land, Sea and Air (supplementing the UN Convention against Transnational Organized Crime), Article 3(a) states: ' "Smuggling of migrants" shall mean the procurement, in order to obtain, directly or indirectly, a financial or other material benefit, of the illegal entry of a person into a State Party of which the person is not a national or a permanent resident' (A/55/383).

5  See www.trafficked-women.org.
6  'Communication from the Commission to the Council and the European Parliament on Trafficking in Women for the Purpose of Sexual Exploitation', Brussels, 20.11.96, COM(96) 567 final, p. 4.
7  IOM News, June 2000, 'Don't get hooked – IOM anti-trafficking campaign in Hungary'.
8  Evidence presented at Europol expert group meeting on 'trafficking in human beings for the purpose of sexual exploitation' (21–22/3/01), The Hague; attended by the author on behalf of CICP, UN Vienna.
9  Interview with office of Dutch Rapporteur on Trafficking in Human Beings, 23/3/01, The Hague.
10 See www.homeoffice.gov.uk/ind/asylum/asylum_home.html.
11 Interview with BKA Trafficking Unit, Wiesbaden, 20/3/01.
12 Information provided at Europol expert group meeting on 'trafficking in human beings for the purpose of sexual exploitation' (21–22/3/01).
13 The Communication encompassed a joint Proposal for a Council Framework Decision on combating the sexual exploitation of children and child pornography; see European Commission (2001) 'Communication from the Commission to the Council and the European Parliament on combating trafficking in human beings and combating the sexual exploitation of children and child pornography', COM(2000) 854 final/2, Brussels (22.1.01).
14 Document 10387/00 COPEN 54 'Draft Framework Decision on the Standing of Victims in Criminal Procedure'.
15 Interview with BKA Trafficking Unit, Wiesbaden, 20/3/01.
16 Evidence presented at Europol expert group meeting on 'trafficking in human beings for the purpose of sexual exploitation' (21–22/3/01), The Hague.

# References

Beare, M.E. (1997) 'Illegal migration: personal tragedies, social problems, or national security threats?', *Transnational Organized Crime* 3, 4: 11–41.
BKA (1999) *Trafficking in Human Beings, Situation Report 1999*. Wiesbaden: Bundeskriminalamt.
Brienen, M. and Hoegen, E. (2000) *Victims of Crime in Twenty-Two European Jurisdictions*. Ph.D. Thesis, Katholieke Universiteit Brabant, Nijmegen, The Netherlands: Wolf Legal Productions.
Council of Europe (1999) *Recommendation R (96)8 on Crime Policy in Europe in a Time of Change*. Strasbourg: Council of Europe Publication.
EC Com (1999) 349 final; Communication to the European Parliament, the Council and the Economic and Social Committee on 'Crime Victims in the European Union: Reflections on Standard and Actions', Brussels.
Goodey, J. (2001) 'Whose insecurity? Organised crime, its victims and the EU', in A. Crawford (ed.) *Crime, Insecurity and Safety in the New Governance*. Cullompton: Willan Publishing, 135–58.

IOM (1995) *Trafficking and Prostitution: The Growing Exploitation of Migrant Women from Central and Eastern Europe*. Geneva: IOM.

Kelly, L. and Regan, L. (2000) *Stopping Traffic: Exploring the Extent of, and Responses to, Trafficking in Women for Sexual Exploitation in the UK*. London: Home Office, Police Research Series, paper 125.

OSCE (1999) *Trafficking in Human Beings: Implications for the OSCE*. Warsaw: Organization for Security and Co-operation in Europe, and Office for Democratic Institutions and Human Rights (ODIHR) Background Paper 1999/3.

Pearson, E. (2001) *The Need for Effective Witness Protection in the Prosecution of Traffickers: A Human Rights Framework for Witness Protection*. Paper presented at the First Pan-African Regional Conference on Trafficking in Persons, Abuja, Nigeria, 19–23 February.

Turnbill, P. (1997) 'The fusion of immigration and crime in the European Union: problems of co-operation and the fight against the trafficking in women', *Transnational Organized Crime* 3, 4: 189–213.

Wergens, A. (1999) *Crime Victims in the European Union*. Umeå, Sweden: The Crime Victim Compensation and Support Authority.

# Part IV

# Current and prospective responses

Implicit in the foregoing arguments about the origins, interpretations and case studies of TOC is a broader controversy in criminological thought over the appropriate conceptualisation of crime and control. At the root of this controversy is a dialogue about the limits of gauging policy change and learning in terms of criminal justice and its enforcement. In one sense it is banal to question the centrality of criminal justice as, by definitional fiat, practices only become 'crimes' when they are proscribed by various criminal legal codes. Yet the limitations of law enforcement as a means of actually controlling practices thus criminalised have been regularly noted in contributions to the first three parts of this book.

Here, however, a key division emerges between those who attribute these limitations to the poor formulation of law and its enforcement and those who attribute them to failures in the theory of control upon which criminal justice is premised. For the former, the implications for policy reform are better law-making and refinements to the devices of criminal justice, such as the omnipresent call for greater 'co-ordination' of law enforcement agencies and judicial dispensations, the provision of mutual judicial aid and resources to enhance the capacity for law enforcement, as in the standardisation of extradition procedures and powers of arrest across national borders, and protocols for the sharing of criminal intelligence. For the latter, as neatly argued by Levi in his contribution to this part of the book, 'In general, criminal justice only looks backwards at fixing blame, not forwards in strategic thinking'. From this perspective, the limitations of criminal justice policy are in its theoretical misconception of 'what works' in controlling crime, which no amount of legal reformulation and implementation reform is likely to allay. To switch policy-oriented learning about the efficacy of crime control away from the reactive mode of criminal justice and towards a more strategic way of thinking is to question the preconditions for crime, to ask what factors facilitate certain criminal practices, and then to consider the potential of alternative strategies for intervening in these preconditions as a means of at least reducing certain crimes. The contributions to this final part of the book examine current and prospective policy responses to TOC in terms of this dialogue over the limitations of using criminal law as an instrument of control and what, therefore, the adoption of a more strategic approach could entail.

Baker, in Chapter 11, considers the utility of criminal justice responses to TOC in terms of the philosophical foundations of criminal law-making. It is argued that TOC is an inappropriate object of criminal law because it is difficult to establish *mens rea* given the diffusion of culpability amongst a broad group of individuals, often the lack of proximity of these actors to particular offences and, therefore, the problem of establishing, beyond reasonable doubt, the conscious intent of suspected offenders. Further, 'At a theoretical level, there is a fundamental link between the norms that are enshrined in the criminal law, the degree of identity with those norms that is felt by the population to which they apply, and the likelihood that law-abiding behaviour will result.' Given the ambiguity of TOC as an object of regulation, it is argued that the promulgation of criminal laws in response is unlikely to enhance citizens' identification with the legitimacy of public authorities per se and may well jeopardise this identification, especially if the perceived consequences are general invasions of privacy and the curtailment of civil liberties. The recent trend of legislators to replace the principle of *mens rea* with conditions of 'strict liability' in relation to certain offences and criminalisation of participation in criminal organisations (apropos the RICO statutes in the United States) will, if anything, exacerbate this legitimacy deficit. It is also argued that criminal law-making in relation to TOC flouts established boundaries between domestic security, which is the appropriate jurisdiction of the criminal law, and protection from external threats which is the appropriate responsibility of foreign and defence policy. Attempts to overcome these jurisdictional barriers to criminal law enforcement measures designed to tackle organised crime, such as asset confiscation and controls on money laundering, are then considered. Baker concludes, however, by arguing that because,

> there is a fundamental mismatch between the basic characteristics of the behaviour concerned and the traditional parameters of the criminal law ... the criminal law should be abandoned and that energy should be devoted instead to the development of an alternative set of legal tools that might be better suited to dealing with such problems.

Chapter 12, by Mitsilegas, discusses the development of such alternative 'hard' and 'soft' legal tools in relation to the emergence of a 'global anti-money-laundering regime'. The rapid emergence of this regime over the past 14 years is traced from the 1988 UN Convention Against Illicit Traffic in Narcotic Drugs and Psychotropic Substances, which provided the first international legal instrument for establishing the laundering of proceeds from drug trafficking as an offence. The purview of counter-measures against money laundering was, subsequently, extended in the 1990s to cover all forms of 'organised crime' and, in the context of the September 11 2001 attacks on the World Trade Center and Pentagon, to the financing of terrorism. Originally the rationale of these counter-measures was to identify where 'dirty' money had come from and to prevent its 'cleansing', as a means of enhancing the prosecution and prevention of organised criminality. Subsequently, the extended remit of these measures – to identify 'clean' money used to support international terrorism – means that financial institutions will now have to monitor 'where money is going to as well as where it has come from', thereby effectively bringing all 'suspicious' financial transactions within the remit of anti-money-laundering controls.

The ambitious scope of this regime is reflected in the number of actors now rendered responsible by 'hard' legal instruments for monitoring and reporting suspicious transactions, such as the EU's Directives on financial management. The Financial Action Task Force (FATF), established by the Group of 7 advanced industrial nations in July 1989, has been the key actor in promulgating 'soft' legal instruments, in the form of ethical principles and recommendations on financial management, for the control of money laundering. As a consequence of these hard and soft legal tools, duties for reporting suspicious transactions have been extended beyond banks and other financial institutions to 'intermediary' professionals, such as accountants, solicitors and company formation agents, thought by the FATF to be potentially responsible for providing, 'the apparent sophistication and extra layer of respectability to some laundering operations'.

Mitsilegas identifies the ethical and practical problems associated with the global scope of this anti-money-laundering regime. The information overload it places on responsible monitors and the consequent necessity of exercising discretion in which clients and transactions are controlled, 'may lead to prejudice and racial discrimination [especially] regarding customers from the Middle East'. The broader salience of this regime is that it undermines principles of confidentiality between financial institutions and their customers and between solicitors and their clients, placing intermediary professionals in the invidious position of having to 'shop' their clients to public authorities. The global reach of this regime has also been criticised for its 'normative imperialism' because it 'disregards the particular social, economic and political situation in developing countries and the fact that they may not have the same economic priorities as the FATF members' who are largely drawn from the Group of 7 states. As a consequence, 'A balance has to be struck between countering money laundering and protecting fundamental legal principles and human rights.'

Levi also takes counter-measures against money laundering, in particular the confiscation of criminal assets, as a focus for debating the limits of, and alternatives to, criminal law instruments for controlling organised crime. Levi reviews the various dimensions of asset confiscation in relation to the proceeds from drug trafficking, considered as the principal activity of what is taken to constitute 'organised crime'. He concludes, however, that there is a stark gap between guesstimates of money-laundering volumes and confiscation orders made, let alone actual confiscation effected. The question this raises is whether, at one extreme, these money-laundering estimates should be discarded as 'gross data' or, at the other extreme, criminal justice agencies are doing 'an exceptionally bad job'. Yet, there is no reliable method for researching this question and arriving at a sensible conclusion.

Levi suggests, therefore, that policy debates should step back from the minutiae of such legal instruments as asset confiscation and question, instead, the usefulness of alternative conceptions of control. As such, his chapter marks an important turning-point in debates over the prospective responses to TOC. Principally, Levi challenges the preoccupation of policy-makers with measures of *activity*, such as seizures, proceeds and arrests, rather than *final outcome* measures, such as lower narcotics consumption and a reduction in harms associated with the 'collateral consequences of *unaffordable* drugs-taking, that is, crime for gain, including wars over distribution rights'. Further implications for re-thinking control follow from this shift of focus. It is necessary to question what is meant by the 'success' of alternative control strategies and this thorny evaluative question can be clarified by distinguishing, 'between (a) ultimate – or 'final' – objectives, and (b) intermediate goals along the way, which are crucial to the achievement of final ones but should not be confused with them.' If the ultimate objective of policy is to reduce harms then intermediate goals, such as seizures, arrests and the confiscation of criminal assets, are 'helpful only if – taken as a whole rather than just looking at any one arrest – [they produce] real incapacitation or general deterrence', and the evidence for this is, as noted throughout this book, negligible.

Focusing on final outcomes suggests, in turn, a re-orientation of the contribution that research can make to evidence-based policy-making, away from the relatively narrow preoccupation with the devices of criminal justice towards a broader social scientific concern with the actual preconditions of crime, on the basis of which more insightful knowledge about the efficacy of alternative control strategies can be generated. From this perspective, the very notion of *transnational* organised crime needs to be eschewed, not just because it is too vague an object for clear law-making but, more profoundly, because it is a contentless abstraction that obfuscates the qualities of the very diverse concrete criminal practices which it is used to refer to. Allied to the proposed shift in focus on the final objectives of policy, therefore, is the necessity of disaggregating TOC and the notion of 'crime' per se into its various sub-categories, such as drug trafficking or trafficking in certain types of narcotic and psychotropic substances, amongst specific populations, in particular places, at particular times and so on. The more concrete research and policy-making can be about certain practices deemed to be harmful, the more likely their causes will be apprehended so as to better intervene against them.

Dorn, however, adopts a different approach to the prospects for policy responses to TOC in Chapter 14. Rather than disaggregate this concept, he chooses to identify the interconnections between the diverse activities that it signifies, such as:

> corruption of state officials or of commercial enterprises; fraud in relation to private parties, the state or the European budget; large-scale evasion of tax; thefts of objects of high monetary value; trafficking in drugs, other prohibited goods or human beings; arms trafficking, and so on.

From this perspective, the limitations of control strategies can be ascertained precisely in their failure to comprehend the 'structurally similar, functionally parallel and empirically overlapping forms of OC'. These interconnections reveal the protean capacity of organised criminals to adapt to the changing environment of controls on their activity. Indeed, in relation to the relatively pedestrian conduct of criminal law enforcement, organised criminals are more reflexive in anticipating and outflanking such controls and manipulating this environment for their own ends. Increasing cognisance of this amongst policy-makers is a key factor behind the emergence of various strategies of multi-agency co-operation. Dorn identifies four generic strategies which, together, define the emerging 'control space' in which organised criminals must act: *law enforcement* through policing operations that result in judicial action under national criminal codes; *disruption* through non-judicial, covert, action, misinformation and so on; *administrative measures* such as civil fines and the confiscation of criminal assets (see Chapter 13 by Levi); and *market regulation* through the withdrawal of various commercial rights and privileges.

Central to understanding the operation of this control environment, and organised criminal adaptations to it, is the sharing of intelligence and 'counter-intelligence'. Dorn argues that prospective research and policy-making on organised crime should focus on the interactive nature of intelligence sharing. In turn, this entails a movement away from specialisation, both in the conduct of agencies engaging in law enforcement, disruption, administrative measures and market regulation, and in the way policy-oriented learning is organised:

> We can no longer rely on experience in any one particular field – be it practical experience in one agency or sector of control, or academic expertise in any one discipline (criminology, law – whether national or European – applied economics, applied accountancy). This is not

just a theoretical observation. On a mundane note, over-specialised approaches are increasingly difficult to market to policy-makers – all the more so since the various administrations are themselves required to work in partnership.

As Dorn acknowledges with reference to his own chapter, 'Too often, the study of crime and control are divorced', when, as already noted, policy change and learning about control needs to proceed from an understanding of the dynamics of crime and, therefore, the appropriateness of alternative control strategies. In the concluding chapter to this part of the book, Ekblom discusses the features of a conceptual framework, the 'Conjunction of Criminal Opportunity' (CCO), and how it can inform policy-oriented learning about the interactions between crime and control. At the epicentre of this framework is the idea that such interactions resemble an 'arms race between preventers and organised offenders', wherein changes in the social and technological environment of crime 'constantly creates new opportunities for offending', where, 'Even successful crime control methods eventually weaken as offenders learn to circumvent them', and where, 'Legislative solutions lag behind changing crime patterns – particularly those requiring international agreement'.

For Ekblom it is, therefore, important to regard organised crime as an 'evolutionary process' and thus to 'gear-up' policy responses to 'catch-up' with existing crime problems that cannot yet be prevented, 'scan' for emergent crime problems and stop them early, 'anticipate' new problems and develop and deploy timely new solutions, and ensure the 'durability' of solutions. In turn, this entails the production of knowledge 'about' the causes and patterns of crime, 'what' preventive measures work in which contexts relative to these causes, 'how' such measures can be tailored to different local circumstances, and 'who' can contribute to this knowledge and effectively participate in preventive strategies. The CCO framework is promoted as a means of organising such knowledge so that, 'we are neither reinventing the wheel of success nor the flat tyre of failure – and the initiatives we produce are most likely to succeed.'

The CCO framework represents an advance in thinking about the interrelationships between crime and control in so far as it emphasises an understanding about the outcomes of these interrelationships and how these are affected by, 'contextual factors like culture, law, environment'. The conception of crime prevention as an 'evolutionary process' in this framework has, however, been subject to certain criticisms in the UK in relation to debates over the efficacy of volume crime reduction programmes, out of which the framework originally developed. It is important to note these criticisms if the CCO framework is to be extended to the control of organised crime. Specifically, the Darwinian metaphor of 'evolution' obfuscates the political content and choices inherent in interrelationships between crime and control. It is argued that 'crime prevention techniques not only embody political assumptions and commitments to particular models of social explanation, they also imply a political context and have political consequences' (Crawford, 1998: 246). Notwithstanding this, the tendency in much crime prevention discourse has been to replace political debate with administrative platitudes on the need for more co-ordination, sustainability, accurate intelligence, sophisticated evaluation and monitoring, ad nauseam. It follows that policy-oriented learning about the outcomes of crime control cannot be divorced from a critical appraisal of the processes through which certain policy responses are formulated and implemented. Rather, the outcomes of policy are inextricably related to these processes; they are implied in alternative narrations of 'the problem', 'the solution' and how this solution is to be accomplished. From this perspective, it is important to discern competing 'governmentalities' in crime control discourse, what their implications for policy-making have been and what, nonetheless, they could be (Edwards and Gill, 2002; O'Malley, 1992; Stenson, 1999). Switching the terms of debate from an administrative to an expressly political discourse enables a more fundamental questioning of the significance of crime control strategies. It is in these terms that we reconsider the frenetic policy-making activity around the perceived threat of TOC in Chapter 16.

## References

Crawford, A. (1998) *Crime Prevention and Community Safety: Politics, Policies and Practices*. London: Longman.

Edwards, A. and Gill, P. (2002) 'The politics of "transnational organized crime": discourse, reflexivity and the narration of "threat"', *British Journal of Politics and International Relations* 4, 2: 245–70.

O'Malley, P. (1992) 'Risk, power and crime prevention', *Economy and Society* 21, 3: 252–75.

Stenson, K. (1999) 'Crime control, governmentality and sovereignty', in R. Smandych (ed.) *Governable Places: Readings in Governmentality and Crime Control.* Aldershot: Dartmouth.

# 11 The legal regulation of transnational organised crime

## Opportunities and limitations

*Estella Baker*

## Introduction

One of the rudimentary propositions that is communicated at an early stage in the career of every aspiring criminologist is that the concept of 'crime' has no objective reality, but is an artificial construct of the criminal law. Implicitly, therefore, when the term 'transnational organised crime' is used, it conveys the message that a policy decision has been taken that the forms of behaviour that it embraces should be the subject of this type of legal regulation. However, it is not an implication that it is safe to draw because, distinct from any technical legal definition, the term also has a colloquial meaning which relies on everyday understanding. Rather like the proverbial joke about the elephant and the pillar-box, we may not be able to define what we mean by transnational organised crime, 'but we recognise it when we see it'. It will be one of the principal arguments of this chapter, however, that the veneer of confidence which this appeal to common sense creates is potentially very unhelpful because it disguises the reality that the phenomenon of transnational organised crime poses considerable challenges for criminal law regulation. At first base, it is very unclear that everything to which the label is applied is in fact criminal, or that it should be. Consequently, the term is used in its colloquial sense throughout this chapter unless specifically stated otherwise. But even where there is a case for criminalisation in principle, questions arise as to which exact aspects of the behaviour involved should be the targets of offences. Moreover, these theoretical issues are not the only ones that are relevant. Separate from them, but having a significant practical bearing on their resolution, is a different type of difficulty from which the chapter's second line of argument will be developed.

Although not habitually described as such, law is a form of intellectual technology and, like all technologies, it has its shortcomings. Consequently, for all that policy-makers might desire to outlaw particular activities or forms of conduct that fall within the bracket of transnational organised crime, the practical reality is that the traditional framework according to which the criminal law operates makes it a less than ideal tool for tackling this type of problem. Its deficiencies have not been over-looked; dissatisfaction with the traditional parameters of operation of criminal law has sparked attempts at modification that are designed to achieve a better fit between its dimensions and those of transnational organised crime. However, they are not entirely satisfactory either. As a result, there is reason to suggest that, in some situations, the effect of legal regulation can be to make matters worse by creating fresh opportunities for those operating outside the confines of legitimate structures to exploit and/or by generating displacement behaviours that exacerbate the problems confronting law enforcement authorities. In order to set the subsequent arguments in context, the first section of the chapter will begin by outlining a number of relevant features of the criminal law.

## Criminal law regulation and the challenge posed by transnational organised crime

In order to understand the nature and depth of the challenge to criminal law regulation that is posed by transnational organised crime, it is helpful to map out four central propositions concerning the application and function of the criminal law. These will then be used to explain how and why the phenomenon of transnational organised crime poses a challenge to criminal law regulation.

The first of the four propositions is that, to be properly made the subject of a criminal offence, an act or omission must be sufficiently harmful (Ashworth, 1999: Chapter 2). Philosophically, it is a statement of principle that follows from the fact that the corollary of criminalisation is to expose those who violate the law to the exercise of coercive force by the state and to the deliberate infliction of suffering in the form of state punishment (Clarkson and Keating, 1998: Chapter 1). For the state to be justified in delivering such hard treatment to its citizens, it ought to have good reason. It is outside the scope of the present discussion to investigate the voluminous theoretical literature devoted to examining the circumstances when such good reasons can be said to exist. However, an important aspect of the argument is the further idea that the harm concerned must be of a nature and degree which means that, at a conceptual level, its effects extend beyond the immediate victim (assuming there is one) to damage the interests of society as a whole. In short, therefore, a crime should constitute both a private and a public wrong.

The second proposition is linked to the first. It is that, in the light of the detrimental consequences of conviction, it is a moral imperative that only those who are rightly regarded as responsible for their actions should be held to blame for their conduct, and so liable to punishment. The technical means by which this imperative is put into effect is through the doctrine of *mens rea*, or 'guilty mind'. It stipulates that, for an individual to be convicted of an offence, the prosecution must prove, not only that he or she performed the prohibited act or omission, but also that the act or omission was accompanied by a specified blameworthy mental state or attitude. The *mens rea* paradigm is becoming undermined by the increasing trend for Parliament to enact offences of 'strict liability' (offences where *mens rea* need not be established in relation to one or more offence elements) (Ashworth and Blake, 1996). However, the doctrine remains substantially intact where serious crimes are concerned and has important ramifications in terms of defining the types of situations in which the criminal law operates as an effective device through which to bring the perpetrators of harm to justice. Specifically, it works well in circumstances where the following conditions are satisfied: individual or small numbers of actors are involved, their participation is proximate to the offence and it occurs in circumstances where a conscious awareness of the enterprise in hand can be established. Conversely, the criminal law copes badly when harm amounting to a criminal act takes place as the result of the collective actions or omissions of a group of individuals or of an organisation, especially where the blame for their occurrence is widely diffused among a body of actors.

The third proposition concerns the constitutional function of the criminal law and, in particular, the role that it plays in defining the concepts of 'citizen' and 'state'. A well-discussed assertion in the theoretical literature is that the state has a 'classic triad' of tasks; namely, the provision of security, of economic well-being and of cultural identity (Shaw, 1998: 296). If the criminal law is considered in terms of this framework then, plainly, it plays a pivotal part in the state's ability to fulfil the first of these. However, it also makes an important contribution to the delivery of the second and third. It follows that one of the sources of the state's claim to legitimate existence in the eyes of its citizens is derived from its promise to provide these fundamental commodities through the exercise of criminal jurisdiction. In the light of this, it is unsurprising that governments appear to perceive the existence of a strong nexus between the latter function and the assertion of sovereign power (Garland, 1996). Meanwhile, on the citizenship side of the equation, the immediate return for the citizen in recognising the state's legitimacy is that he or she receives such protection as the criminal law provides. This protection has both a particular and a general aspect which picks up the notion of a crime as simultaneously a private and a public wrong. On the one hand, in so far as an individual occupies the position of potential victim, his or her personal assets and interests are the object of particular protection; on the other, in so far as crime occurs in the community at large and therefore threatens the internal security of the state, the individual is the beneficiary of the general contribution that the criminal law makes towards preserving the peaceful order of society. This latter benefit, of course, is also one in which the state shares a powerful vested interest. Moreover, recent work has begun to show just how deeply these interests are inter-connected. At a theoretical level, there is a fundamental link between the norms that are enshrined in the criminal law, the degree of identity with those norms that is felt by the population to which they apply, and the likelihood that law-abiding behaviour will result (Bottoms, 2002; von Hirsch *et al.*, 1999). This suggests that the state stands to reap a significant security dividend by ensuring that the content of the criminal law constitutes a good match with the values and interests of its citizens.

The final proposition needs only to be touched on briefly. Although there are a few longstanding exceptions, the normal premise has been that the criminal law applies just to those acts and omissions that are committed within the territory of the state and that the criminal courts have no jurisdiction over events occurring abroad (Simester and Sullivan, 2000: 315–17). It can be seen that this is consistent with the established conception of the criminal law as concerned with internal security, by contrast with foreign and defence policy that is designed to protect the state from external attack.

## The difficulties presented by transnational organised crime

At heart, the explanation for why transnational organised crime poses such a profound challenge for criminal law regulation is that it makes a bad 'fit' with the propositions that have just been sketched out. The reasons why this is so, some of which are more obvious than others, will now be examined.

Beginning with the matter of criminalisation, a key question concerns the identification of what exactly it is about the phenomenon of transnational organised crime that is harmful and should be the target of offences. There are a number of possibilities, which are not necessarily mutually exclusive. One is that it is the range of damaging activities in which relevant organisations engage; what might be termed the 'end behaviours' (drug trafficking, fraud, smuggling and so on). However, putting jurisdictional difficulties caused by the transnational element to one side for the present, there must be more to the issue than this because an abundance of offences exists to deal with such problems. Therefore, it is necessary to consider a second possibility; that there is something inherently, or additionally, threatening about the organised nature of the behaviours concerned, and it is this which ought to be the target of the law.

It is certainly possible to find recognised arguments to the effect that the conscious organisation of crime makes it worse. For example, under English sentencing law an offence is regarded as aggravated, and thus deserving of greater punishment, if it is organised. The rationale is that such crimes are more likely than others to involve premeditation and planning as well as an enhanced potential for causing harm (Ashworth, 2000: 136). It might also be added that organised groups are likely to be able to muster greater resources than individuals and therefore to be able to perpetrate more ambitious crimes than would otherwise be possible as a consequence. Beyond these arguments based on harm, there are also policy grounds in favour of framing a criminalisation strategy in terms of the organisation of crime. From the perspective of crime prevention, logic suggests that an approach aimed at the level of the organisation is likely to produce greater crime reduction dividends than one which requires dissipated law enforcement efforts across a spectrum of individual end behaviour offences. Added to this, especially where criminal organisations of any hierarchical complexity are concerned, it may be difficult to establish criminal liability for the commission of specific 'end behaviour' offences on the part of certain individuals if the extent of their participation in those offences is minimal, even though their aggregate involvement in the organisation's activities is great. A form of criminalisation that focuses on association with the organisation may get round this difficulty.

A third perspective on the harm caused by transnational organised crime suggests that its truly invidious character stems not so much from its immediate activities nor from their organised nature, but from the potential of such organisations to accumulate a concentration of illicit power of such magnitude that they can begin to challenge the authority of the state. The criminological literature provides some evidence that criminal organisations can become culturally embedded in a manner that threatens legitimate economic and social structures or draws sustenance from their inherent weakness (Passas and Nelken, 1993; Shelley, 1996, 1999; Wiles, 1999). Interestingly, the sorts of conditions that appear to contribute to this parasitic process verge on a description of the opposite of those that are achieving recognition as calculated to induce stability in law and order (Bottoms, 2002). They include the existence of a critical mass of individuals who share a rival set of values from those of mainstream society, or who have merely become disaffected from those values and from the rule of law, together with the accompanying absence, decay or collapse of official state apparatus to provide the means by which a reasonable living standard may be secured. In combination, these features seem to create a fertile environment for organised crime to flourish by establishing an unofficial, alternative infrastructure which provides a substitute system of social order and, more generally, replaces the amenities and services which the state is failing to supply.

On one level this process might sound relatively benign. However, the underlying qualitative nature of the organisations concerned should not be overlooked. What is being described is a situation in which illicit organisations acquire the potential to achieve a position in which they are able to exercise a system of governance over a community, thus acquiring a stronghold from which to perpetrate their unlawful activities. Not only is this state of affairs liable to generate crime in the local environment since, for transparent reasons, the mode through which social control is exercised is likely to rely heavily on fear, intimidation and violence (Arlaachi, 1998) but, as the alternative culture becomes entrenched, the socially corroding activities with which it is associated are likely to spread outwards into surrounding communities, including across borders (Shelley, 1996, 1999).

Reviewing the analysis above, the unsurprising conclusion emerges that a variety of reasons exists for categorising transnational organised crime as harmful. But perhaps less obviously, it can also be seen that, potentially, this means that there is a complementary set of interlocking strategies that might be adopted towards its criminalisation. Whether they are feasible in practice, however, is another matter, and is dependent on the need to take account of their compatibility with the other propositions concerning the criminal law that were sketched out in the previous section. As regards the first two perspectives on harm, the source of the difficulties that they present for criminalisation can be reduced to two fundamental issues: the technical problems associated with framing suitable offences to combat the organisation of crime and the traditional jurisdictional parameters placed on the application of the criminal law. These points will now be enlarged upon. The structural breakdown analysis that underpins the third perspective requires separate consideration, and will be dealt with afterwards.

Turning, then, to the matter of the organisation of crime, a useful way to illustrate the issues that it presents is to consider the consequences of taking the apparently straightforward step of literally criminalising participation in transnational organised crime. It is an approach found in the United Nations Convention against Transnational Organised Crime. Despite carrying the ostensible endorsement of this powerful body, however, a cursory reflection is sufficient to show that it is fraught with difficulty. As a matter of ordinary everyday understanding, whenever two individuals conspire together to commit an offence, the resulting crime can be said to be 'organised'. However, small-scale criminal enterprises of this type fall well short of the conceptual image of offending behaviour under consideration here. A contrast is often drawn between Mafia-type organisations and their activities, on the one hand, and 'ordinary decent organised crime', on the other, with a view to discriminating between the nature and magnitude of the threat that each represents. Empirically, however, it has been pointed out that it is far from clear that these phenomena are as distinct as they are commonly painted (Stelfox, 1998). Second, the notion of 'organisation' conjures up a sense of stability over time and of coherence of membership, both in terms of there being criteria by which those who belong can be distinguished from those who do not and some kind of longevity. Again, however, the available evidence casts significant doubt on the validity of these assumptions with respect to the gamut of enterprises that are responsible for the commission of transnational organised crime.

These points return attention to the definitional problems that were alluded to in the introduction, exposing the deficiencies of the common sense 'we know it when we see it' approach. Quite simply, the term 'transnational organised crime' is too conceptually imprecise to be legally satisfactory and can even be regarded as dangerous when regarded from a civil liberties perspective. Its use in defining the group of offenders against whom specially designed measures are intended to be targeted carries an inherent risk that, unintentionally, many 'ordinary' offenders will be drawn into the scope of highly coercive law enforcement measures despite the fact that their criminality does not justify their application. It also risks violating important issues of principle. For instance, it is a basic requirement of the rule of law that the criminal law should be sufficiently clear for individuals to be able to discriminate between those acts that will infringe the norms that it lays down and those which will not (Ashworth, 1999: 76–8). Vaguely drafted crimes with the potential to cover an enormous breadth of conduct contradict this tenet. Moreover, in so far as the problem of such over-inclusiveness might be rectified by the courts giving relevant offences an artificially narrow reading, they risk the allegation that they have overstepped their proper constitutional role by usurping the function of the legislature to determine the content of the criminal law (ibid.: 60).

An alternative approach to the criminalisation of the organisation of crime, which avoids some of these pitfalls, is to focus on the substantive 'end behaviour' offences that crystallise from the organisation's activities and then trace liability back to include those with a hand in their commission, planning and execution. In essence, this is the model adopted by the English law of complicity, according to which it is an offence to 'aid, abet, counsel or procure' a substantive offence. However, this strategy, too, is not without practical and theoretical difficulties. One important issue, for example, concerns the point at which the transition occurs between conduct that is too remote from a completed crime for it to be legitimate for the criminal law to intervene, to circumstances that are sufficiently proximate for such regulation to be appropriate. Related to it is a second question as to just how much an individual has to do in order to be included in the net of those who are regarded as accountable under the criminal law for bringing an offence about. Difficulties also arise in connection with the attribution of *mens rea*. If an actor is not directly responsible for the resulting harm that springs from the commission of an offence, just what and how much must she or he know, believe or suspect for it to be just to regard her or him as blameworthy? And what if she or he has a change of mind? Should it be possible to withdraw from involvement in the criminal enterprise, thereby avoiding liability for it, especially once an offence has been embarked upon; and, if so, how? That these are genuinely searching questions is borne out by the fact that they continue to trouble the courts even though the legislation that underpins this area of law, the Accessories and Abettors Act, dates back to 1861 (Ashworth, 1999: Chapter 10).

Compounding all of the difficulties in crafting adequate and effective criminal laws that have been outlined so far is the further hurdle presented by the fact that the behaviour in issue is transnational in character. Immediately it can be seen that this poses a challenge to the strong traditional presumption that criminal liability is founded in national territoriality. It means that perpetrators can slip through the law enforcement net because discrete elements of relevant offences occur in different jurisdictions, because they are less likely to be detected than other crimes and because, even if detected, they are less likely to be the subject of law enforcement effort. There is little incentive for law enforcement agencies to invest resources in pursuing the investigation of offences if it is clear that a conviction is never likely to result. Furthermore, even where offences are completed within a single jurisdiction, offenders may escape justice by fleeing across borders so as to be beyond the reach of the applicable criminal courts. And, as if this catalogue of difficulties was not enough, there is evidence that well-informed intending offenders sometimes select particular jurisdictions in which to perpetrate their crimes on the grounds of the comparative ineffectiveness of law enforcement and/or leniency of their penal laws (Sevenster, 1992: 30). In short, offenders are known to 'forum shop'.

Before examining the sorts of steps that have been taken to address these deficiencies, it is necessary to say something about the third level at which transnational organised crime can be categorised as harmful: the structural breakdown perspective. Despite the fact that this analysis provides the most convincing account of why a response is needed in the interests of social defence, it is difficult to see that the criminal law provides a suitable mode of response to the type of fundamental harm that it describes. Rather, the analysis would appear to invite a governance solution that is targeted at restoring a legitimate infrastructure and combating the underlying causes of social and structural decay which permitted the power vacuum to arise (Baker, 2002).

## Adaptations of criminal law to deal with transnational organised crime and their limitations

Consistent with the analysis in the previous section, the measures that have been adopted to try to modify the criminal law into a more suitable tool for responding to transnational organised crime fall into two broad areas: measures that are designed to tackle the organised nature of the behaviour and measures that are targeted at overcoming the jurisdictional barriers to law enforcement. Each will be considered briefly.

Starting with attempts to address the organisation of crime, a lot of the fresh thinking has been devoted to identifying ways in which the criminal law can be used to remove the incentives for offending and/or to disturb the infrastructure that enables it to be carried out. A prime example is the criminalisation of money laundering. There are persuasive arguments that money laundering is a harmful activity in its own right because, for instance, of its potential to destabilise currency markets and to ferment bribery and corruption. However, over and above these considerations, a case for its criminalisation can be made on the twin grounds that the motivation for much organised crime is financial and, second, that a major source of strength of relevant organisations is derived from their economic power. Therefore, effective anti-money-laundering measures should simultaneously remove a key inducement for engaging in the criminal enterprise and weaken the organisations concerned (Gilmore, 1995). A number of other features of anti-money-laundering legislation also reinforce these central strategic goals. One of them is the way in which it affects professional groups. The difficulty of disposing of significant amounts of capital in the absence of assistance from bankers, accountants, lawyers and other professionals has been recognised. Consequently, legal responsibilities have been conferred on these groups to develop anti-money-laundering policies and practices; responsibilities that are backed up by the threat of criminal sanctions for breach. These professionals, of course, are private individuals and/or undertakings. Thus it can be seen that a further important aspect of this approach is the introduction of compulsory obligations on the private sector to participate in policing the legislation.

Just as with the more conventional applications of the criminal law that were examined above, it has become evident the implementation of this new type of approach is not unproblematic. To give a flavour, one issue that has arisen has been the encouragement of displacement activity. Instead of channelling capital through banks and other primary financial agencies, once these became subject to effective regulation, the launderers adapted to the new conditions of the marketplace by investing in other forms of property. Consequently, it proved necessary to broaden the net of legal regulation to incorporate a broader span of the financial and property sectors. Nor is displacement a phenomenon that is unique to the money laundering context. It has also been detected in relation to the legislative controls on precursor chemicals that are used in the manufacture of illicit drugs, with similar consequences in terms of pressure for more extensive regulation. Unfortunately, however, the drive for greater regulation generates additional problems in its wake because of its intrusive impact on legitimate business and associated commercial costs. Moreover, beyond the practical drawbacks, these types of approach also provoke civil liberties concerns. For example, with respect to money laundering, the legislation places obligations on affected professionals to disclose certain information about clients and customers to law enforcement agencies in a manner that is contrary to the normal presumption of confidentiality (Levi, 1991).

Turning to measures that are targeted at overcoming the jurisdictional barriers to law enforcement, a variety of techniques is being used. With respect to a small number of offences the decision has been taken to permit the courts to exercise jurisdiction over events that have occurred abroad. However, this approach is unusual. The main focus of attention has been in the field of mutual legal assistance and other measures designed to improve co-operation between law enforcement authorities, including the development of information networks to enable intelligence to be shared across jurisdictions. Some of the most sophisticated initiatives are being developed by the European Union as part of its programme to create an 'Area of Freedom, Security and Justice' within its territory. Apart from measures that are targeted at specific forms of transnational organised crime, moves are afoot to achieve a situation in which the principle of mutual recognition governs the dealings between the police and judicial authorities of the member states (European Union, 1999; Rees and Webber, 2002).

Once more, the steps that have been taken in this area are not entirely satisfactory. Serious practical difficulties arise in attempting to put mutual legal assistance into effect and it remains to be seen whether the European Union's ambitious goal to implement mutual recognition will prove possible. In order for it to work, the relevant authorities will have to cultivate a high degree of trust in one another and to overcome cultural differences in approach as between their policing and legal systems (Nelken, 1994). On a broader plane, there is also concern that initiatives of this type place a disproportionate premium on the interests of law enforcement, while the need to afford adequate protection to the rights of suspects and defendants remains relatively neglected. Lastly, it is possible to interpret measures that enhance cross-jurisdictional co-operation as undermining the traditional nexus between criminal jurisdiction and statehood. For those who believe in the desirability of the latter link, they therefore represent a significant threat to the principle of national sovereignty.

## Conclusion

Despite the fact that the term 'transnational organised crime' has fallen into colloquial use, it is clear that it poses a host of problems as far as its regulation through the criminal law is concerned. In part this is because of a failure of legal technology: there is a fundamental mismatch between the basic characteristics of the behaviour concerned and the traditional parameters of the criminal law. However, it is also symptomatic of a conceptual failure that applies to a growing variety of cross-jurisdictional threats which are not of a nature to be suitable for a conventional defence response. Consequently, it is increasingly apparent that the traditional dichotomy drawn between matters of internal and external security is breaking down, so that what were once regarded as separate issues are becoming fused. Hypothetically, this might suggest that the criminal law should be abandoned and that energy should be devoted instead to the development of an alternative set of legal tools that might be better suited to dealing with such problems. However, for the present at least, governments have chosen to seek modifications to the criminal law to try to fashion it into a more suitable vehicle for addressing transnational security issues. They thus appear to remain confident that its mechanisms and infrastructure can be manipulated so as to yield viable solutions to these problems.

# References

Arlaachi, P. (1998) 'Some observations on illegal markets', in V. Ruggiero, N. South and I. Taylor (eds) *The New European Criminology: Crime and Social Order in Europe*. London: Routledge.

Ashworth, A.J. (1999) *Principles of Criminal Law*, 3rd edn. Oxford: OUP.

—— (2000) *Sentencing and Criminal Justice*, 3rd edn. London: Butterworths.

Ashworth, A.J. and Blake, M. (1996) 'The presumption of innocence in English criminal law', *Criminal Law Review* 306–17.

Baker, E. (2002) 'Criminal jurisdiction, the public dimension to "effective protection" and the construction of community–citizen relations', in A.A. Dashwood *et al.* (eds) *Cambridge Yearbook of European Legal Studies Volume 4*. Oxford: Hart Publishing.

Bottoms, A.E (2002) 'Morality, crime, compliance and public policy', in A.E. Bottoms and M. Tonry (eds) *Ideology, Crime and Criminal Justice: A Symposium in Honour of Sir Leon Radzinowicz*. Cullompton: Willan Publishing.

Clarkson, C.M.V. and Keating, H.M. (1998) *Criminal Law: Text and Materials*, 4th edn. London: Sweet & Maxwell.

European Union (1999) Conclusions of the Tampere European Council, 15 and 16 October 1999, *Bulletin of the European Union*, Bull.EU 10–99.

Garland, D. (1996) 'The limits of the sovereign state: strategies of crime control in contemporary society', *British Journal of Criminology* 36: 445–71.

Gilmore, W. (1995) *Dirty Money: The Evolution of Money Laundering Counter-Measures*. Strasbourg: Council of Europe.

Levi, M. (1991) 'Regulating money laundering: the death of bank secrecy in the UK', *British Journal of Criminology* 31: 109–25.

Nelken, D. (1994) 'Whom can you trust? The future of comparative criminology', in D. Nelken (ed.) *The Futures of Criminology*. London: Sage.

Passas, N. and Nelken, D. (1993) 'The thin blue line between legitimate and criminal enterprises: subsidy and frauds in the European Community', *Crime, Law and Social Change* 19: 223–43.

Rees, G.W. and Webber, M. (2002) 'Fighting organised crime: the European Union and internal security', in A. Crawford (ed.) *Crime and Insecurity: the Governance of Safety in Europe*. Cullompton: Willan Publishing.

Sevenster, H. (1992) 'Criminal law and EC Law', *Common Market Law Review* 29: 29–70.

Shaw, J. (1998) 'The interpretation of European Union citizenship', *Modern Law Review* 61: 293–317.

194 Estella Baker

Shelley, L. (1996) 'Criminal kaleidoscope: the diversification and adaptation of criminal activities in the Soviet successor states', *European Journal of Crime, Criminal Law and Criminal Justice* 4: 243–56.
—— (1999) 'Crime of the former socialist states: implications for Western Europe', in G.J.N. Bruinsma and C.D. van der Vijver (eds) *Public Safety in Europe*. Enschede: University of Twente.
Simester, A.P. and Sullivan, G.R. (2000) *Criminal Law: Theory and Doctrine*. Oxford: Hart Publishing.
Stelfox, P. (1998) 'Policing lower levels of organised crime in England and Wales', *Howard Journal of Criminal Justice* 37, 4: 393–406.
von Hirsch, A., Bottoms, A.E., Burney, E. and Wikström, P.-O. (1999) *Criminal Deterrence and Sentence Severity*. Oxford: Hart Publishing.
Wiles, P. (1999) 'Troubled neighbourhoods', in G.J.N. Bruinsma and C.D. van der Vijver (eds) *Public Safety in Europe*. Enschede: University of Twente.

# 12 Countering the chameleon threat of dirty money

'Hard' and 'soft' law in the emergence of a global regime against money laundering and terrorist finance

*Valsamis Mitsilegas*

## Introduction

Recent years have witnessed an unprecedented international mobilisation towards the elimination of the flow of 'dirty' money into the global financial system. International initiatives in the field first emerged in the late 1980s, in the context of the war on drugs, targeting the laundering of proceeds from drug trafficking. This was achieved via the 'traditional' route of an international Convention, leading to binding, 'hard' law obligations for the parties ratifying it. In parallel to that, the perceived threat of dirty money to the stability of the financial system, has led to the promulgation of 'soft' law instruments, in the form of ethical principles and recommendations, which were not legally binding but aimed at encouraging action by credit and financial institutions. Since then, both 'hard' and 'soft' law avenues have been used in the development of a global, multi-level anti-money-laundering regime,[1] with money laundering countermeasures being constantly updated and expanded. This chapter aims to examine the role and relationship between 'hard' and 'soft' law in the evolution of this example of legal globalisation, which has been legitimised through a securitisation discourse associating 'dirty' money with transnational threats such as corruption, organised crime and, lately, terrorism. By focusing on this ongoing 'securitisation' process, the chapter will critically evaluate the development of these measures and the challenges they pose to well-established legal principles, as well as society and the economy.

## Fighting the 'war on drugs'

The first international attempts to counter money laundering were made in the context of the escalation of the 'war on drugs' in the 1980s. This decade was characterised by a policy shift – largely led by the United States – towards global repressive, law enforcement-led measures aimed at combating drug trafficking. This 'internationalisation' of the war on drugs (term used by Stewart, 1990) led to the adoption in 1988 of the United Nations Convention Against Illicit Traffic in Narcotic Drugs and Psychotropic Substances, which was described by George Bush, then President of the United States, as 'of fundamental importance to effective international co-operation to combat drugs' (cited in Gilmore, 1999: 50). Along with criminalising drug trafficking, the Convention is the first international law instrument to establish an offence of laundering the proceeds of drug trafficking (Article 3(1)). It also included a series of provisions on confiscation, extradition and mutual legal assistance in relation to these offences.

The criminalisation of money laundering was deemed to be an effective weapon in the international war on drugs. It was justified in the Preamble to the 1988 Convention by the aim of depriving traffickers of the proceeds of their crimes 'and thereby eliminate their main incentive for so doing' (Preamble, 6th recital). This 'deterrence' objective was coupled with the need to facilitate international law enforcement and judicial co-operation in order to detect and prosecute the offences established by the Convention. The introduction of an international money laundering offence was deemed paramount to the achievement of this aim. According to the US delegation:

> Because all Parties are obligated to establish Article 3, paragraph 1 offences as criminal offences in their domestic law, any requirements of dual criminality, that is that the offence is criminal in both jurisdictions, in a Party's extradition law should be met. Although there has been almost universal recognition that illicit drug trafficking offences are extraditable offences, narcotics related money laundering is a new criminal offence for many states and has not been traditionally recognised as an extraditable offence. The universal recognition of narcotics related money laundering as an extraditable offence is one of the most important aspects of this article.
>
> (Cited in Commonwealth Secretariat, 1991: 6)

Article 3(1) of the Convention, upon which subsequent international and regional criminalisation initiatives are modelled, defines money laundering as:

i   The conversion or transfer of property, knowing that such property is derived from any of the drugs offences established by the Convention, or from an act of participation in such offences, for the purpose of concealing or disguising the illicit origin of the property or of assisting any person who is involved in the commission of such an offence to evade the legal consequences of his actions;

ii  The concealment or disguise of the true nature, source, location, disposition, movement, rights with respect to, or ownership of property, knowing that such property is derived from any of the drugs offences established by the Convention or from an act of participation in such offences (Article 3(1)(b));

iii   and, subject to the constitutional principles and the basic concepts of the Parties' legal systems, the acquisition, possession or use of property, knowing, at the time of receipt, that such property was derived from Convention drugs offences or from an act of participation in them. Participation in, association or conspiracy to commit, attempts to commit, and aiding, abetting, facilitating and counselling the commission of any of these offences is also criminalised (Article 3(1)(c)(i) and (iv)).

It is evident that the Convention defines money laundering in a broad manner. While knowledge of the origin of proceeds is expressly required for the *mens rea* of all of the laundering offences to be established, money laundering, which is perceived as a sophisticated, complex and multi-layered process,[2] can be the mere possession or use of drug money, or even the less clear 'acquisition'. The wording of this provision (Article 3(1)(c)(i)) raised concerns to a number of Convention delegates, which resulted in the safeguard clause allowing its adoption subject to national constitutional and fundamental legal principles.

The requirement of knowledge for the establishment of a money laundering offence is of pivotal significance. Without the element of knowledge, most of the acts criminalised by the Convention (such as the conversion or transfer of property and its possession or use) constitute, at first sight, everyday, ordinary commercial transactions, which are not only commonplace, but also 'outwardly innocent behavior [sic]' (Abrams, 1989: 35). What renders this behaviour punishable is purely the mental state of the offender: the law demands from those involved in financial transactions to take a moral stance against drug money. At the same time, through its connection with the threat of drug trafficking, money itself is stripped of its neutrality: it becomes 'dirty'.

## Protecting the integrity of the financial system

The criminalisation of drug money laundering was accompanied by growing awareness of the use of the banking and financial system for the achievement of the launderers' aims. This realisation has led to concerns regarding the negative impact that the flow of 'dirty' money could have to the integrity and stability of the international financial system. This led to the mobilisation of international financial regulators, aiming to establish guidelines to protect the financial system from the laundering threat. An initiative towards this aim was put forward by the Basle Committee on Banking Supervision, whose purpose is to provide regular co-operation between its member countries on banking supervisory matters. This is achieved not through the adoption of legally binding norms (as the Committee does not have such powers), but through the issuance of guidelines which members are encouraged to apply (Alford, 1993: 247).[3] In the same year as the publication of the UN drug trafficking Convention, the Committee issued 'a general statement of ethical principles' aiming to encourage banks' management to put in place effective procedures to ensure: that all persons conducting business with their institutions are properly identified; that transactions that do not appear legitimate are discouraged; and that co-operation with law enforcement agencies is achieved (Preamble, 6th recital).

The Basle principles constitute the first major attempt by the developed world to shift bankers' 'liberal' attitude in doing business towards a more 'regulated' model which requires enhanced diligence regarding customers and transactions, as well as co-operation with the police. It is interesting to note the justification of these guidelines, as the Committee notes that:

> Public confidence in banks, and hence their stability, can be undermined by adverse publicity as a result of inadvertent association by banks with criminals. In addition, banks may lay themselves open to direct losses from fraud, either through negligence in screening undesirable customers or where the integrity of their own officers has been undermined through association with criminals.
>
> (Cited in Gilmore, 1992)

The moral undertones of the passage are easily discernible: not only is action needed in order to protect the stability of the system, but it is acknowledged that bankers may themselves be responsible for this through their association with criminals. In this manner, the seemingly different worlds of 'clean' and 'trustworthy' financial systems and the innocent public are associated with 'dirty' money, 'undesirable' customers and criminals. As these worlds intermingle, the boundaries become blurred: the 'illegitimacy'/'immorality' of criminals is transferred to banks. The more 'dirty' money gets 'cleansed', the more 'contaminated' the financial system becomes.

The Basle principles were a precursor to action undertaken by the G-7 in the field. At the July 1989 Paris Summit, the G-7 leaders decided to create the Financial Action Task Force (FATF), an independent international body whose Secretariat is housed at the OECD. Its mandate was 'to assess the results of co-operation already undertaken in order to prevent the utilisation of the banking system for the purpose of money laundering, and to consider additional preventative efforts in this field, including the adaptation of the legal and regulatory systems so as to enhance multilateral judicial assistance' (Gilmore, 1998: 34).[4] Action by the FATF was not justified solely on police efficiency grounds: as was noted by a former FATF President in 1992, 'combating money laundering is not just a matter of fighting crime but of preserving the integrity of financial institutions and ultimately the financial system as a whole' (cited in Gilmore, 1999: 83).

The examination of the nature of the money laundering phenomenon and existing countermeasures has led, in 1990, to the adoption by the FATF of 40 Recommendations for action. The Recommendations were not legally binding, but rather a 'soft law' instrument aiming to provide a blueprint for global standards in the field. They were grouped under three central objectives: the improvement of national legal anti-money-laundering systems, most notably in the field of criminal law; the strengthening of international co-operation; and the enhancement of the role of the financial system in the fight against money laundering. It is with regard to this third objective that the Recommendations had the greatest impact, as they expanded considerably both the content and the scope of the Basle principles. The Recommendations call for both credit and financial institutions to undertake a series of duties related to:

- *customer identification and record keeping rules* – credit and financial institutions should not keep anonymous accounts or accounts in obviously fictitious names, and identify their customers on the basis of reliable documentation; to obtain information regarding beneficial ownership of accounts; and to maintain, for at least five years, transaction records (Recommendations 12–14), and
- *increased diligence* – financial institutions should *inter alia* pay special attention to complex or unusual transactions, whose background and purpose must be examined; and they are permitted/required to promptly report to the competent authorities their money laundering suspicions. They should not warn their customers about the existence of these reports and should comply with instructions from the authorities and develop programmes against money laundering (Recommendations 15–20).

These far-reaching Recommendations complemented the UN Convention, which did not include any provisions on the prevention of money laundering. Although not legally binding, they were immensely influential in the development of subsequent international and regional initiatives (such as the 1991 EC money laundering Directive), have been implemented by FATF members and, as will be seen later in this chapter, have been exported to non-FATF countries as well. They brought about unprecedented changes in commercial relationships: credit and financial institutions are now obliged to keep detailed files, report suspicious transactions to state authorities and keep investigations secret from their clients. This shifts considerably the balance in the banker–customer relationship, as the former have to reduce the protection of the customers' privacy in order to co-operate with the state not only reacting to requests, but also proactively, by reporting suspicious transactions.

It has been mainly the imposition of proactive reporting duties to financial institutions which led commentators to speak of the 'death of bank secrecy' (Levi, 1991). Along with implications for legal principles of confidentiality, privacy and everyday commercial life, the new duties have a major impact in the re-negotiation of the relationship of the individual and the private sector with the state (Mitsilegas, 2003). The discourse underlying calls for action against money laundering by the private sector has combined the need to protect the financial system (which, in the case of the European Community, served also to justify the adoption of EC legislation, as the EC did not have competence to adopt criminal law measures) with a moral crusade geared towards financial institutions. The latter cannot afford to follow the 'amoral' laws of business any more, as even their negligent association with the 'dirty' money from drugs makes them morally stigmatised and, thus, criminal. They have no choice but to co-operate with the state in the fight against crime.

This 'new policing' (Levi, 1997) is a clear example at the global level of what Garland calls the 'responsibilisation strategy', whose recurring message is the displacement of the state's responsibility for preventing and controlling crime. The state cannot fulfil these tasks alone and thus requires the active co-operation of citizens: the latter 'must be made to recognise that they too have a responsibility in this regard, and must be persuaded to change their practices in order to reduce criminal opportunities and increase informal controls' (Garland, 1996: 453). This does not imply, however, a relaxing of state controls: in reality, informal controls (which in this case result in a flow of large volumes of everyday financial information towards financial intelligence units) occur in parallel and in addition to state controls, thus reinforcing them.

## Countering organised and serious crime

In view of the aforementioned developments, one would expect action in the 1990s to have focused on the implementation of the UN Convention provisions and the FATF Recommendations. However, such implementation did not stop the development of further money laundering countermeasures globally. This continuous production of anti-laundering norms is inextricably linked with the emergence of organised crime as perhaps the most serious global threat in international policy discourse. The perceived need to counter the organised crime threat legitimised the extension of the global anti-money-laundering framework. At the same time, work by the FATF and the United Nations, constantly evaluating the implementation of the measures and the development of money laundering trends and typologies, has led to calls for the adaptation of the existing framework to the new reality. This had as a result the considerable widening and deepening of global anti-money-laundering measures.

### Extending the criminalisation of money laundering

The debate here concerned criminalising the laundering of proceeds not only from drug trafficking (as stipulated by the 1988 Convention), but from all serious crime. An *impetus* in that direction could be provided by the 1990 Council of Europe Convention on Laundering, Search, Seizure and Confiscation of the Proceeds of Crime (see Nilsson, 1991). The Convention largely follows the wording of the UN instrument, but extends criminalisation to the laundering of proceeds of 'any predicate offence' (Articles 6(1) and 1(a) and (e)). According to the Explanatory Memorandum to the Convention, one of its purposes is 'to facilitate international co-operation as regards investigative assistance, search, seizure and confiscation of the proceeds from all types of criminality, especially serious crimes, and in particular drug offences, arms dealing, terrorist offences, trafficking in children and young women ... and other offences which generate large profits' (cited in Gilmore, 1999: 125). This extension to an all-crimes-laundering offence is however not obligatory, as parties to the Convention may formulate reservations regarding its scope (Article 6(4)). It was noted, however, in the late 1990s, that the trend was to criminalise 'all-crimes' money laundering (Csonka, 1998: 96).

A similar trend can be discerned in the implementation of the EC money laundering Directive by EU member states. The 1991 Directive followed a 'minimum standard' approach. It prohibited the laundering of the proceeds of drug trafficking, while leaving to member states the discretion to extend criminalisation to further offences. None of them restricted the offence to the proceeds of crime, with some opting for the inclusion of a broader list of predicate offences and others for an 'all-crimes' laundering offence (Commission, 1998). This Directive has now been replaced by its amended version, adopted at the end of 2001 (*OJ* L 344, 28.12.2001, p. 76). It criminalises the laundering of proceeds of drug trafficking, organised crime, (at least serious) fraud, corruption, offences 'which generate substantial proceeds and are punishable by a severe custodial sentence' by member states, and, by December 2004, all serious crime as defined in the 1998 Joint Action on confiscation.

This extension of the predicate offences has also been influenced by work done within the framework of the FATF. In its revised Recommendations of 1996, following an assessment of the implementation of the 1990 version, the criminalisation of non-drug-money laundering is made mandatory. Recommendation 4 states that 'each country should extend the offence of drug money laundering to one based on serious offences', which will be defined by each member. The role of the FATF in this context has been welcomed, as it has 'played an important part in the efforts to decouple money laundering from the initial preoccupation with drug trafficking thus ensuring that this aspect of crime control strategy is now much more widely available in efforts to counter other activities generating substantial international concern' (Gilmore, 1998: 38).

The criminalisation of the laundering of the proceeds of all crime signifies the transformation of the money laundering offence from a tool limited to the fight against major international threats such as drug trafficking, to countering any 'serious crime' and perhaps eventually 'all crime'. This is welcomed by those believing that the division of criminal money into categories is artificial and hinders investigation and prosecution of money laundering (United Nations, 1998: 66). However, it is difficult to balance the broad criminalisation of money laundering – which has been deemed essential to combat serious transnational threats – with the fight against less serious offences. Moreover, in view of the push towards a global money laundering definition in order to enhance international judicial and police co-operation, this extension is not unproblematic. It is unclear what 'serious crime' is, as this may be defined differently in different jurisdictions. This may cause significant problems of legal certainty, which has to be observed in view of the nature of information exchanged.

### The widening of reporting duties

A noticeable trend in money laundering typologies in the 1990s has been the use by money launderers of institutions and professions – both inside and outside the financial sector – that were not covered by the anti-money-laundering framework. Along with the lack of regulation, this trend has been associated with the increasing sophistication of money laundering activities, which involve a wide range of intermediary professions of varied expertise. According to the FATF:

> Accountants, solicitors, and company formation agents turn up even more frequently in anti-money laundering investigations. In establishing and administering the foreign legal entities which conceal money laundering schemes, it is these professionals that increasingly provide the apparent sophistication and extra layer of respectability to some laundering operations.
>
> (FATF, 1997: para. 16)

The FATF addressed these developments in its revised 1996 Recommendations. Recommendation 8 (ex. 9) was revised to include an additional indent calling on member states to ensure the application of anti-money-laundering standards to non-bank financial institutions which are not subject to a formal prudential supervisory regime in all countries, such as *bureaux de change*. Recommendation 9 (ex. 10), on the other hand, extends the Recommendations' duties to 'the conduct of financial activities as a commercial undertaking by businesses or professions which are not financial institutions, where such conduct is not allowed or not prohibited'.

The extension of the *ratione personae* scope of the prevention measures has also been the subject of heated debate, especially in view of the application of the duty to report suspicious transactions to the legal profession. The changes brought in the early stages of the money laundering countermeasures were unprecedented in challenging bank confidentiality and the nature of the banker–customer relationship. The same challenges apply here, only reinforced: in most countries the relationship between the lawyer and his or her client enjoys a higher level of protection than the banker–customer relationship and is subject to strict confidentiality rules. Although the protection varies from country to country, the confidential nature of the lawyer–client relationship has been acknowledged, albeit in a specific context, to be a common legal principle in the European Union (case *AM & S Europe Ltd v Commission* [1982] ECR 1575), with a constitutional foundation in a number of countries (Xanthaki, 2001). Even in English law, where legal privilege was not considered to be as far reaching as in civil law jurisdictions, a recent House of Lords judgment recognised it as a fundamental human right (*Regina v Inland Revenue Commissioners, Ex parte Morgan Grenfell and Co Ltd, The Times,* 20.5.2002).

The extension of reporting duties to lawyers places them in a very difficult position as they have to balance their paramount duty to defend their client's interest and their duty to co-operate with the authorities in the fight against crime. This balance is shifted considerably, as now the lawyer has not only to respond to police inquiries, but also to proactively report suspicions and not to tip off her client of a pending money laundering investigation. This not only has important privacy implications, but may also jeopardise the defendant's right to a fair trial. The issue is the subject of a constitutional challenge in Canada.[5] In the EU, the inclusion of lawyers in the revised money laundering Directive has been the subject of heated controversy, leading to more than two years of negotiations. The compromise reached in the Conciliation procedure between the Council and the European Parliament includes lawyers only when they participate in a series of specifically enumerated financial transactions. However, member states are not obliged to apply reporting duties to lawyers in the course of ascertaining the legal position for their client or performing their task of defending or representing their client in judicial proceedings (Mitsilegas, 2003). It remains to be seen how the Directive will be implemented in member states and what kind of balance the legislator and the judiciary will strike between the conflicting interests at stake.

## Countering tax evasion

A matter of controversy regarding the definition of 'serious crime' concerns the inclusion of tax evasion in the list of predicate offences. Its inclusion is highly problematic, in view of the thin line that divides it with – potentially legitimate – tax avoidance schemes. It is further acknowledged that both tax evasion and international exchange of tax information 'are politically sensitive issues even for the FATF membership', with none of the 40 Recommendations being tax specific (Gilmore, 1999: 112). Tax offences represent a challenge to money laundering policy-makers as tax activities – even if illegal – are essentially economic and can thus be viewed separately from criminal offences such as drug trafficking, which occur *outside* the legal marketplace, with the proceeds then filtered into the financial system. Further, tax evasion involves taking *legally* earned income and either hiding its very existence or disguising its nature (United Nations, 1998: 5). In extending the offence, money laundering would thus cover legal income that has *become* illegal through tax evasion.

The absence of references to money laundering from tax evasion seems paradoxical in view of the increased action by the FATF against offshore financial centres. Pressure in this direction has been intensified by the decision by the FATF to establish a 'black list' of non-co-operative countries and territories, including all countries (both inside and outside the FATF) 'whose detrimental practices seriously and unjustifiably hamper the fight against money laundering' (FATF, 2000: 6). Action against 'non-co-operative' countries is based on the assumption that there needs to be a uniform global regime against money laundering, whose enforcement has been elevated as the main task of the FATF. Uniform global standards are justified on the basis of the need to 'ensure the stability of the international financial system' which is jeopardised by the competition between offshore centres (ibid.: 1).

The emphasis on the financial impact that offshore centres have on the stability of the financial system signifies a shift of emphasis from the use of money laundering countermeasures as a tool against crime to their use in order to impose the G-7 financial standards world-wide and to discourage tax evasion. According to the *Economist*, 'some critics reckon that the hidden agenda behind the attack on money laundering is for big countries to make it much harder for their citizens to evade taxes by cutting off those offshore centres that offer low taxes from the international payment system' (*Economist*, 2001). This is confirmed by a United Nations study, which states that 'the greater the domestic clamp down on taxation and the more resentful that citizens are about paying taxes . . ., the greater will be the demand for banking secrecy' (UN, 1998: 51).

The FATF has been drawing up 'black lists' of 'non-co-operative' jurisdictions since 2000.[6] 'Blacklisting' seems an effective way to ensure global compliance with anti-money-laundering standards by putting jurisdictions that are deemed to be 'non-co-operative' under the threat of severe economic sanctions. These may include, according to a statement by the G-7 in July 2000, conditions or restrictions on financial transactions and support from international financial instruments (Levi and Gilmore, 2002: 357). It is evidently a one-sided process, aimed at imposing, within the limited flexibility offered by the FATF Recommendations, the G-7/FATF model of financial regulation on the rest of the world. It is striking to note that it is an *ad hoc* body consisting of 'rich' countries, and not an international organisation, which evaluates, on the basis of soft law, action taken by sovereign states. What is striking in this regard is that the criteria for this evaluation are more demanding than the standards set out for the FATF members by the Recommendations (Levi and Gilmore, 2002: 358), thus reinforcing a 'double standard'.[7] This manner of creating global norms – through the unilateral stigmatisation of 'non-co-operative' states – has attracted major criticisms from the countries assessed. The latter may view the assessment process as a form of 'normative imperialism' which disregards the particular social, economic and political situation in developing countries and the fact that they may not have the same economic priorities as the FATF members. In the context of the Caribbean countries, the following quotation from the Director of Public Prosecutions in Barbados is worth noting:

> Efforts by small Caribbean states to diversify their economies are now being labelled as harmful taxation policies by the . . . OECD countries. The onslaught of global crime on such fragile economies in the face of such hostility by developed countries could undermine the democratic traditions of these states. The globalization of crime must be attacked by all states participating in mutually-respected multilateral fora. The March 2000 U.N. Offshore Forum in the Cayman Islands suggested that the United Nations is the best broker for the establishment of mechanisms and standards for the offshore centres.
>
> (Leacock, 2001: 277).

## Attacking terrorism

A further impetus for the extension of money laundering countermeasures has been created by the attacks of September 11. Along with the adoption of specific counter-terrorism measures world-wide, these events also accelerated legislative action in fields potentially related, but broader than terrorism. In the context of the European Union, this is exemplified primarily by the speedy adoption of the Framework Decision on the European Arrest Warrant, which, although covering in one way or the other most criminal offences, has been primarily justified as an emergency counter-terrorism response post-September 11. A similar story can be told with regard to the adoption of the revised money laundering Directive. At the time of the

attacks on the Twin Towers, the Directive was the matter of heated controversy between the Council and the Commission on the one hand, advocat-
ing *inter alia* a general extension of the Directive duties to the legal
profession, and the European Parliament, which resisted this move on the
basis of its potential impact on human rights and civil liberties. Pressure
post-September 11 resulted in a last-minute compromise, with the Parliament consenting, under a number of conditions, to the inclusion of lawyers
in the scope of the Directive in order to fight terrorism. As the Parliamentary Civil Liberties Committee noted, 'on the substance, the events of 11
September in the USA changed dramatically the point of view on the issue
because from that date on the money laundering Directive was widely considered as part of the fight against terrorism' (document A5–0380/2001,
cited in Mitsilegas, 2003). Although the Directive did not include specific
provisions on terrorism, the events leading to its adoption demonstrate that,
post-September 11, money laundering countermeasures are considered
essential to counter the terrorist threat by attacking terrorist funds.

International action geared at combating terrorist finance preceded
September 11, with the United Nations adopting a Convention for the
Suppression of the Financing of Terrorism. Article 2(1) criminalises
action by any person who by any means, directly or indirectly, unlawfully
and wilfully, provides or collects funds with the intention that they should
be used or in the knowledge that they are to be used, in full or in part, for
terrorist purposes. However, this commitment towards a broad criminalisation of terrorist finance has been reiterated after the events in New
York by the UN Security Council Resolution 1373(2001) of 28 September
2001, which calls for member states to prevent and suppress terrorist
finance, repeats the commitment of the 1999 Convention to criminalise it
and provides for the freezing of terrorist assets.

A similar commitment was made on September 25 in a statement by the
G-7 Finance Ministers, who stressed the importance of more vigorously
implementing UN sanctions on terrorist financing and called on the FATF
to encompass terrorist financing into its activities. This call, combined
with pressure from the US government[8] resulted in the swift adoption by
the FATF of a series of Special Recommendations on terrorist financing.
These should be combined with the 40 Recommendations on money laundering and call for: the ratification and implementation of UN instruments; the criminalisation of terrorist finance and associated money
laundering; freezing and confiscation of terrorist assets; reporting suspicious transactions related to terrorism; and international co-operation.
The Recommendations further call for the regulation and licensing of
persons or legal entities involved in alternative remittance schemes,
enhanced scrutiny regarding wire transfers and a focus on the role that
non-profit organisations can play in terrorist finance.

The FATF Special Recommendations were not the only soft law initiative to counter terrorist finance. In a move reminiscent of the crusade

against drug money laundering in the late 1980s, these Recommendations were followed by action by the Basle Committee, and the Wolfsberg Group of financial institutions, a group of eleven major international banks originally convened to issue global anti-money-laundering guidelines for international private banks in response to financial scandals concerning corrupt leaders of developing countries (Graham, 2001; Hinterseer, 2001).[9] Echoing the late 1980s discourse, action against terrorist finance has been justified by the need for financial institutions to cooperate with the authorities in the fight against terrorism (Wolfsberg principles), with terrorism perceived as a 'threat to financial stability' (Basle Committee, 2002: 1). According to the FATF, business relationships with terrorists could expose financial institutions to 'significant reputational, operational, and legal risk' (FATF, 2002: 1).

Notwithstanding the similarities in the justification and content of measures against terrorist finance with money laundering countermeasures, there is a fundamental difference: terrorist finance is not necessarily 'criminal', as it may often stem from perfectly legitimate sources.[10] This is acknowledged by the FATF, which states that a financial institution knowingly carrying out a transaction involving terrorist funds is guilty of an offence 'regardless of whether the assets involved in the transaction were the proceeds of criminal activity or were derived from lawful activity but intended for use in support of terrorism' (FATF, 2002: 1). In this manner however, the concept of 'dirty' money that needs to be monitored by financial institutions is extended to include *legitimate* funds, which are tainted by their potential use to support terrorism.

As has been eloquently stated, this means that financial institutions will now have to monitor 'where money is going to as well as where it is coming from' (Peel and Willman, 2001). This is, however, an extremely complex task, and pressure on financial institutions to report people who may have been engaged in perfectly lawful transactions may lead to prejudice and racial discrimination regarding customers from the Middle East (Peel and Willman, 2001). It may also lead to the blanket targeting of charities or non-profit organisations, which are targeted by the FATF in its Special Recommendations (FATF, 2002: 5–6). While the scope of monitoring is significantly extended, the fact that it may involve legal funds makes it more difficult for financial institutions to establish a well-founded suspicion. The danger of reporting suspicions on innocent customers in the name of the fight against terrorism is evident.

## Conclusion

The proliferation of money laundering countermeasures in the international arena in a relatively short period is an impressive feat, resulting, in less than two decades, in a comprehensive global anti-money-laundering regime. This has been the outcome of a policy consensus by the developed countries, but its establishment and constant expansion is inextricably linked with the framing of money laundering as a security issue and its association with all the evils which emerged in international policy discourse as global security threats after the end of the Cold War. Money laundering countermeasures were deemed to be essential in order to combat drug trafficking (in the late 1980s), organised and serious crime (in the 1990s) and, lately, terrorism. Underlying this threat discourse has been the goal to protect the stability of the international financial system.

This expanding 'securitisation' process has resulted not only in a quantitative, but also in a qualitative shift in anti-money-laundering policies. The concept of 'dirty' money, which has been the target of such policies, has assumed chameleon qualities during this shift. In early years 'dirty' money meant proceeds from drug trafficking, but the definition has since expanded to include proceeds from organised, serious and, ultimately, all crimes. However, 'dirty' money is not only criminal money: it may be legitimate money rendered illegal through tax evasion, or even legitimate proceeds which are tainted by their use to support terrorist organisations. The line between legality and illegality thus becomes thinner and thinner, with money laundering countermeasures potentially applying to everyday lawful activities. This may also be the case in view of the expanding scope of controls, to cover non-financial professions such as lawyers. A balance has to be struck between countering money laundering and protecting fundamental legal principles and human rights.

This may be a complex task in view of the way that money laundering countermeasures are developing. Their association in political discourse with the need to fight global threats such as organised crime and terrorism makes derogation from established legal principles seem acceptable. However, in balancing the conflicting interests at stake, it is essential to assess whether money laundering per se poses an equal threat to the public interest as its predicate offences. While proceeds of crime can undoubtedly be used to sustain criminal organisations, the question of whether the infiltration of 'dirty' money from any crime to the financial system has a destabilising effect to democracy and the state – as organised crime may have – is more complex. Equally complex is the issue with regard to legitimate charity funds that may fall under a broad definition of terrorist finance. On the other hand, a more direct threat may be established vis-à-vis the stability of the international financial system which must be protected. It remains to be assessed, however, whether the extensive criminal and preventive measures in place are proportionate to the achievement of this aim and whether the latter may be paramount to the protection of fundamental rights.

An equally important challenge surrounding the emergence of a global regime against money laundering and terrorist finance is one of legitimacy. The issue is closely associated with the way in which global norms are produced and enforced in this context. The main motor for the evolution of a global regime has been the FATF, in adopting guidelines and enforcing them world-wide. A fundamental issue in this regard, however, is that the FATF represents the interests of the developed world and thus its policies may fail to take into account the specific needs of countries outside of this club. The unilateral imposition and evaluation of standards by an *ad hoc* body differs significantly from negotiations and agreement of sovereign states within the auspices of an international organisation. The issue has broader implications, as the FATF standards are not only linked with the formation of economic policy, but have major implications for the receiving countries' legal systems, which have to implement guidelines that may still be controversial in the exporting countries. While a global response to money laundering is essential in view of the transnational nature of the phenomenon, this response would be more effective if based on as broad a consensus as possible.

## Notes

1  The term 'international regime' has been summarised as 'a system of norms, standards, procedures, institutions and rules of conduct that constrain and shape state behaviour in a particular issue area' (Alexander, 2001: 231). For an excellent analysis of 'global prohibition regimes' see Nadelmann, 1990.
2  The money laundering process consists of three stages: *placement*, where cash derived directly from criminal activity is first placed either in a financial institution or used to purchase an asset; *layering*, where there is the first attempt at concealment or disguise of the source of the ownership of the funds; and *integration*, where the money is integrated into the legitimate economic and financial system and is assimilated with all other assets in the system (Gilmore, 1999: 29).
3  Its members come from Belgium, Canada, France, Germany, Italy, Japan, Luxembourg, the Netherlands, Sweden, Switzerland, the United Kingdom and the United States.
4  FATF membership has been expanding since its establishment. It currently has 29 members: Argentina; Australia; Austria; Belgium; Brazil; Canada; China; Denmark; Finland; France; Germany; Greece; Hong Kong; Iceland; Ireland; Italy; Japan; Luxembourg; Mexico; the Netherlands; New Zealand; Norway; Portugal; Singapore; Spain; Sweden; Switzerland; Turkey; United Kingdom; and the USA. Two international organisations are also members: the European Commission and the Gulf Co-operation Council.
5  Many Canadian provincial courts granted temporary exemptions to the application of the suspicious transaction reporting requirements to lawyers pending the determination of the constitutionality of the legislation at federal level (the first case in November 2001 being *Law Society of British Columbia v Canada [2001] BCJ No 2420*). In May 2002 the Canadian government finally agreed to suspend the application of the reporting duties until their constitutionality is determined. This is still pending.
6  The current list (as of 17.02.2003) is as follows: Cook Islands; Egypt; Grenada; Guatemala; Indonesia; Myanmar; Nauru; Nigeria; Philippines; St Vincent and the Grenadines; and the Ukraine.
7  It has been argued that this 'double standard' also appears within the FATF, in

the context of its mutual evaluations. Greater pressure has been placed on countries like Turkey and Austria than, say, the USA, 'whose evaluations in 1997 and subsequently might appear to merit more severe treatment than it has received' (Levi and Gilmore, 2002: 355).

8 See Testimony of Juan C. Zarate, Deputy Assistant Secretary, Terrorism and Violent Crime, US Department of the Treasury, in Hearing of the US Committee of Financial Services on 'Patriot Act Oversight', cited in Alexander and Musch, 2002: 201.

9 The members of the Wolfsberg Group are: ABN Amro, Banco Santander, Bank of Tokyo-Mitsubishi, Barclays Bank, Citigroup, Credit Suisse Group, Deutsche Bank, Goldman Sachs, HSBC, J.P. Morgan Chase, Société Générale and UBS.

10 Another difference being of course that, unlike criminals, the principal motivation for terrorists is not financial gain: see Biersteker, 2002: 83.

# References

Abrams, N. (1989) 'The new ancillary offences', *Criminal Law Forum* 1, 1: 1–39.

Alexander, K. (2001) 'The international anti-money-laundering regime: the role of the financial action task force', *Journal of Money Laundering Control* 4, 3: 231–48.

Alexander, Y. and Musch, D.J. (2002), *Terrorism: Documents of International and Local Control.* Dobbs Ferry, New York: Oceana.

Alford, D.E. (1993) 'Basle Committee minimum standards: international regulatory response to the failure of BCCI', *George Washington Journal of Law and Economics* 26: 241–91.

Basle Committee on Banking Supervision (2002) *Sharing of Financial Records between Juridictions in Connection with the Fight Against Terrorist Financing,* www.bis.org.

Biersteker, T.J. (2002) 'Targeting terrorist finances: the new challenges of financial market globalization', in K. Booth and T. Dunne (eds) *Worlds in Collision: Terror and the Future of Global Order.* Basingstoke and New York: Palgrave, 74–84.

Commission of the European Communities (1998) *Second Commission Report to the European Parliament and the Council on the Implementation of the Money Laundering Directive,* COM (1998) 401 final, Brussels 1.7.1998.

Commonwealth Secretariat (1991) *Combating International Drugs Trafficking: The 1988 United Nations Convention Against Illicit Traffic in Narcotic Drugs and Psychotropic Substances.* London.

Csonka, P. (1998) 'Organised and economic crime (an overview of the relevant Council of Europe activities)', in P.J. Cullen and W.C. Gilmore (eds) *Crime Sans Frontières: International and European Legal Approaches.* Edinburgh: Edinburgh University Press, 93–9.

*Economist* (2001) 'Through the Wringer', 14 April: 85–7.

Financial Action Task Force on Money Laundering (FATF) (1997) *Annual Report 1996–97,* downloaded from www.oecd.org/fatf.

—— (2000) *Report on Non-Cooperative Countries and Territories,* 14 February, downloaded from www.oecd.org/fatf.

—— (2002) *Guidance for Financial Institutions in Detecting Terrorist Financing,* 24 April, downloaded from www.oecd.org/fatf.

Garland, D. (1996) 'The limits of the sovereign state: strategies of crime control in contemporary society', *British Journal of Criminology* 36, 4: 445–71.

Gilmore, W.C. (ed.) (1992) *International Efforts to Combat Money Laundering*. Cambridge: Grotius.

—— (1998) 'The G-7 and transnational drug trafficking: the task force experience', in P.J. Cullen and W.C. Gilmore (eds) *Crime Sans Frontières: International and European Legal Approaches*. Edinburgh: Edinburgh University Press, 30–8.

—— (1999) *Dirty Money. The Evolution of Money Laundering Countermeasures*. Strasbourg: Council of Europe Publishing.

Graham, T. (2001) 'What's behind the Wolfsberg Principles?', *Journal of Money Laundering Control* 4, 4: 348–9.

Hinterseer, K. (2001) 'The Wolfsberg anti-money laundering principles', *Journal of Money Laundering Control* 5, 1: 25–41.

Leacock, C.C. (2001) 'Internationalization of crime', *New York University Journal of International Law and Politics* 34, 1: 263–80.

Levi, M. (1991) 'Regulating money laundering: the death of bank secrecy in the UK', *British Journal of Criminology* 31, 2: 109–25.

—— (1997) 'Evaluating the "new policing": attacking the money trail of organized crime', *The Australian and New Zealand Journal of Criminology* 30: 1–25.

Levi, M. and Gilmore, B. (2002) 'Terrorist finance, money laundering and the rise and rise of mutual evaluation: a new paradigm for crime control?', *European Journal of Law Reform* 4, 2: 341–68.

Mitsilegas, V. (2003) *Money Laundering Countermeasures in the European Union. A New Paradigm of Security Governance Versus Fundamental Legal Principles*. Kluwer Law International (forthcoming).

Nadelmann, E.A. (1990) 'Global prohibition regimes: the evolution of norms in international society', *International Organization* 44, 4: 479–526.

Nilsson, H.G. (1991) 'The Council of Europe laundering convention: a recent example of a developing international criminal law', *Criminal Law Forum* 2, 2: 419–41.

Peel, M. and Willman, J. (2001) 'The dirty money that is hardest to clean up', *Financial Times*, 20 November, downloaded from www.ft.com.

Stewart, D.P. (1990) 'Internationalizing the war on drugs: the UN Convention Against Illicit Traffic in Narcotic Drugs and Psychotropic Substances', *Denver Journal of International Law and Policy* 18, 3: 387–404.

United Nations Office for Drug Control and Crime Prevention (1998) *Financial Havens, Banking Secrecy and Money Laundering*. New York.

Xanthaki, H. (2001) 'The duties of lawyers under the draft European Union Money Laundering Directive: is confidentiality a thing of the past?', *European Journal of Law Reform* 3, 2: 111–29.

# 13 Criminal asset-stripping

## Confiscating the proceeds of crime in England and Wales

*Michael Levi*

## Introduction

The 1990s have witnessed increased attention to income from crime and what is done with the money, particularly by the various forms of what is commonly called 'organised crime', which still consists principally of the multi-layered activity compressed into the pseudo-homogeneous term 'drugs trafficking' (Levi, 1998; 2002a). This development can be observed, first, in the legislation on the confiscation and forfeiture of the proceeds of crime and anti-money-laundering legislation in most industrialised countries (Alldridge, 2003; Fisse *et al.*, 1992; Gilmore, 1999; Levi, 1991; Levi and Osofsky, 1995; Meyer *et al.*, 1989; Mitsilegas, Chapter 12, this volume; Stessens, 2000); and, second, in the growth of policing (including customs and excise) involvement in financial investigation. Despite shifts due to the global 'War on Terrorism' (and terrorist finance, see Levi and Gilmore, 2002), this is still mainly in the drugs field, though with the targeting of *persons* rather than simply *activities*, the precise context in which prosecutions and asset confiscation occur has become flexible. This has implications for differentials in powers and procedures that occur when, for tactical reasons, prosecutions for offences other than drugs arise.[1]

Enthusiasts for following the money trail historically have been motivated by the desire to tackle what they believe to be pyramidal structures of criminal organisation such as the Italian Mafia or the American–Italian Mafia. Motivated offenders face the following problems, some of which are made more difficult by the 'new financial policing':

1 financing the criminal opportunity;
2 obtaining the prerequisites of whatever crime they are contemplating and carrying out the crime (from precursor chemicals, through 'market ready' drugs, to credit cards and other generators of criminal income such as burglary);
3 transforming the physical results of crime into a desired form (one presumes that drug sales are for cash, though they may involve barter);

4   storing the funds until needed (for personal consumption, transfer or investment); and
5   evading conviction.

The focus of this chapter will be shifts in dealing with the proceeds of crime and the way that this feeds or does not feed into measures to deal with 'organised crime' and, more usefully in analytical terms, into the organisation of serious crimes (Levi, 2002b). The confiscation of proceeds of crime is best understood in the context of money laundering regulation, for it is in this way as well as from the normal methods of 'intelligence-led' serious crimes investigation – criminal informants, electronic and other surveillance, undercover policing and stop-and-search powers – that the transparency of criminal funds and their confiscation comes about. Such crime control methodologies are taking on an increasingly international dimension, whether reflecting changes in the organisation of crimes or not, but a focus on the organisation of crime renders problematic the notion that particular cases or even criminal events 'belong' to particular countries. In principle, at least prior to the development of the European arrest warrant within the EU, nationality-basis of prosecution and extradition notwithstanding, some of these international crimes could take place in *any* of the countries involved in the financing, planning, direct commission, laundering and asset-holding components of the *process* of crime commission. The totality of the case can still occur wholly within any individual country: for example, if the non-drugs case was committed by and against persons from the same country or the vice (including synthetic drugs production and sale) occurred between consenting nationals, and the funds were frozen in the domestic bank account or the domestic home into which they were deposited.

There are some rare jurisdictions – as I write in early 2003, solely common law ones – that grant civil as well as purely criminal confiscation/forfeiture/recovery powers: the Irish Republic, New South Wales, the Ontario province of Canada, South Africa, the United Kingdom and United States. But elsewhere, confiscation can occur only following a criminal conviction determination and, to the extent that the most sophisticated offenders remain unconvicted, it is not possible to deprive them of their suspected crime proceeds other than by taxation or civil lawsuits by those with standing and means to sue. Essentially, except in fraud and corruption cases where there usually is considerable paperwork (though not all of it is genuine), the paper trail for the financial aspects in most completed UK drugs trafficking cases prosecuted is modest.

In England and Wales, during 1999, police and customs investigators discovered suspected criminal assets approaching £100 million within the English courts' jurisdiction in the course of their investigations. To this must be added substantial sums discovered in overseas accounts. Here a general point that applies throughout the European Union must be emphasised. Particularly in a cash business such as drugs or prostitution, it is almost impossible to reconstruct the money movements after the fact unless one has an insider in the business. In other sorts of 'paper trail' cases, as the UK Serious Fraud Office has discovered, there may be intentional breaks in the pursuit of the chain of money, not least through Liechtenstein *anstalts* and other offshore finance centres. In one case in 1996, £5 million was wired from the UK to an organised crime group in the Third World by a Money Transmission Agent, and up to four times this sum have been transferred in this way. (Far greater sums, though often not with an obvious criminal origin, have been discovered in the aftermath of terrorist finance investigations.) There is relative ease of collection of funds in destination countries and a low risk of disclosure. Some criminals have taken over existing money transmission agents or founded new ones, in order to launder their own funds, and until 2002 there was no regulation of the industry for money laundering purposes. Directors, auditors and banking facilities can be registered in differing jurisdictions in order to increase legal and administrative difficulties for investigators, and beneficial ownership may not be required to be disclosed. The use of nominee directors is widespread, and until this loophole was closed, some people on the Island of Sark in the Channel Islands were directors of some 1,300 companies. Company formation agents and estate agents make few disclosures, though this may change following formal regulation under the Proceeds of Crime Act 2002. However, as with other areas, the relationship between theoretical risk and actual incidence and prevalence of crime is unknown.

In any event, the offenders may not be known as offenders at the time (otherwise they would have found it harder to commit fraud). So the capacity to follow the money trail depends on competence and powers in the international arena, on how many investigators are available, and on the stage at which the financial investigation occurs relative to the dates of crime commission. It may also depend on what is found on suspects' persons and in their homes if and when they are arrested, which return may be improved if competent financially trained persons are present, since they know better what to look for than do ordinary uniformed officers or even detectives.

The NCIS's Organised Crime Threat Assessment Report 2002 provides an alarming view of the flexibility of laundering risks, despite the passage of the Proceeds of Crime Act 2002:

> In response to revised powers for cash seizure, serious and organised criminals may look for alternatives to the use of couriers on commercial flights, for example private transport. They may put greater emphasis on placing cash within the UK financial sector before transferring seemingly legitimate funds overseas. However, the risks in

each case will have increased significantly, and one consequence may be that serious and organised criminals come to rely more heavily on professional help and advice.

(NCIS, 2002: Sections 6.17–18)

Trend analysis of this kind always runs the risk of conflating changes in the organisation of crime with changes in the organisation of intelligence about crime. For the second key dimension of attacking the money trail, let us now turn to proceeds of crime confiscation and recovery.

## Confiscation law: developments in England and Wales

Once we move beyond forfeiture of the instrumentalities of crime, or of physical cash at the airport that has not been declared when required, confiscation presents a series of logistical and legal pitfalls. Since relatively few judges or, for that matter, counsel ever get to deal with many cases, there is the additional difficulty of relatively low reinforcement for learning how to do it properly: a combination of analytical complexity, low frequency of need, and relatively little positive praise for getting things right is disastrous for motivation.[2] Historically, levels of prosecution for money laundering per se have been very modest in England and Wales – about 12 cases annually before the late 1990s, and these mostly for the simple deposit of funds into a bank account rather than anything much more complex. Interviews suggest that before this century there were few local police or even national crime squad investigations where the *known* realisable assets constitute more than cash found or the matrimonial home. In one case – *In re P* – a racehorse was not allowed to be sold because the court was persuaded that it was a family pet, and the Receivers were required to keep it looked after even though this was loss-making. In Serious Fraud Office and non-SFO cases in which, by definition, large sums are involved, the money laundering is usually of interest only as evidence of an unwillingness or inability to repay creditors, though there are an increasing number of money laundering prosecutions by the SFO, sometimes including solicitors (Serious Fraud Office, 2002). Furthermore, the cases often reach the Serious Fraud Office only after investigation by accountants and/or lawyers has failed to recover funds.

Forfeiture of the instrumentalities of crime remains popular with some magistrates and even judges, though the defendants and counsel did not know or care who had the benefit. The Advisory Council (1970) intended that crime prevention should be the principal purpose of the Powers of Criminal Courts Act 1973, and consequently, s.43 allows forfeiture not just of property actually used but of that *intended to be used* in committing or facilitating the commission of any offence. Despite the fact that property not used or intended to be used in the commission of an offence cannot be forfeited, it was on this basis that, not long after the coming into force of the Drugs Trafficking Offences Act 1986, the Court of Appeal held in *O'Farrell* (1988) 10 Cr. App. R. (S.) 74 that the defendant's 'working capital for future dealings in drugs' could be forfeited under s.43 PCCA 1973.

The Drug Trafficking Act 1994 (s.42(1)) permits a constable or customs officer to seize and detain sums of £10,000 in 'cash which is being imported into or exported from' the UK if 'he has reasonable grounds for suspecting that it directly or indirectly represents any person's proceeds of drug trafficking or is intended by any person for use in drug trafficking'. Following representations by HM Customs and Excise and case examples of assets returned, the Proceeds of Crime Act 2002 extended the powers to seize cash inland, if no satisfactory account of its legitimate origin is provided. Historically, the sums of drugs cash recovered by Customs have been very small – around £3 million in 1999/00 – whereas the sum of cash estimated to have left the country to pay for illegal drugs supply in, for example, 1994 was £970 million. Once transferred to locations where anti-money-laundering controls are less rigorous, currency can be entered into the banking system and transferred back to the UK with relatively little risk of detection or disclosure.

The importance of cash exports in understanding what happens to the proceeds of crime is illustrated by a UK Customs experiment in tracking such proceeds over a three-month period, which discovered that £150 million was exported from the UK to Turkey alone in cash. A Jamaican money launderer caught with £750,000 when boarding a return flight to the Caribbean forfeited the money rather than seek to account for its legitimate origin: a Customs receipt for the money confiscated demonstrates to his domestic contacts that he had not simply stolen the money and therefore did not merit severe punishment (though presumably, there will develop a market for counterfeit receipts).

*Sentencing*

The court first imposes the sentence and then can consider the confiscation, but the confiscation process must precede the making of any monetary order. No statistical data are yet available on how often the opportunity to delay confiscation hearings for up to six months after conviction is taken up, but interviews suggest that it is very common. Table 13.1 shows the figures for confiscation orders imposed *in drug trafficking cases only* in England and Wales. Note that very few of these cases will have been money laundering prosecutions, which totalled some 52 in 1998. (Curiously, these data, like non-drugs confiscations, are not available regularly in the general or drugs crime statistics.) The figures below also indicate the modest sums of money detected as realisable assets and the attitudes of judges in imposing these as realisable orders. In the past three years, an average of 13 orders for drugs trafficking of £100,000 or over

Table 13.1 Confiscation orders in England and Wales, 1996–2001

|  | 1996 | 1997 | 1998 | 1999 | 2000 | 2001 |
|---|---|---|---|---|---|---|
| Total sentenced for drug trafficking offences | 7,373 | 8,370 | 6,998 | 6,577 | 6,458 | 6,683 |
| Confiscation order *not* made | 581 | 6,904 | 5,755 | 5,568 | 5,622 | 5,876 |
| Confiscation order made under £1,000 | 1,117 | 1,032 | 855 | 682 | 525 | 454 |
| Confiscation order made £1,000–£29,999 | 399 | 417 | 352 | 291 | 279 | 279 |
| Confiscation order made £30,000–£99,999 | 32 | 19 | 26 | 23 | 20 | 30 |
| Confiscation order made £100,000–£299,999 | 6 | 6 | 7 | 9 | 11 | 10 |
| Confiscation order made £300,000 plus | 3 | 2 | 3 | 4 | 1 | 4 |
| Total ordered to be confiscated (million) | 10,471 | 5,620 | 6,971 | 16,107 | 5.002 | 7,980 |
| Average confiscation order | 6,725 | 3,834 | 5,608 | 15,964 | 5,984 | 10,270 |

suggests either that few major offenders are being convicted (in a conviction-based system such as England and Wales), or that financial investigations are not being very successful, or that the sentencing process is not working so as to maximise the amount recovered from offenders and their families and associates, or all three. And this is without reviewing the attrition between the amount ordered to be confiscated and that actually obtained from offenders, which is high not only in the UK but elsewhere in Europe.

### Enforcement and penalties for non-payment

Once the Crown Court sets the amount of the confiscation order, the defendant is faced with a choice. Since UK confiscation orders operate *in personam* (on the person) rather than *in rem* (on the property), nothing in the order dictates what property must be used to satisfy the order. Instead, it is up to the defendant to choose which property to use. Where there are insufficient funds to pay the order, any assets – whether acquired honestly or not – can be used in satisfaction. This is important because, until the offender has paid over sums equal to his (assessed) proceeds, the prosecution can always go back to the High Court to order him to repay more money, even though at the time of sentence, his 'realisable property' was lower than his assessed proceeds and therefore was given a lighter confiscation certificate.[3] The initial assumption was that a long spell in jail would stiffen offenders' motivation to repay. However, this has not always proven to be the case, and although there is merely anecdotal evidence which I have been unable to test or extend, some offenders would rather 'do extra time' so as to avoid punishment from angry conspirators who do not want their share to disappear, and also because the prospect of coming back to the money on their eventual release sustains them (and their prestige among their peers) throughout their stay (Levi and Osofsky, 1995). Hence, the legislation now holds that the order is not expunged by time spent in jail for non-compliance.

The system of enforcement is uneven or chaotic, and, as the Home Office (1998) and the Performance and Innovation Unit (2000) indicates, some serious reform was required in a 'system' that was never designed for the complexities of international or even national extraction of funds from high-level offenders (see also Levi and Osofsky, 1995) and has difficulty extracting repayment from minor offenders. Receivers (for example, liquidating accountants) can be appointed to deal with the funds – and they tend to be appointed in the more complicated cases – but the costs involved tend to deter the CPS and Customs at both the restraint and the confiscation stages. (Though it is impossible to know how much better the performance under the old legislation would have been if the funds spent on the Asset Recovery Agency in 2003 had been available for them.) Furthermore, reflecting the disparate process of enforcement, no data are available on the number of cases in which prison sentences are imposed. I was informed of last minute applications for imprisonment 'in lieu' when the law enforcement or prosecuting authority happened to learn that offenders who had not co-operated or paid up were about to be released.

### Assets held overseas

An obvious thing for offenders to do, especially if they have laundered their funds in a sophisticated way rather than simply put money in a bank account, is to keep it overseas. Restraint orders *can* apply to property outside the jurisdiction, and defendants or third parties outside the jurisdiction may have restraint orders made against them and – with leave of the court – may have orders served upon them outside the jurisdiction (Order 11 r.1(1)(q)/s). The Vienna Convention, Council of Europe Convention and the various bilateral and Commonwealth provisions are relevant here, and this is likely to be a key area of development for EU action. Once countries have ratified, Orders in Council can be made and co-operation can commence. Finally, unless there is some specific asset-sharing agreement, to encourage co-operation, the funds normally rest where they fall. For this reason, there is substantial pressure to develop asset sharing agreements internationally. Let us now turn to examine the *effectiveness* of the policing of the money trail.

## The objectives of financial policing and confiscation

If criminals are convinced that 'crime does not pay' and that (if caught) they will be unable to retain their ill-gotten gains, then, presumably, at least some criminals will be deterred from committing certain crimes. Some of my interviews with offenders would suggest that many view the proceeds of crime as their 'entitlement', and removing this presumed entitlement would naturally cause resentment and be seen as 'punishment'. *Prima facie*, however, there seems no reason to expect that such confiscation will lead such individuals to abstain from crime in future – it might simply lead to greater determination to 'get their just desserts' (as they see them) though, as in snakes and ladders, they may find it hard to get back to where they were before. Moreover if – as is the view of the police as well as myself – many of the proceeds of crime are spent before arrest (and *a fortiori*, before confiscation), the deterrent as well as punitive and reparative effects will be modest. Finally, in the so-called 'war against *organised* crime' (as opposed to organised *white-collar* or *political* crime), it is believed that asset forfeiture (as it is termed in the USA) or confiscation (in the UK) will incapacitate the organisation by removing its financial lifeblood, eliminating its capacity to trade and attractiveness to recruits. (Though if one accepts the model of *dis*organised crime (Reuter, 1983) or networked crime (Levi, 2002b) the likely impact on 'criminal organisations' is more problematical and we fall back to the more individual deterrent effect.)

For mixed philosophical and pragmatic purposes – including the far from negligible populist attraction of seeing people without visible legitimate incomes or wealth[4] being stripped of their luxury homes, cars and lifestyle – 'taking the profit out of crime' has been an important rhetorical *motif* in the English-speaking developed world for the past decade. It also carries with it the potential for making some areas of police investigation financially self-sufficient, though this was never the motivation behind the confiscation legislation in England and Wales, where hypothecation (assigning income to particular expenditure functions) is conventionally disallowed.

In addition, depending on the importance attached to the concern about the socio-political effects of 'organised crime', one might look at measures to ensure that former 'organised criminals' do not get 'purchase' upon important elements of the economic system. On the assumption that most organised crime is motivated by profit – though some offenders may also get emotional satisfaction from frightening and killing – then 'following the money' has always had the potential to be the appropriate way forward. Nevertheless, when the individual crime has been solved and the suspect has been brought to trial, and even when a confiscation order has been made, the accumulated knowledge and experience frequently 'evaporates' because new tasks have to be carried out and most organisations have little or no memory (Levi and Osofsky, 1995). Staff changes and losses to the higher paid private sector in countries such as Canada, the Netherlands, UK and US contribute to this loss of collective memory.

When assessing the overall effect of asset confiscation, the stark gap between guesstimates of money laundering volumes and confiscation orders made, let alone actual confiscation effected, is evident, even though it is seldom drawn attention to in official reports (see, for example, Home Office, 1998). (For European data and reviews, see Kilching, 2002.) If it is the case, for example, that there is $85 billion generated *annually* by the all-drugs trade in the US and Europe, as the Financial Action Task Force Report for 1990 asserted,[5] and that some £1 billion is spent *annually* on illegal drugs in the UK,[6] then the £37.3 million remitted to the Consolidated Fund from drugs trafficking confiscation over the period 1989–96 looks pathetic. Even the £25.4 million ordered to be confiscated in the peak year of 1994 (due to one order being made for £15.3 million) represents only a tiny percentage of the sum estimated to arise from the drugs trade *that year*. (We do not know what the results are of that particular order, but it is estimated that about 40 per cent of funds ordered to be confiscated are actually remitted.) In 1997 an almost record *low* figure for the 1990s of £5.6 million was ordered to be confiscated, and the average sum almost halved to £3,834 from the previous year, which itself was at the low end for the decade. The sums rose slightly the following year, but not by much (see Table 13.1). In no year during the 1990s was the median sum confiscated over £20,000, indicating that (subject to under-resourced financial investigative input into the discovery process) the great majority of offenders were low-level traffickers or had few identified assets remaining. The proportion of drug trafficking convictions that led to asset confiscation orders declined from 25 per cent to 18 per cent between 1994 and 1999. This is despite the reasonable expectation that those convicted of dealing in drugs have enjoyed benefit from their crimes. Assets confiscation orders are made in an average of only 0.3 per cent of other crime cases, although about 70 per cent of all crimes are acquisitive. (However, it should be noted that, in most cases, proceeds of crime are modest and may never even be placed in any savings or investment account, let alone reintegrated except in the form of expenditure without return in a gaming business.)

Even where the courts make confiscation orders, the amounts actually collected are much lower than the amounts ordered to be confiscated, running at an average of only 35 per cent. Overall, the amount of criminal assets recovered in a year (for example, £17 million in 1999) is tiny by comparison with estimates made of the amount of criminal funds in circulation of 2 per cent of GDP (i.e. approximately £18 billion). At the other extreme, assuming there to be some correlation between seriousness of involvement in drugs trafficking, expertise and resources put into financial investigation, and realisable benefit from trafficking, we should note that since 1992, only 13 drugs trafficking confiscation orders have exceeded £1 million: apart from 1995, the maximum number of orders in any one year has been two. Whether this is the result of inadequacies in the policing, courts, and/or financial investigation processes cannot readily be determined in this study, but it is this sort of frustration that gave impetus to the recommendations of the Performance and Innovation Unit (2000), followed by the Proceeds of Crime Act 2002.

The question to which there is no research-led answer is whether, at one extreme, the money laundering estimates should be discarded as merely gross data or whether, at the other extreme, law enforcement, prosecutors and courts are doing an exceptionally bad job of turning criminal investigations into money or other assets. One way of approaching this is through comparison of how other countries are doing, but this logically can only occur in the context of their own offending population. Hypothetically, one should look not just at one's domestic criminal markets as the sole source of 'convictable, asset-full' persons but also at foreigners operating into and out of the UK and domestic persons (lawyers, bankers) who are laundering the proceeds of crime committed entirely overseas. All of this makes estimating the maximum likely UK criminal income and realisable assets intellectually hazardous. Of course, under the present legislation, the population of convicted persons and their *detected attributable and realisable* assets defines the limits of realistic proceeds of crime capable of being confiscated: the less 'efficient' the conviction process *for those 'offenders' who have substantial assets*, the lower the potential impact of confiscation is. However, under a system freed of the necessity to convict before forfeiture, the much larger volume of estimated proceeds is the relevant one. Given these very different denominators, one could easily end up with a civil forfeiture system under which, although the *ratio* of forfeited funds to proceeds of drugs sales was much lower than under the present system, the *absolute amount* forfeited was much higher than at present. It is within this perspective that one must see the role of financial investigation.

The impact of the disruption of money flows can be observed by its displacement to countries other than where it is carried out. An example is the attack of the British and Dutch authorities on the *bureaux de change* in their countries during the mid-1990s. These bureaux were only a link in the cross-border circuits of the crime-money, changing, for example, English, Scottish and Irish currency into Dutch guilders. The attack on the Dutch money change facilities resulted in a shift of the activities to Belgium and later back to Britain. Thus, in March 1999, a Kurdish bureau chief operating in London was jailed for 14 years for acting as a vast cash laundry for major Liverpudlian traffickers with strong Dutch connections. (The fact that they had to or chose to change the money in London rather than closer to home may be significant; nor do we know what disruption the incarceration of that 'flexible' money exchanger will have caused.) The suspicion is that British buyers prefer to settle their accounts in the Netherlands: if you are being reported for a suspicious transaction by the bank, it probably feels safer to let it happen abroad and be off before anyone follows up the 'unusual' or 'suspicious' transaction report, if they do at all (Gold and Levi, 1994).

## Judging the effectiveness of interventions: some general comments and conclusions

Many measures used are *activity measures* – such as seizures of drugs or, for that matter, proceeds of crime or even arrests of major offenders – rather than *final outcome* measures, such as lower narcotics consumption. Although final outcome measures tend to be demotivating, because demonstrating effects is often hard, they are important. By stressing the importance of judging performance against objectives, incrementalism is not dismissed: enormous increases in international transparency and in functional equivalence in regulation have been achieved, and to reduce harm is itself a considerable benefit even if harm (whether it takes the form of serious drug abuse or fraud and corruption) is not eliminated altogether. But to give an example, even if one vigorously attacks 'organised crime' and puts away some key players, then the amount of crime may not reduce. Is this success or failure? For retributivists, the conviction of serious offenders and/or the deprivation of their proceeds of crime is an inherently good thing, but it is an empirical question whether or not such actions lead to less crime: the very concept of organised crime along the model of an illicit corporation is that the removal of executives may make only a modest difference to the continuation of the 'business', though anecdotal evidence suggests that individuals *do* matter.

Finally, one must examine what one might mean by 'success' and how one could recognise it if one saw it. It can be helpful to distinguish between (a) ultimate – or 'final' – objectives, and (b) intermediate goals along the way; these are crucial to the achievement of final ones but should not be confused with them. But one must beware of pseudo-objectives. It may be morally tenable for some people to lock up people simply because they have done bad things, irrespective of other impacts on crime. But if one's final objective is the reduction of narcotics *consumption*, then the arrest of offenders for 'drugs trafficking' (which can be just growing a bit of cannabis in the loft, assisted by Dutch hydroponics) or even for money laundering is helpful only if – taken as a whole rather than just looking at any one arrest – it produces real incapacitation or general deterrence. In the particular case of *drugs* money laundering and asset confiscation, the 'final objectives' are surely reduction in drug-taking and in the collateral consequences of *unaffordable* drugs-taking, that is, crime for gain, including wars over distribution rights.

It is important to disaggregate the concept of crime and think of sub-categories of crime. My interviews, as well as the modest amount of systematic research (Pearson and Hobbs, 2002), suggests that most drug offenders spend most of their money on entertainment and home improvements, plus some lifestyle symbols such as boats which can still be purchased unmonitored for cash in many parts of the world. (This will be even more true if money laundering controls on suspicious transactions spread.) Except for the major international syndicates, relatively little narcotics sales money may end up being laundered: it is simply spent in criminal 'running expenses' (such as hedonistic pursuits, holidays paid for cash) once the house has been refurbished with gold taps. Whether such funds ever enter the banking system before they are deposited by sellers of legitimate services 'for value' is questionable.

In short, the 'savings ratios' of offenders may vary depending on personality and on income levels: the marginal utility of savings rises with criminal as with legitimate income. Drugs traffickers may have to work harder to establish front companies or use existing genuine businesses to merge their large cash deposits into. Anecdotal interviews suggest that more cash is being kept nowadays, and it seems plausible that this is due to the difficulties of placement.

Currently, we have only a modest idea about how much the proceeds of so-called victimless crimes (drugs trafficking and vice) constitute; how much offenders save from crime; and what they do with their money. The empirical foundation for the Financial Action Task Force and IMF estimates is illusory. The more long-term covert operations (including electronic surveillance) that law enforcement agencies do, and the more offenders are interviewed about what they do with the money side of their crimes, the more we will find out about such operations: but current debriefing of offenders about this by busy police or customs investigators is very modest in England and Wales. In general, criminal justice only looks backwards at fixing blame, not forwards in strategic thinking. Only if we devote some serious resources, including strategic analysis of data, will we be able to start to think more clearly about evaluating the impact of financial investigation, but even then we will have to decide whether we are reviewing the impact of investigation, prosecution and/or asset confiscation:[7]

1    on 'crime' generally,
2    on particular forms of crime (whose accurate measurability also varies), or
3    on 'organised criminals'.

Conceptual and technical aspects of confiscation law are dealt with elsewhere (Aldridge, 2003; Mitchell *et al.*, 2002).

Prior to the Proceeds of Crime Act, 2002, the major causes of low proceeds of crime confiscation in England and Wales have been:

1    moderate investigative knowledge, due to the inherent secrecy of the activities and inadequate resource allocation to financial aspects of crime;
2    inadequate co-ordination and intelligence exchange between police and the revenue department, due partly to legislative prohibitions on data sharing but also reflecting differences in cultural and policy objectives;
3    inadequate use made of suspicious transaction reports by the police and customs agencies due to a lack of resources and the inherent difficulty of following up many reports without contacting the account-holder for an explanation;
4    inadequate powers to detain cash of unexplained origin other than drugs money at borders (though suspects may be reluctant to justify the cash as the proceeds of other crimes and may choose to lose it anyway);
5    inadequate funds and staff resources to restrain proceeds;
6    judicial reluctance to apply the law rigorously, especially the reversal of the burden of proof post-conviction, and especially where the family home may have to be sold (though the evidence here is anecdotal); and

7 lack of transparency in beneficial ownership of funds held offshore or even onshore which, combined with secrecy provisions in some jurisdictions unless high proof levels exist connecting funds to specific offences (often excluding tax), mean that funds are difficult to discover and to repatriate.

To the extent that these elements remain unreformed, the problem of proceeds remaining unrecovered will remain. The new Asset Recovery Agency set up in 2003 will have a target of recovering £64 million in proceeds of crime. What the impact of higher recoveries will be on the level and organisation of serious crimes remains to be seen.

## Notes

1 Ideally, it would be interesting to look at the offences for which a sample of NCIS/NCS/Customs targets were prosecuted, to examine the extent to which this principle of tactical flexible prosecution operated in practice. *Ex hypothesi,* one might anticipate that drugs trafficking would still predominate, but this might understate the extent to which information about drugs involvement precipitated the priority ranking of the individual(s) as targets.
2 This may be a warning for the widespread implementation of confiscation since the Proceeds of Crime Act 2002.
3 The position in fraud cases is, however, different. There, confiscation orders can be reopened only if there is evidence that the court has underestimated the offender's benefit from the crimes.
4 Obviously it is arguable that contemporary 'organised criminals' are by no means the only possible 'undeserving' targets for such asset-stripping, but this takes us beyond the theme of this book.
5 Other 'estimates' go higher, to $500 billion, but converting these global figures into *national* ones is highly speculative, especially if one includes proceeds of crime money flows that can legitimately be double counted as they pass through different jurisdictions.
6 With illegal income of heroin/crack users being especially high – £10,000–£12,000 annually (Tackling Drugs, 1998: 9).
7 One can have substantial asset confiscation without criminal proceedings, as in the US, where much confiscation takes place under civil parts of the Racketeer Influenced Corrupt Organizations legislation.

## References

Alldridge, P. (2003) *Money Laundering Law.* Oxford: Hart Publishing.
Fisse B., Fraser, D. and Coss, G. (eds) (1992) *The Money Trail.* Sydney: The Law Book Company.
Gilmore, W. (1999) *Dirty Money,* 2nd edn. Amsterdam: Council of Europe Press.
Gold, M. and Levi, M. (1994) *Money-Laundering in the UK: an Appraisal of Suspicion-Based Reporting.* London: The Police Foundation.
Home Office (1998) *Third Report: Criminal Assets.* Home Office Working Group on Confiscation.
Kilchling, M. (ed.) (2002) *Die Praxis der Gewinnabschöpfung in Europa.* Freiburg in

Breisgau: Kriminologische Forschungsberichte aus dem Max-Planck-Institut für ausländisches und internationales Strafrecht Band 99.

Levi, M. (1991) 'Pecunia non olet: cleansing the money launderers from the Temple', *Crime, Law, and Social Change* 16: 217–302.

—— (1998) 'Perspectives on organised crime: an overview', *The Howard Journal of Criminal Justice* 37, 4: 335–45.

—— (2002a) 'Money laundering and its regulation', *The Annals of the American Academy of Social and Political Science*, July 582: 181–94.

—— (2002b) 'The organisation of serious crimes', in M. Maguire, R. Morgan and R. Reiner (eds) *Oxford Handbook of Criminology*, 3rd edn. Oxford: Oxford University Press.

Levi, M. and Gilmore, W. (2002) 'Terrorist finance, money laundering and the rise and rise of mutual evaluation: a new paradigm for crime control?', *European Journal of Criminal Law Reform* 4, 2: 337–64.

Levi, M. and Osofsky, L. (1995) *Investigating, Seizing and Confiscating the Proceeds of Crime.* Crime Detection and Prevention Paper 61. London: Home Office Police Research Group.

Meyer, J., Dessecker, A. and Smettan, J.R. (1989) *Gewinnabschöpfung bei Betäubungsmitteldelikten.* Wiesbaden: BKA-Forschungsreihe.

Mitchell, A., Taylor, S. and Talbot, K. (2002) *Confiscation and the Proceeds of Crime.* London: Sweet & Maxwell.

NCIS (2002) *Organised Crime Threat Assessment Report 2002*, Public Version. London: National Criminal Intelligence Service.

Pearson, G. and Hobbs, D. (2001) *Middle Market Drug Distribution*, HORS 227. London: Home Office.

Performance and Innovation Unit (2000) *Recovering the Proceeds of Crime*, www.cabinet-office.gov.uk/innovation. London: Cabinet Office.

Reuter, P. (1983) *Disorganized Crime: Illegal Markets and the Mafia.* Cambridge, MA: MIT Press.

Serious Fraud Office (2002) *Annual Report.* London: Serious Fraud Office.

Stessens, G. (2000) *Money Laundering: an International Enforcement Model.* Cambridge: Cambridge University Press.

Tackling Drugs (1998) *Tackling Drugs to Build a Better Britain.* London: Home Office.

# 14 Proteiform criminalities

The formation of organised
crime as organisers' responses to
developments in four fields of
control*

*Nicholas Dorn*

## Introduction[1]

Following the Second World War, different state agencies (the police, the
Customs, secret services, fiscal and other administrations, market regulators, and so on) have generally regarded their concerns as non-
overlapping, and the sharing of information between them was *ad hoc*.
Increasingly, however, these agencies consider themselves all to be
involved, to some extent, in a common fight against the various facets of
an extended and dangerous phenomenon, that of 'organised crime'
(henceforth, 'OC'). This chapter first develops a framework for asking
questions about intelligence development by, and intelligence sharing
between, diverse agencies. It then invokes the general assumption (drawn
from enforcement practice and social theory) that the forms taken by
criminal enterprises are at least partly the result of criminal organisers'
counter-measures to strategies of control. This raises a practical question
for research and for policy: what new forms of criminality and social risk
arise as unintended side-effects of, and reactions to, multi-agency intelligence exchange? Today's intelligence environment also raises questions
about the future of research.

## Historical emergence of co-operation

In previous decades, diverse forms of economic activities – marginal,
irregular, 'grey' and/or criminal (such as corruption of state officials or
of commercial enterprises; fraud in relation to private parties, the state
or the European budget; large-scale evasion of tax; thefts of objects of
high monetary value; trafficking in drugs, other prohibited goods or
human beings; arms trafficking, and so on) – were seen as separate
and distint from each other. These and other problems were seen as

* This chapter is an English language version of a paper originally published as, 'Du renseignement au partage des informations: l'intelligence protéiforme', in *Les Cahiers de la Sécurité Intérieure*, 1999, no. 34.

non-overlapping, certainly meriting some kind of action, but generally unco-ordinated action, by separate control agencies.

But from the mid-1990s onwards, from the points of view of many policy-makers, administrators, regulators and police officers interacting together at international, European and national levels, these economic phenomena have increasingly been seen as structurally similar, function-ally parallel, and empirically overlapping forms of OC.[2] One observer has coined a provocative phrase, *une criminalité proteiforme*, to describe this development.[3] This shift in perceptions of OC has gone hand-in-hand with a trend for greater co-operation between the diverse agencies and bodies, not only in the public sphere but also in the market and civil spheres of society that are concerned in various ways with the regulation and/or sup-pression of economic crime and related phenomena.

What has propelled this meshing of the hitherto separate control spheres? It is beyond the scope and intention of this chapter to try to weigh the arguments, which on the one hand refer to the possibility of a rise in objective threats posed by OC in global, regional and national situ-ations and, on the other hand, refer to a process of social construction of threat. Commonly it is proposed that the collapse of communism has led to a degeneration of economic and political life in some countries, leading to 'robber baron' forms of capitalism, international gangsterism and a collapse of boundaries between crime and business. Similar observa-tions have been made in relation to the conduct of politics and business life in many developing countries. And, of course, there have been major scandals in the developed world, as corporate scandals in the USA and elsewhere have illustrated. However, other commentators suggest that, whilst there are many objective threats, nevertheless the dangers have been exaggerated – either by popular and political cultures that may 'need' strong outside threats, or more specifically by state security agen-cies that seek new roles in a post-communist world.[4]

Suffice it to say that there do seem to be global, regional and national threats that overlap political and economic boundaries; and there may be tendencies in our culture, politics and media for enthusiastic celebration of such threats. The overall effect is that OC is defined as being large-scale, wide-ranging and crossing not only geographic boundaries but also economic sectors.

## Spheres of inter-agency co-operation today

What the OC 'phenomenon' means (and legitimises) is that there is a tremendous motivation to get agencies to co-operate in order to combat the forms of OC which now seem to confront them all. The most recent form of co-operation – and, it is here argued, eventually the most pro-found – is in relation to information, which, when shared, exchanged, combined and acted upon, becomes 'intelligence'. Intelligence is now detaching itself from the specific, separate and limited spheres that previously generated it; intelligence about OC is, by definition, multi-agency intelligence. There seem to be four main 'players'. Here we focus not so much on who they are, but on what they do:

i the police, Customs and other agencies having a role in the enforcement of criminal laws, acting in investigatory roles, often involving undercover action, when the intention is to collect enough evidence to bring criminal charges against their targets;[5]

ii police and other agencies, but this time pursuing the currently fashionable 'disruption tactics', where the aim is either to disrupt temporarily the operations of suspected criminal targets, to degrade the capabilities of the criminal organisation or to dismantle it permanently, through covert action, mis-information, etc;[6]

iii other state authorities of many kinds, when exercising their administrative powers to impose non-criminal fines (for example, the administrative fines of the tax authorities, called 'civil fines' in Britain), to confiscate the proceeds of crime or suspected proceeds (Home Office Working Group on Confiscation, 1998 and see Mitsilegas and Levi, Chapters 12 and 13 respectively, this volume) or to withhold or suspend various economic permissions or privileges (Dorn 1999b);

iv regulatory agencies, such as state agencies and public/private hybrid agencies, when involved in regulating important parts of commercial life, notably the competition and anti-cartel authorities of the European Commission and of member states, and bodies regulating financial services[7] or international trade.[8]

These four sectors of control define the control environment within which OC must operate and are shown in Figure 14.1.

The historical evolution of co-operation between such agencies can be traced through several stages:

i informalism, or personal contacts;

ii operational formalism, between similar agencies;

iii multi-agency intelligence sharing, that is to say between diverse agencies and;

iv action and plans of the European Union.

### Informalism

Twenty years ago, co-operation between police, administrative and other state agencies would have been limited to occasional and informal contacts between individuals working in these agencies, and who had learnt to trust a very limited number of individuals in other agencies (and, indeed, in the world of crime). That was the era of informalism in police

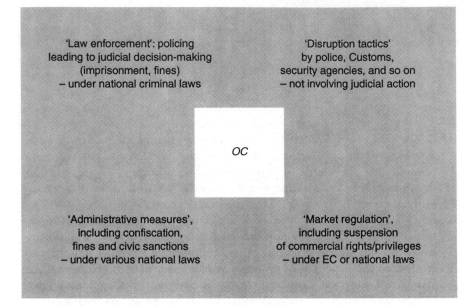

*Figure 14.1* The organised crime control space.

co-operation and in prosecutors' investigations. It allowed great steps forward in some arenas, for example in the courageous work of well-known investigating judges in Italy. But the same lack of formalisation and mutual oversight could too easily form a breeding-ground for police corruption.

### Operational formalism

From the 1980s onwards – although, no doubt, the story varies considerably from place to place – more formalisation of working relationships between agencies began, both within and between states, which now co-operate more often and more routinely at an operational level. Here the linkage occurs between teams, indeed between systems (not just between individuals), and it becomes enmeshed in rules. This is formalism in police co-operation. Within the European Union, this stage is still developing today (see below, pp. 231–2).

### Intelligence sharing

For the 1990s, it may be proposed that the most significant opening up of co-operation between the diverse agencies concerned with OC was (and continues to be) in relation to intelligence. Intelligence development, the process by which intelligence is constructed by one agency, is increasingly becoming synonymous with intelligence sharing between agencies. Since OC today is perceived to cover so many diverse arenas and so many forms of economic activities – spanning both licit and illicit economies, and many sectors and trades – so it must be combated by a comprehensive mapping of its contours, across all administrative, judicial and geographical boundaries. So runs the argument that broke surface in the 1990s (and was reinforced following 2001) in the discourse on co-operation on intelligence, risk and OC in Europe and internationally. And although this development may evoke a number of concerns (see pp. 235–7), it will not easily be turned back.

### The post-Amsterdam agenda

With the creation of the Schengen area and the wider Single Market, the European Community and the member states stepped up co-operation on the control of economic crime. After the Treaty on Economic Union signed at Maastricht, although there has been considerable discussion of the institutional difficulties, there have also been practical developments (Dorn and White, 1997). Following the Amsterdam Treaty[9], 'an area of freedom, security and justice' is the overarching aim. This is being pursued through a wide variety of measures, with legal bases in the first pillar and third pillar. An *Action Plan* agreed by the Justice and Home Affairs Council in December 1998 summarises the work to be done over five years (European Union, 1998). In relation to police and judicial co-operation in criminal matters, the Action Plan states:

> The aim is to give citizens a high level of protection as provided for in the Treaty of Amsterdam and to promote the rule of law. This implies greater co-operation between the authorities responsible for applying the law with due regard for legal certainty. It also implies giving practical form to a judicial area in which judicial authorities co-operate more effectively, more quickly and more flexibly. Encourage an integrated approach through close co-operation, of judicial, police and other relevant authorities in prevention and combating crime, organised or otherwise.
>
> (European Union, 1998: Article 42)

The Action Plan says that recent experience in European Customs co-operation is to be taken as 'a model' for wider co-operation between agencies. This is to be 'extended with national police forces and gendarmerie and in closer co-operation with judicial co-operation'; and there will be an examination of 'whether and how Europol could have access to the Customs Information System' (European Union, 1998: Art. 44(c) and 48(v)). Indeed it seems that Customs services – which in some but not all member states have responsibilities under both criminal and administrative laws – have functioned as a laboratory for co-operation on the exchange of administrative information, in particular. Another focus for intelligence sharing has been the anti-fraud activities of OLAF (previously UCLAF), the European Union body having responsibility for protection of the financial interests of the European Community. Because of the overlapping interests of diverse agencies, such as Customs and OLAF, the information exchange system SCENT (System Customs Enforcement Network), set up in 1985, has been absorbed into a wider system, AFIS (Anti Fraud Information System).[10] Within this, there are various levels of sensitivity, security and access, and various closed groups. The work of Europol should also be borne in mind.

More generally, the fact that, in EU member states, different agencies may have responsibilities for different aspects of criminal, administrative and civil matters, means that European co-operation brings together traditionally separate groups: police have to talk to Customs; prosecutors have to talk to investigators; legally-trained people have to talk to non-legal administrators; criminal law people have to talk with regulatory people, and so on. Evidently, the European dynamic, increasingly linking action across many EU first pillar and third pillar aspects, gives further impetus to the national tendency for information exchange between diverse agencies.

## Framework: intelligence as interaction

Too often, the study of crime and of its control is divorced. Indeed this is uncomfortably the case in the present chapter, due to practical limitations and the author's decision to keep the perspective as broad as possible. This inevitably steers us more towards control than to crime, since control is increasingly convergent – whilst crime still bears the diverse marks of its origins (Paoli, 1997).

Nevertheless, a step forward is taken if one tries to see information/ intelligence as an *interactive* phenomenon: the constitutive aspect of a fast-growing environment occupied by a variety of control agencies and by OC itself. It is of considerable interest to assess the forms of OC that emerge as criminal organisers react to the widening of intelligence sharing. Clearly, if intelligence sharing becomes more important for control and regulatory agencies, then there are implications for criminals and others. Of course, it is through intelligence that the control agencies seek to prevent, deter, disrupt or capture OC. Equally, however, the criminal organiser, through his or her own intelligence and actions, seeks to circumvent or evade the actions of the agencies. Beyond these protective responses, the more competent and ambitious criminal organisers seek actually to manipulate control agencies, through the medium of intelligence. These responses may be characterised as *counter-intelligence*. Research on this issue so far is fragmentary, and much of it remains hidden within individual control agencies, inaccessible to the other partners. Indeed, there is a general question about the extent to which research (as distinct from intelligence) is shared between agencies today, and how much it should be in future.[11]

To move towards a coherent programme of European research on OC and its reactions to multi-agency intelligence sharing, we have first to develop a framework within which we can picture (a) the relevant control/regulatory agencies, (b) OC in all its economic and organisational forms and, (c) the interactions between all these parties. In such a framework, intelligence can be seen as being interactive in two senses:

- first, under certain conditions, intelligence is passed between agencies. This has a tendency to promote development of that information;
- second, there is a flow of information – an antagonistic flow – between the agencies (on the one hand) and the organisers of OC (on the other hand).

On the first point, it will be understood that putting together two or more pieces of information about a suspected party (henceforth called 'target') may not always lead to better information, or even to more information. For example, only one of the data holders who agree to pool information may actually hold information on a particular target. In that case, something more might need to be done to increase the stock of information. Possibly, the information held by different agencies might be contradictory: that might lead to further checks. Or, another alternative, the information might be wrong in one or both cases, without this being apparent to either party. There is nothing intrinsic in the mere act of passing information from one agency to another that does anything to increase its quality.

Nevertheless, the point is that transmission of information by Agency A to Agency B – and any checks that Agency B may initiate or ask Agency A to initiate because of good or bad 'fit' with the information already held by Agency B – has a general tendency to increase the complexity of information. One aspect of this is that the total stock of intelligence on any particular target becomes more diverse, spread over a number of different fields. Whilst specialist control units (for example, those dealing with only one type of crime or irregularity, such as drug trafficking or tax evasion) naturally tend to record information most relevant to these specialised interests, intelligence shared between diverse agencies has a tendency to become much broader, to cover a multiplicity of fields.

This is one aspect of the interactive nature of intelligence and is illustrated by Figure 14.2. In this figure, the second column represents the increasingly important field of multi-agency information-sharing, resulting in intelligence that spans the interests of the police and other agencies

| Stage 1 | Stage 2 | Stage 3 | Stage 4 |
|---|---|---|---|
| INFORMATION SIMPLEX | INFORMATION COMPLEX | FORMAL OR INFORMAL INTERVENTION | LEGALITY AND JUDICIAL CONTROL |
| Intelligence collation and development *within specific fields of control*: | Information is further developed by exchange *between fields of control*: | Intervention occurs through one or more of: | Some unsettled issues: |
| • information for case-making for court | **The arena of interactive intelligence** | Criminal courts | Questions about judicial oversight of criminal intelligence |
| • information for disruption or dismantlement | | Disruption | Lack of legal basis for disruption, and so on |
| • information for administrative actions, fines ... | | Administrative action | Proportionality and procedural rights in confiscation, and so on |
| • information for market regulation | | Regulatory action | Strong market players restrict regulatory powers |

*Figure 14.2* The information process (overview from the control perspective).

involved in criminal prosecution including all agencies concerned with disruption or dismantlement of suspected OC; with procurement or tax collection and regulators of markets and professions. In the light of the possibilities for interaction of such diverse information, we could refer to the emergence of *renseignments proteiformes*, in parallel with the development of *une criminalité proteiforme*.

Some problems of judicial control, legality, and so on, are represented by the fourth column of Figure 14.2. Amongst these issues are some relating to data protection. Whether or not the guarantees that should be applied are always applied is open to question. In any case, there are many possibilities for information exchanges which are legitimised by various permitted exceptions to data protection rules, based on public security and anti-crime rationales. For the purposes of the present discussion, the main point is that both the propensity to exchange information and the technical possibilities for doing so are increasing.

## Process: the contested nature of intelligence

We have observed that the first characteristic of intelligence as an *interactive* phenomenon is that it passes between control agencies, becoming 'broader' as it does so. The second characteristic is that there is a flow of information between the agencies (on the one hand) and the organisers of OC (on the other hand). This is a hostile flow. The agencies collate information on OC, which they hope to be accurate, and they try either to deny information to OC, or to feed it inaccurate information. For their part, the organisers of OC seek to hide information about their activities, or to give information which is misleading, and whilst doing this they seek to collate information about the activities and intentions of the control agencies. For example, in the context of work carried out in Britain (Dorn *et al.*, 1998), the author came across some instances of when convicted criminals interviewed in prison, and informants of Customs who were interviewed incognito, proposed the idea that criminal organisers who operate behind the façade of legitimate businesses are wise to be prompt in their payment of taxes (direct and indirect). The aim of prompt payment is said to be to prevent the triggering of any investigation by the tax authorities – which might, in turn, lead to an investigation by Customs or police. At least, this is what those interviewed suggested.[12] There seems no reason for us to accept that tax authorities or other authorities necessarily think in such a manner – the point being made is that some criminals think that they do and that they draw practical conclusions for their conduct. The ways in which different OC enterprises react will of course differ, depending on their assessment of the situation and their leads about the likely beliefs and actions of the authorities. We need to know more about these assessments, as they evolve.

### *Overflowing the criminal/non-criminal distinction*

The private sector finds itself more and more in a moral category alongside, and overlapping with, that of serious criminality. For example, the prevention of fraud against the public purse – both at national level, in procurement, and at European level, in the protection of the financial interests of the European Community – is high amongst current concerns about OC. There is a paradox here, or a contradiction. On the one hand, it is perhaps here, in particular, that the threat of OC to the state itself is most manifest, as far as the threat to the integrity of elected politicians and public officials (as well as the private sector) is concerned. On the other hand, precisely because powerful people and big corporations are involved, there is extreme nervousness about preventive measures that might cut across legitimate rights and expectations. So, for example, although the term 'blacklisting' has been in use in many administrative contexts, in order to designate firms suspected of involvement in corruption or fraud, this term creates nervousness. It implies that an economic entity might be denied a contract, merely on suspicion – in other words, on the basis of information that is untested. Other mechanisms, such as positive inclusion on an 'approved list', may sometimes be preferred. The construction of such a list may involve a process in which potential contractors are asked to give information about their anti-corruption and anti-fraud procedures: a self-certification process that may be subject to checking on the basis of random sampling and/or risk assessment. As the private sector is more routinely scanned for signs of OC, so questions about quality and justifiability of anti-OC intelligence development and sharing become more prominent.

Just as the private sector finds itself in intelligence systems that overlap with criminal intelligence, so criminals find themselves the focus of an information gathering process that is wider than 'traditional' criminal intelligence. The tactic of disruption or dismantlement of criminal organisations, which has gained favour in EU member states, has particular implications for the development of intelligence gathering. In Britain, this method is accepted enough for a Performance Indicator already to be in operation for disruption of drug traffickers by Her Majesty's Customs and Excise and the National Crime Squad (police managed on a national basis, previously organised as Regional Crime Squads). When such measures are adopted by internal or external security services it is possible for disruptions to be 'credited' to police and/or Customs, in order to reach a national total. Information to be used in disruption operations is, by its nature, 'softer' than information to be used for criminal prosecution, in the sense that it does not have to withstand challenge and adjudication. So it seems possible that a wide tranche of information from administrative and civil agencies – information which is indicative, rather than being 'beyond reasonable doubt' – could be especially useful for the purposes of identifying targets for disruption.

Several issues can now be summarised. First, information sharing may be a prelude to criminal law action, disruption, confiscation of assets, administrative fine or exclusion of a call for tender. Second, a wide range of agencies are becoming involved in sharing information that may be used for putting people out of business. Third, legitimate and reputable economic enterprises may become a target for intelligence gathering, or they may believe themselves to be so targeted.[13] Fourth, enterprises already use private security firms for a variety of purposes, amongst them checking whether they may be under investigation by control and regulatory agencies and finding out what information is held on them. It is possible that such private checking will increase. The role of private security firms in relation to multi-agency information is important though too complex to be discussed here but, clearly, they can be on either side. Fifth, both reputable and disreputable enterprises may wish to take action in order to prevent administrative or regulatory action or to compensate for its negative impacts on their business. Sixth, such targets may have no recourse under the criminal law (because this may not be used against them), but they may have recourse under judicial review, administrative law, civil law or regulatory guidelines. Seventh, enterprises may wish to take preventive action by calling upon all information collectors to validate the information they hold.

### Implications for criminal intelligence

There should be implications, in the longer term, for the categories and quality of information exchanged by different agencies (criminal law, disruption, administrative, regulatory). As the systems of information tend to converge, it is more and more difficult for each system to continue to have different criteria for inclusion of data, methods of intelligence development, internal assessment of quality, external scrutiny, challenge, redress for bad information, and so on. Diverse criteria and diverse standards become more difficult for both practical and legal reasons. The practical reasons are straightforward: how can information be exchanged when it is incomparable? Already, intelligence systems are being designed more for standardised categories of information, and less for free text.[14]

The legal reasons are more debatable: multi-agency intelligence – which is a hybrid of commercial, administrative and criminal information – may one day come under the eye of the European Court of Justice (despite the reluctance of most EU member states). Meanwhile, the European Court of Human Rights already has some jurisdiction on surveillance methods and hence on aspects of intelligence because of the development of the case law on legitimate expectations of privacy. It may be found that the usual 'get out' clauses in data protection legislation – which typically exempt data collected for purposes of safeguarding national security or preventing serious crime – may not be applicable when economic operators are disrupted rather than being subjected to administrative penalties. We may have to await future legal action to resolve some of these issues.

In summary, for practical and legal reasons, the convergence of intelligence systems which we are seeing today, conjoining information across the categories of criminal law, disruption, administrative action and regulation of markets, inevitably leads to a debate over criteria, methods, quality, justifiability and oversight systems. In other words, the management of criminal intelligence is being radically affected by its increasing overlap with non-criminal information.

### Conclusion

In conclusion, we can say that, in both analytical and practical terms, today it would be too restrictive to see intelligence as something which only the control agencies 'do'. Both sides 'do intelligence'. It is simply that the control agencies structure it more powerfully, on an increasingly wide front (for criminal prosecution, disruption/dismantlement, administrative action and for regulatory action) and on an increasingly global scale. By contrast, OC is more fragmented and more reactive, seeking out sanctuaries, contradictions and opportunities in the sea of intelligence. Questions about formal objectives, constraints, data protection and legal oversight of intelligence systems and practices remain to be fully addressed at national and European levels. Also remaining are questions about counter-measures adopted by managers and operators of economic enterprises which may be involved in aspects of OC, questions about the forms of OC which result and questions about the prospects for more effective control.

These dynamic developments are at the core of European research on organised crime. There are manifest implications for the ways in which research is done. The collapse of geographical and sectoral boundaries means that the old demarcation lines between practitioners and researchers are as dead as the proverbial Dodo. The phenomena which interest us are clearly much too wide-ranging for our analysis of them to succeed if it is corralled within boundaries which have been overrun by history. We can no longer rely on experience in any one particular field – be it practical experience in one agency or sector of control, or academic expertise in any one discipline (criminology, law national or European, applied economics, accountancy). This is not just a theoretical observation. On a mundane note, over-specialised approaches are increasingly difficult to market to policy-makers; all the more so since the various administrations are themselves required to work in partnership. This presents us with analytical opportunities but also practical research problems: how to work in teams that are dispersed in terms of geography, administrative bases, occupational backgrounds, life experiences, ways of thinking and, of course, languages.

Finally, the development of intelligence is itself blurring the line between practitioners and researchers – partly because of the (rather wary) forms of assistance that some give each other, partly because the expansion of the private sector helps open doors and also partly because of the emergence of the intermediate category of the intelligence analyst. Intelligence analysts are employed by control agencies to sift and analyse not only tactical intelligence (relating to particular operations against OC), but also to develop strategic intelligence (descriptions of the general development and dynamics of OC). This occupation, which is expanding, sits between, and overlapping with, the roles of academic researchers and practitioners in agencies concerned with the regulation and control of OC. At a debate that I was privileged to observe between officials and other representatives of EU member states, following on from and commenting on two days of deliberations by academic experts on aspects of OC, one of the questions eventually posed was this: how much more can the independent researchers tell us about OC, that intelligence analysts cannot (or maybe the latter can tell us more)? This, of course, is an interesting question, one that it would be stimulating to explore in a structured manner, but the point for this conclusion is that, as intelligence becomes proteiform, so it is reshaping the world of the researcher, as well as that of the policy-maker, and that of the thief.

## Notes

1 The author is grateful to the editors of *Les Cahiers de la Sécurité Intérieure* for the stimulus to write the first version of this chapter (Dorn, 1999a).
2 For a general review, see Van Den Wyngaert (1998).
3 With full acknowledgement for the concept to Alexandro Missir di Lusignana, previously with Directorate General 20 of the European Commission.
4 The events and aftermath of September 2001 are outside the scope of this chapter. Nevertheless, clearly, they rather undercut sceptical positions and give a further boost to international co-operation whilst, at the same time, perhaps loosening the degree of attention to be paid to economic criminality that is reckoned not to be closely related to terrorism. These themes and contradictions will be taken up elsewhere.
5 Limitations of space forbid an excellent discussion of issues arising in policing practice, but a stimulating review is given by Brants and Field (1995). For a comprehensive review of legal issues arising in police co-operation, see Van Den Wyngaert, op. cit., sections 3–6.
6 See successive annual reports of Her Majesty's Customs and Excise, and the sections on Performance Indicators from the UK government's ten-year drug strategy (Cabinet Office, 1998).
7 Notably, from a UK perspective, see Ryder (1995: 1–11) and, on comparative issues, Johnstone (1998).
8 One issue too complex to be dealt with here is the vexed question of 'extra-territoriality', meaning any claim that may be made by the regulatory authorities of one state to have jurisdiction over another state's trade with a third state. This issue is familiar in the form of actions by US authorities to enforce trade sanctions.
9 Neither the subsequent Treaty of Nice nor the mooted 2003 Convention much affect the EU's approach to organised crime.
10 Source: European Commission, Secretariat General, 1998.
11 The question of the extent to which criminal and administrative control agencies share the results of internally commissioned strategic research on OC is an interesting one. The author's impression is that agencies are quite often unaware of each other's internally commissioned research or consultancy on aspects of OC. We may have arrived at the situation where operational intelligence about specific OC targets is considered less sensitive, and easier to share, than non-operational research and development done for an agency's own strategic or planning purposes. The EU Action Plan's commitment within five years to 'set up a research and documentation network on cross-border crime' (Article 48(ii)) and other initiatives may help to unblock this situation, if new ways of working can be found.
12 At other times it has been suggested to me that too prompt payment of sums routinely due to state authorities could be equally suspicious.
13 Such targeting may occur, for example, because of the suspicion of a regulatory or control agency that the economic enterprise may be used as a 'front' by employees, or may be manipulated by third parties.
14 This is the case with AFIS, see p. 232.

# References

Brants, C. and Field, S. (1995) *Participation Rights and Proactive Policing: Convergence and Drift in European Criminal Process*, Nederlandse Vereniging voor Rechtsvergelijking, number 51. Deventer: Kluwer.

Cabinet Office (1998) *Tackling Drugs to Build a Better Britain.* London: HMSO.

Dorn, N. (1999a) 'Du renseignement au partage des informations: l'intelligence protéiforme', *Les Cahiers de la Sécurité Intérieure* 34, 4ᵉ trimestre, pp. 91–108.

—— (ed.) (1999b) *Regulating European Drug Problems: Administrative Measures and Civil Law in the Control of Drug Trafficking, Nuisance and Use.* The Hague: Kluwer.

Dorn, N., Oette, L. and White, S. (1998) 'Drugs importation and the bifurcation of risk: capitalization, cut-outs and crime', *British Journal of Criminology* 38, 4: 537–60.

Dorn, N. and White, S. (1997) 'Beyond Pillars and Passerelle debates: the European Union's emerging crime prevention space', *Legal Issues of European Integration* 1: 79–93.

European Union (1998) 'Action Plan of the Council and the Commission on how best to implement the provisions of the Treaty of Amsterdam on an area of freedom, security and justice'. Text adopted by the Justice and Home Affairs Council of 3 December 1998, *Official Journal of the European Communities*, 23 January, C 19/1, EN.

Home Office Working Group on Confiscation (1998) *Third Report: Criminal Assets.* London: Home Office Organised and International Crime Directorate.

Johnstone, P. (1998) 'Financial crimes in England and Wales: the criminal and civil interface', *European Financial Services Law* 5, 9: 196–203.

Paoli, L. (1997) 'The pledge of secrecy: culture, structure, and action of Mafia associations', unpublished Ph.D. Thesis, European University Institute.

Ryder, B. (1995) 'Civilising the law: the use of civil and administrative proceedings to enforce financial services law', *Journal of Financial Crime* 3, 1–11

Van Den Wyngaert, C. (1999) 'The transformations of international criminal law as a response to the challenge of organised crime', *International Review of Penal Law* 70: 133–221.

# 15 Organised crime and the Conjunction of Criminal Opportunity framework

*Paul Ekblom* *

## The challenge of preventing organised crime

Organised crime is especially challenging to control. It is:

- complex,
- dispersed and invisible – forming networks more than gangs,
- invasive and progressive,
- subversive and self-protective – disabling and corrupting crime control systems,
- persistent,
- adaptive and durable,
- entrepreneurial and well-resourced,
- innovative.

These features confront us with a pernicious combination of moving targets and shifting ground. They set the scene for an arms race between preventers and organised offenders (Ekblom, 1997, 1999), especially where social and technological change constantly creates new opportunities for offending – new targets, environments, business models, tools and information sources. Even successful crime control methods eventually weaken as offenders learn to circumvent them. Legislative solutions lag behind changing crime patterns – particularly those requiring international agreement.

* This chapter is based on material developed during a project supported by the Falcone Fund of the European Union, 'The Identification, Development and Exchange of Good Practice for Reducing Organized Crime'. The project involved colleagues in Europol, the Swedish National Crime Prevention Council (BRÅ), the UK Home Office and National Criminal Intelligence Service, Cardiff University and Corporate Solutions Ltd. Particular thanks to Mike Sutton and Dick Oldfield formerly of Research, Development and Statistics Directorate, Home Office; Bram Dekker of Europol; Michael Levi and Mike Maguire of Cardiff University; Dermot Browne of Corporate Solutions; and Lars Korsell of BRÅ. This chapter © UK Crown Copyright 2002. Reproduced by permission of the Controller of Her Majesty's Stationery Office. The views expressed are those of the author and do not necessarily reflect the views or policy of the UK Home Office or any other UK Government Department.

We must therefore improve our performance against organised crime – cost-effectiveness, responsiveness, sustainability and scope (the range of crime problems controlled). But beyond incremental advances, we must *gear up* to:

- catch up with existing crime problems we cannot yet prevent,
- scan for emergent crime problems and stop them early,
- anticipate new crime problems and develop and deploy timely new solutions,
- make solutions durable, striving to maintain them whilst preparing for obsolescence.

Gearing up involves treating organised crime control as an *evolutionary* process (Ekblom, 1997, 1999) and becoming adaptive and innovative ourselves – aiming to outpace offenders (or at least to follow close behind, for they can take the initiative and have fewer constraints on manoeuvrability). We, too, can organise better – for example, through the UK's National Intelligence Model and Europol's Analytical Guidelines. However, the main challenge is to gain the edge and then keep it sharp. What can we do that organised criminals usually cannot? We can be:

- systematic – in analysing crime problems and criminal organisations, and in designing solutions.
- scientific and professional – using evidence and ideas distilled from research on the causes of crime and evaluation of crime reduction, and blending this with the 'craft' competencies of detectives and crime analysts.
- strategic – analysing, planning and acting at different levels – from preventing individual criminal events to putting criminal organisations out of business, to pursuing career criminals, to disrupting entire criminal markets.
- contextual – customising action to local circumstances.
- cumulative – building reliable and durable knowledge.
- current – keeping up to date on crime and crime reduction and prepared for obsolescence of existing preventive measures; pursuing a succession of momentary advantages rather than vainly seeking permanent solutions.
- communicative – sharing know-how and broader capacity.
- collaborative – working in partnership with diverse agencies, to pool complementary resources (the same reason why criminals themselves link up).

*The role of knowledge in improving crime prevention performance*

Knowledge is vital in gearing up performance. It takes several forms (Ekblom, 2002a):

- *know-about:* crime problems, patterns of criminality, risk factors, theories and causes, consequences.
- *know-what:* what works in prevention, how cost-effectively and sustainably, in what context.
- *know-how:* practical processes of analysing crime, its patterns and causes, customising preventive interventions, implementation, mobilisation and evaluation.
- *know-who:* contacts with generic expertise, access to wider resources, and those in the wider public and commercial community who can take on particular preventive tasks.

This chapter centres on 'know-what'. However, this cannot be detached from 'know-how,' and a single conceptual framework can support all kinds of knowing. A knowledge base of what works should help practitioners maintain the effectiveness of existing interventions, replicate in diverse contexts, innovate and anticipate. The aim is to learn from past experience, so we are neither reinventing the wheel of success nor the flat tyre of failure – and the initiatives we produce will be more likely to succeed.

Replication is the main function of a knowledge base, but even that is not straightforward. The Kirkholt Burglary Prevention Project (Forrester *et al.,* 1988, 1990) was a notable success in 'ordinary' crime prevention. Developed by top academics working with talented police and probation staff, a range of interventions – covering target-hardening, target removal, neighbour surveillance, tackling offender motives and community development – reduced domestic burglary by 65 per cent. Several attempts were made to replicate this – but a major review (Tilley, 1994) showed disappointing results. Reasons included:

1   *transferability* of knowledge is problematic. What works in one context may not work elsewhere – especially if we know little about the influence of contextual factors (like culture, laws, environment). No knowledge base of case studies, however well-evaluated or well-populated, can cover all contextual contingencies for replication. We must therefore make the best guess on prior knowledge, pilot the intervention and use rapid and good-quality *feedback* until we get the intervention right, or abandon it. Replication thus resembles innovation – entering the unknown. The necessary knowledge is best distilled into *generic principles* to be applied in designing interventions for new contexts. Such principles also resist obsolescence.

2  the replicators copied the end product, instead of the intelligent process of identifying problems/risks, diagnosing causes, identifying solutions and customising these to problem and context. Cookbook replication will not work and 'know-what' is of limited value without 'know-how'.

These are not unusual problems. The current UK Crime Reduction Programme is also finding that implementing successful schemes, originally developed by academics, into routine mainstream roll-out, is extremely challenging (Ekblom, 2002a). A similar issue besets Problem-Oriented Policing in UK and USA.

### Conceptual framework needed

This 'replication gap' partly reflects insufficient practitioner training, wider supportive climate and infrastructure for prevention. But more fundamental is the failure of prevention to develop into a professional discipline (Ekblom, 1996), and beneath that, the lack of an overall, integrating conceptual framework.

Without conceptual frameworks to guide the development of good practice, progress is hindered (Ekblom, 2002a):

- 'what works' knowledge bases are limited in content and utility, especially if users have different languages and working contexts.
- communication and collaboration between diverse partners are inhibited: police may use one term, local government another.
- strategic thinking remains compartmentalised and 'method-oriented' or 'organisation-oriented' rather than 'problem-oriented'.
- practice fails to test and refine theory, and theory to inform practice.
- education and training lack coherence. Instead of the integrated generic principles advocated in this chapter, there are a haphazard assortment of cases and 'star' schemes. Practitioners act more like narrow technicians than professional consultants applying a range of knowledge to a problem. Interventions are often superficial and prone to fashion.

## The Conjunction of Criminal Opportunity framework

The *Conjunction of Criminal Opportunity* (CCO) framework aims to alleviate these problems and support the development of crime prevention as a professional discipline. CCO originated in efforts to describe and classify some 2,000 diverse 'ordinary' crime prevention schemes from England's Safer Cities Programme. The framework has been adapted, and adopted, by various UK committees on training and education of crime prevention professionals, and accompanies the development of 'toolkits' for crime reduction practitioners in the UK (see www.crimereduction.gov.uk/learningzone/cco.htm).

CCO bridges two major 'cultural gaps' that have divided crime prevention practitioners, policy-makers and theorists:

- between *situational* versus *offender-oriented* prevention – understanding the offender is vital to our capacity to intelligently manipulate the crime situation;
- and between *criminal justice/enforcement/repressive* approaches versus *'civil'* prevention.

CCO aspires to serve as a precision tool for:

- systematic thought in crime prevention policy and practice – for analysis, response, feedback and adjustment and connecting 'know-about' with 'know-what' and 'know-how'.
- communication and partnership working.
- supporting detailed to synoptic views, and tactical to strategic action.

More specifically, CCO can supply consistent terminology to describe the content of preventive action, its implementation, and the detailed causal mechanisms by which it works. Specifying such mechanisms of intervention is vital for evaluation and replication (Tilley, 1994; Pawson and Tilley, 1997). The framework's integrating structure helps to systematically capture descriptive and evaluative information on preventive interventions, support the storage and retrieval of cases, distil generic principles and transfer and apply good practice. This makes it an appropriate platform for a knowledge base (Ekblom and Tilley, 1998; Ekblom, 2000a, 2002a).

The framework was not designed with organised crime in mind. However, the following version was adapted to accommodate organised crime problems identified during the Falcone-sponsored project. While such evolution will continue, the ultimate proof is the utility of the framework for improving the practice and extending the scope of organised crime prevention – not just by a small margin but in giving practitioners the capacity to gear up to a higher level of performance altogether.

### Definitions, perspectives and levels

CCO starts by defining crime prevention in an open-ended way that links intervention to theory in general, but avoids restriction to specific theories in particular. Crime prevention reduces the risk of occurrence, and the potential seriousness, of crime and disorder events by intervening in their causes.

Organised crime can be prevented at the level of tackling the many individual criminal events it generates. However, focusing on criminal events exclusively is too tactical and reductionist. The criminal career and planning activity of the individual offender spans multiple events; and the persistence, invasiveness and growth of organisational careers and networks, structure of the market, and so on involve causes operating at higher, emergent levels. Ignoring these higher levels would limit the practical utility of our tools for thought. CCO must therefore evolve to handle them, by starting from the lowest and simplest, namely the molecular approach of criminal events, then rigorously, systematically and parsimoniously building up to higher structures and processes. This chapter aims to begin that development, with special emphasis on knowledge base issues.

### The preventive process

This is the central 'know-how' part of CCO. The competencies and knowledge to convey are less a matter of circumscribed technical skills and universally applicable 'facts', and more an expert way of viewing the world and applying a problem-identifying and problem-solving procedure. From the crime event focus, the approach adopted is the *preventive process*, which is closely related to SARA in Problem-Oriented Policing and 'problem profiles' within the UK National Intelligence Model:

- identifying symptoms – specific crime problems.
- setting objectives of reducing the frequency or seriousness of the chosen problem.
- diagnosis – interpreting the causes of the problem.
- specifying the intervention in principle – devising preventive action to tackle the most tractable of the identified causes of the problem, using knowledge of cost-effective solutions and sound crime-prevention principles, adjusted to local circumstances.
- implementing the action in practice – through *targeting* of the intervention on the selected causes of the crime problem, *designing a practical intervention method* (the action that actually disrupts the causes) and *insertion* (mobilising appropriate people or agencies to take responsibility and act).
- monitoring and fine-tuning implementation.
- evaluation through

   i   assessing *impact* on the target crime problems, and *cost effectiveness*;
   ii  developing a clear picture of *how it worked* – exactly what changes were needed to trigger the intervention mechanism (Pawson and Tilley, 1997) and what aspects of the local context were 'hidden ingredients' necessary to make the intervention work elsewhere.

- adjustment of the action, abandonment if failing, replication elsewhere if successful.

A knowledge base to support replication must capture information on both know-how and know-what.

### The symptoms

In dealing with specific crime problems the first stage identifies crime risks. Figure 15.1 schematically shows typical results of crime pattern analysis in terms of a 'problem space' covering the nature of the offence, offenders, modus operandi and circumstances, for a simple 'non-organised' offence such as domestic burglary or assault. The same set of features can be used to specify operational objectives and targets of crime reduction activity – for example, 'reduce burglary by young people, by 10 per cent'.

Some criminal events are simple – such as spontaneous assaults. Others involve offenders successfully negotiating several *scenes* and employing appropriate *scripts* to attain a sequence of goals (Cornish, 1994; Cornish and Clarke, 2002) – for example:

- preparation – discover a bank's security procedures, steal getaway car, forge security pass;
- execution – rob bank;
- escape – drive off, swap cars;

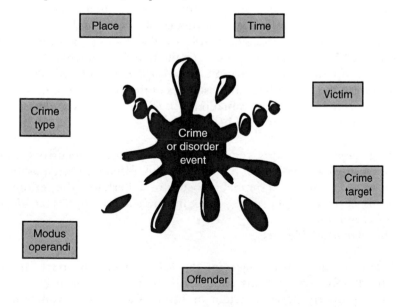

*Figure 15.1* Problem space: a map of symptoms and crime reduction objectives.

- cover tracks – hide weapons, destroy DNA evidence, intimidate witnesses, corrupt officials;
- consummation – sell stolen goods, enjoy loot, launder money.

### Diagnosis

Diagnosis involves identifying the immediate causes that combine to generate the events – the *Conjunction of Criminal Opportunity* itself. This is a 'universal story' of the criminal event, in which a ready, willing and able offender encounters, seeks or engineers a crime situation comprising a vulnerable and attractive target of crime, in a favourable environment and in the absence of alert, motivated and empowered preventers. Remoter causes like the price of car spares, or societal influences on child-rearing quality, are diverse and many but all ultimately act through the immediate ones.

The CCO owes much to Cohen and Felson's (1979) Routine Activities Theory, but suitably extended to identify 11 generic kinds of *immediate causal precursor*. On the *offender* side, these comprise:

- their *criminality* – longer-term, personality-based influences predisposing them to crime – perhaps amplified through recruitment into a criminal career.
- *lack of skills to avoid crime* – for avoiding conflict, resisting social pressures to offend, or gaining a legitimate living.
- shorter-term influences on their *readiness to offend* – motives and emotional states (need money, stressed out) as determined by current life circumstances and conflicts, and influence of alcohol and drugs.
- offenders' *resources for committing crime* – skills, courage, knowledge of targets and M.O.s, tools, weapons and collaborative networks.
- their perception and anticipation of *risk, effort, reward* and *attacks of conscience* in the immediate circumstances of the criminal event.
- their *presence* in the crime situation (or telepresence, via electronic means, or through traditional henchmen).

Envisaging *corporate offenders* requires adjusting some precursors (for example, instead of individual criminality the offending organisation could have a persistent criminal subculture). Perhaps the criminal event/transaction could be understood through a *Conjunction of Illegal Business Opportunity*.

On the *situational* side are:

- the *target* – the central object of the crime (through attack, theft, counterfeiting, illegal transaction, possession or trafficking) – the person, property, service, system or information that is vulnerable, provocative or attractive.

- the *target enclosure* – compound, building or container that is vulnerable to penetration and encloses suitable targets.
- a *wider environment* logistically/tactically favourable for offenders and unfavourable for preventers, and which may attract or generate the offence, e.g. by containing suitable targets or setting the scene for conflict.
- the absence of *crime preventers* – people or organisations, formal or informal, who make the crime *less* likely by action before it (like locking doors or dissuading youngsters from theft), during it (interdiction or arrest), or after (reporting crime, giving witness statements, remedying revealed vulnerabilities in a financial system).
- the presence of *crime promoters* – who make crime *more* likely, whether unwittingly, carelessly or deliberately – for example by supplying tools, information or other criminal services before or after the crime. Promoters may furnish outlets for stolen goods and link up in distinct criminal markets; and supply role models, moral justification for offending, practical help to offenders' families should imprisonment happen, recruitment and training in criminal skills.

*Victims* feature indirectly because they play remarkably diverse roles: owner of targets of property crime, target of crime against the person, legal complainant, crime preventer and (careless or provocative) crime promoter. Likewise, people acting as *illegal migrants* are: promoters – paying to support the crime of trafficking; targets of that crime – the human commodities being illegally transported; and offenders themselves through the crime of illegal entry. The lesson is to unpick the diverse roles people play.

The 11 generic, immediate causes are shown in Figure 15.2 (more details are in Ekblom, 2000b). This is a diagnostic map for practitioners deciding how to tackle a particular local crime problem or risk (or alternatively how to conduct a crime impact assessment or crime proofing exercise – Ekblom, 2002b).

The causal precursors can be customised for each crime problem addressed (with vehicle crime, for example, cars are the *target* for the crimes of 'theft of' or damage, and the target *enclosure* for 'theft from'). Each precursor can be further subdivided to indicate more detailed elements for preventive practitioners to address (for example, in burglary, the home, as target enclosure, can be divided into boundary, entry points and interior). Other aspects of causation particularly connect with organised crime.

### Resources for committing crime

'Opportunity' is normally seen as a feature of the environment – something 'out there' to be exploited. In fact, an opportunity is just as much determined by the resources offenders are able to deploy in overcoming

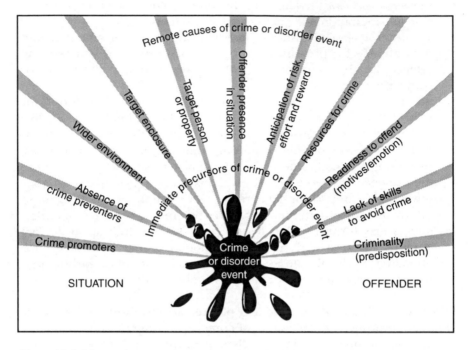

*Figure 15.2* Diagnosis space: the conjunction of criminal opportunity.

resistance and solving various logistical problems in committing the crime (Ekblom and Tilley, 2000). An open third-floor window is an opportunity only to someone with courage, agility and a ladder; and a loophole in a financial computer network only to someone knowing the password, the target and how to cover tracks. Through collaboration, organised criminals can deploy more, and more diverse, resources; or subcontract, recruit or train specialists.

### CCO in cyberspace

The Internet presents a new environment for crime. Cyberspace removes constraints of inertia, time and reproduction of property and information. The CCO can stretch to accommodate this – for example:

- target – information, pirated electronic commodity, IT system.
- target enclosure – firewall.
- environment – IT/financial system.
- preventer – intelligent fraud-detecting software.
- promoter – computer virus, intelligent agent.
- offender resources – code-cracking software.
- offender presence – remote hacker.

*Crime as process*

Supplementing the static, *anatomical* picture of causes in Figure 15.3 is the *physiological* view of crime as a dynamic process:

- offender, preventer and promoter may *interact* – threat, attack, surrender.
- each makes *decisions* based on their diverse perceptions of risk, etc., including what each thinks the others will do.
- they may interact through *move and countermove*. What brings CCO alive is the *modus operandi* – the characteristic ways offenders apply their resources in preparing, executing and completing a criminal event to minimise effort and risk and maximise reward. M.O. relates to Cornish's (1994) concept of the *script*.
- scripts/M.O.s may not be linear, but branching and contingent on what offenders encounter during the crime. This ranges from tactical manoeuvring to *displacement* or *strategic adaptation, innovation and crime 'arms races'* between thieves and crime preventers. Organised criminals may be adept at this. They will also be better able to *replace* offenders removed from crime situations through imprisonment, whether new bosses muscling into vacated territories or new recruits replacing arrested 'mules'.
- many organised crimes involve offenders navigating a series of *scenes* – preparation, execution and consummation.

Scenes are vital for understanding organised crime. The same diagnostic map of causes applies to the event completing each scene (Figure 15.3). (What may be a target in one scene – a car to steal – may be a resource in the next – getaway car in a robbery.) We can intervene at any stage – perhaps several. Scene diagrams serve as flowcharts for helping to think strategically about how well-resourced, organised criminals could bypass blockages/disruptions by seeking alternative routes to their ultimate goal.

*Factors bringing the Conjunction of Criminal Opportunity together*

Remote causes rarely operate through a single, analytic ray of Figure 15.3. Nor is the conjunction like tramlines inevitably converging on the criminal event. The causal prerequisites of the event are brought together through social, economic and psychological processes described by many a criminological theory. These processes involve macroeconomic influences, subcultural factors and the market demand for goods or illegal services; channelling by the built environment and transport; victims' and offenders' current life circumstances, routine activities and lifestyle which cause them to encounter each another regularly in time and space; and

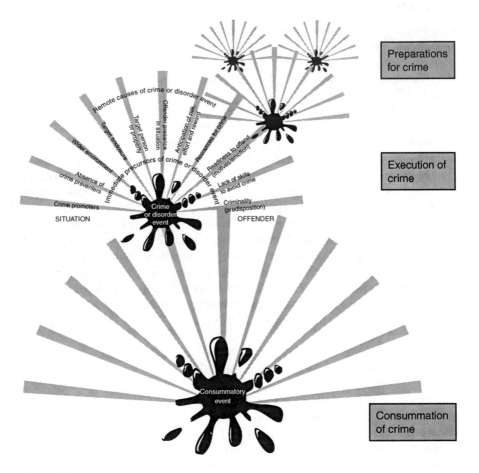

*Figure 15.3* Scenes.

long- or short-term conflicts such as between gangs or ethnic groups. Of course, active offenders, especially if organised, will be planning and preparing – seeking opportunities and creating them by bringing the causal preconditions of crime together. At one end of the scale they will be setting up a sequence of scenes for specific criminal enterprises; at the other, invasively establishing a supportive environment for crime through building contacts, developing trust and corrupting officials.

A key strategic concept is the *niche* for offending (or for promoting crime, for example via money laundering services). Borrowed from ecology, it is an identifiable concentration or flow of wealth from which offenders can make a living, using the resources at their disposal to exploit it whilst maintaining acceptable levels of effort and risk. The idea of controlling offending by controlling the niche is advanced by Paul and Jeff Brantingham (1991); Cohen *et al.* (1995) suggest related ideas. The significance of the niche connects with offender replacement – arrest 'Mr Big' the drug dealer, and 'Mr Notsobig' swiftly fills his place, because that place is available for anyone with the resources to exploit it. The Brantinghams argue that cuts in crime that outlast offender replacement require reducing the available niches. Albanese (2000) poses the closely related question: 'do criminals organise around opportunities for crime or do criminal opportunities create offenders?' Answering this question requires considering the causes of organised crime at different levels:

> *Level 1* – the *components* of the Conjunction of Criminal Opportunity or subsidiary scenes (offender, preventer, etc.).
> *Level 2* – the *individual scene* and the causes that combine to make it happen.
> *Level 3* – the *logistical structure of scenes* – the flowchart of M.O. and scripts, in which the criminal events are embedded.
> *Level 4* – the *day-to-day operation of a criminal enterprise* in generating the flow of profitable events/transactions and associated scenes.
> *Level 5* – *wider structures:*

- the *career of the criminal enterprise* – initiation, growth, decline, splitting, merger, adaptation to new threats and criminal/legitimate business opportunities.
- the *niche.*
- *criminal networks* for transaction, collaboration, and service provision.
- specific *markets* for stolen or illegal goods.

> *Level 6* – the *whole ecosystem* of organisational/individual careers in the context of networks, markets and niches.

### Specifying interventions in principle

Having diagnosed the causes and processes of the crime problem, practitioners must choose how and where to intervene. Figure 15.4 shows a 'universal story of a preventive scheme' in which an intervention, at some point upstream of the criminal event, disrupts the CCO, reduces the risk of criminal events and if successful, ultimately reduces their actual frequency. Benefits for community safety and economic well-being (such as regeneration or higher tax yield) may follow. From an organised crime perspective multiple interventions in multiple scenes may be desirable, but the same basic descriptive sequence can be used repeatedly and linked together in a structured description.

Again 11 generic kinds of 'molecular' intervention can be mapped onto the causes they are ultimately intended to block, weaken or divert – even if, as with early childhood schemes, the intervention is way upstream of the criminal events to be prevented. On the *situational* side, are:

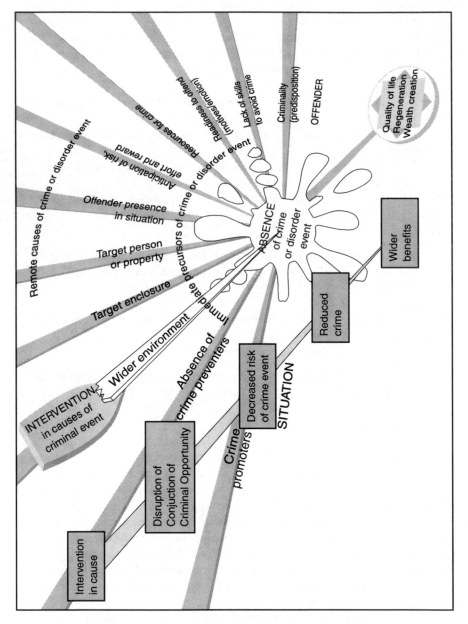

*Figure 15.4* A crime prevention intervention.

- *target hardening, target removal, value reduction,* and so on.
- *perimeter access and security.*
- *environmental design, planning and management* including aiding surveillance, resolving conflicts and setting rules.
- *boosting preventers* – their presence, alertness, competence, motivation and responsibility, whether through formal control (like patrolling), informal social control, self-protection and/or avoidance. Stopping preventers becoming promoters is important. With organised crime, this may involve preventing corruption and protecting and cultivating witnesses and informants.
- *discouraging and deterring crime promoters* and awakening their *conscience* – through naming and shaming, civil liability, prohibiting rechipping of stolen mobile phones, tackling criminal subcultures, procedural controls or market reduction; reduction of existing corruption.

On the *offender* side are:

- *excluding offenders* from crime situations – for example, keeping young offenders under curfew or incarcerated, stopping corrupt company directors from running businesses, excluding shady companies from winning public contracts or restricting licences to operate printing presses or bureaux de change.
- *deterrence* – raising perceived risks and costs of detection; *discouragement* – making the effort to offend seem too great and the reward too small; *awakening conscience.*
- *restricting resources for offending* – control of weapons, tools and information on targets, and transfer of criminal know-how. Control of criminal organisations' recruitment, growth and efficiency by disruption of trust and logistics.
- *reducing readiness to offend* – changing offenders' current life circumstances – alleviating drug problems, stressors like poor housing, and conflicts; limiting organisational pressures on individual members.
- *supplying resources to avoid crime* – training offenders in social and work skills. At the corporate level, helping companies verging on illegal behaviour towards legitimate profit (Pettersson and Lundgren, 2002).
- *reducing criminality* – intervening in early lives to reduce known risk factors, enhancing known protective factors through family, school and peer groups; and supplying remedial treatment for those already convicted. These all limit the scope for recruitment to criminal networks and organisations.

With the map of interventions in Figure 15.5, practitioners have the main options laid out, and can then delve into further detail to match interventions to crime problems (and specific scenes), their causes and context. Again, interventions targeted on individual offenders or co-offenders could be complemented by interventions on corporate offenders.

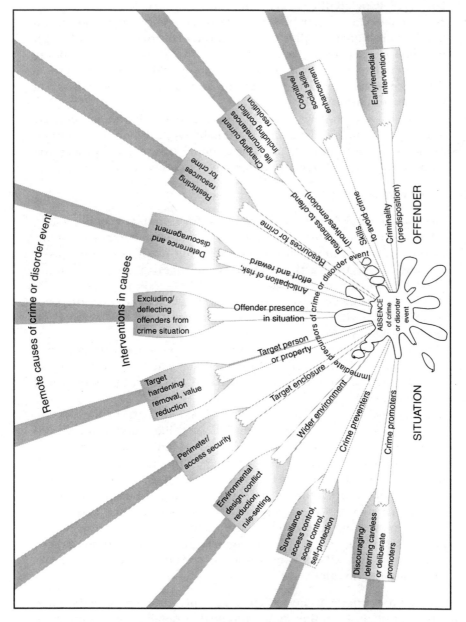

*Figure 15.5* Intervention space: crime prevention and the Conjunction of Criminal Opportunity.

These are highly-specific 'molecular' interventions against specific crime problems. The interventions make specific crime opportunities more risky, more effort and less rewarding, or focus on disrupting, inhibiting, removing or reforming specific offenders. Even repeated, temporary disruption of offending reduces the average yield to criminals and limits the rate of growth of their activities. However, as previously stated, preventing organised crime must extend to higher strategic levels to incapacitate and permanently reduce the activity of illegal enterprise. Without this, we may win the battles but still lose the war. Something more than just single blockages and disruptions is needed because illegal enterprises can circumvent individual barriers, and new organisations will replace those closed down if the niches are still available and the markets persist. Strategic interventions tackling the higher levels of causation include:

- targeting 'lynchpins' in an offender network.
- tackling those crimes (for example, vehicle crime) that lead to individual criminal careers, aid recruitment to organised crime, or financially nourish more serious and organised crimes like terrorism.
- considering wider patterns of displacement and offender replacement which may limit the sustainability of specific interventions.
- tackling multiple scenes in a complex organised crime.
- simultaneously disrupting several aspects of a market for contraband, stolen or illegal goods.
- establishing a linked system of barriers collectively hard to bypass. (Damming a stream eventually requires blocking off the whole valley. But studies of displacement of crime (Barr and Pease, 1990; Hesseling, 1994) suggest that offending does not overflow forever – eventually the effort to maintain the rewards of crime relative to the risk increases so much that offenders choose to channel their activities legitimately.)
- designing out *niches* for offending – concentrations or flows of wealth which inevitably draw offenders to exploit them (for example, warehouses full of expensive computer chips, funds flowing routinely through particular channels) – e.g. by dispersing targets and making the average level of risk and effort unacceptable with the resources available to the offenders.
- generally tackling crime as a business enterprise (but for limitations see Levi and Taylor, 2000) and reversing all central/local government's knowledge about supporting enterprise *without* harming legitimate companies. Here, the planning and development/construction control systems are strategically important.
- the Market Reduction approach – disrupting specific markets for stolen goods (Sutton, 1998).
- preventing/resolving sustained *conflicts* between gangs, ethnic groups, and so on, which generate persistent crime problems.

Despite the importance of these high-level interventions, the last word is that they usually work through a structured set of activities at the lower, molecular levels – right down to erecting barriers to individual crime scenes.

### Implementing prevention in practice

Much that practitioners should know about implementation is prosaic (project management, media handling, and so on). But know-how and know-what information specific to crime prevention must also be captured. Space prevents this chapter from covering aspects of implementation such as targeting causes, designing methods and delivering the right interventions to the right causes of crime efficiently, effectively, sustainably and acceptably (see Ekblom, 2001, 2002a). However, we must clarify the relationship between interventions in principle and methods in practice.

### From interventions in principle to real-world methods

Whether interventions are implemented in a strategic or tactical context, the immediate *principles* or *mechanisms* by which they are intended to work can be described using the 11 generic categories listed above (pp. 253–5), linked and extended to cover higher-level causes. But real-world *methods* of intervention are more complex. Remote methods may work through long causal chains before influencing the immediate precursors. A single method (like putting fences around a factory) can work through many mechanisms (physically blocking access, discouraging offenders, helping preventers – site guards) – see Figure 15.6, illustrating this 'solution space'.

Individual intervention methods may be combined in a package (see Figure 15.6) that may combine interventions, sometimes at different levels, which address multiple causes of a particular crime problem; or tackle causes common to diverse crime problems involving use of a common resource such as forged passports, or a criminal network. Holistic approaches can confer synergy and efficiency. But the more holistic a package, the greater care practitioners should take to focus on specific arrays of intervention mechanisms. All-inclusive initiatives with unclear and drifting means and ends are to be avoided.

Holistic approaches can confer synergy and efficiency. But the more holistic a package, the more practitioners should focus on specific problems, their causes and interactions. All-inclusive initiatives with unclear and drifting objectives are to be avoided.

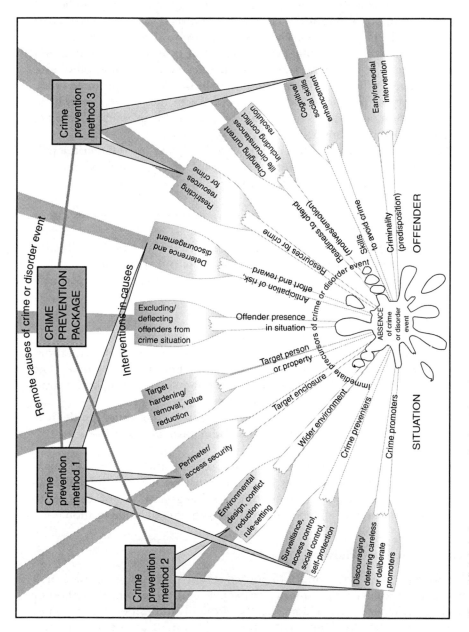

*Figure 15.6* Solution space: methods and packages.

*Involvement of the community*

Formal crime preventers such as government agencies and local partnerships cannot operate alone but must *act at a distance* – mobilising other public and private institutions and ordinary citizens better-placed to perform particular roles and tasks in prevention. The tasks may involve directly intervening in the causes of crime, facilitating interventions of others by motivating and enabling them or alleviating constraints. Besides boosting these preventive roles, we must influence those who accidentally or recklessly promote crime by their everyday private, public or commercial activities. We especially need to protect those in positions of formal responsibility for prevention, who are at risk of corruption, thus becoming crime promoters.

Acting at a distance involves a sequence of steps to *insert* the crime prevention tasks in the community. These can be systematically planned under the acronym CLAMED (see Ekblom, 2001):

*   *Clarify the crime reduction roles and tasks* requiring external agents rather than in-house delivery.
*   *Locate the preventive agents* – identify institutions and individuals with the potential to carry out the tasks effectively and acceptably.
*   once located, secure their co-operation and enhance their performance by:

    *   *Alerting* them to the crime problem;
    *   *Motivating* them to accept the Crime Reduction task;
    *   *Empowering* them – building capacity through competence (know-what, know-how and technical aids), operational resources like funds, staff, information and legal powers; alleviating constraints, but establishing checks and balances against excess;
    *   *Directing* them (if appropriate) to follow particular guidelines, select particular targets or implement particular activities.

Given the many interdependencies within society, and the need to establish multiple barriers, applying CLAMED must go beyond isolated individuals or institutions – engendering an integrated set of actions to co-ordinate a range of agents and establish a climate of collaboration.

## The structure of knowledge bases

Knowledge bases to support organised crime prevention must switch between the analytic mechanism perspective, and the practical method or package perspectives (Ekblom, 2002a; Ekblom and Tilley, 1998). They must reflect the five kinds of knowledge identified at the start of this chapter, and particularly cover both know-what and know-how. They should also capture information on the levels at which the interventions act. The 'ordinary' version of CCO confines itself to distinguishing 'social levels' of action. That concept characterises the methods employed in mobilising, implementing and intervening in the causes of criminal events, as acting on or through a diverse set of 'entities' in the wider world. These entities range from the individual offender or target of crime, to family, community or institutions such as companies and schools, and (already) markets (Ekblom, 2001). This structure can be built upon to capture the entities and processes relevant to organised crime prevention.

## Conclusion

The CCO framework is not based on simple 'aide-memoire'-type slogans and diagrams like the 'Problem Analysis Triangle' (Hough and Tilley, 1998). No other profession (public health or architecture, say) would send its practitioners into the field and expect them to deliver with such limited conceptual resources! The CCO philosophy is that high invest-ment in practitioner familiarisation and training produces high yield in geared up performance against organised crime. Once trained, practition-ers acquire the general schema; the transfer of individual items of know-ledge about particular preventive methods is far more efficient and less of a mental burden than when a whole new way of thinking must be grasped at the point of consulting a knowledge base. Products like the UK's National Intelligence Model indicate that the police are not afraid of com-plexity where it is judged necessary to help them tackle crime. But the competition between simple and sophisticated frameworks is ultimately a question to be resolved by practical development and evaluation.

The CCO framework can potentially support a 'what works' knowledge base for preventing organised crime in several ways. It can aid the main-tenance and replication of good practice, innovation and anticipation by facilitating entry, storage, retrieval and synthesis of knowledge on:

- crime problems, scene by scene,
- operational objectives of schemes and programmes,
- the causes of crime (potentially at a range of levels),
- interventions,
- practical methods and strategies of prevention, and their implementa-tion and insertion in the community,
- evaluation of process and impact.

The CCO can also facilitate the pooling of knowledge between those who prevent organised and 'ordinary' crime. But the knowledge base can be much more than a dry repository of individual case studies. It can be a dynamic, organised body of evidence-based expertise distilling generic principles that empower professional practitioners to tackle diverse crime problems in diverse contexts. The very structure of the knowledge base can convey the necessary ways of thinking to users. We will need this knowledge and these ways of thinking to keep up with sophisticated, organised criminals.

What are the next steps? The Falcone-funded study (Browne *et al.*, 2001) considered the utility of CCO in structuring a knowledge base on what works in organised crime prevention. CCO appeared to work rather well in handling and capturing the complexity of organised crime in the example of a multi-scene scam involving a range of different actors with diverse resources in the export of stolen Mercedes cars to Africa. However, the Falcone research principally revealed great difficulty in obtaining more than a handful of detailed good practice examples to study. On the one hand, this means CCO has yet to be tested extensively as a knowledge-base framework, promising though it seems. On the other, it suggests further opportunities to try CCO out because, behind the lack of good practice examples, there appeared to be an absence of the kind of routine and systematic approach to reducing organised crimes that CCO can support. For this, CCO would have to be tested and refined at an operational level, and developed into a user-friendly toolkit, for example as an 'intelligence product' within the terms of the UK National Intelligence Model (NCIS, 2000).

## References

Albanese, J.S. (2000) 'The causes of organised crime: do criminals organise around opportunities for crime or do criminal opportunities create new offenders?', *Journal of Contemporary Criminal Justice* 16: 409–23.

Barr, R. and Pease, K. (1990) 'Crime placement, displacement and deflection', in M. Tonry and N. Morris (eds) *Crime and Justice*, vol. 12. Chicago, IL: University of Chicago Press.

Brantingham, P. and Brantingham, J. (1991) 'Niches and predators: theoretical departures in the ecology of crime'. Paper presented at Western Society of Criminology, Berkeley, California.

Browne, D., Levi, M., Maguire, M. *et al.* (2001) 'The identification, development and exchange of good practice for reducing organised crime'. Unpublished report to European Commission of Falcone-funded research project.

Cohen, L. and Felson, M. (1979) 'Social change and crime rate trends: a routine activity approach', *American Sociological Review* 44: 588–608.

Cohen, L., Vila, B. and Machalek, R. (1995) 'Expropriative crime and crime policy: an evolutionary ecological analysis', *Studies on Crime and Crime Prevention* 4: 197–219.

Cornish, D. (1994) 'The procedural analysis of offending and its relevance for situational prevention', in R. Clarke (ed.) *Crime Prevention Studies*, vol. 3. Monsey, NY: Criminal Justice Press, pp. 151–96.

Cornish, D. and Clarke, R. (2002) 'Analyzing organised crimes', in A. Piquero and S. Tibbetts (eds) *Rational Choice*. London: Routledge, pp. 41–63.

Ekblom, P. (1996) 'Towards a discipline of crime prevention: a systematic approach to its nature, range and concepts', in T. Bennett (ed.) *Preventing Crime and Disorder: Targeting Strategies and Responsibilities*, Cambridge Cropwood Series. Cambridge: Institute of Criminology.

—— (1997) 'Gearing up against crime: a dynamic framework to help designers keep up with the adaptive criminal in a changing world', *International Journal of Risk, Security and Crime Prevention* 214: 249–65. Online: http://www.homeoffice. gov.uk/rds/pdfs/risk.pdf (accessed 30 April 2002).

—— (1999) 'Can we make crime prevention adaptive by learning from other evolutionary struggles?', *Studies on Crime and Crime Prevention* 8: 27–51. Online: http://www.bra.se/extra/studies/ (accessed 30 April 2002).

—— (2000a) 'A formal and systematic description of a preventive scheme and its components', unpublished paper.

—— (2000b) 'Preventing organised crime: a conceptual framework'. Presentation at Europol workshop on Organised Crime, The Hague, May.

—— (2001) *The Conjunction of Criminal Opportunity: a Framework for Crime Reduction Toolkits*. Online: http://www.crimereduction.gov.uk/learningzone/cco.htm (accessed 30 April 2002).

—— (2002a) 'From the source to the mainstream is uphill: the challenge of transferring knowledge of crime prevention through replication, innovation and anticipation', in N. Tilley (ed.) *Analysis for Crime Prevention, Crime Prevention Studies*, vol. 13. Monsey, NY: Criminal Justice Press, pp. 131–203.

—— (2002b) 'Future imperfect: preparing for the crimes to come', *Criminal Justice Matters*, 46 Winter 2001/02, 38–40.

Ekblom, P. and Tilley, N. (1998) ' "What works" database for community safety/ crime reduction practitioners – towards a specification for an ideal template', unpublished paper.

—— (2000) 'Going equipped: criminology, situational crime prevention and the resourceful offender', *British Journal of Criminology* 40: 376–98.

Forrester, D., Chatterton, M. and Pease, K. with the assistance of Brown, R. (1988) *The Kirkholt Burglary Prevention Project, Rochdale*, Crime Prevention Unit Paper 13. London: Home Office.

Forrester, D., Frenz, S., O'Connell, M. and Pease, K. (1990) *The Kirkholt Burglary Prevention Project: Phase II*, Crime Prevention Unit Paper 23. London: Home Office.

Hesseling, R. (1994) 'Displacement: a review of the empirical literature', *Crime Prevention Studies* 3: 197–230.

Hough, J. and Tilley, N. (1998) *Getting the Grease to the Squeak: Research Lessons for Crime Prevention*, Police Research Series Paper 85. London: Home Office.

Levi, M. and Naylor, T. (2000) 'The organisation of business and the organisation of crime.' Research essay on CD-ROM published with *Turning the Corner*, Foresight Crime Prevention Panel Report. London: Office for Science and Technology, Department of Trade and Industry.

NCIS (2000) *National Intelligence Model*. London: NCIS.

Pawson, R. and Tilley, N. (1997) *Realistic Evaluation*. London: Sage.

Petterson, L. and Lundgren, V. (2002) *Just in Time. Economic Crime in the Road Haulage Industries of Sweden and Norway*. English summary of *Just in Time. Ekobrottslighet inom svensk och norsk långtradartransport*. Report 2002: 6 Stockholm: Swedish National Crime Prevention Council.

Sutton, M. (1998) *Handling Stolen Goods and Theft: a Market Reduction Approach*, Home Office Research Study 178. London: Home Office.

# 16 After transnational organised crime?

## The politics of public safety

*Adam Edwards and Peter Gill*

Dates provide an alluring framework for historical and political analysis; for example, we routinely compare the nineteenth and twentieth centuries as though the numbers 1800 and 1900 can actually do any more for explanation than provide convenient bookends. So, here, it is tempting to identify the decade 1991–2001 as, in international political terms, the decade of transnational organised crime. Even more precisely, the bookends might be formed, at one end, by the failure of the conservative coup in Russia in August 1991 or the decision of several republics to form the Commonwealth of Independent States in December and, more clearly at the other, September 11, 2001, when hijacked planes were flown into the World Trade Center in New York and the Pentagon in Washington, DC.

The events, debates and policies of the period 1991–2001 do provide much of the substance of the chapters in this book; indeed, as explained in the Introduction, they provided the impetus for setting up the seminars in the first place. But dates *are* just bookends and it is important to acknowledge the longer gestation of these issues. For example, Ethan Nadelmann (1993) traced what he called the 'internationalization' of American law enforcement from the late eighteenth century onwards, a process that accelerated from the early 1970s particularly with respect to drugs. Similarly, in Europe, the earliest moves to achieve some form of multi-lateral co-operation on criminal matters regarding drugs trafficking came in 1972 with the formation of the Pompidou Group consisting of the then-EC states plus others and STAR (translated as 'Permanent Working Group on Drugs') which involved some EC countries plus the USA (specifically the Drugs Enforcement Agency). Until the 1980s, European policy initiatives remained relatively discrete – drugs from 1972, 'terrorism' in Trevi from 1976 onwards – but then issues began to be conflated into what Bigo (1994) identified as the 'security continuum' taking in terrorism, drugs, illegal migrants and asylum seekers. In 1989, EC Interior Ministers drew up the PALMA document with recommendations for action on all these security issues and, in 1992, the move to formalise the intergovernmental TREVI forum was completed in the Maastricht Treaty establishing the 'third pillar' for justice and home affairs and the decision to establish the European Police Office (Europol) for information exchange and the development of intelligence.

So, when the end of the Cold War opened up the political or security space for new developments, there was already a considerable institutional architecture in place within which governments could operate. The dominant theme accompanying the ensuing occupation of this space by diverse security, law enforcement and military agencies was the seriousness of the threat from 'transnational organised crime'. Thus an issue that had, for the previous 20 years, been discussed primarily in technical terms in various inter-governmental arenas became, within just a few years, the subject of a special United Nations Conference. As several of our chapters have indicated, it is problematic to explain the rapid emergence of this issue through reference to any measurable increase in cross-national criminality, but the indications are that the period 1992–4 saw an emerging coincidence of interests between key actors in both the US and Europe, though, in the latter, there were certainly worries about the impact of the collapse of the old regimes, especially in Russia and Yugoslavia.

It is recognised in political theory that authorities do not simply respond, in a more or less enlightened fashion, to pre-given problems but must, of necessity, define these problems in order to render them thinkable for the purposes of government (Barry *et al.*, 1996; Burchell *et al.*, 1991; Smandych, 1999). In crime control discourse, the definition of a problem and the promotion of certain policy responses is, therefore, an inherently political enterprise; strategies of control embody political assumptions, entail certain political contexts and have political consequences (Crawford, 1998; Stenson, 2000). The contribution that social scientists can make to policy change and learning is, therefore, restricted by work that accepts as axiomatic prevailing definitions of the scope and dynamics of a governmental problem. Rather, a more 'reflexive' scrutiny of what we study, how we study it and to what ends is required (Rhodes, 1997). Yet much criminological discourse continues to treat such scrutiny as a caveat that can be bracketed-off from more forensic discussions of the technologies of control and their *modus operandi* (Felson and Clarke, 1998; Pease, 2002; Tilley, 2002). Conversely, the ways in which policy-oriented learning is organised *presuppose* certain technologies and the interpretation of their outcomes, whilst obfuscating, if not negating, others (Edwards and Gill, 2002b).

Our interest in the problem of transnational organised crime (TOC) is, therefore, to explicate the underlying governmentality of policy responses, how this narrates the problem of TOC, privileges particular strategies and attendant technologies of control and then organises the interpretation and appraisal of these strategies to contain policy change and learning within certain parameters (Edwards and Gill, 2002a, b). In this concluding chapter we develop this approach further by contrasting the governmentality of TOC with the criticisms it has attracted throughout the UK Economic and Social Research Council (ESRC) seminar series, on which this book is based, and through reference to the broader literature generated by the frenetic policy activity around this perceived problem over the past decade. Through this contrast, it is possible to distinguish three generic narratives on the interrelationships between crime and control, which differ in terms of their belief in the intelligibility of TOC as an object of government and how this and/or other threats to 'security' can and should be controlled.

## The governmentality of organised crime control

The need for reflexivity in thinking about the problems of government forms part of a broader turn in the philosophy of social science, away from positivist thought and the presumption that observers, especially 'experts', can have a view of social objects such as crime that is unmediated by the values these observers have about that which should be observed and how it should be interpreted. Notwithstanding the substantial criticism that positivist thought has received from interpretative social science, much governmental discourse continues to be dominated by the belief that its objects are unproblematic and that objective knowledge can be obtained through methodological innovations in the measurement of these objects so defined. This is especially the case in relation to official discourse on the problem of 'crime' and its control. This 'orthodox conception of the aims of science' can, however, be contrasted with a 'critical theory conception' that insists knowledge should proceed from a questioning of the ontology of objects, which is to question the possibility and conditions of their existence and how these can be apprehended (Sayer, 1992: 232ff).

As noted in the Introduction, controversy over the very existence of 'transnational organised crime' informed the establishment of the ESRC seminar series and, throughout this book, the status of TOC is contested. Is it useful to collate diverse practices, such as trafficking in drugs, people, armaments, the corruption of public officials, tax evasion, fraud, money laundering, and so on, under this omnibus category (see chapters by Burnham, Gregory, Dorn in this volume) or is it preferable to replace the over-homogenised imagery of TOC with a focus on harmful practices on the presumption that they are conceptually discrete, entail different dynamics and require 'customised' interventions (see chapters by Stelfox, Klerks, Levi and Ekblom in this volume)? This ontological disagreement is complicated further by those who argue that a preoccupation with 'crime' reproduces a narrow concern with practices that are proscribed, in a particular place and moment, by criminal legal codes, and thereby precludes debate over the need to intervene against activities that may be legal, such as the operation of de-regulated markets, but are nonetheless harmful according to broader criteria of social justice and public safety (see chapters by Woodiwiss, Elvins, Sheptycki, Rawlinson, Bogusz and King in this volume).

In order to explore the implications of the contested nature of TOC, we have found useful political and criminological studies of the governmentality of crime control. Studies of governmentality are concerned with 'governance as a mentality or rationality of rule, stressing that phenomena have to be intellectually and linguistically represented as a certain kind of problem in order for them to be governed' (O'Malley, 2001: 134; Dean, 1999). As such, the conduct of certain individuals, groups and populations has, of necessity, to be defined by public authorities and, inherent in this definition, are specific value judgements about the kinds of conduct that should be proscribed and how this conduct should be controlled. Such value judgements are, in turn, informed by political rationalities of rule, such as neo-liberalism, conservatism and social democracy, which specify the ends of government, such as 'individual freedom', 'moral authority' and/or 'social solidarity', and strategies for the accomplishment of these ends and their related technologies (Barry *et al.*, 1996; Stenson, 1999, 2000). In elucidating the political mentalities inherent in specific strategies of control, the study of governmentality enables us to think beyond that which already exists in order to imagine alternative ends and/or means of government.

Studies of governmentality can be elaborated further through reference to the ways in which competing policy coalitions employ political rationalities to *translate* problems of government and their resolution (cf. Callon, 1986). We have, in earlier work, employed this focus on the translation of crime and its control to distinguish official from critical narrations of TOC (Edwards and Gill, 2002b). In the light of arguments conducted through the ESRC seminar series and in the broader criminological literature, it is possible to refine this distinction further to identify three discrete narratives which conceive TOC as an external threat, as a consequence of increased opportunities for crime and as a challenge generated by the internal dynamics of market societies. In the remainder of this chapter we discuss the distinctiveness of these narratives and their implications for prospective policy change and learning in terms of the ways in which they define particular objects of threat and security and thus prioritise certain control strategies and technologies over others.

## External threat

Research into the origins of TOC has traced its provenance as a priority for governmental intervention back to the influence of American conceptions of organised crime as an external threat by ethnically defined groups who act against the integrity of western political-economies (Nadelmann, 1993; Woodiwiss, Chapter 1, this volume). Whilst different outsider groups, such as the 'Colombian Cartels', 'Chinese Triads' and, more recently, the 'Russian Mafya' have been added to the longer-standing suspicion of the 'Italian Mafia' and their US relations, the 'Cosa Nostra', this alien conspiracy theory has remained the connecting thread in the crime control policies of post-1945 US Federal Administrations. The successful generalisation of this theory, beyond its use in US domestic criminal justice to key international policy-making fora such as the United Nations and G7/P8, is essential to understanding the emergence of TOC as an object of global governance and as exemplifying a 'new global pluralist' theory of threats to the security of western political-economies post-Cold War (Woodiwiss, Chapter 1, this volume).

It has been suggested that the definition of TOC represented more of a coincidence of interests amongst US Administrations and member states of the European Union, who had, simultaneously, been developing policies for international co-operation in law enforcement, security and intelligence since the early 1970s in response to fears over political violence, immigration and, subsequently, over the criminogenic consequences of the 'freedom of movement' across national borders entailed in the Single European Market (Bigo, 2000). Nonetheless, these interests coalesced around the new global pluralist theory of the security threats posed by ethnically-defined criminal groups.

Within the European Union, recent policy initiatives have begun to challenge this theory; it is recognised in the New Millennium Strategy for the *Prevention and Control of Organised Crime* that, whilst there is an increasing threat from organised criminal groups outside the territory of the EU, nationals and residents of member states pose 'a significantly greater risk' (see Elvins, Chapter 2, this volume). Even though organised crime is portrayed more as an 'enemy within' rather than as an alien conspiracy, the New Millennium Strategy still perpetuates the preoccupation of official discourse with a 'pyramidal' conception of organised crime as the activity of hierarchically structured, ethnically-defined groups who collaborate for prolonged periods of time and whose pursuit of profit and political power threatens an otherwise satisfactory political economy, whether from within or without (see Levi, Chapter 13, this volume).

At a more profound level of understanding, this official discourse embodies a 'criminology of the other' (Garland, 1996: 461–3) in that it produces an exogenous understanding of the causes of organised crime. This is explicitly the case in the very etymology of trans*national* organised crime, where security is defined in relation to the external threats encountered by nation states. Even where the prefix 'transnational' is dropped, as in the EU New Millennium Strategy, organised crime is still portrayed as an attack on political-economies that are assumed to be satisfactory, or at least non-criminogenic, and should, *ipso facto*, be secured in their existing format. In the longstanding tradition of criminologies of the other, criminality is assumed to be a consequence of pathological actors who are essentially different from 'us', the normal, law-abiding, consensual majority. In this 'essentialising of difference' lies the tacit political uses of threat to affirm the righteousness of a particular social order and displace responsibility for its problems onto 'deviant' others (Young, 1999).

To problematise crime in terms of the demonising of others pre-supposes certain strategies of control, whilst negating others. For, having defined certain ethnic and social groups as the problem, any responsibility that specific political-economic arrangements may have for generating criminality and other social harms is obviated. Security becomes, instead, the business of enforcing, punishing, containing, disturbing and dismant-ling these outsider groups (Adamoli *et al.*, 1998: 131ff.). The denial of the responsibility that such arrangements may have for crime and social harm reaches its apogee in the strategy of 'securitisation' (Bigo, 1994; Buzan *et al.*, 1998). Problems of government can be located along a spectrum from non-politicised (there is no public debate and public authorities disavow their involvement) through politicised (where the issue is subject to ongoing democratic debate) to securitised where, 'the issue is presented as an existential threat, requiring emergency measures and justifying actions outside the normal bounds of political procedure' (Buzan *et al.*, 1998: 23–4). Various contributions to this book have documented the securitisation of policy responses to organised crime and the consequent deployment of control technologies, such as the extension of intelligence and surveillance operations to cover all financial transactions, electronic and mobile telephonic communications and the confiscation of purport-edly criminal assets, formulated by policy-making bodies such as the Financial Action Task Force (FATF) and the EU's Multi-Disciplinary Group on Organised Crime (MDG), which are not subject to any demo-cratic oversight and whose evidential basis for these policies remains insu-lated from public scrutiny (see chapters by Elvins, Sheptycki and Mitsilegas in this volume).

The problematisation of TOC in terms of pyramidal groups and their 'kingpins' or 'core nominals' not only presupposes control strategies of enforcement, punishment, containment, disturbance and dismantling, it also constrains the interpretation and appraisal of these strategies. Intelligence-led policing, for example, has been criticised for its 'self-replicating and self-guiding' character in focusing on measures of activity, such as arrest rates, seizures of illicit goods and the confiscation of pro-ceeds (see chapter by Sheptycki). Whereas measures of the outcomes of such strategies, for example reductions in the consumption of illicit nar-cotics and associated harms, question the very raison d'etre of law enforce-ment and open-up the political space for devising alternative strategies of control (see chapters by Levi and Ekblom), measures of activity are self-serving in that they imply the need for more enforcement, the further extension of surveillance and greater investment in intelligence gathering, and so on.[1]

## Increased opportunities

Disenchantment with criminal justice alone as a crime control strategy has been a key factor in the rise of an alternative paradigm, which switches the focus away from the punishment of pathological offenders toward the prevention, or at least reduction, of opportunities for the commission of particular types of crime, in specific situations, at certain moments by 'rational' actors (Clarke, 1997; Graham and Bennett, 1995: 47–70). Counterpoised to the 'criminology of the other', this 'criminology of the self' regards offenders as essentially the same as their victims and certain implications for defining the objects of control follow from this (Garland, 1996: 461–3).

Instead of investigating the attributes of 'core nominals' or criminal organisations and deducing problems of crime from these attributes, this narrative is concerned with those factors that make certain organised crime events possible (see Stelfox in this volume). It assumes there will be a 'supply of motivated offenders' and argues that it is less important to understand the dispositional qualities of their motivation than to identify how this supply coincides with the availability of 'suitable targets' and the absence of 'capable guardians' in particular places at certain moments to produce crime (Felson, 1994). As such, patterns in the incidence, prevalence and concentration of organised crime are interpreted in terms of social trends that generate increased opportunities. For example, technological innovations in communication and intelligence sharing amongst criminal fraternities (see Dorn in this volume) and the abolition of border controls create suitable targets for crime such as electronic commerce and the evasion of customs and excise duties, whilst negating, or enabling the circumvention of, capable guardians.

This narrative has also influenced the re-definition of criminal organisations in terms of protean social networks rather than immutable, pyramidal, hierarchies (Coles, 2001). From this perspective organised crime is enabled through the episodic co-operation of actors with a diversity of skills and resources and this, in turn, is facilitated by intermediaries, or 'criminal contact brokers', who supply criminal entrepreneurs for the purposes of accomplishing particular jobs (see Klerks in this volume). These intermediaries have been central to replenishing the capacity of criminal co-operatives after particular actors have been removed by law enforcement operations and are identified, therefore, as key targets for control hitherto obscured by the pyramidal conception of organised crime and the consequent focus on 'bosses'. In this narrative a further distinction is made between the 'molecular' and 'strategic' objects of opportunity reduction (see Ekblom in this volume). Molecular objects of control include those specific social networks and proximal circumstances involved in the commissioning of particular crimes. Strategic objects refer to the broader social contexts, such as markets for the production, exchange and consumption of illicit goods and services, which generate the supply of motivated offenders, presence of suitable targets and absence of capable guardians.

This emphasis on the need to understand the contexts of certain crime events marks a key difference with the narrative of organised crime as an external threat. To emphasise contexts that generate increased opportunities for crime is to recognise that crime events are embedded in particular places and experienced at specific moments; they are woven into the everyday routines of social relations (Felson, 1994). Whereas the external threat narrative invariably proceeds by enumerating checklists of abstract features that provide a content definition of organised crime and then deduces organised crime from these features (Adamoli *et al.*, 1998: 4–10), the increased opportunities narrative 'retroduces' the causes of crime from an examination of specific events and seeks to tailor various technologies of crime prevention to the diverse local contexts and thus routines in which they occur (Pawson and Tilley, 1997; Ekblom in this volume).

Again, certain strategies of control are presupposed in this problematisation, an exemplar of which is the strategy of 'market reduction' (Sutton, 1998). Once overly homogeneous concepts such as TOC are disaggregated into more concrete objects of control, such as the illicit trafficking of narcotics, the different dynamics of production, exchange and consumption entailed in the markets for such goods and services can be realised. From this perspective it is argued that control strategies have been preoccupied with curtailing the supply of illicit goods and services, through operations against 'core nominals' and organised crime groups (OCGs), whereas a more effective focus for control is the exchange and consumption of such goods and services. Reducing the opportunities for exchange and consumption will, it is presumed, reduce the motivation to provide illicit goods and services on behalf of offenders. From this axiomatic principle, the market reduction approach (MRA) argues that the basic aims of control should be to instil in offenders an appreciation that dealing in illicit goods and services is at least as risky as offending in the first place and to make the purchase, exchange and consumption of illicit goods and services more risky for all concerned (Sutton *et al.*, 2001: vii). Increasing the risks associated with the exchange and consumption of illicit goods and services can be accomplished by disabling key intermediary actors in illicit markets, especially 'fences' – those who knowingly purchase illicit goods and services with the intention of selling them on to end consumers – such as commercial enterprises (jewellers, pawnbrokers, second-hand dealers, etc.), residents (who organise local illicit markets) and hawkers (often the offenders themselves who sell directly to consumers). Although the MRA was initially developed, as with other opportunity reducing technologies, to control volume crimes such as domestic burglary and automobile theft, it is argued its principles can be generalised to other kinds of illicit markets, especially those in narcotics, so long as the particular dynamics and contexts of the markets in question are appreciated (Sutton *et al.*, 2001: 4) and has, subsequently, been identified as a potentially important innovation in the control of organised crime (see chapters by Stelfox and Ekblom in this volume).

Although this narrative can be credited with pinpointing the need for 'multi-agency' initiatives against crime, it has been criticised for the limits to its introspection of the causes and control of crime and other social harms. It is argued that criminologies of the self are adaptive to, rather than critical of, the social orders within which they are deployed (Garland, 1996: 463ff.). The strategy of opportunity reduction and its attendant technologies of control are defined through a critique of criminal law enforcement as a partial and blunt instrument of control, but not through a critique of the ends of control per se, which are 'provisionally accepted' as a reduction in those behaviours proscribed by the criminal law (Pease, 2002: 970). It is acknowledged, however, that without an ethical foundation, the deployment of opportunity reducing technologies can undermine social relations of trust and tolerance whilst exacerbating inequalities in the provision of security and the experience of victimisation (ibid.: 970–2).

For all the rhetorical insistence in the 'increased opportunities' narrative on the need to contextualise crime and its control, the image of offending that is produced by criminologies of the self is one of ahistorical rational actors abstracted from the particular social context and cultural milieu in which they *acquire* an understanding of who they are, what is in their 'rational' interests and how these can be advanced (Edwards and Gill, 2002b: 248; Hobbs, 1998a, b, 2001). The retort of advocates of opportunity reduction is that such 'dispositional' questions are impossible to answer and are, in any case, irrelevant to an understanding of how crime events can be prevented (Clarke, 1997). Yet it is precisely for this eschewal of dispositional analysis that the increased opportunities narrative can be criticised as contradictory: policy-makers are simultaneously encouraged to tailor control to the specific contexts in which crime events occur but are asked to do so using models of offending behaviour that negate contextual understanding (cf. Taylor, 1999).

## Internal challenge

From this perspective a more sociological understanding of interactions between crime and control as the products of certain kinds of social, economic and political arrangements can be derived. Crime is endogenous to particular social orders and it is in this sense that problems of crime are regarded as an 'internal challenge' rather than as an alien threat. The internal challenge narrative is also distinct from the idea of crime as a consequence of increased opportunities in that it replaces a focus on the rational choices of atomised individuals, abstracted from their actual social contexts, with a focus on the differential cultural, political and economic *associations* between individual and collective actors in historically specific contexts.

Reference to the differential associations entailed in criminal activity reflects the influence of Edwin Sutherland's thinking on this narration of transnational organised crime (Ruggiero, 2002). Sutherland's proposition that 'white-collar crime' belies the deterministic correlation between disadvantage and offending and the suggestion that criminal behaviour per se 'is learned in association with those who define it favourably and in isolation from those who define it unfavourably' (1949: 234) has provided a conceptual foundation for an alternative problematisation of TOC. Criminal activity is regarded as the outcome of interactions infused with a subcultural valorisation of offending as legitimate conduct. However, beyond Sutherland's social psychology of how certain individuals or small groups of actors become criminal, it is argued that criminal associations embody the cultural values of, and are enabled by, entire social formations, especially free market societies (Taylor, 1999: 156–63). Further, the dissemination of the 'entrepreneurial spirit' throughout civil society and into the routine, everyday activities of commerce coupled with the relentless competitive pressures of the global marketplace generates greater incentives for corruption and the contravention of regulations on trade, for example in the armaments industry (Taylor, ibid.; Ruggiero, 2000: 99–105).

Inspired by Sutherland's work, this narrative has also questioned the interdependencies between nominally licit and illicit entrepreneurs in market societies. It is argued that criminal associations are not contained within an 'underworld' or 'dirty' marketplace that parallels the 'upperworld' of 'clean' business. Rather, they segue into 'grey' markets of exchange between licit and illicit actors as in, for example, the role of certain financial institutions in laundering the proceeds of criminal organisations and the employment of criminal organisations by licit business to circumvent environmental protection laws and dump toxic industrial waste (Block, 1991; Ruggiero, 1998). The presence of grey markets also suggests a broadening of the entrepreneurial activities, beyond those formally proscribed in criminal legal codes, which should be encompassed in policy responses to 'social harm' rather than the narrower signifier of 'crime'. Critics of policy responses to TOC that depict organised criminal activity as external to the operation of licit markets, also note how the activities of multi-national business and the consequences of licit market exchange, whilst not illegal can, nonetheless, be considered harmful to civil society according to criteria of social, not just criminal, justice (Slapper and Tombs, 1999: 131–62; Rawlinson, 2002 and in this volume).

Interdependencies between 'dirty' and 'clean' markets have also been examined in terms of the stretching of criminal associations across different spatial scales. In these terms there is a certain ambiguity over the status of TOC in the internal challenge narrative. Some acknowledge its utility in so far as it updates Sutherland's ideas for the era of globalisation by recognising that opportunities for licit wealth creation enabled by the growth of transnational commerce, the deregulation of international markets and the construction of continental trading blocs (ASEAN, EU, NAFTA) in which internal border controls are weakened or abolished, also enable abundant opportunities for illicit transnational commerce, especially in the trafficking of narcotics (Ruggiero, 2002: 180–1). Even so, the over-homogenised imagery of TOC is deconstructed to reveal that globalisation is selective in its distribution of licit, illicit and grey market opportunities for accumulation. With regard to licit business, the transnational corporations that are successfully exploiting the opportunities of deregulated markets are, emphatically, Western. The converse of Western corporate capital's mobility is the immobility of entrepreneurs and the wider citizenry in the developing world. It is, therefore, a moot point as to whether the demons of TOC, the Columbians, Chinese, Russians, Turks, and so on, are as mobile as their licit Western counterparts in transnational commerce (ibid.).

The selectivity and unevenness of globalisation has, in the broader sociological literature, been argued to accentuate the importance of localities, rather than nations, as the new 'nodal' points and basic units of analysis in social and political change (Hirst and Thompson, 1996: 170ff.; Lash and Urry, 1994: 279–313). Thinking from within this tradition some commentators have eschewed the very idea of TOC as a contentless abstraction that is 'devoid of [actual] relations'; rather, 'Unlike previous eras, contemporary organised crime with its emphasis upon drugs, fraud and counterfeiting, simultaneously occupies both the local and the global. It is ... "local at all points"' (Hobbs, 1998a: 143). As a consequence the imbrication of licit and illicit enterprise occurs within 'glocalities' whose diverse cultural, political and economic histories shape the possibilities for this enterprise (ibid., 1998b).

This focus on 'glocal' rather than 'transnational' organised crime implies a further revision to the concept of human agency deployed in the narratives of 'external threat' and 'increased opportunities'. In place of the 'ethnic other' or the 'rational self' models of agency, it is argued that criminal associations entail not just instrumental–rational but also affective and habitual dispositions. These embody routines, prejudice, amorous attachments, and so on, on the basis of which entrepreneurs decide who to trust and do business with. If this is the case with licit enterprises, which may collapse precisely because they *fail* to adopt rational, utility-maximising approaches to the calculation of the risks, efforts and rewards associated with particular ventures, then such cultural qualities of interaction are accentuated for illicit entrepreneurs operating in hostile, law enforcement environments where trust is at a premium (Hall, 1997; Hobbs, 2001; Klerks in this volume).

The narrative of organised crime as an internal challenge to certain social formations has not accomplished the same degree of influence over official discourse as have narratives of external threat or, as is increasingly the case, of increased opportunities (cf. NCIS, 2000). Nonetheless, it can still be understood as a governmentality in so far as its problematisation presupposes certain governable places and actors and technologies for their control. This narrative presupposes interventions against the social preconditions for the formation and reproduction of criminal associations. Ethnographic research into the dynamics of criminal networks in English localities has, for example, identified the operation of local housing and labour markets as central to an understanding of how networks are formed and reproduced or disabled (Hobbs, 1998b; Hobbs and Dunningham, 1998). The implication of this is that social policy interventions should be prioritised in official discourse on crime and control. In addition it is argued that policing and criminal justice interventions can have perverse, unintended consequences in generating lucrative markets for organised crime (see Stelfox, Rawlinson in this volume). Another policy implication of this narrative is the need for action research into the structures of different markets, how they unevenly distribute cultural, political and economic capital amongst competing entrepreneurs and the contribution of policing and regulation to the creation, stagnation or collapse of such markets (Edwards and Gill, 2002a; Gill, 2002).

A more profound implication of the internal challenge narrative, however, is that such technologies of control should be deployed towards the end of social, not just criminal, justice. This is, arguably, the key quality distinguishing this from the other two narratives discussed in this chapter. For, in their domination of official discourse, criminologies of the other and self have disassociated strategies of control from political debate over the ends of government; instead they promulgate, 'policies for managing the danger and policing the divisions created by a certain kind of [neo-liberal] social organisation' (Garland, 1996: 463–6). Others have noted the dangers inherent in a 'criminalisation' of social policy (Crawford cited in Pease, 2002: 964); we would suggest it be replaced by the 'socialisation' of criminal justice.

## Conclusion

The advantage of examining policy debates over TOC in terms of competing governmentalities is that diagnosis of the implicit truth claims advanced in different narratives on crime and control is facilitated. As a consequence innovation is enabled by thinking beyond what is apparently the case to imagine how such problems of government could, nonetheless, be apprehended and governed otherwise. However, as advocates of governmentality studies have acknowledged, 'This process of displaying the truth claims of government, and their contingent nature, is the operation of "diagnosis" that displaces critique' (O'Malley, 2001: 135). As a consequence there is a division within the study of governmentality between those who advocate this study as a precursor to 'realist' inquiry into the actual, messy, often inchoate conduct of government (Garland, 1997; Stenson, 1998), and those who resist realist critique of what actually happens and why, who does what and with what consequences etc., in the belief that this precludes innovative thinking (O'Malley, 2001; Rose, 1999). Whereas the former seek to arbitrate between the claims of competing governmentalities, the latter believe there are no super-ordinate criteria for advancing the claims of a particular narrative other than normative political beliefs in, for example, neo-liberalism or social democracy.

This chapter has been an exercise in diagnosis through which we have sought to elicit the truth claims of competing narratives about TOC to, in turn, facilitate thinking about the 'reality' of this concept and represent the broader repertoire of concepts, strategies and technologies of security discussed in the ESRC research seminar series and in the wider literature. We do not accept, however, that diagnosis and critique are mutually incompatible. Rather, diagnosis can be used both as a means of thinking 'beyond the present' and as a precursor to more concrete research into the actual conduct of government.

There is insufficient space to elaborate fully on a future research agenda but let us give some examples of how research may provide the links between these competing narratives and improvements to the knowledge base and hence, possibly, to reductions in harmful activities. Studies of governmentality have demonstrated the contestable nature of the truth claims of competing narratives of crime and crime control (Smandych, 1999) but they have not analysed adequately the gulfs that exist between what governments say and what they actually do. These 'implementation gaps' have been explained in different ways, for example, arising from authorities' need to provide '*symbolic* reassurance' to masses while negotiating the *real* impact of policies with elites (Edelman, 1964) or, in more recent scholarship, signifying the decline in 'sovereignty' enjoyed by states so that they are more dependent on non-state political actors (Kooiman, 1993; Latour, 1986; Rhodes, 1997). Thus, all research must take into account the extent to which authorities depend on others for the realisation of security and that all policies (not just those specifically aimed at crime) must be examined for their potential impact on crime and other forms of social harm. The UK Crime and Disorder Act, for example, requires each local authority to exercise their functions recognising, 'the need to do all that it reasonably can to prevent crime and disorder in its area' (s.17); the extension of this to central government as recommended by the DTI Foresight Crime Reduction panel (DTI, 2000) would be an interesting basis for such research.

Within the general context of political authorities' power-dependency, more specific research can proceed. It is clear from the contributions in this book that understanding the diverse phenomena that have come to be labelled as 'transnational organised crime' requires concrete study of specific activities in many contexts, across different markets and in various localities. For example, whether degrees of harm caused are adequately reflected by prevailing legal definitions must be examined. The pre-eminent example of this is drugs where, encouragingly, in the UK the pro-hibitionist stranglehold on policy appears to be weakening. Clearly, education, employment and health specialists must be involved as much as those from law enforcement and security if a serious reduction is to be made in the degrees of harm caused by uncontrolled addiction and the consequential victimisation of property-holders in the pursuit of cash.

Research directed at assessing the impact of organised crime must develop more realistic measures. Several of our chapters have demonstra-ted the futility of many of the estimates reproduced in official reports. The problem is that they measure the 'output' of law enforcement (arrests, seizures, and so on) but not the impact of crime. While they might provide data for performance-measurement that may or may not aid the agencies in budgetary negotiations, they provide scant basis for policy change and learning. Further, their use may be misleading as to the precise consequences of law enforcement policies. It cannot be assumed that any amount of arrests or seizures constitute more than temporary set-backs to specific traders within expanding marketplaces. Businesses, whether legal or illegal, do not sit by passively while regulators or police enforce their laws; they respond, they innovate – or, at least, the strongest do. The chapter by Dorn in this volume, on the protean nature of crim-inal organisations, encapsulates this idea and we have written elsewhere developing the point that policing/regulation and marketplaces interact dynamically (Edwards and Gill, 2002a).

We suggested earlier in this chapter that the core framework for the examination of the 'internal challenge' represented by organised crime should be the differential associations between entrepreneurs, firms and marketplaces and how they interact with those authorities seeking their regulation (or suppression). A significant corollary of this, indeed, an important part of the interaction between traders and regulators, is the issue of corruption. This should not be viewed simplistically as 'external threat' from criminals seeking to evade enforcement by intimidating or bribing previously honest officials (though that certainly happens). It must also include demands by officials for pay-offs or promises to 'turn a blind eye' from those to whom they are empowered to issue licences or against whom they enforce laws and regulations. For some authors, indeed, it is the threat posed to the *polity* rather than to the *economy* that distinguishes 'organised crime' from other forms of criminal preda-tion (Gill, 2000: 67–9). In some areas of the world this is argued to be so extensive as to constitute 'criminal states' (e.g. Voronin, 1997) or 'kleptocracies' but even those places that like to think of themselves as far removed from such problems are hardly immune from less dramatic routines of corruption. What does require future research are the especially problematic relationships that are accruing as the dominance of the 'law enforcement' response to TOC results in the ever greater deployment of covert information gathering against individuals and traders whose businesses are so profitable. Pressure from authorities on enforcers to deliver (via 'performance indicators' and 'what works' programmes) encourages investigators to cut corners while traders are able to offer them unprecedented rewards for looking the other way. Such dangers make transparency within the whole process crucial at the very same time that other pressures actually decrease the avenues of public accountability. For example, we see the increased use of security and military forces (who are even more used than domestic law enforcement agencies to operating secretly) in operations against TOC and the increased use of 'disruption' as a technique rather than arrest and prosecution, thus obviating the necessity of any accounting in the public forum of a trial (Gill, 2000: 254–6). On the world stage this development has been furthered since September 11, 2001. It is precisely in such periods of heightened perceptions of insecurity that authorities are most likely to push forward the barriers to 'executive' or covert action.

In the heightened sense of insecurity since September 2001 it becomes even more important to avoid the simple conflation of various threats (some much more real than others) into a generalised fear of transnational crime and terrorism. While there are areas of the world in which local insecurities are intimately bound up with terrorism (for example, pockets of Northern Ireland, more extensive areas of Colombia, much of Israel and Palestine), in most of the world they are not. It remains important to disentangle organised crime and the harm it causes to specific communities from more generalised perceptions of security threats, especially those emanating from terrorism. Thus the challenge remains to resist the siren call of ever-greater securitisation; if communities (whether local or national) become convinced that they must place their futures in the hands of 'securocrats' then they will become ever more demoralised in the futile pursuit of some crime-free and violence-free future. Rather, they must retain some sense of control over their own destinies by embarking on realistic analyses of the causes of social harms and indulging in debates about the most appropriate responses, including, crucially, the optimum balance of public and private power in reducing those harms.

# Note

1 The evaluation of enforcement strategies becomes circular. The actual total of, for example, illicit narcotics imported into a country is, by definition, unknown. It emerged in one of the seminars that, in order to provide an estimate, authorities will normally subject the amount seized by a multiplier of ten. So, by definition, the authorities will never achieve greater than 10 per cent success in their aim of eliminating drug importation!

# References

Adamoli, S., Di Nicola, A., Savona, E.U. and Zoffi, P. (1998) *Organised Crime Around the World.* Helsinki: HEUNI.

Barry, A., Osborne, T. and Rose, N. (eds) (1996) *Foucault and Political Reason: Liberalism, Neo-Liberalism and Rationalities of Government.* London: UCL Press.

Bigo, D. (1994) 'The European internal security field: stakes in a newly developing area of police intervention', in M. Anderson and M. den Boer (eds) *Policing Across National Boundaries.* London: Pinter.

—— (2000) 'Liaison officers in Europe: new officers in the European security field', in J. Sheptycki (ed.) *Issues in Transnational Policing.* London: Routledge.

Block, A. (1991) 'Organized crime, garbage and toxic waste: an overview', in A. Block, *Perspectives on Organized Crime: Essays in Opposition.* Dordrecht: Kluwer.

Burchell, G., Gordon, C. and Miller, P. (eds) (1991) *The Foucault Effect: Studies in Governmentality.* Brighton: Harvester Wheatsheaf.

Buzan, B., Wæver, O. and de Wilde, J. (1998) *Security: a New Framework for Analysis.* London: Lynne Rienner.

Callon, M. (1986) 'Some elements of a sociology of translation: domestication of the scallops and the fishermen of St. Brieuc Bay', in J. Law (ed.) *Power, Action and Belief.* London: Routledge and Kegan Paul.

Clarke, R.V. (1997) 'Introduction', in R.V. Clarke (ed.) *Situational Crime Prevention: Successful Case Studies,* 2nd edn. Guilderland, NY: Harrow and Heston.

Coles, N. (2001) 'It's not what you know – it's who you know that counts: analysing serious crime groups as social networks', *British Journal of Criminology* 41, 4: 580–94.

Crawford, A. (1998) *Crime Prevention and Community Safety: Politics, Policies and Practices.* London: Longman.

Dean, M. (1999) *Governmentality: Power and Rule in Modern Society.* London: Sage.

DTI (2000) *Turning the Corner,* Foresight Crime Prevention Panel Report. London: DTI.

Edelman, M. (1964) *The Symbolic Uses of Politics.* Urbana, IL: University of Illinois.

Edwards, A. and Gill, P. (2002a) 'Crime as enterprise? The case of "transnational organised crime"', *Crime, Law and Social Change* 37, 3: 203–23.

—— (2002b) 'The politics of "transnational organized crime": discourse, reflexivity and the narration of "threat"', *British Journal of Politics and International Relations* 4, 2: 245–70.

Felson, M. (1994) *Crime and Everyday Life.* Thousand Oaks, CA: Pine Forge Press.

Garland, D. (1996) 'The limits of the sovereign state: strategies of crime control in contemporary society', *British Journal of Criminology* 36, 4: 445–71.

—— (1997) '"Governmentality" and the problem of crime: Foucault, criminology, sociology', *Theoretical Criminology* 1, 2: 173–214.

280    *Adam Edwards and Peter Gill*

Gill, P. (2000) *Rounding Up the Usual Suspects: Developments in Contemporary Law Enforcement Intelligence.* Aldershot: Ashgate.

—— (2002) 'Policing and regulation: what is the difference?' *Social and Legal Studies* 11, 4: 523–46.

Graham, J. and Bennett, T. (1995) *Crime Prevention Strategies in Europe and North America.* Helsinki: HEUNI.

Hall, S. (1997) 'Visceral cultures and criminal practices', *Theoretical Criminology* 1, 4: 453–78.

Hirst, P. and Thompson, G. (1996) *Globalization in Question: The International Economy and the Possibilities of Governance.* Cambridge: Polity Press.

Hobbs, D. (1998a) 'The case against: there is not a global crime problem', *International Journal of Risk, Security and Crime Prevention* 3, 2: 139–43.

—— (1998b) 'Going down the glocal: the local context of organised crime', *The Howard Journal* 37, 4: 407–22.

—— (2001) 'The firm: organizational logic and criminal culture on a shifting terrain', *British Journal of Criminology* 41, 4: 549–60.

Hobbs, D. and Dunninghan, C. (1998) 'Glocal organised crime: context and pretext', in V. Ruggiero, N. South and I. Taylor (eds) *The New European Criminology: Crime and Social Order in Europe.* London: Routledge.

Kooiman, J. (1993) 'Findings, speculations and recommendations', in J. Kooiman (ed.) *Modern Governance: New Government–Society Interactions.* London: Sage.

Lash, S. and Urry, J. (1994) *Economies of Signs and Space.* London: Sage.

Latour, B. (1986) 'The powers of association', in J. Law (ed.) *Power, Action and Belief.* London: Routledge and Kegan Paul.

Nadelmann, E. (1993) *Cops Across Borders: The Internationalization of U.S. Criminal Law Enforcement.* University Park, PN: Pennsylvania State University Press.

NCIS (National Criminal Intelligence Service) (2000) *The National Intelligence Model.* London: NCIS.

O'Malley, P. (2001) 'Governmentality', in E. McLaughlin and J. Muncie (eds) *The Sage Dictionary of Criminology.* London: Sage.

Pawson, R. and Tilley, N. (1997) *Realistic Evaluation.* London: Sage.

Pease, K. (2002) 'Crime reduction', in M. Maguire, R. Morgan and R. Reiner (eds) *The Oxford Handbook of Criminology*, 3rd edn. Oxford: Oxford University Press.

Rawlinson, P. (2002) 'Capitalists, criminals and oligarchs – Sutherland and the new "robber barons"', *Crime, Law and Social Change* 37, 3: 293–307.

Rhodes, R.A.W. (1997) *Understanding Governance: Policy Networks, Governance, Reflexivity and Accountability.* Buckingham: Open University Press.

Rose, N. (1999) *Powers of Freedom.* Cambridge: Cambridge University Press.

Ruggiero, V. (1998) 'Transnational criminal activities: the provision of services in the dirty economies', *International Journal of Risk, Security and Crime Prevention* 3, 2: 121–9.

—— (2000) *Crime and Markets: Essays in Anti-Criminology.* Oxford: Oxford University Press.

—— (2002) 'Introduction – fuzzy criminal actors', *Crime Law and Social Change* 37, 3: 177–90.

Sayer, A. (1992) *Method in Social Science: a Realist Approach*, 2nd edn. London: Routledge.

Slapper, G. and Tombs, S. (1999) *Corporate Crime.* Harlow: Longman.

Smandych, R. (ed.) (1999) *Governable Places: Readings on Governmentality and Crime Control.* Dartmouth: Ashgate.

Stenson, K. (1998) 'Beyond histories of the present', *Economy and Society* 29, 4: 333–52.

—— (1999) 'Crime control, governmentality and sovereignty', in R. Smandych (ed.) *Governable Places: Readings in Governmentality and Crime Control.* Dartmouth: Ashgate.

—— (2000) 'Crime control, social policy and liberalism', in G. Lewis, S. Gewirtz and J. Clarke (eds) *Rethinking Social Policy.* London: Sage.

Sutherland, E. (1949) *White-Collar Crime.* New York: Holt, Rinehart and Winston.

Sutton, M. (1998) *Handling Stolen Goods and Theft: A Market Reduction Approach,* Home Office Research Study 178. London: Home Office.

Sutton, M., Schneider, J. and Hetherington, S. (2001) *Tackling Theft with the Market Reduction Approach,* Home Office Crime Reduction Series Paper 8. London: Home Office.

Taylor, I. (1999) *Crime in Context: A Critical Criminology of Market Societies.* Cambridge: Polity Press.

Tilley, N. (2002) 'The rediscovery of learning: crime prevention and scientific realism', in G. Hughes and A. Edwards (eds) *Crime Control and Community: the New Politics of Public Safety.* Cullompton: Willan Publishing.

Voronin, Y.A. (1997) 'The emerging criminal state: economic and political aspects of organized crime in Russia', in P. Williams (ed.) *Russian Organized Crime: the New Threat?* London: Cass.

Young, J. (1999) *The Exclusive Society: Social Exclusion, Crime and Difference in Late Modernity.* London: Sage.

# Index

Note: Where a page number is followed by an '*n*' it indicates a reference to an endnote; when followed by a '*t*' it indicates a reference to a table.